973.731
FUR

D1112236

DOLTON PUBLIC LIBRARY DISTRICT
708 849-2385

ALSO BY ERNEST B. FURGURSON

Ashes of Glory: Richmond at War

Chancellorsville 1863: The Souls of the Brave

Hard Right: The Rise of Jesse Helms

Westmoreland: The Inevitable General

Not War But Murder

Not War But Murder

Cold Harbor 1864

ERNEST B. FURGURSON

Alfred A. Knopf
New York
2000

This Is a Borzoi Book
Published by Alfred A. Knopf

Copyright © 2000 by Ernest B. Furgurson
Maps copyright © 2000 by Random House, Inc.
All rights reserved under International and Pan-American
Copyright Conventions. Published in the United States by Alfred
A. Knopf, a division of Random House, Inc., New York,
and simultaneously in Canada by Random House of Canada Limited,
Toronto. Distributed by Random House, Inc., New York.

www.aaknopf.com

Knopf, Borzoi Books, and the colophon are registered trademarks
of Random House, Inc.

Library of Congress Cataloging-in-Publication Data
Furgurson, Ernest B.
Not war but murder: Cold Harbor 1864 / by Ernest B.
Furgurson.—1st ed.
p.   cm.
Includes bibliographical references (p.   ) and index.
ISBN 0-679-45517-5 (alk. paper)
1. Cold Harbor (Va.), Battle of, 1864.   I. Title.
E476.52.F87 2000
973.7'37—dc21   99-37147   CIP

Manufactured in the United States of America
First Edition

To

James Stallings Pogue
Jesse Levi Furgurson II
Kemper Dennison Pogue

—may they never see such things

Contents

16 pages of illustrations will be found
following page 176

List of Maps

All maps drawn by George Skoch.

Preface

FROM JUNE 3, 1864, to this day, for those who know anything about the American Civil War, the name Cold Harbor has been a synonym for mindless slaughter.

U. S. Grant admitted that he never should have ordered the all-out attack against Robert E. Lee's entrenched troops there on that Friday, and afterward he did his best to pretend that it had never happened. One of Lee's staff colonels called the one-sided Southern victory "perhaps the easiest ever granted to Confederate arms by the folly of Federal commanders." When the North realized how seriously the Union army was bloodied there, the muttered barroom description of Grant as butcher swelled into the public prints. Speaking as newspapers ran long lists of the dead and wounded, Abraham Lincoln, who would have fired any previous commander after such a debacle, grieved that "it can almost be said that the 'heavens are hung in black.' " His closest friend in the press, Noah Brooks, reflected the mood in Washington when he wrote that "those days will appear to be the darkest of the many dark days through which passed the friends and lovers of the Federal Union." A hundred years later, Bruce Catton called Cold Harbor "one of the hard and terrible names of the Civil War, perhaps the most terrible one of all."

Those words, among the many written about Cold Harbor, remain true. It was Grant's worst defeat, and Lee's last great victory. Thousands of soldiers who survived agreed with Confederate general Evander Law that "It was not war, it was murder." But it was much more than one head-on attack and ruthless repulse.

The Cold Harbor campaign, from the Union army's crossing of the Pamunkey River to its departure for the James, was more than two weeks of infantry and cavalry clashes, each sharp enough to stand in history as a separate battle if it had come at some other time and place. The climactic fight of June 3 was more complicated than alleged by earlier writers, and it lasted longer than the ten minutes, twenty minutes, or one hour so often reported by veterans who witnessed only their own part of the struggle.

Too often brushed past as barely a chapter in the story of the 1864 overland campaign, Cold Harbor demands much closer study than most historians have given it. The *West Point Atlas of American Wars,* for example, devotes six maps to First Bull Run, where about one-fourth as many casualties were suffered on both sides as at Cold Harbor. It covers the Wilderness with nine maps, and Spotsylvania Court House with eight. Cold Harbor proper gets one half-page, small-scale map, in which the action covers about two inches at the upper margin. That is roughly the same proportion of attention that Grant gave to Cold Harbor in his official report of the campaign and his memoirs. Less than 10 percent of the published Official Records of the overland campaign, from the Rapidan River to the crossing of the James, are from the Confederate side, a fact that has strongly influenced later assessments of what happened.

Strategically and tactically, Cold Harbor was a turning point of the Civil War. After it, the war of maneuver became a war of siege; stand-up attack and defense gave way to digging and trench warfare, the beginning of tactics that became familiar in France half a century later. And psychologically, Cold Harbor provided a case study of command relationships that should be taught in every military academy. When Grant arrived from the West to become general-in-chief of all Union armies, he believed that the prowess of Lee and the Army of Northern Virginia was a myth that could be shattered by unrelenting pressure. As it turned out, his relations with George G. Meade, commander of the Army of the Potomac, and Edwin M. Stanton, secretary of war, may have been as crucial to what happened as his misreading of their stubborn enemy.

I AM DEEPLY indebted to Robert E. L. Krick, historian at the Richmond National Battlefield Park, for guiding me on the field, and to him and his colleague, Michael Andrus, for their valuable comments on my manuscript. My appreciation also goes to the many archivists and librarians who have done more than their duty to help, particularly at the Virginia Historical Society, the Library of Congress, the Museum of the Confederacy, the National Archives, and the U.S.

Army Military History Institute. I have leaned more than usual on my friends the historian Nathan Miller and the wordsmith Thomas N. Bethell, who were always there with advice and encouragement. I am grateful for the friendship and professionalism of my editor at Alfred A. Knopf, Ashbel Green; his associates Asya Muchnick, Anthea Lingeman, and Melvin Rosenthal; and my literary agent, David Black. And as ever, I have depended on the support and understanding of Cassie Thompson Furgurson.

E.B.F.

Not War But Murder

Prologue

The Circumstances
of the Case

BLACK AGAINST the pale hot sky, they drifted into sight by ones and twos, floating high above the overgrown creek bottoms and zigzag trenches. Gradually there were dozens of them, wheeling, banking, slowly spiraling lower, slipping down toward the fields so thickly dotted with Union blue. Some of the Northern boys in the rifle pits facing west toward Richmond, survivors of battle keeping watch across the trenches, had never realized before that there were two kinds of buzzards. Turkey vultures they knew, birds with bare red heads, graceful in flight, big as eagles but soaring with wings angled in a shallow V, seldom pumping, constantly tilting on columns of heat rising from the battlefield. But as the scavengers glided lower, soldiers in the lines on both sides of no-man's-land could see that some had black heads, shorter tails, silver patches on wings that flapped more often—birds that seemed more hellish because they looked so clumsy. These were black vultures, up from the deeper South, drawn to the carnage of eastern Virginia. Both kinds of buzzards circled silently, their ugly heads turning, considering, choosing targets as far as possible from the thousands of live soldiers aiming at one another across the festering acres between them. Among the helpless wounded, the most unlucky lay facing the sky, watching the wicked shapes descending, hoping that death came first. When the first bird braked to earth, someone in the Yankee lines shouted a curse and a musket popped. The vulture took off with a noisy flapping, but soon another slipped down, and another.

Never before and never again in the American Civil War were so many wounded soldiers left so long to suffer in plain sight of their comrades, their enemies, and the birds of carrion. Never did generals so blatantly place concern for their own reputations above mercy for

their soldiers lying dying in the sun. Never between the opening cannon at Fort Sumter and the stacked muskets at Appomattox Court
House was another major battle so shamefully one-sided as that in the
first week of June 1864, at the country crossroads of Cold Harbor,
Virginia.

How could such a thing happen?

THREE MONTHS earlier, on a raw afternoon in early March, the
White House had seemed as gloomily gray as the clouds scudding low
over Washington. Three senators stepped from their carriage onto the
north portico and announced themselves to the president.

Mr. Lincoln received them politely, but with something less than
brotherly affection. The senior among them, the coarse and self-
important Benjamin Franklin Wade of Ohio, had been ranting since
the first days of war that the president and his army were not aggressive enough. Only slightly less openly, he and his companions,
Zachariah Chandler of Michigan and freshman senator Benjamin
Franklin Loan, a former militia brigadier from Missouri, were hoping
to replace the president with a more radical Republican.

That these three would come to the White House seeking favors,
or even courtesy, seemed far-fetched early in this election year of 1864.
But on the matter at hand, Lincoln had very nearly anticipated them
the summer before. Now, bringing what they called "overwhelming
evidence," they came to urge him to do what he had not done then.

As chairman of the Joint Committee on the Conduct of the War,
Wade had led his radical colleagues all winter in efforts to besmirch
the commander of the Army of the Potomac, Major General George
Gordon Meade. From unhappy generals displaced or offended by
Meade, they solicited secret testimony about his alleged "want of
heart, of earnestness of purpose." Most of his army lacked faith in
him, said these witnesses, and the officers who did support him were
suspected of pro-Southern "Copperheadism." From this, the radical
committeemen concluded what they had set out to conclude. They
"believed it to be their duty" to lay their case before the president and
the secretary of war, and "in behalf of the army and the country,
demand the removal of General Meade. . . ."

Lincoln heard them out patiently, without surprise. And who, he
asked, was qualified to replace Meade? Their answer did not surprise
him either. Well, the senators said, they "would be content with General Hooker, believing him competent." But, "not being advocates of

any particular general," they would be satisfied with anyone the president considered better.

The glaze of civility over the conversation nearly cracked when the senators warned that unless the president acted promptly, "it would be their duty to make the testimony public . . . with such comments as the circumstances of the case seemed to require."[1]

Lincoln was not an extravagant admirer of George Meade; he had almost fired him for failing to crush the Confederate army after defeating it at Gettysburg the previous July. But the president was not about to replace him with the radicals' favorite, the conniving "Fighting Joe" Hooker, whom Meade had succeeded following Hooker's defeat at Chancellorsville. Before Meade's appointment, command of Union forces in the East had changed five times in the first twenty-six months of war. The army needed stability, and Lincoln had no intention of responding to this brazenly political threat by his congressional enemies. Yet he did act, on a decision made weeks earlier.

That very day, he sent orders west for Major General Ulysses S. Grant to report to Washington. Five evenings later, the tired, disheveled Grant arrived in the capital, checked in at Willard's Hotel, and went to the White House to meet Lincoln for the first time. Amid a reception in the East Room, he stood on a sofa to escape the crush of a cheering crowd. The next morning, he was promoted to lieutenant general, a rank that only George Washington and Winfield Scott had held before him.

Appointed general-in-chief of all Federal armies, Grant headed out immediately to visit the Army of the Potomac in its winter lines above the Rapidan River in Virginia. He meant to take the advice of his leading lieutenant in the West, Major General William Tecumseh Sherman, who had written to him warning of "the buffets of intrigue and policy" in the capital. "For God's sake and your country's sake come out of Washington," said Sherman. Grant did not need to be persuaded. He would make his headquarters in the field, with the Army of the Potomac, beside Meade, a man as unlike him as any officer in the same uniform could be. And largely because he did, there he would suffer the worst defeat in his illustrious military career.[2]

1

The Rising Sun

ON COLD AND rainy March 10, 1864, U. S. Grant crossed the Potomac River to introduce himself to the Union army in Virginia, proud birthplace of presidents as revered as George Washington and Thomas Jefferson, of generals as exalted as Winfield Scott and Zachary Taylor. Now those heroes were consigned to history, and the Old Dominion was renowned not as birthplace but as burial ground, for tens of thousands of soldiers from North and South. The only great Virginian on Grant's mind that day was Robert E. Lee.

As the train clacked west and then south along the tracks of the Orange & Alexandria Railroad, Grant gazed out over the ravaged, winter-dreary countryside and thought of what lay ahead. Villages, streams, and crossroads eased by, places he had never seen before, though their names were familiar to him and everyone who read the newspapers: Fairfax, where the Confederate raider John Mosby had kidnapped a Union brigadier in bed one winter morning; Bull Run, where overconfident Union armies had twice been soundly whipped; Manassas Junction, where Stonewall Jackson's men had plundered and burned a Union supply depot; Bristoe, where one of Lee's corps had been mauled as he maneuvered the Union army into a forty-mile retreat; Catlett's, where Jeb Stuart's jaunty horsemen had captured General John Pope's dress coat and headquarters files; the Rappahannock River, along whose banks Lee had turned back the Union army in the bloody battles of Fredericksburg and Chancellorsville. Puffing steam, the train halted at Brandy Station, where Union horsemen had at last held their own in the biggest cavalry battle ever fought on the North American continent. Each checkpoint on the way had been a reminder of Union defeat, frustration, or, at best, marginal success, and thus a reminder of why Grant had come.

George Meade was nursing a severe cold and cough on the day the new general-in-chief arrived. Because he had been ill with pneumonia earlier in the winter, he sent his chief of staff, Andrew A. Humphreys, to escort his guest on the muddy way from the rail station to the head-quarters of the Army of the Potomac. Major General Humphreys, a serious fifty-three-year-old career soldier, had never met Grant before. He was not sure what to think about this newcomer who had graduated twelve years behind him at West Point, who had made one reputation in a struggle with John Barleycorn and another in besting the inferior Confederate generals beyond the Appalachians. The two men found little to say on their way to Meade's command post. As they arrived, Humphreys had the feeling that "it was the visit of a rival commander to a rival army, or at least the meeting of the commanders and officers of rival armies."[1]

Grant himself, though now in supreme command, may have heightened that tension. He had known Meade slightly during the Mexican War but had not seen him since. He was concerned that he might find the same kind of resentment among Meade's officers that the braggadocious Major General John Pope had created when he arrived to take command in Virginia in 1862. "I have come from the West, where we have always seen the backs of our enemies," Pope had proclaimed, as if sneering at the troops he was to lead; he came, he added, from "an army whose business it has been to seek the adversary, and to beat him when he was found; whose policy has been attack and not defense." Within weeks, Pope had been thoroughly outgeneraled by Lee and transferred to the Northwest, seldom to be heard from again.[2]

Grant's traveling companion must have created some nervousness on their arrival, too: he was the famously assertive Major General William F. "Baldy" Smith, whose performance at Chattanooga had won Grant's admiration and inspired talk that he was about to replace Meade. "It is said he is greatly smitten with Baldy Smith," Meade wrote to his wife on the eve of Grant's arrival—which might mean that Smith was to replace him. "Of this I am indifferent, but [for] my reputation I will battle to the last."[3]

Though these things were on Meade's mind, he gave no hint of it as he rushed out into the rain to greet Grant before he could dismount. Grant's lack of pomp quickly erased any fear that another Pope had come, and before he and Meade sat to talk and smoke at dinner, Smith had departed.

Without waiting, Meade tried to anticipate Grant's mission by

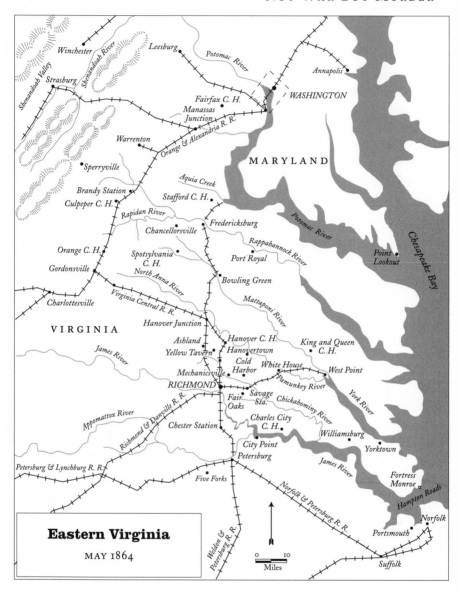

Winchester
Leesburg
Potomac River
Annapolis
Strasburg
Shenandoah River
Fairfax C. H.
WASHINGTON
Shenandoah Valley
Manassas Junction
Warrenton
Orange & Alexandria R. R.
MARYLAND
Sperryville
Aquia Creek
Brandy Station
Stafford C. H.
Culpeper C. H.
Rapidan River
Fredericksburg
Potomac River
Chancellorsville
Rappahannock River
Orange C. H.
Spotsylvania C. H.
Port Royal
Point Lookout
Gordonsville
North Anna River
Bowling Green
Chesapeake Bay
Charlottesville
Virginia Central R. R.
Mattaponi River
VIRGINIA
Hanover Junction
James River
Ashland
Hanover C. H.
King and Queen C. H.
Yellow Tavern
Hanovertown
Cold Harbor
White House
West Point
Mechanicsville
Savage Sta.
Pamunkey River
RICHMOND
Fair Oaks
Chickahominy River
York River
Appomattox River
Richmond & Danville R. R.
Chester Station
Charles City C. H.
Williamsburg
City Point
Yorktown
Petersburg & Lynchburg R. R.
Petersburg
James River
Five Forks
Fortress Monroe
Norfolk & Petersburg R. R.
Hampton Roads
Norfolk
Portsmouth
Weldon & Petersburg R. R.
Suffolk

Eastern Virginia

MAY 1864

0   10
Miles

suggesting that the new chief might want someone he knew, a general from the West, like Sherman, to take over the Army of the Potomac. The work ahead was so important that nobody's personal feelings should stand in the way, said Meade; he himself would do his best wherever placed. This offer to step aside made an even more favorable impression on Grant than had Meade's victory at Gettysburg. Although Grant had clearly come east thinking of Smith for the post, he assured Meade that he had no intention of replacing him. Lincoln had not pressed the matter, and Grant had no desire to start his new assignment with a political ruckus over demoting the man who had won the greatest battle of the war. He returned to Washington the next day, and ten days later he announced that Meade was secure in his job.

But on that first visit, Grant had dropped a surprise that would often make Meade wish he had been replaced—a bomb with a long fuse, which would do its damage weeks later, deep in Virginia. Without asking Meade's opinion, he informed him that he would not make his headquarters in Washington, as his predecessor, Henry W. Halleck, had done. Halleck would stay there, with the lesser title of chief of staff, but Grant, as general-in-chief, would travel with the Army of the Potomac. Though responsible for all the armies of the United States, he would give his personal attention to the one commanded by Meade.

When Meade wrote home the following night, he tried to be generous. He said he was "very much pleased with General Grant," who had shown "more capacity and character than I expected," and had paid Meade compliments in declining his offer to be replaced. But Grant's announced intention of campaigning beside Meade took the shine off his kind remarks. From now on, Meade told his wife, she would see "the Army of the Potomac putting laurels on the brows of another rather than your husband."

Looking back, Grant would acknowledge that "Meade's position afterwards proved embarrassing to me if not to him." This was most disingenuous; he had to know that if he was embarrassed, Meade must be many times more so. If he had read Meade's letters home that spring, he would have realized that *embarrassment* was a feeble word to describe how the commander of the Army of the Potomac came to feel as he served in the shadow of the general-in-chief.[4]

· · ·

GRANT LATER summed up the situation he found in Virginia: "the armies . . . confronting each other had already been in deadly conflict for a period of three years, with immense losses in killed, by death from sickness, captured and wounded; and neither had made any real progress toward accomplishing the final end. . . . here was a stand-off."[5]

Soldiers of both armies understood that Grant had come to break that standoff, and they dreaded what spring would bring. The naïve expectations of 1861, that this would be a quick war of parades and cheers and welcome-home kisses, were long forgotten. Union soldiers were frustrated by defeat and stalemate; Confederates suffered from hunger and cold. Dug in along the Rapidan in that winter of 1863–64, they had prepared for the next season of war in their separate ways. Thousands, unable to satisfy the needs of their bodies, became more concerned for their souls. Some grubby ordinary soldiers, living in makeshift huts, found ways to show their resentment toward officers who flaunted their luxuries. More dutiful officers went home to recruit new strength for their riddled regiments. Some ambitious generals, with plenty of time for intrigues, fought rear-guard actions in press and Congress to uphold their reputations and tear down others. All, from private to general, looked at the vacancies around them and real-ized that in the next battle, or the one after that, they were increas-ingly likely to join their departed friends.

In the early months of war, clergymen from home had preached to soldiers en route to battle, and many became chaplains with regiments at the front. Great religious revivals swept through the stationary armies in Virginia in the two middle winters of the war. Soldiers heard more preaching in camp than they ever had at home, and became con-noisseurs of pulpit oratory. While some welcomed the word of the Lord however delivered, others were as discriminating as if they had paid good money to see a stage play in New York or Richmond. John D. Follmer, of the Sixteenth Pennsylvania Cavalry, had become so jaded by early 1864 that he set unrealistically high standards, perhaps because church services, like inspections, were considered mandatory duty in his regiment.

"There are some of the poorest preachers whom we are compelled to listen to," he wrote in his diary. "Some of them have missed their calling, greatly. They might make fair shoemakers or auctioneers, but it is plain that they will never make preachers. . . . I think sometimes that these men are talking on a subject they aren't acquainted with." That day's service had been unusually uninspiring: the minister opened with "some of the old graveyard hymns, and then [spoke] of death and judgment etc. as if the soldier was particularly afraid of death. He should see some of the grand charges the men make and see how they fear death."[6]

By well-established tradition, Union officers often brought wives and less legitimate lady friends down from Washington for fancy-dress soirees behind the lines, in halls built and decorated by lone-some, loveless privates. At least once, the ordinary troops' hard feelings about the privileges of rank burst into flame. Wilbur H. Proctor, a musician with the Tenth New York Battalion, exulted when a theater used by the troops burned to the ground: "The officers wanted it for a ball room so the boys rather than give it to them burnt it down it served them right it maid a great blaze we thought it was Mosbys men making a raid. . . ."[7]

Between privates and officers, generals and politicians, soldiers and civilians, the lines of authority and loyalty shifted as the war dragged on. During the long muddy season, some Virginians within the Union lines opened their doors to friendly intruders in hopes of tapping the bulging Federal commissary, and some because they had abandoned their allegiance to a Confederate government unable to defend their homes and crops. For Southern soldiers, each probe and skirmish along the front produced prisoners and gossip about how boots, beef, and coffee seemed inexhaustible on the Northern side. Some Rebels who had hung on through ghastly fights like Chancellorsville and Gettysburg could not face another campaign on rancid bacon and stale cornbread.

In late April, a Virginia soldier of Pegram's artillery battalion instructed his wife in Richmond to write him that she was lying ill "at the point of death." When he took leave to attend to her, she had a false passport waiting for him, and with it he made his way across the Rappahannock and Potomac to southern Maryland. Debriefed by Federal officers, he gave them fifteen pages of solid information and wild speculation.

"Troops have plenty of shoes, such as they are, made out of horse-hide and lasting about a week's march," the Rebel reported. "All other clothing was scarce—no jackets nor pants, don't issue hats at all. . . ." His battery had only twenty-five of its usual seventy-five horses left; fodder was limited to a pound of corn and a pound and a half of hay a day. Medical supplies were scant.

The deserter, identified by his questioners as Captain James Bellew, had intimate knowledge of the Confederate army's shortages. But he offered a confused order of battle, and his report of Rebel plans for the spring campaign wandered far beyond mere confusion. According to him, Lee would attack westward toward Pittsburgh and Wheeling, while Richmond would be left to defend itself with a skimpy force under General Pierre G. T. Beauregard.[8]

If the artilleryman had not taken such an elaborate route to desert, he would seem to have been another of the soldiers whom Lee occasionally sent across the lines to mislead Union interrogators. Two nights earlier, Private John Camper of the Thirty-seventh Virginia had sneaked directly across the Rapidan into Union hands and confided that his regiment had received "orders directing great care to be had in answering questions, if any men are made prisoners of war." Apparently disarming his questioners with that preamble, he then told them enough about Lieutenant General James Longstreet's movements en route from Tennessee back to Lee's army to convince Meade that "it looks as if Longstreet was going to make a diversion *down the* [Shenandoah] *valley* to threaten our rear."[9]

Lee was planning no such thing. Facing Grant's growing accumulation of troops with still-skimpy supplies and transport, he had asked President Davis for reinforcements wherever they could be found. His concerns were widespread, but his plans were local: he intended to strike the Federal center on the Rapidan and follow success by piling in troops from either flank. But under its new management, the Union army did not wait to see what Lee would do.[10]

GRANT, UNLIKE his predecessors as general-in-chief and his Confederate counterparts, could see the war whole. The Army of the Potomac's role in Virginia was one part of his war-wide plan, coordinated to prevent the Confederates from moving strength from one threatened front to another as they had done against separate Federal efforts in the past. Rather than committing Union forces to uncoordinated offensives that allowed the Confederates to mass against them, he would concentrate his army's operations in time, moving against several objectives at once. The overstretched Rebels would not be able to deal with simultaneous attacks on different fronts.

Since the war began, "On to Richmond!" had been the rallying cry of the North, and for three years the Federal army had been trying to get there. The Confederates had turned back every general Lincoln had sent to do the job: Irvin McDowell at First Manassas in 1861;

George B. McClellan in the Peninsula campaign, John Pope at Second Manassas, and Ambrose E. Burnside at Fredericksburg in 1862; Joe Hooker at Chancellorsville in 1863. It was Lee who had administered most of those defeats, winning a reputation for aggressiveness and tactical surprise that must have been worth a division of infantry. Before working out details of the 1864 campaign, Grant told Meade that not Richmond but "Lee's army will be your objective point. Wherever Lee's army goes, you will go also."[11]

Lee's victories in the first three years of war had come on one battlefield at a time; now Grant, with superior numbers and materials, prepared to move everywhere at once. While he with Meade attacked Lee, five other Union generals were to take the offensive. Sherman would push into Georgia toward Atlanta, and Nathaniel P. Banks toward Mobile on the Gulf. Franz Sigel would march up the Shenandoah Valley into central Virginia, and George Crook with a force of cavalry and infantry would work eastward to meet him, destroying railroads along the way. Meanwhile, Benjamin F. Butler, coordinating with Grant's and Meade's overland drive, would move an army up the James River to cut off Richmond from the south. Grant's decision to make his headquarters with Meade's army left no doubt about which of those offensives he considered most important.[12]

Early on May 4, the Army of the Potomac started across the Rapidan and Rappahannock with 118,000 men, plunging into the thick Wilderness astride the Orange-Spotsylvania county line, near where Lee had routed Hooker in the Chancellorsville campaign a year earlier. One of Grant's aides saw the place as "a tangled forest the impenetrable gloom of which could be likened only to the shadow of death. . . . Directions were ascertained and lines established by means of the pocket-compass, and a change of position often presented an operation more like a problem of ocean navigation than a question of military manoeuvers. . . ."[13]

Grant wanted to hurry his army through that Wilderness as fast as possible; Lee, with only 62,000 troops, wanted to attack him there, where the Union advantage in numbers and guns would matter less. Partly because the long Federal wagon train crept so slowly along the narrow, crisscrossing forest roads, the armies collided early on May 5. Only two of Lee's three corps, under Richard S. Ewell and A. P. Hill, were at hand. That afternoon, they fought to a bloody stalemate against elements of three Yankee corps. Bursting shells set the woods afire, roasting many of the dead and wounded. Lee expected

Longstreet's corps to cover the twenty-plus miles from near Gordonsville before action resumed, but Longstreet was still off to the west when Union forces attacked at first light on May 6.

The Federal offensive was crumpling Lee's flank when Longstreet's troops at last came up in a savage counterattack. Longstreet scouted ahead and was badly wounded by his own troops, much as Stonewall Jackson had been shot four miles away a year earlier. The contest was so close that Lee himself rode forward, ready to lead a charge across a farmhouse clearing as if he were a regimental commander; he desisted only when the Texas soldiers around him, shouting, "Lee to the rear!" vowed that they would not go ahead until he went back.

The two-day Battle of the Wilderness was costly to both sides: Lee lost almost eleven thousand in killed, wounded, and missing, including his senior corps commander, while Grant lost about eighteen thousand. Like all battles, it was also a learning experience, and at that point Grant had far more to learn than did Lee.

By then, the Confederate commander knew his own subordinates intimately; when Longstreet was disabled, Lee quickly appointed Richard H. Anderson, who had led a division through many fights under him, to command that corps. Grant, however, was just getting acquainted with most of his generals, beginning with Meade.

He had brought with him from the West a substantial staff and the profane, pugnacious Philip H. Sheridan, whom he made his cavalry chief. But he was unfamiliar with the men leading three of his four corps and his infantry divisions. Winfield Scott Hancock (Second Corps), Gouverneur K. Warren (Fifth), and John Sedgwick (Sixth) were all distinguished veterans of the war in the East, but they were very different from one another. In theory, the personalities of corps commanders might not have been of direct concern to Grant, because his chain of authority as general-in-chief ran downward through Meade, commander of the Army of the Potomac. The only exception to this was Ambrose Burnside, whose Ninth Corps had returned from duty elsewhere as the spring offensive started. By date of rank, Burnside was senior to Meade; he had commanded this army at Fredericksburg, when Meade headed a mere division. Thus, to respect Burnside's feelings, Grant kept the Ninth Corps nominally separate as the campaign began. But under stress in the field, the protocol of who formally commanded whom would often be ignored. The personal traits of all Grant's generals, especially the dissatisfied Meade caught in between, would matter more each day.

As Grant learned more about his eastern generals, they were learning about him, about this soldier who had fought his war beyond the mountains. Some had known him at West Point and as a lieutenant in Mexico, where he had won brevet promotion to captain. But later, during lonely duty on the West Coast, he had drunk too much and resigned to avoid a court-martial. He lurched from farming to selling real estate to clerking in a customs house before going home to Galena, Illinois, to work in his father's leather store. When the Civil War began, he had to beg for weeks for a commission—while his eventual opponent, Colonel Robert E. Lee of the First U.S. Cavalry, was being offered command of the whole Union army, and turning it down. Finally, Grant was appointed colonel of the Twenty-first Illinois, and once given his chance, he rose fast. As brigadier general, he took Forts Henry and Donelson; as major general, he fought not wisely but stubbornly at Shiloh, then showed bold innovation in capturing the Confederate strongholds of Vicksburg and Chattanooga. After working with him in those campaigns, Sherman felt that Grant's most valuable trait was a "simple faith in success . . . which I can liken to nothing else than the faith a Christian has in a Savior."[14]

Grant modeled himself on the plain and steady Zachary Taylor, under whom he had served first in Mexico, rather than on his later commander, Lee's mentor, the grandiose and brilliant Winfield Scott. Quite possibly, he also remembered that "Old Rough and Ready" Taylor had gone on to the White House, but "Old Fuss and Feathers" Scott was overwhelmingly defeated in the 1852 election. At first sight, a Fifth Corps artillery officer had found Grant "stumpy, unmilitary, slouchy, and Western-looking; very ordinary in fact." Curious officers read character even in the way he wore his campaign hat: "he neither puts it on behind his ears, nor draws it over his eyes; much less does he cock it on one side, but sets it straight and very hard on his head. His riding is the same . . . he sits firmly in the saddle and looks straight ahead, as if only intent on getting to some particular point."[15]

At the Wilderness, these officers got their first impressions of what lay beneath Grant's appearance, of his performance under pressure. In two days of pitched battle, he seemed to uphold his reputation as a calm, determined bulldog. His aide, Lieutenant Colonel Horace Porter, wrote of how an eastern officer approached the general-in-chief the night of May 6 to warn that Lee was likely to cut the Union army's communications. Grant replied, "Oh, I am heartily tired of hearing about what Lee is going to do. Some of you always seem to think he is suddenly going to turn a double somersault, and land in our rear and on both of our flanks at the same time. Go back to your com-

mand, and try to think what we are going to do ourselves, instead of
what Lee is going to do." The next morning, according to Porter,
Grant awoke looking "thoroughly refreshed after the sound sleep he
had enjoyed," and sat whittling, smoking his ever-present cigar, while
coolly analyzing the battle.[16]

But two of Grant's staff officers who had come with him from the
West, Brigadier General John A. Rawlins and Major Theodore S.
Bowers, believed that the brutal fighting the night before had "tested
Grant's fortitude and self-control more seriously than any event of his
past career." When Grant mused that Confederate general Joseph E.
Johnston would have fallen back after "two such days' punishment,"
another aide commented that "*Lee* won't retreat." At this, Grant "went
into his tent and, throwing himself face downward on his cot, gave
way to the greatest emotion." Rawlins said the general-in-chief "was
stirred to the very depths of his soul"—though still concealing such
inner doubts from others.[17]

Grant was learning about Lee, and Lee about Grant—and on the
morning after the Wilderness fell quiet, one fact emerged that mat-
tered more than anything else that either general learned there. As
Grant had said, Joe Johnston would have retreated after such a vicious
battle. And as Lee might have said, Irvin McDowell, George McClellan, John Pope, Ambrose Burnside, or Joe Hooker would have done
the same. But just as Lee was unlike Johnston, Grant was unlike those
Union generals who had preceded him in the East: though the Army
of the Potomac had once again been roughly handled by a much
smaller force, he did not give up the initiative. At 6:30 a.m. on May 7,
he issued orders to Meade—not to withdraw, but to push his damaged
army on to Spotsylvania Court House, to get between Lee's army and
Richmond.

A new war had begun.

THAT EVENING, when Federal troops saw their general-in-chief and
his entourage pass by riding south, they understood what it meant
and broke into cheers. The night before, a rumor had circulated
that Meade had urged Grant to fall back across the Rapidan after
the bloody fight in the Wilderness. "The enlisted men, one and
all, believed it," a Pennsylvania artilleryman recalled. "None of the
enlisted men had any confidence in Meade as a tenacious, aggressive
fighter. . . . many of them openly ridiculed him and his alleged military ability."[18]

George Meade had more character than personality; he never won the kind of popularity among his troops that leaders like McClellan and "Uncle John" Sedgwick inspired. A junior officer at his headquarters said that he had "that marvelous instrument, a rich, cultivated voice," but his "high-bred" manners "reared a barrier around him which cut him off from the love of his army." Another aide, Colonel Theodore Lyman, who watched him as closely as anyone, noted that on routine days, Meade "is in excellent spirits and cracks a great many jokes and tells stories." But during a movement, "he is like a firework, always going bang at someone, and nobody ever knows who is going to catch it next, but all stand in a semi-terrified state. There is something sardonic in his natural disposition, which is an excellent thing in a commander; it makes people skip round so." Since the army that spring was constantly in motion, Meade's temper was constantly on display.[19]

As a boy, Meade had never aspired to be a soldier; he went to West Point because his once-wealthy father lacked funds to send him to college. He had finished nineteenth among fifty-six members of the class of 1835, and after little more than a year, resigned his commission to become a civilian engineer. That put him behind his classmates when he returned to the army as a lieutenant in 1842, then served under Taylor and later Scott in Mexico. After years spent surveying borders and building lighthouses, he finally made captain in 1856, twenty-one years after graduating from the military academy.

When war began, he got nowhere in his pleas for a command until after First Bull Run, when his wife's Philadelphia connections helped him gain a brigadier's star. Leading his Pennsylvania brigade in the Seven Days battles, he was seriously wounded at Glendale, in the lowlands outside Richmond. Though one bullet entered just above his hip joint, nicked his liver, and exited near his spine, and another struck his arm, Meade stayed in command until he had lost so much blood that he had to leave the field. Before fully recovering, he returned to fight at Second Bull Run, then headed a division at South Mountain, Antietam, and Fredericksburg, and commanded the Fifth Corps at Chancellorsville. His steadiness there led some of his peers to push him as Hooker's replacement, a change that Lincoln made over Meade's protests. As Lee marched into Pennsylvania, three days before Gettysburg, Meade became commander of the Army of the Potomac.

At that moment, he also became the prime target of jealous generals, and of radical Republicans who had made Hooker their favorite. Though Meade defeated the vaunted Lee at Gettysburg, his foes in

the Union army, Congress, and the press determined to oust him
because of his performance at and after that battle. The legislators'
grievances reached back even further, to Detroit in the days after Fort
Sumter, when strict soldier Meade, avoiding politics, refused to order
his command to retake the oath of allegiance at the behest of local
officials. That earned him the lasting personal enmity of Senator
Chandler, who became the dominant force on the Joint Committee
on the Conduct of the War and eventually led the effort to replace
Meade. There was also the matter of Meade's relatives: his wife's sister
was married to the flamboyant secessionist, Virginia governor, and
Confederate brigadier general Henry A. Wise; one of his own sisters
had been married to a Confederate navy captain killed at New
Orleans, and another was the wife of a Philadelphian turned Mississippi gentleman whose plantation had been ruined and two sons killed
by Yankees.[20]

The Joint Committee called disgruntled friends of Hooker who
alleged that an overcautious Meade had made plans to retreat from
Gettysburg while the battle was in progress, had failed to crush Lee's
army afterward, and had bungled operations along the Rapidan, and
that he generally lacked zeal for his mission. The reason, they darkly
suggested, was that Meade was too close to McClellan and the Peace
Democrats who sought a negotiated end to the war.[21]

Because of these earlier accusations, most of them unfair, many soldiers found it easy to believe the rumor of Meade's pressing for withdrawal after the Wilderness. Not only the troops but at least one
newspaperman heard it and later alluded to it in print, a decision he
came to regret.

RUMORS NOTWITHSTANDING, the Union army headed south from
the Wilderness, proving that if Meade had indeed offered such advice,
Grant had rejected it. As the troops marched, they began singing so
loudly that Grant hushed them, lest the noise alert Lee to what was
happening.

But Lee found out soon enough, and so did his troops. Their reaction was not singing, but "surprise and disappointment," wrote the
sergeant major of a Virginia battery. Here was a new Federal commander "so ill-informed as to the military customs in our part of the
country that when the battle of the Wilderness was over, instead of
retreating . . . he had the temerity to move by his left flank to a new
position, there to try conclusions with us again. We were . . . full of

curiosity to know how long it was going to take him to perceive the impropriety of his course."[22]

Once assured that Grant was on the march, Lee quickly ordered Longstreet's corps, now under Anderson, to head south for Spotsylvania Court House. And Anderson, in his first move as corps commander, made a horseback decision that may have prolonged the war in Virginia for nearly a year. Because the woods along the nearby roads were still smoldering, instead of letting his troops sleep there he started them south four hours earlier than ordered, and kept them marching until they halted at first light within sight of the courthouse village.

As they collapsed around campfires, Anderson's men did not realize that they had been in a race with Warren's Union corps, and had won. If they had lost, if the Yankee infantry had gotten ahead, Lee would have been cut off from Richmond and the war might have been decided at Spotsylvania. But on the way there, the Federal foot soldiers had been slowed by Sheridan's cavalry clogging the road—a run-in that would inflame relations among Grant's generals when word of it reached headquarters. After horsemen of both sides fought back and forth through the little county seat, Anderson's troops held off exhausted Union infantry while the rest of the two armies converged for the battles of Spotsylvania Court House.

In bursts of furious action, the struggle went on for almost two weeks. Grant's divisions pounded the thoroughly dug-in Confederates first here, then there, with little effect beyond more bloodshed on both sides. The heaviest fighting began the day after Grant sent to Washington the famous dispatch that said, "I . . . propose to fight it out on this line if it takes all summer." Whether he meant the line that his troops then held or the line of march toward Richmond was not questioned by the president and all the North, who cheered the general's promise. But Grant's bold talk did nothing to improve Meade's disposition. The army's provost marshal, Brigadier General Marsena R. Patrick, found Meade "cross as a Bear, at which I do not wonder, with such a man as Grant over him."[23]

Early on May 12, Hancock's corps attacked out of the predawn mist, surprising the Rebels and driving in a "mule shoe" salient that Lee had unwisely stripped of artillery in anticipation of another Union move southward. The Federals captured some three thousand men of Ewell's corps, including two generals and most of the famed Stonewall Brigade; sixteen Yankees were later awarded the Medal of Honor for taking Confederate flags that morning. Lee rallied his troops and built a line across the base of the salient. The murderous hand-to-hand struggle at the "bloody angle" left corpses piled before the earthworks. Further clashes lengthened the list of those killed, wounded, and missing. After a final effort to break through at the angle, Meade wrote that the Confederates were "so strongly entrenched that even Grant thought it useless to knock our heads against a brick wall, and directed a suspension of the attack."[24]

The results at Spotsylvania: another eighteen thousand Federal and almost ten thousand Confederate casualties, on top of those lost at the Wilderness. Once again, there was a terrible toll on the leadership of both armies. Union general Sedgwick was killed by a sharpshooter only seconds after telling nearby soldiers that the Rebels "couldn't hit an elephant at this distance." Regretfully, Meade turned over Sedgwick's Sixth Corps to Major General Horatio G. Wright.[25]

Since the start of the campaign, five Confederate generals had been killed; nine, including Longstreet, were wounded, and two captured. When A. P. Hill fell ill, Lee gave Jubal Early temporary command of his corps. Most conspicuous among the dead was the charismatic, irrepressible cavalryman J. E. B. Stuart, of whom Lee said sadly, "He never brought me a piece of false information."[26]

Union brigadier general James H. Wilson would write in his official report that Stuart's death heralded "the permanent superiority of the national cavalry over the rebels." But for months before Stuart was killed, attrition and lack of forage had weakened his brigades; they were running their irreplaceable horses into the ground, while the Federal riders seemed to have an endless supply of fresh mounts. Stuart's passing confirmed a gradual shift that had been going on for months, based first on logistics.[27]

In a peculiar way, his death grew out of the confusing traffic jam of Union cavalry and infantry on the road to Spotsylvania Court House. After it, Meade furiously blamed Sheridan, but this time he had met his match in temperament. The five-foot-five, 115-pound cavalry commander may have been the most aggressive general in the Union army; he and Grant's senior aide, Lieutenant Colonel Cyrus B. Comstock, urged an unremitting offensive wherever the enemy could be found. "Smash 'em up! Smash 'em up!" was Comstock's constant advice at headquarters, and Sheridan, when provoked, was just as quick to take on a rival general as he was to fight the Rebels.[28]

When Meade faulted the cavalry for the mix-up on the road, Sheridan roared back at him in language "highly spiced and conspicuously italicized with expletives," declaring that he could whip Stuart if only

Meade would let him. But since Meade insisted on giving the cavalry its orders, he said, henceforth he could do so without Sheridan's involvement. Meade, nearly exploding with anger, reported this insubordination to Grant—and instead of cracking down, the general-in-chief looked up and asked with interest, "Did Sheridan say that?" Assured that he had, Grant said, "Well, he generally knows what he's talking about. Let him start right out and do it."[29]

Turned loose, Sheridan set off with a thirteen-mile-long column of horsemen, slashing south toward Richmond. Just outside the Confederate capital, Stuart's hard-riding cavalry blocked him at Yellow Tavern. In a running clash there on May 11, Stuart fell mortally wounded, and what General Wilson said was true: the Confederate cavalry would never be the same. But Grant, by overruling the senior Meade on behalf of his cocky favorite from the West, had ensured more serious friction within his command, farther down the road to Richmond.

AT MASSAPONAX, about six miles east of Spotsylvania Court House, Grant's headquarters soldiers lifted pews out of the little brick church and made a rough circle of them, a place for the staff to rest in the shade of twin poplars as they decided what to do after Spotsylvania.

Grant, the only officer with three stars on each shoulder, sat at the end of a pew facing the church, with the dirt road behind him. Except for those stars, he looked as ordinary as any middle-aged quartermaster. He was wearing no sword; to say that he was five feet eight was stretching it, and his uniform was less grand than those of the captains and colonels in his retinue. Like everything else within miles of the army's march route, his dark beard, blue coat, and tall cavalry boots were filmed with the powdery white dust of the Virginia countryside. He slumped slightly forward, listening with blue eyes downcast, a fresh cigar between his teeth, as a staff colonel stood within the circle reading the latest reports of enemy movements.[30]

Many of the twenty-five or so officers seated around him were paying only casual attention, some leaning on their swords, a few reading newspapers just arrived from New York and Washington. Some examined folded maps as they followed the colonel's report. A dozen soldiers stood beside the road watching the proceedings, trying to hear. Among them were a handful of men in civilian clothes, with the rough look of scouts or spies. A train of Fifth Corps wagons stopped alongside, and its teamsters stood with reins in their hands, wanting a look at the famous generals.

One of these generals was Meade, who wore the brim of his high-crowned campaign hat turned down all around. That added to the impression of height and glumness made by his long Roman nose and pointed, frosty chestnut beard, and the capacious purplish bags beneath his blue eyes. He had something to be glum about; he had already read the newspapers.

The army that he had commanded for almost a year had now been fighting and marching for seventeen straight days, through two of the fiercest battles in American history. Though that army had lost tens of thousands of men, it had not turned back. It was ready to move again; indeed, as the colonel read his report, a stream of supply wagons rumbled past, heading south, billowing more dust onto generals and teamsters alike. All the North was reading about this campaign, which all hoped would be the last. But as Meade scanned the papers, he became glummer still.

Day after day, headlines trumpeted news of "Grant's Army" and "Grant's March." Even official dispatches from the War Department, where they should know who commanded what, were all Grant, Grant, Grant. Nowhere did the commander of the Army of the Potomac, so far the only general who had ever soundly defeated Robert E. Lee and the Army of Northern Virginia, find his own name.

THAT NIGHT, as almost every night, in camp or on the march, Meade wrote to his wife at home in Philadelphia. It was a habit he had stuck to since his post–West Point days as a civilian surveyor in the Florida swamps, along the Louisiana-Texas and Maine-Canada boundary lines, and as military engineer with General Taylor in the Mexican War. He was devoted to Taylor and to his comrades on the trail, but he opened himself only to his alter ego, the cultured Margaretta. Daughter and granddaughter of distinguished congressmen, she spoke four languages and was a talented pianist. Since their wedding in 1840, the Meades had had seven children. One of them, Captain George Meade, a twenty-year-old West Point dropout, was with his father as military aide. But the general would never confide in anyone the way he did in Margaret.

Barely a month after Grant was appointed, Meade had grumbled to her about the way "the whole public press, even including that very loyal sheet the [Philadelphia] Inquirer, has ever since Grant's arrival here been so uniform & consistent in endeavoring to make him out the actual commander of this army." Unconvincingly, Meade wrote that "there have been so many offensive and lying paragraphs that I have ceased to notice them or allow them to influence me." A little later, he added, "You would be amused to see the worshipping of the Rising Sun by certain officers in this army but Grant behaves very handsomely and immediately refers to me all the letters & communications he gets from my subordinates, who apply to him when they have axes to grind."[31]

Meade's awkward position obsessed both him and his wife; hardly a letter between them failed to complain about it. Stirred by what she was hearing and reading in Philadelphia, Mrs. Meade was apparently more aggrieved than he was. The week before the fighting began, she had urged him to resign rather than tolerate the situation. Meade replied that not only would that be wrong, but leaving "would be fatal to my reputation." If he had known how relations with Grant would develop, he might have resigned earlier on the pretense of illness, but to depart on the verge of battle was something "no man should do under any circumstances." Otherwise, if he could somehow be at home with Margaret and the children, he "would willingly let Grant gain victories, have all the credit & be made President"—to which he added, "Perhaps before long this may come about."[32]

All this was not just paranoia, escalating back and forth between Meade and his wife; other, more objective officers also felt the problem, even before the campaign began. On the day the Union army crossed the Rapidan, Meade's chief of staff, General Humphreys, wrote that Grant had not ignored or slighted him in any way. But, he said, it was obvious that while he and Meade would work as hard as ever, "the reputation justly due to those labors, responsibility and deeds will go to General Grant and not to General Meade, much less to myself. General Grant will reap all the glory, all the reputation of success, and share none of the obloquy of disaster if such should befall us."[33]

Within days, unknown to Meade and Humphreys, Grant's headquarters officers were urging the general-in-chief "with much force" to assume direct control of the army around him. At the height of the Spotsylvania conflict, his staff asserted that crucial time was being lost in passing orders through Meade, that instructions could be garbled, and that no matter whether Meade failed or succeeded, in his "somewhat anomalous position" he would never get proper blame or recognition. Besides, his short temper alienated the officers he had to work with, while Grant's easy disposition won willing cooperation.

Grant listened to these arguments, and conceded that "some embarrassments" resulted from the arrangement. But, he said, as general-in-chief, he was responsible for all the Union armies, and he could not risk neglecting others by personally commanding the Army of the Potomac. Besides, Meade was highly respected in Pennsylvania, which had sent more men into Union service than any other state except New York. He had been with this army in all its ups and downs. For Grant to relieve him so soon after arriving from the West might damage morale in the army and on the home front. Grant concluded by saying that he and Meade worked smoothly together, and Meade was "capable and perfectly subordinate," which gave the supreme commander time to deal with his broader obligations. He promised that "I will always see that he gets full credit for what he does."[34]

But under the circumstances he did not, indeed could not. For one thing, official bulletins on the war in Virginia were not based on Grant's messages to Chief of Staff Halleck, but on dispatches to Secretary Stanton from his observer at Grant's headquarters, Charles A. Dana. In Washington, Stanton summarized and rewrote them for public consumption, seldom even acknowledging Meade's existence. For another thing, newspaper correspondents and editors (and later historians) naturally focused on the rough-cut new chief from beyond the mountains, rather than on the touchy, too-familiar patrician from Philadelphia. And for another, everything Grant's headquarters officers said about the hazards and inconveniences of overlapping command was true—made more so by their own exasperation with Meade and the mutual resentment of the duplicate staffs. Despite what Grant promised, from that day on "he gave a closer personal direction in battle to the movements of subdivisions of the armies." Meade saw this clearly, and so did the rest of the world.[35]

Three days after that debate within Grant's command post, Meade noted to his wife that "the papers have counted me out entirely. . . . I presume therefore we might as well make up our mind to this state of things and be reconciled to it." When the Spotsylvania battle was over, two visiting senators complimented him and told him that in Washington "it was well understood that these were my battles." Meade demurred, saying that at first he had maneuvered the army, "but that gradually & from the very nature of things, Grant had taken the control, and that it would be injurious to the army to have two heads." One newspaperman had written that "Grant does the grand strategy and I the grand tactics," a version with which Meade seemed to agree. Another writer said the Army of the Potomac was "directed by Grant, commanded by Meade, and led by Hancock, Sedgwick and Warren," which Meade told his wife "about hits the nail on the head." But none of this made him feel any better. Scoffing again at how some officers were "worshipping the Rising Sun," he told his wife, "I think Dearest we might as well make up our minds that our sun has passed his meridian. Let us try however to make it set in the clearness of honesty & purity, disdaining to keep it up by resorting to falsehood & clap-trap."[36]

IT WAS IN this frame of mind that Meade sat through the council of war outside Massaponax Church on May 21. Above the circle of officers, in the church steeple, the renowned photographer Timothy O'Sullivan adjusted his cumbersome camera to take in the scene below. A tall cavalryman wearing a kepi instead of a campaign hat rode up, handed his horse to an orderly, and started to tell the circle of planners what he had discovered out ahead of the army. Meade, peering at his map, apparently asked a question. As the scout stepped toward Meade and traced his finger across the map, Grant rose, walked around behind Meade's pew, and leaned over his shoulder. At that moment, O'Sullivan snapped one of the war's most famous photographs, in which Grant unconsciously blocks Meade from the view of the camera, and thus symbolically from the view of posterity.

2

We Must Strike Them a Blow

THE TIME WAS long past when Robert E. Lee needed to prove himself to his troops in the Army of Northern Virginia. When he had first taken command in 1862, some soldiers had grumbled at his seemingly defensive attitude when he assigned them to what they considered slaves' work, deepening the fortifications around Richmond. He silenced them in seven days of roaring counterattacks against McClellan, proving that, as one subordinate said, "his very name might be audacity." At the Wilderness and again at Spotsylvania Court House, the adrenaline of the moment drove him to risk his life by riding ahead of his attacking soldiers, until they refused to go forward unless he went to the rear. Though he was usually a model of dignified self-control, when he rode into a desperate situation, he spurred his warhorse Traveller alongside the men in front. In those crises, he was thinking only of what he saw, of rallying the men in the ranks immediately around him. Yet word of his impetuosity had its effect throughout the army, lifting morale in hard times.

During the Spotsylvania struggle, an infantryman named Jesse Frank wrote to his father in North Carolina that "Mr. Grant is the worst whipd man ever trod the soil of Va—but he is fighting for honer not to save life but . . . he keeps his carcass out of danger. You would be astonished to see Moss Bob always ride along the lines in the thickest of the fight he should not expose himself so but it is his will to do so. . . ." Whether it was Lee's considered will is doubtful, for he certainly realized how foolish it was for an irreplaceable commander to ride out front as if he were the rashest lieutenant, making a target that enemy gunners could not resist. (At Spotsylvania, his horse reared just as a round shot from a Yankee cannon passed under his stirrups.) One of his artillerymen wrote, "He had the combative instinct in him as strongly developed as any man living." When that instinct burst out, Lee's officers explained it to one another with both admiration and dismay: "His blood was up."[1]

Lee was fifty-seven, and three years of war had aged him dramatically. In 1861, when he arrived in Richmond to take charge of Virginia's forces, his mustache had been black, his face beardless, his hair showing only streaks of gray. Now he looked older than his age. He was sleeping little; in the field, he might retire to his cot between 9:00 and 10:00 p.m., rise about 3:00 a.m., and be on the move at daybreak. At any waking hour, he was likely to be off inspecting his lines, talking with a colonel about the angle of his breastworks, or advising a battery officer to drop in a few rounds to probe a Federal position. One aide, after riding through the night to corps and division headquarters and finding every officer he sought already slumbering, returned to Lee's tent, to discover the chief of staff on his knees praying and the commander wide-awake, squinting at a map by the light of a candle stuck in a bottle. "Does he never, never sleep?" the officer asked himself.[2]

One reason why Lee rested so little was that he had such a small, relatively junior military staff. His Union counterparts sometimes used generals who could command corps as their chiefs of staff, and erstwhile division commanders in lesser headquarters jobs. But in this as in so much else, Lee was old-fashioned; his formative combat experience had been in Mexico as understudy to General Scott, who believed in the morale value of personal leadership. The officers closest around Lee were lieutenant colonels, who seemed to function mostly as dictationists when they were not off delivering orders. Lee wanted to see the battlefield for himself. At the same time, he concerned himself firsthand with problems that in a modern staff system would have been delegated to separate personnel, intelligence, operations, and logistics sections. Now, pushing his army to stay ahead of Grant, Lee rode through the night, sleeping little. The pounding of hour after hour in the saddle, together with mosquitoes, skimpy, greasy food, and bad water, sapped his vigor and sometimes even shook the granite composure that had been his hallmark.

The hurried march east, then south from Spotsylvania, had the same effect on tens of thousands of younger soldiers. Yankees and Rebels followed roughly parallel roads, forced to press on past dawn and dusk, often asleep on their feet. When there was no rain, the fine dust stirred by companies and regiments, cavalry and cannon, choked the plodding infantry. When there was rain, the clinging mud made each weary leg lift a ton of added weight in a day's march. Costly experience had taught the soldiers of both sides to dig in before they ate or slept.

Night marching and digging were particularly hard on the garrison troops Grant had summoned as reinforcements after the first days of bloodletting. To men like those of the Second Connecticut Heavy Artillery, who until then had served their country comfortably in the fortifications around Washington, "it was almost beyond the limits of endurance." Ordered to the front as infantry, they had done as so many other green soldiers had done, setting out loaded down with extra clothing, supplies, and equipment that they soon dropped along the roadside. Before they heard a shot fired by the enemy, they got "a savage hint of the hardships of campaigning . . . and much more terrible experiences were close at hand."[3]

They also trudged into the miasma of uncertainty where combat soldiers traditionally live. They knew that Grant's objective was Lee's army—or Richmond, or both, depending on when the question was asked and who answered it. Beyond that, men in the ranks could only guess where they were at any given hour, and where they were going. Milton Myers, a compass-conscious foot soldier in the 110th Ohio, made entries in his journal at almost every break in the march. After departing the Spotsylvania lines, he wrote, "Have crossed or re-crossed two streams (perhaps the Po and N.Y.) and are now posted . . . in the woods, apparently not far from the position we occupied just previous to crossing what we thought was the Po River." (Like many travelers before and since, Myers was confused by the Mat, Ta, Po, and Ni rivers, which combine downstream into the Mattaponi. He thought he had fixed his location between the Ta and the Po when the latest *Harper's Weekly*, containing war maps, made its way to the army.) Later the same day, Myers added, "Back where we started from last night. . . . I felt disheartened this morning while on the 'back track,' as we thought, wondering if General Lee had outgeneraled General Grant."

Fresh beef was issued; at nightfall, the regimental band's "Hail, Columbia" cheered the camp, and Myers went on speculating: "Lying in line of battle—third line, I think, facing northwest. . . . We have probably not marched more than a couple miles, in a southwesterly direction. . . . It is said the enemy are but a little way out front. . . . It seems to me almost probable. . . . Our general course has been about S. by S.W. . . . This P.M. we crossed a stream which may or not be the one we crossed early this morning." On a special occasion when half a gill (two ounces) of whiskey was issued, Myers did not drink his, but did what he had read that a wise traveler in Russia did—rubbed it with candle tallow on his sore feet.[4]

Yet many of the soldiers who later recalled that trek felt a little lighter as they tramped out of the war-stripped country near Fredericksburg, crossing into relatively unravaged Caroline County. "Forests were standing untouched, farm lands were protected by fences, crops were green and untrampled, birds were singing, flowers blooming—Eden everywhere."[5]

Abolitionist Yankees resented leaving such idyllic countryside in the hands of undeserving secessionists. In the county seat of Bowling Green, Hancock's soldiers threw open the jail, liberating four convicts who had been sentenced to death. Then they appropriated a cache of hams, and gutted an apothecary shop just because "we disliked the chin music of its proprietor." When their regimental commander chastised them, saying it was unmanly to take medicine from the needy, John Haley of the Seventeenth Maine "made some pointed remarks concerning a couple of ducks that the colonel's cook was at that moment preparing for his palate. I see no great difference between the sins of stealing medicines or stealing ducks," Haley wrote, "but [Lieutenant] Colonel [Charles B.] Merrill is a lawyer, and he doubtless can discriminate."

Farther down the road, Haley helped ransack the well-furnished home of "a divine who must be a person of 'culture and means,' " noting that the clergyman seemed to have "more business capacity than faith." Haley selected for himself a fine china plate, though an infantryman could hardly expect to preserve such a fragile bit of loot through the travails of a single day. However, he clearly was less interested in enriching himself than in punishing the absent landlord. "It is in keeping with our mission to destroy his kind of theology," he confided in his diary. "A theology that sanctions slavery savors too strongly of Satan to be tolerated."[6]

Though many Virginians in territory long occupied had learned to be accommodating to Yankees, citizens were less hospitable here, where the Federals had always been transients. When the *New York Herald* correspondent Sylvanus Cadwallader stopped at a farmhouse in lower Caroline, his reception by the women there "bordered on positive incivility" until Generals Grant and Meade rode up. The arrival of such impressive rank softened the ladies' manners, but not their Southern loyalty. Meade said affably that he "supposed they had never seen so many live Yankees before," to which one hostess replied, "Oh, yes I have—many more." "Where?" asked the general. "In Richmond," she snapped—Richmond, where thousands of live Yankees were prisoners of war.[7]

DESPITE CASUALTIES, Grant and Meade were still pushing south, but while the Army of the Potomac was fighting at Spotsylvania Court House, Confederates had blunted the other prongs of Grant's Virginia offensive. South of the James River, hastily gathered and out-numbered Rebels under General Beauregard had counterattacked Ben Butler's forces at Drewry's Bluff, then bottled them up in the neck of land called Bermuda Hundred, while in the Shenandoah Valley, Major General John C. Breckinridge had turned back Franz Sigel at New Market. Thus the Union threats to cut off Richmond from the south and west settled into stalemate. As they did, both Lee and Grant sought to refill their ranks with troops from those fronts, to throw all their might into their next confrontation.

Before leaving Spotsylvania, Lee had written a long confidential dispatch to Davis, promising to keep looking for opportunities to strike, but adding that "neither the strength of our army nor the condi-tion of our animals will admit of any extensive movement with a view to drawing the enemy from his position." Grant was merely waiting for reinforcements, Lee suggested, and he was likely to get all he needed. "The importance of this campaign to the administration of Mr. Lincoln and to General Grant leaves no doubt that every effort and every sacrifice will be made to secure its success. . . ." Grant could bring up enough men to replace all his heavy losses, Lee said. Shortly afterward, in case that wording did not seem urgent enough, he added a thought that had always gotten a response from Davis: "The ques-tion is whether we shall fight the battle here or around Richmond. If the troops are obliged to be retained at Richmond I may be forced back."[8]

Both commanders expected their next collision to be at the North Anna River, which seemed the most defensible natural barrier between the Union army and Richmond. Along the way, Grant sent Hancock's corps ahead, thinking Lee might dare attack it and so expose his own army to a crushing counterblow. But the battered Confederates kept moving on the inside track, while most of the Fed-erals made a rough quarter-circle to their east. Grant's divisions had to march farther, but both armies left thousands of exhausted stragglers in their wake as they pushed on toward the North Anna.

The problem was always worse on the brink of battle. On the

Union side, Brigadier General John Gibbon wrote, "Immense numbers of men would quit the ranks upon the slightest pretext or none at all, leaving the more faithful to do the fighting." This problem became "so serious an evil" that the steely Gibbon, who had repeatedly returned to duty after major wounds and illness, urged Meade to order one out of every hundred stragglers summarily executed. Meade did not take this advice, but he did order summary court-martials for such offenders, and on the last day at Spotsylvania, Gibbon wrote with some satisfaction in his diary that one of his soldiers who ran away every time his regiment went into battle had been tried one day and shot at seven o'clock the next morning.[9]

Again, the Confederates got to the next battlefield first. On May 22, Grant notified Washington that Lee was ahead of him, already on the south bank of the North Anna. Federal troops had picked up prisoners from the first elements of Major General George E. Pickett's division, sent to Lee from Petersburg, and Breckinridge's, brought east from the Valley. Under the circumstances, Grant said, Butler should retain only enough Union force to "keep a foothold" on the James, and send the rest to him. At the same time, Lee was telling Jefferson Davis that Beauregard should come up to join him because "it seems to me our best policy to unite upon [Grant's army] and endeavor to crush it"—the farther from Richmond, the better.[10]

But telling Washington what the Union army should do and telling Richmond what seemed best did not produce automatic results. Both Grant and Lee had to deal with self-important fellow generals who were stubbornly possessive of whatever troops they could grasp. Grant, though general-in-chief of all Union armies, put up with repeated delays by Butler, who consistently exaggerated the number of Confederates facing him. Lee's situation was worse, for though he would become the Confederacy's general-in-chief in the final weeks of war, he now commanded only the Army of Northern Virginia. Davis insisted on clinging to a system of geographical departments whose heads reported independently to Richmond, which meant that the overworked Confederate president himself effectively controlled every transaction among his ranking commanders. Thus Lee could only request cooperation from Beauregard, not order it—and Beauregard, at Petersburg, on the main railroad lines from farther south, could argue over every detachment he forwarded to Lee.

Barely twenty-three miles above Richmond, Lee set up his new headquarters at Hanover Junction, where the Virginia Central Railroad curved west across the tracks of the Richmond, Fredericksburg &

Potomac. And there on May 23, life in the field had so drained Lee that on his first personal reconnaissance below the North Anna, he presented a sight his troops had never witnessed before: tired and sick, he inspected the ground not from his steady horse Traveller, but in a borrowed civilian carriage.

Grant and Meade were physically healthier, but their command relationship had not improved. Meade still missed no opportunity to be offended by whatever intentional or accidental slights he perceived. On the way south, when the two generals and their staffs were conferring on pews at Mount Carmel Church, a dispatch came from Sherman in Georgia. It reported his success on the road to Atlanta and said that if Grant's inspiration could make the Army of the Potomac do its share, great things lay ahead. Charles Dana, the former managing editor of Horace Greeley's *New York Tribune,* now serving as assistant secretary of war and Stanton's official informant with the army, perhaps intentionally made the mistake of reading the Sherman message aloud. At this, "the eyes of Major-General George Gordon Meade stood out about one inch as he said, in a voice like cutting an iron bar with a handsaw: 'Sir! I consider that despatch an insult to the army I command and to me personally. The Army of the Potomac does not require General Grant's inspiration or anybody else's inspiration to make it fight!' " Meade would not drop the subject; still unhappy during dinner with his own staff, he called the western army "an armed rabble."[11]

While Meade was fuming, Union troops had reached the North Anna and captured the Telegraph Road bridge, on the main route to Richmond. Farther upstream, the whole Fifth Corps got across unchallenged at Jericho Mills. These Federals on Lee's left were starting to bivouac when A. P. Hill threw a surprise attack against them at suppertime. In confused fighting, the Yankees repulsed this effort and dug in to hold their position on the south side of the river. Lee, seeing the threat of being turned on one or both flanks, focused on his map. He could no longer defend the river line—not only were the Yankees already across on right and left but from the higher north bank their artillery could dominate most of the potential battlefield. Only at one position, Ox Ford, between the two enemy crossing points, did topography favor the Confederates. There the river was perhaps seventy-five yards wide and three or four feet deep, overlooked by a wooded ridge on the south that ran up to about 130 feet.[12]

Grasping this, Lee devised one of the cleverest tactical schemes of his career: while holding Ox Ford, he angled Hill's corps back on his left, and Anderson's and Ewell's on his right, making an inverted V, with its point on the high ground overlooking the ford. Hill would dig in on a line running southwest to steep bluffs at the Little River; Ewell's line on the far right would be anchored on a swampy creek bottom above Hanover Junction. This layout would invite the Union army to advance on both flanks, effectively separating it into three parts—one still north of the river, facing Ox Ford, and one across the river on each flank. If all went well for Lee, he could strike either of those wings and crush it before Grant could respond, because for Union regiments to move from one flank to the other, they would have to cross and then recross the North Anna. But if the Federals attacked first, Lee could shift strength quickly to either side of his V.

Grant very nearly stepped into this trap. Because his flank elements had crossed the river so easily, he thought Lee was falling back toward Richmond. On May 24, he sent Warren's Fifth and Wright's Sixth Corps ahead on the Union right and Hancock's Second on the left. Burnside, brought under Meade's formal command in the Army of the Potomac the same day, was ordered to take Ox Ford in the center. That evening, the firmly entrenched Confederates shattered assaults by Burnside and Hancock before Grant, realizing what Lee had contrived, halted the attack and ordered his army to entrench quickly before the Confederates took the offensive.

But Lee's expected counterattack never came. Early that day, he had gone in his carriage to Hill's lines to learn why the previous evening's effort against the Fifth Corps had failed. In a most uncharacteristic outburst, he demanded of Hill, "Why did you not do as Jackson would have done—thrown your whole force upon these people and driven them back?" Stonewall had been dead more than a year, but Lee still missed him every day, repeatedly holding other good officers to the impossible standard left in his mind by Jackson. On this occasion, he blamed Hill, who had recently retaken command of his corps after days of illness, for the shortcomings of subordinate generals the night before.[13]

Lee's own illness helped explain this display; his temper flared when his body let him down, and now he was trying to control severe diarrhea. Frustrated, unable to spring the trap he had so cunningly laid, he seems to have overlooked what he had accomplished on the North Anna: he had blocked Grant's direct route toward Richmond and retained control of the vital Virginia Central rail line to the Shenandoah Valley. Back at his tent, he lashed out at his professorial staff officer Lieutenant Colonel Charles S. Venable. The colonel emerged to say, "I have just told the old man that he is not fit to command this army, and that he had better send for Beauregard."[14]

Lee would do no such thing, nor even hint at his condition in dispatches to Richmond. Instead, he lay exhausted on his cot, telling his staff, "We must strike them a blow—we must never let them pass us again—we must strike them a blow!" As Venable wrote, "Lee confined to his tent was not Lee on the battlefield."[15]

There was no immediate solution to Lee's physical or command problems. Diarrhea was rampant in both armies among soldiers who sometimes had to drink dirty water from the bottom of their trenches and had only the vaguest understanding of sanitation. It weakened men so that they became easy victims of other ailments—one Confederate doctor wrote, "No matter what else a patient had, he had diarrhoea." Another reported that "chronic diarrhoea and dysentery . . . not only destroyed more soldiers than gunshot wounds, but more soldiers were permanently disabled and lost to the service from these diseases than from the disability following the accidents of battle."[16]

William H. Taylor, a surgeon with the Nineteenth Virginia, told how he practiced healing on the march: "Diagnosis was rapidly made, usually by intuition. . . . In one pocket of my trousers I had a ball of blue mass, in another a ball of opium. All complainants were asked the same question, 'How are your bowels?' If they were open, I administered a plug of opium; if they were shut, I used a plug of blue mass [calomel]." Taylor's prescriptions were enlightened, by modern standards, but other would-be remedies for the most common complaint varied from the horrifying (cauterizing the rectum) to the primitive (teas of blackberry, chinquapin, dogwood, sweet gum, black oak, or pomegranate leaves).[17]

What medicine was given to Lee, if any, was not recorded. But he was largely immobilized as the opportunity to strike Grant at the North Anna slipped away. For a series of good reasons, Lee refused to pass temporary command to Beauregard. Had he been unable to function at all, he might have reluctantly turned over his beloved army to someone in whom he had full confidence—the lamented Jackson might have qualified, and perhaps Longstreet, but now he was out of action, too. Lee had no personal rapport with the courteously contentious Beauregard, who had never been part of his Army of Northern Virginia. And after the costly struggles at the Wilderness and Spotsylvania, he was reassessing his corps commanders for the tests that lay close ahead.

The cool, modest South Carolinian Dick Anderson, forty-two

years old, had been with Lee in every fight since the Peninsula campaign of 1862. He had led a division since Second Manassas, coming
back promptly after a wound at Sharpsburg. After Chancellorsville,
Lee had told President Davis that Anderson was "a capital officer"
who would make a good corps commander when needed. That came
true when Anderson replaced the wounded Longstreet at the Wilderness and made the fortunate decision to keep his corps marching to
Spotsylvania. There he had handled his divisions with steady skill. But
that was only days earlier; though he was now a senior major general,
he was Lee's least experienced corps commander.[18]

On field after field, A. P. Hill had won a reputation for aggressiveness and initiative, for marching his men hard and meeting crises
without waiting for orders. Of Jackson's division commanders, he may
have been the one most like Stonewall himself. But the hot-tempered
thirty-eight-year-old Virginian had also crossed Jackson more than
once, privately describing him to Jeb Stuart as "that crazy old Presbyterian fool." There had been friction with Longstreet, as well. At
Spotsylvania, Hill had been so ill that he managed his corps from an
ambulance close behind the lines, and he was not long back in the saddle when his evening attack failed at the North Anna. Though Lee
may have regretted his resulting outburst at Hill, the disappointment
there was fresh in his mind.[19]

Then there was Dick Ewell. Early in the war, especially in the
Shenandoah Valley campaign of 1862, he had been the Jackson lieutenant who fought most like his commander. In personality, "Old Bald
Head" was the opposite of Jackson—he was peppery and profane,
while Stonewall was dour and devout. But in action, Ewell had been a
lesser Jackson, quick and hard-hitting, until losing a leg at Second
Manassas. Since returning to the field to take over Jackson's corps
after Chancellorsville, he had had to be lifted and strapped into his
saddle. On the first day at Gettysburg, his hesitation under Lee's order
to go forward "if practicable" became a factor in the Confederate
defeat. Forty-seven years old during the current campaign, he was
showing strain in both health and temper. At Spotsylvania, he took a
bad fall when his horse was hit, and he furiously cursed his troops as
cowards when trying to rally them at the "mule shoe." Lee, coming up
beside him, asked, "How can you expect to control these men when
you have lost control of yourself? If you cannot control your excitement, you had better retire."[20]

On May 27, as the Union army moved south again, nature and Lee
made Ewell's retirement decision for him. When Ewell, too, was dis-

274-4070 Dolton Public Library District

abled by diarrhea, he had to ask Jubal Early to manage his corps. Two
days later, with a new fight developing, Lee gave Early formal command. A protesting Ewell was placed on indefinite leave, and later put
in charge of local Richmond defenses.

"Old Jube" Early at forty-seven was sarcastic and agnostic, yet
devoted to the reverent Lee, and never let him down. He had resigned
from the army a year after graduating from West Point in 1837, then
returned briefly during the Mexican War, only to miss the fighting. As
a civilian, he had argued against Virginia's secession at the state convention in 1861, but once the war began, he fought with rare vigor.
Wounded in the Peninsula campaign, he had led a division since
Sharpsburg, had filled in more than once as corps commander, and
was as qualified for full promotion to that level as anyone in Lee's
army.

Not only was Lee himself ailing, and two of his three infantry corps
under new command; he also was without a cavalry chief as he organized for fighting closer and closer to Richmond. Rather than immediately replacing Jeb Stuart in that role, he ordered his major generals
of cavalry—his son W. H. F. "Rooney" Lee, his nephew Fitzhugh Lee,
and the towering South Carolinian Wade Hampton—to report
directly to him until further notice.

But the senior Lee was not as concerned about his own health and
his command structure as he was about the dwindling size of his army
compared to Grant's. So far in May, the Army of Northern Virginia
had suffered approximately twenty thousand casualties, and the Army
of the Potomac about forty thousand, which by itself would mean that
the Union advantage was lessening. But Lee had known for days that
massive Union reinforcements were arriving, and a Northern newspaper had reported that Butler's two corps from below the James were
coming to bolster Grant and Meade.

The Confederacy could not hope to send Lee such manpower.
True, the rest of Pickett's division had come up, with their general
reporting his troops "much worn for want of food. . . . The men are
calling loudly for bread. . . . We must get something, or this division
will be worse than useless." His plaint rang hollow among other officers whose men had been fighting and marching on short rations for
nearly a month. Breckinridge's two brigades had also arrived, plus
another separate brigade and a contingent of green South Carolina
cavalry. But together, these additions totaled only about eleven thousand infantry and eleven hundred horsemen. Lee needed more. As
his enemy started around his right flank again, trying again to get

between him and the fortifications protecting Richmond, he looked ahead grimly.[21]

"We must destroy this army of Grant's before he gets to the James River," he told Early. "If he gets there it will become a siege, and then it will be a mere question of time."[22]

3

Rely Upon It the End Is Near

"LEE'S ARMY is really whipped," Grant told Washington on May 26. "The prisoners we take now show it, and the action of his army shows it unmistakably."[1]

That was Grant's opinion as he pulled away from the trap set for him on the North Anna. During that fight, a returning cavalry officer found Union headquarters so quiet that he could hardly believe anything serious was in the air. There was the general-in-chief with one leg of his trousers slipped down over his boot, "his coat in confusion, his sword equipments sprawling on the ground, not even the weight of sleep erasing that persistent expression of his lip holding a constant promise of something to be done." Here was Meade, pondering, with his hat brim "turned down about his ears, tapping a scabbard with his fingers, gazing abstractedly into the depths of the earth through eye-glasses that should become historic." Staff colonels, artillerymen, orderlies, and horses crowded the grove; the army's quartermaster toyed with his riding whip as he dropped a casual comment into the conversation. "A drowsy and curious scene," mused the cavalryman.

Sleep deprivation may have contributed to that seeming calm. Beneath it was more tension than the visitor could see—the tension of waiting for word from the lines, where Union attacks were being thrown back on left and right.[2]

The next morning, Grant acknowledged that he was checkmated. He ordered his troops to recross the North Anna quietly, then march southeastward into King William County to cross the Pamunkey River, trying again to loop behind the Confederates. In his urgency to move before Lee realized what was happening, Grant abandoned any pretense that he was merely overseeing Meade's management of the campaign. He issued detailed instructions, telling Meade which corps should march when, on which roads, across which bridges. Talking with his staff as he moved his command post from one country church to another, he could conceive only one reason why Lee had let him get away from the North Anna without a major counterblow: obviously the Rebels were "really whipped."[3]

"A battle with them outside of intrenchments cannot be had," Grant reported to army chief of staff Halleck in Washington. "Our men feel that they have gained the morale over the enemy and attack with confidence. I may be mistaken, but I feel that our success over Lee's army is already assured. The confidence and rapidity with which you [Halleck] have forwarded re-enforcements have contributed largely to the feeling of confidence inspired in our men and to break down that of the enemy."[4]

By then, this was the consensus at Union headquarters, endorsed by dispatches from Dana, Secretary Stanton's observer at the front. "The rebels have lost all confidence and are already morally defeated," Dana wrote. "This army has learned to believe that it is sure of victory. Even our officers have ceased to regard Lee as an invincible military genius. On part of the rebels this change is evinced, not only by their not attacking, even when circumstances seem to invite it, but by the unanimous statement of prisoners taken from them. Rely upon it the end is near as well as sure."[5]

Meade was not quite as optimistic. "We undoubtedly have the *morale* over them, and will eventually, I think, compel them to go into Richmond," he wrote to his wife—"after that, *nous verrons.*"[6]

Grant's wishful thinking inspired Northern press reports such as an item of "highly important and glorious intelligence" that appeared in the *Washington Republican,* reprinted in the *Philadelphia Bulletin.* Lee, it said, had "commenced a hasty retreat . . . pursued with real vigor by Grant. The latter is in the saddle all the time, day and night, directing general movements in person. Grant is evidently embarrassing Lee. Unless Lee stops to fight today, we shall hear next of a grand conflict for the city of Richmond, before or in the works of that capital. Advices say that Jeff. Davis and his Cabinet left Richmond some days ago. There is little doubt that Richmond by this time is pretty well cleaned out of its inhabitants, and that it is nothing less than a fortress. . . ." The *New York Times* reprinted the article, too, but under the realistic heading "Mischievous and Exaggerated Reports."[7]

.　.　.

WARTIME governments always feel political pressure to improve the news from the battlefield. In election years, the pressure is intensified—and in 1864, Abraham Lincoln was facing a reelection campaign in the midst of civil war, a situation that history had never witnessed before. In May, as Grant and Dana were sending their glowing reports to Washington, the public was reading long casualty lists in newspapers across the North, and "multitudes of wounded" were jamming Washington hospitals. At the same time, the president was challenged politically from within and without his own party. Anti-Lincoln radical Republicans and impatient War Democrats, agitating for harsher military and reconstruction policies, were about to nominate former major general John Charles Frémont to run against him. Peace Democrats, urging negotiation or some other bloodless way to end the war, were looking for leadership from that other resigned warrior, Major General George Brinton McClellan. And now, in less than two weeks, the National Union Convention, an amalgam of Republicans and less angry War Democrats, would gather in Baltimore to anoint its presidential candidate. Lincoln, his cabinet, and his general-in-chief knew that only one thing—some shocking turn of events at the front—might prevent his renomination there.

To head off any such shock, the domineering secretary of war kept a tight grip on official information from the armies. In 1862, Stanton had moved the telegraph office into the War Department specifically "to control the military news and have it censored, and to prevent it from reaching the enemy, or the press. . . ." Stanton himself, according to his confidential secretary, "became the only reliable reporter the press had." Though Stanton could not black out the news of setbacks, he could and did filter and delay it, cushioning its impact on the home front and on interested powers abroad. His regular communiqués were based on Dana's reports to him, and released in the form of letters to Major General John A. Dix, commander of the Department of the East, based in New York.[8]

But Stanton, back in Washington, could censor only what passed through his office—Dana's reports, official news from the army, whatever moved from the field by telegraph. He could not directly control reports from the correspondents lingering at various headquarters, mingling with the troops, and collecting gossip at relay points between the army and cities of the North. He or the generals could banish any or all reporters from the front, threaten them with summary punishment, and render ex post facto judgment against publishers after the correspondents' work was printed. But then, as now, the press was irrepressible.

Before the spring campaign began, Grant's hometown friend and congressional booster, Representative Elihu Washburne, had visited his headquarters and introduced William Swinton, a writer whom Grant did not know. As Grant recalled it, Swinton "was presented as a literary gentleman who wished to accompany the army with a view of writing a history of the war when it was over. [Washburne] assured me that he was not present as a member of the press." Grant accepted Swinton on that basis, noting, "We received Richmond papers with about as much regularity as if there had been no war, and knew that our papers were received with equal regularity by the Confederates. It was desirable, therefore, that correspondents should not be privileged spies of the enemy within our lines."

Swinton would indeed write a valuable history of the Army of the Potomac. But before and after his introduction to Grant, he was a star correspondent of the *New York Times*. As Grant put it, "I soon found that he was corresponding with some paper (I have now forgotten which one), thus violating his word either expressed or implied." Shortly after the army crossed the Rapidan, Grant said, he had given spoken instructions to a staff officer, and three days later he saw them quoted verbatim in a Richmond paper. He obviously blamed Swinton. A few nights after that, Grant had conferred with Meade and staff well outside his headquarters tent, "thinking our conversation should be private." One of Grant's colonels spotted someone leaning against a stump in the darkness, listening. Pulling the man into the firelight, the colonel saw that it was Swinton, whose explanation was "evasive and unsatisfactory." But the only result at that time was a warning against "further eavesdropping." Much more would be heard from Swinton; he would stay with the Army of the Potomac long enough to write a superb account of the climactic action ahead, including one paragraph that got him into still deeper trouble.[9]

Whatever Grant's own feelings about the press, he was its greatest beneficiary as the campaign moved south, and Meade was its victim. At first, this was merely because the new general-in-chief got coverage and credit, while the familiar Meade was virtually ignored. But gradually, Meade's resentment of this contrast made it worse. He and Mrs. Meade did not imagine the favoritism, however; others saw it, too, perhaps more clearly.

James C. Biddle, a loyal Philadelphian and major on Meade's staff, blamed reporters more than he did Stanton's censorship. "Meade has fought [the campaign] and all these stories in the newspapers about Grant are disgusting," he wrote to his wife during the struggle at Spotsylvania. "I do not want you to be deceived. . . . They are made up of untruths. The reporters who make public opinion are the scum of creation and there is not one of them whom any gentleman would associate with. . . . There is one thing I do not like Grant has five or six reporters around him at his headquarters whilst Meade has not and never has had one. Is it not heartsickening to think that one's reputation depends on such a lot of scum . . . ?"[10]

Reporters wanted to spend their time around Grant not only because he was general-in-chief but also because there they were treated with more or less civility. As Biddle made clear, that was not the case at the headquarters of the Army of the Potomac, and Meade suffered for it.

POLITICALLY, if not militarily, Jefferson Davis's situation in those months seemed firmer than Lincoln's. Davis had been reinaugurated in 1862 for a six-year term as president of the "permanent" Confederate government. He had to endure vicious criticism from congressmen, restive governors, and the Southern press, which editorialized much more freely than did newspapers up north. But in the one-party Confederacy, there was no organized political opposition. Now, with the Union army shifting south around Lee, the sound of guns would soon be heard again in the Confederate capital, as loud as it had been two years earlier. Home-guard companies from across the state had been ordered to the Richmond defenses. Yet, contrary to rumors peddled in Washington, Davis had not fled; he was in his office, worrying over details as compulsively as if he were general-in-chief, secretary of state, and three-dollar-a-day government clerk combined. And the Confederate Congress was at work in Thomas Jefferson's state Capitol, cracking peanuts and spitting tobacco, about to approve extension of military conscription to boys as young as seventeen and men as old as fifty.[11]

As the Union army marched day and night to get across the Pamunkey River, its generals must have shivered as they rethought how close they had come to disaster at the North Anna. To Grant, the fact that Lee had not mounted a full-scale attack under such tempting circumstances meant that he could not. Considering casualties—each side had lost about 2,500 more men at the North Anna—there was some truth in this. Lee was so weakened in numbers that he could no longer afford to risk counterstrokes as bold as those at Second Manassas and Chancellorsville. For Washington to spread the idea that this meant "the end is near" might be useful at a time of political nervousness, and for privates in the ranks to believe that their enemy was demoralized might help them press on despite casualties and fatigue. But for the Union generals themselves to assume that what had not happened at the North Anna meant a moral collapse among Confederate soldiers could be a dangerous mistake.

That assumption was understandable if they were comparing gaunt Confederate prisoners to the well-fed Union replacements arriving from the North. A long list of full-strength regiments had been added to the Army of the Potomac before its vanguard reached the Pamunkey River on May 27. No doubt some captured Rebels were so impressed by the sight of all those fresh Yankees that they sounded hopeless—and they had not yet seen the mightiest single contingent of Union reinforcements, soon to start arriving from Butler's Army of the James.

BEFORE DEPARTING the North Anna, Grant had told Washington to "send Butler's force to White House to land on north side and march up to join this army . . . leave nothing more than is absolutely necessary" to hold the Union position south of the James River. "The enemy will not undertake any offensive operations there, but will concentrate here."[12]

Since opening the campaign in the Wilderness, the Union army had used Virginia's tidal rivers, flowing into Chesapeake Bay, to bring men and matériel and take back casualties. From Aquia Creek and Belle Plain on the Potomac above Fredericksburg, Grant had changed his supply point to Port Royal on the Rappahannock. Now, as he approached Richmond, he was shifting it to White House Landing, on the winding Pamunkey above its exit into the York. McClellan had used White House this way in 1862 until Lee drove him southeast, away from Richmond, a retreat that the Union commander famously euphemized as "changing his base" to ports on the James River. Now Grant was forcing the 1864 campaign onto the same rolling, swampy terrain over which the two armies had fought the bloody Seven Days battles two years earlier.

Sheridan's cavalry, which had ridden on to the James after its mid-May raid into the Richmond suburbs, resupplied down the river and

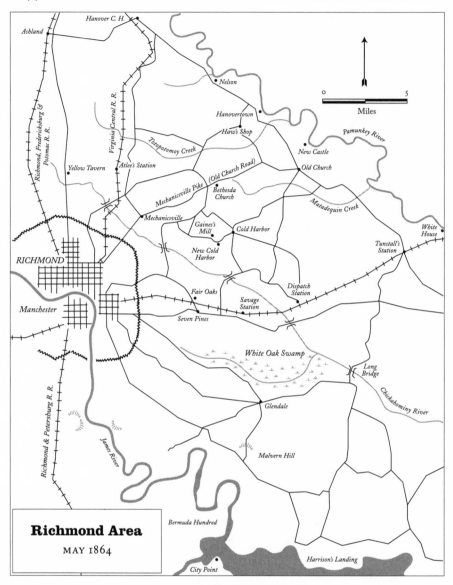

Richmond Area

MAY 1864

After being checked at the North Anna River, the Army of the Potomac raced to cross the Pamunkey at Hanovertown and Nelson's Crossing in another effort to get between Lee and Richmond. South of the James, Beauregard held off Butler's Union army at Bermuda Hundred.

returned to the Army of the Potomac in time to cover Grant's move from the North Anna across the Pamunkey River. Grant, hoping to get around Lee without being detected, had left skirmishers behind and sent his army arcing southeast toward Hanovertown, its troops wondering, as usual, where they were headed. "It seems to me it must require an extraordinary military genius to comprehend the reason for all the movements that we make, and their result," wrote Wilbur Fisk of the Second Vermont. His complaint might have been recorded by any foot soldier from Alexander the Great's time to today: "We take up a position one day and fortify it, and the next day we abandon it altogether. Sometimes we think we are about to make a regular attack on the enemy, and sometimes we think they are about to make an assault upon us. We make all preparations for a fight, but no fighting is done. If we think we are going to have a day's rest, we are pretty sure to fall in immediately and commence to march, and when a day's rest does come, it comes quite unexpectedly."[13]

Despite inferior maps, there had been no noticeable confusion over place names by the two infantry corps headed for Hanovertown, which is about twelve air miles down the Pamunkey from Hanover Court House, which is about eight miles below Hanover Junction. The other two corps would cross a couple of miles upstream from Hanovertown, at Nelson's Crossing. To reach those points, the Union infantry had to march much farther; from the North Anna, Burnside's trailing corps covered twenty-seven miles in off-and-on rain to approach Hanovertown.*

---

* Only three of Burnside's four divisions moved with the rest of the army. From the Rapidan to the James, Grant assigned Brigadier General Edward Ferrero's division, whose two infantry brigades were made up of seven regiments of U.S. Colored Troops, to guard the army's supply routes in the rear.

The high command's attitude toward Ferrero's division may have been reflected by Theodore Lyman, Meade's aide, who wrote during the struggle at Spotsylvania: "As I looked at [the black troops], my soul was troubled and I would gladly have seen them marched back to Washington. Can we not fight our own battles, without calling on these humble hewers of wood and drawers of water, to be bayonetted by the unsparing Southerners? Ah, you may make speeches at home, but here, where it is life or death, we dare not risk it. They have been put to guard the trains and have repulsed one or two little cavalry attacks in a creditable manner; but God help them if the grey-backed infantry attack them!" (Theodore Lyman, *Meade's Headquarters*, p. 102.)

As early as October 1862, U.S. Colored Troops had been committed to action farther south and west, and on May 24, 1864, they repelled an attack by Fitz Lee's cavalry on the Federal outpost at Wilson's Wharf, on the north bank of the James River. But except for rear-area skirmishes, they played no serious combat role in Virginia until the assault on Petersburg in mid-June.

The army's long wagon trains jammed the roads and forced infantrymen to slog in the dark across muddy fields and bottomlands. To light the way, soldiers piled fence rails into bonfires and set tall pines ablaze like torches. Thousands of men fell out exhausted, or failed to wake to march again at one of the inevitable stops and starts in the accordionlike column.

"The boys would, every one of them, in two minutes after the halt was made, be lying beside the road fast asleep," recalled one of Burnside's soldiers. "Those fellows once behind may have quite a little trouble in finding their regiments again; but they go straggling along inquiring for their regiments, brigades or perhaps their army corps." Even in their semiconscious exhaustion, some of them kept a sense of defiant humor. When a "very important and arrogant" officer prodded one of the sleeping troops and asked his regiment, the private woke and shouted, "The 279th Rhode Island!" This woke another sleeper, who piped up, "That's a blasted lie, this is the 119th Ireland!" More than once, wagons rolled over sleeping forms invisible in the darkness.[14]

ON MAY 27, the glory-bound twenty-four-year-old Brigadier General George Armstrong Custer led a surprise attack that drove away perhaps a hundred Maryland Confederate horsemen guarding the Pamunkey River crossing at Hanovertown. The First Regiment of his Michigan cavalry brigade rode ahead, yelling and peppering the defenders to protect men of the Fiftieth New York Engineers, who unloaded their pontoon boats and carried them on their shoulders to the riverbank.

Custer, too impatient to wait for the fast-working engineers to lay their bridges, tried to ford the swollen Pamunkey, a "stream fifty or sixty yards wide, water clayey, yellowish, current somewhat rapid." When his struggling horse threw him at midstream, he went flailing downriver and the troopers behind yelled, "Help the general! Help the general!" But Custer shouted back, "Hurry across there and get those Rebs. I can take care of myself!" and eventually he did, dragging himself to land "looking like a drowned rat." Despite his inglorious appearance, his men cheered. Soon Sheridan rode up, laughing, and asked how he had liked his bath. "I always take a bath in the morning when convenient," Custer told him, "and have paid a quarter for many not so good as this." With some Confederate guards still firing from the south bank, the bedraggled brigadier remounted to wait for the bridge, shouting, "Give it to them, boys, give 'em hell! See them run, the secesh sons of bitches!"[15]

The first of two bridges was done in an hour, and Custer's troopers led Brigadier General A. T. A. Torbert's cavalry division across. Probing toward Hanover Court House, these Yankees rode into more Maryland horsemen a few miles west of the pontoon bridges and pressed the defenders back past the boggy bottomlands of Crump's Creek. These cavalry collisions were Grant's army's first engagements south of the Pamunkey, the opening clashes in more than two weeks of action properly defined as the Cold Harbor campaign.[16]

Lee, still ailing and riding in his carriage rather than aboard Traveller, heard of the fighting as he moved his army down Telegraph Road toward Atlee's, only nine miles above Richmond. There he was so sick that he accepted a nearby family's offer to make his headquarters indoors for the first time since Grant had crossed the Rapidan. Lee did not know yet whether the reported contact meant that Federal infantry as well as cavalry had crossed the Pamunkey to his east. Until he found out, he was reluctant to turn his army that way, lest Grant's main force swing around his left, straight down into Richmond. Holding his three corps near Atlee's, he ordered his cavalry to make a reconnaissance in force the next morning, to see whether Union infantry was already across into Hanover County.[17]

By that time, it was. From dawn until past midnight on May 28, all four corps of the Army of the Potomac poured across, unimpeded, at Hanovertown and Nelson's. As troops of the Second Corps filed over the pontoon bridges, Grant himself stood watching with Meade and Hancock. The commanding general clearly was tired, expressionless, his teeth clamped on a dead cigar; the night before, he had had a sick headache and tried to soothe it with chloroform. Meade was deep in contemplation, stroking his chin, while Hancock spoke with his usual animation. The column of bone-tired soldiers stared at Grant, and he stared back as they dragged on without saluting or cheering.[18]

The lead Federal infantry brigades had already started digging in below the Pamunkey when Brigadier General David McMurtrie Gregg's cavalry division collided with the strong Confederate force of horsemen sent scouting by Lee. For seven hours, the two sides fought head-on near Enon Church and a road junction called Haw's Shop. There the Hanovertown-Richmond road crossed a lesser road connecting Hanover Court House to New Castle Ferry, White House,

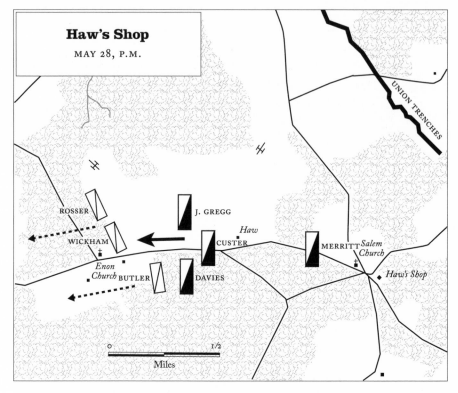

*To feel out the enemy, both commanders send out cavalry units, which collide
along the road between Haw's Shop and Enon Church. The struggle seesaws
back and forth until Custer's Michigan riders break the Confederate center,
giving the Federals control of the important road junction.*

and Cold Harbor, all to become significant sites in the developing
campaign.

THAT MORNING, Charles Dana had reported to Washington that
"Rebel cavalry is exceedingly demoralized, and flees before ours on
every occasion."[19]

He spoke too soon.

Just after passing Haw's Shop, Gregg's Federals struck two brigades of Major General Fitzhugh Lee's horsemen, commanded by
Brigadier Generals Williams C. Wickham and Thomas L. Rosser.
These Virginians were bolstered by part of Brigadier General Matthew Calbraith Butler's untried cavalry brigade, which, after lengthy
negotiations between state officials and Richmond, had just arrived
from South Carolina.

After a few dashes back and forth on horseback, troopers of both sides dismounted to do their serious fighting. Gregg sent Brigadier General Henry E. Davies, Jr.'s brigade ahead until it struck a Rebel line formed along a slight rise amid heavy timber. He quickly found out that these Confederates were not demoralized; in his own words, they put up an "exceedingly stubborn" fight. Against this stiff resistance, General Gregg moved up his second brigade, commanded by Colonel J. Irvin Gregg. The seesaw contest continued until midafternoon, when four of Custer's regiments came forward between Gregg's brigades, centering their advance along the road. On the Confederate side, the fresh South Carolina troopers moved in beside Rosser after Wickham's troopers were hit hard.[20]

Behind the lines, as these "new issue" Carolinians trotted past Virginia veterans of Jeb Stuart's adventures, they had endured mile after mile of teasing about their "city look," their bright equipment and healthy horses. They also had heard enough horror stories to put them in a vengeful mood. In Richmond two days earlier, John Cumming of the Fifth South Carolina Cavalry had written home that "the Yankey raiders wherever they go destroy every thing leave the families one meel of provisions and burn and distroy the rest they treat the young women most shamefully compell them to submit to there brutal lust in the preasents of there Husbands or Fathers and I have been told that the yanky Negro raiders will take white women and carry them . . . with them as long as they want them it is a shocking state of affairs. . . ."[21]

The South Carolinians were so incensed by the time they reached the field at Haw's Shop that they charged in yelling, which announced them to the enemy. They were armed with British Enfield muzzle-loaders, requiring much more manipulation and thus exposure to operate than the Federals' breech-loading carbines; Sergeant Robert Hudgins of Wickham's brigade said he saw more men wounded in the arm that day than anywhere else. But afterward, Union general Custer acknowledged that "These Carolinians fought very gallantly in this their first fight. . . ."[22]

Custer's troopers ran into a damaging cross fire and fell back more than once before leading a charge that drove the Rebels from the woods on one side of the road. This exposed the flank of the South Carolinians, giving the Michiganders clear targets for their seven-shot repeaters as the Rebels pulled away across an open field. Confederate general Fitz Lee apparently ordered the withdrawal because he thought the dismounted Union troopers were infantry. But amid the smoke and racket one of the South Carolina officers, determined to stand fast on his first day under fire, refused to obey the order. General Rosser argued with him until a shot sang between them, clipping the officer's saber knot, at which Rosser said, "If you're fool enough to stay here, you can do so," and departed. Next day the officer apologized to Rosser, explaining that he had believed he was to take orders only from Major General Wade Hampton, another South Carolinian, to whose division the new regiments were assigned. Whether from stubbornness or inexperience, his delay had caused a captain and about a squadron of his men to be captured. The proud Charleston Light Dragoons went into the fight with forty-seven men and lost twenty-one, only one of them taken prisoner.[23]

Custer acknowledged that his brigade's loss at Haw's Shop was "greater than in any other engagement of the campaign." One of the mortally wounded Federals was forty-eight-year-old Private John Huff, of the Fifth Michigan, a former Berdan's Sharpshooter credited with putting Jeb Stuart out of action seventeen days earlier. Colonel John W. Kester of the First New Jersey said that "the severest cavalry fighting of the war" took place at Haw's Shop. In fact, though cavalrymen did the fighting, following the first skirmishes they did it almost entirely on foot. So severe was it that afterward, both sides far overestimated the size of the force against them. "Three of our brigades had whipped their whole corps," wrote a correspondent of the *New York Herald*. "The numerical forces in this fight must certainly have been five to one" in the Federals' favor, wrote "Orlando" in the *Charleston Daily Courier*. Other cavalry units had operated on the margins of the fight and the Union Second Corps had moved up in close support. But the heavy combat involved only Gregg's division plus Custer's brigade on one side and Fitz Lee's division plus the South Carolinians on the other.[24]

The Haw family, whose house was in an oak grove half a mile from the battle line, never forgot that harrowing day. In the morning, the Yankees used the kitchen in an outbuilding as a hospital while the family and servants hid in the shallow cellar. As surgeons were operating, a Rebel shell knocked a cartload of bricks out of the chimney above, and another slammed beneath the table but did not explode. Later, the Federals set up a battery of horse artillery in the yard, which drew so much return fire that Joseph Haw said he counted forty-four dead horses close by.[25]

Some of the wounded troopers died in the woods, and some survived for no better reason than the whimsy of battle. Nineteen-year-old St. George Tucker Brooke, a Second Virginia cavalryman, was sitting his horse broadside to the enemy, talking to his lieutenant, when a Minié ball smashed his thighbone just as the Yankees began a countercharge up the road. Brooke toppled from his saddle, his saber straps catching the pommel and suspending him halfway to the ground. As his comrades retreated, he dangled there for long seconds, his broken leg bent at a crazy angle. He clutched the horse's mane, trying to soothe the panicky beast and not fall into the road. Then the straps broke and he dropped, his leg twisted nearly around his neck, and the oncoming Federals charged over him. Somehow not a hoof touched him as a whole squadron raced across his body.

Two Union sharpshooters followed the horsemen. One pointed to Brooke and casually bragged to the other, "I shot that man." To Brooke, the Yankee sounded as if he bore no more ill feeling toward him than toward some squirrel he had plinked as a boy. An ambulance approached, and two other Yankees moved Brooke within the protective zigzag of a roadside fence. There he lay, his shattered leg jerking uncontrollably, until the ambulance crew returned and lifted him aboard beside a moaning Union trooper. They left him in the yard of the Haw house, the only Confederate among dozens of Federal wounded. When a solicitous chaplain in blue asked Brooke what regiment he was from, he refused to answer. He lay helpless and twitching as the nearby Union battery opened fire and Rebel shells came crashing into the house, mangling tethered horses and knocking down bricks and branches. As the battle faded toward evening, the Yankees departed, taking their wounded. Brooke lay alone and scared, expecting to die less than a day's ride from his home in Richmond, when the Haw family peeped out of the cellar.

The aged parents and a young woman were the only Haws at home; four sons were away at war. Two black servants carried Brooke indoors. The next day, Union surgeons briefly returned, and cut the flattened bullet out of his thigh. They said amputation would mean sure death, so they dressed and splinted the inflamed and swollen leg and left Brooke there. He stayed for three months while the Haw family nursed his suppurating wound and bedsores and fed him the best of what was left after Union scavengers moved on. The dead horses outside were barely covered with litter because no one was there to bury them, and all the household tools had been taken. "The flies eat the horses, the chickens eat the flies and we eat the chickens,"

Brooke wrote. "By that house-that-Jack-built process of reasoning I can prove that we lived that summer on putrid horses." But live he did, a long life, with one leg shorter than the other.[26]

The ringing clash at Haw's Shop had answered Lee's question: yes, Union infantry was across the Pamunkey, in strength. Though it had not been directly involved in the cavalry fight, it had pushed up so close behind the Federal horsemen that Confederate outriders had taken prisoners from at least two corps. The Federals had driven the Southerners back past Haw's Shop, gaining the option to march straight at Lee through that intersection, or to try to cut around him by roads running northwest or south. While the guns were roaring at Haw's Shop, Lee was turning his army to deal with those possibilities. He kept his left near Atlee's and the Virginia Central Railroad, on the lessened chance that Grant might still come that way to drive at Richmond from the north. From there, he deployed his army more than four miles east-southeastward, along the low ridges behind Totopotomoy Creek.

On the way there, Lee's troops were only slightly less exhausted than the Yankees who marched the longer route. Yankees and Rebels alike fought fatigue and hunger by trying to make sport of their misery. Joseph Eggleston, a Virginia cannoneer with Anderson's corps, told of seeing a man drop asleep in the act of lifting food to his lips. At North Anna, he wrote, "for several days both sides had a lot of fun in heavy skirmishing. Nothing had to be very ridiculous to raise a laugh among these veterans on both sides, even when it involved loss of life."[27]

Below Ashland, in the black of night, Anderson's corps halted, with orders to draw rations, cook, eat, and be ready to march in two hours. Eggleston had somehow gotten soda and salt, and when bacon and flour were issued, he set out to find water while his messmate made a fire. "The only possible way to do my part was to walk continually down grade, in no matter what direction, until I found a stream. Of course this meant being utterly lost and the countless fires made the confusion all the greater." Filling the canteens, he tried to find his way back by walking steadily uphill. When he wandered among strange troops, he began calling out for "Haskell's battalion!" and then "Lamkin's battery!" "Hundreds of others were doing the same, and the effect was weird indeed," he recalled. But he did find his messmate, and they made dough on their oilcloth groundsheet, cooked it in a skillet, split the bread, and then stuffed it into their haversacks in time to set off with their battery through the darkness. Somehow, they remembered it as fun.[28]

Indeed, Eggleston's brother George, his battery sergeant major, would write that the ability to laugh at adversity, "trifling of that kind . . . constant among the men throughout that terrible campaign . . . has always seemed to me the most remarkable and most significant fact in the history of the time. It revealed a capacity for cheerful endurance which alone made the campaign possible on the Confederate side. With mercenary troops or regulars the resistance that Lee was able to offer to Grant's tremendous pressure would have been impossible. . . . The starvation and the excessive marching would have destroyed the *morale* of troops held together only by discipline."[29]

Totopotomoy Creek is much like the next barrier river to the south, the Chickahominy. Between those two streams, the next great battles would be fought. Union soldiers remembered the Chickahominy from 1862 almost as a medieval moat protecting the capital fortress, "a wet ditch in front of the outer fortifications of Richmond." There, McClellan's army had bogged down, and his troops referred to the agues and ailments that sapped them as "Chickahominy fever." Grant hoped to get around Lee and force him to fight in the open, or if not, to drive him below the Chickahominy, pin him down, and start a siege that could have but one end.[30]

But first he had to deal with the Totopotomoy—and "a most discouraging place it was," wrote Lieutenant Frederick Mather of the Seventh New York Heavy Artillery. He was so exhausted that on the first morning there, he awoke in a pool of water without knowing it had rained—"without tents or other shelter, we could sleep with the rain pelting in our faces."[31]

Though the Totopotomoy is not an imposing stream, some of the low bluffs along it are steep, and especially in the rainy weeks of spring, the creek becomes wide and marshy. Lee's groundwise troops dug in, making skillful use of the overlooking ridges. They had ample time because Grant, after his superbly executed dash to cross the Pamunkey without interference, had made his most serious mistake of the campaign thus far: he cautiously dug in to protect his bridgeheads rather than pressing on before Lee could turn to face him. By May 29, this Union trench line ran from the Pamunkey south past Haw's Shop to the Totopotomoy. That morning, Meade ordered what he called a "reconnaissance" by three corps on the roads leading westward toward Hanover Court House and Shady Grove Church.

After moving out near noon, the leading Federal divisions met nothing more substantial than the Confederate cavalry screen, and by three o'clock Meade was convinced that Lee had indeed pulled his army back beyond the Chickahominy. But soon afterward, Hancock's corps reported striking infantry pickets, and Grant concluded correctly that "they are probably only covering whilst getting everything well ready to receive us on the south side of [Totopotomoy] creek."[32]

Everything was "well ready." Lee had Jubal Early, newly commanding Ewell's corps, on the Confederate right near Pole Green Church. Dick Anderson was in support behind him, ready to move in any direction. Beyond a swampy branch, John Breckinridge's skimpy division held the center. A. P. Hill's corps was on the Confederate left, stretching to the Virginia Central near Atlee's Station. That afternoon and into the evening, Union troops probed these positions. Marching west on the Union right, Wright's Sixth Corps met few Rebels and reached out toward the Virginia Central. But Hancock's Second and Warren's Fifth Corps both ran into increasing resistance, setting off crackling skirmishes but no sustained combat. Even after these encounters, the Federals still were unsure whether Lee's main force had dropped below the Chickahominy.

Dana reported to Washington that "Grant means to fight here if there is a fair chance." But, he added, "he will not run his head against heavy works."[33]

4

Damn Them Let Them Kill Me Too

BY TORCHLIGHT at 2:00 a.m. on May 28, troops of Major General William Farrar Smith's Eighteenth Corps started groping their way aboard steamboats at City Point, the James River landing that had become the main logistical base of Ben Butler's army. Soon after dawn, the first transports set out down the river. The soldiers on board were not sure where they were headed, but the educated among them understood that they were now players in more than two and a half centuries of James River legend. An officer of the Twenty-seventh Massachusetts wrote, "A trip down the James, at any time, is not uninteresting; but when accompanied by a fleet of vessels laden with troops, through scenes renowned in American history, as well as for recent bloody conflicts, all other travel touches the level of stupidity."

Past "the ruined mansions and broad acres of Virginia's opulent aristocracy," past the original English settlement at Jamestown, past the sites of McClellan's frustration in 1862, an assortment of schooners, steamboats, and barges carried Smith's command to Fortress Monroe. From Butler's army south of the James, Smith was bringing two of his own divisions and one from the Tenth Corps, the three to operate as the Eighteenth Corps while with the Army of the Potomac. At Fortress Monroe, Smith got word that Grant had now crossed the Pamunkey, so he should bring his force up the York River, then on up the Pamunkey to White House. The fleet puffed up the looping lower reaches of the Pamunkey, where "some of the transports appeared to be headed north, some south, some east, and some west"—and some hung up on snags, and some got stuck in the mud until pulled off by tugs.[1]

This slow going meant that Smith and his staff did not reach White House until 11:00 a.m. on Monday, May 30. That night, he got two-day-old instructions to march his command "direct to New Castle, on the south side of the Pamunkey, and there await further orders." There was limited dockage at White House; some of Smith's troops had to be lightered ashore; then his supplies and ordnance were further delayed. He waited until 3:30 p.m. on May 31, after getting further orders from Grant, to start some ten thousand infantry, plus his artillery, on the road to New Castle Ferry. He left 2,500 men under Brigadier General Adelbert Ames to garrison White House Landing.

The heat was hard on Smith's unconditioned troops, there was much straggling, and they bivouacked near Old Church, two miles short of their objective. At daylight, Smith reported, he got further orders to "proceed at once to New Castle Ferry, and place myself between the Fifth and Sixth Corps." Only then did Smith, finally "deeming time to be of great importance," order his men to move out without taking time to boil coffee. But at New Castle Ferry, he found no sign of the Fifth and Sixth. Puzzled, he dispatched his topographical engineer, Captain Francis U. Farquhar, to ask Grant for clarification. Meanwhile, he started to lay a bridge back across the Pamunkey, just in case.[2]

Originally, the instructions that Smith received on arriving at White House made some sense. They specifically located Smith's destination: "move direct to New Castle, on the south side of the Pamunkey, and there await further orders." From there, he could march to either flank of the Union army, as events demanded. The problem was that those orders were two days old when he got them—issued the day Grant crossed the Pamunkey. Grant had reiterated them late on May 30; now that message, too, was overtaken by events; the war had moved on. But the order Smith received on the morning of June 1, telling him again to hasten to New Castle rather than to Cold Harbor, was a shining error. We cannot tell whether it occurred in dictation or in transcription, whether the mistake was committed by Grant himself or by chief of staff Rawlins, who signed it. In his *Memoirs*, Grant says it happened "by some blunder," but he does not say whose.[3]

Personal opinions about Rawlins, some of them motivated by jealousy, figured in later speculation about who was to blame for the blunder. James Biddle, of Meade's staff, considered Rawlins "one of the roughest, most uncouth men I ever saw. He knows no more of military affairs than an old cat." The previous year, when Rawlins had been a lieutenant colonel and Grant's adjutant, Dana had found him industrious and conscientious, a man who "never gives himself any indulgence except swearing and scolding." Rawlins was a lawyer from Grant's hometown of Galena, Illinois. Dana wrote that he "watches [Grant] day and night, and whenever he commits the folly of tasting liquor hastens to remind him" that when war started, Grant "gave him his word of honor not to touch a drop as long as it lasted." For this service, one of Meade's staff officers thought that Rawlins's name "should be carved on every monument erected to Grant, for it was through him . . . that Grant's good angel reached him her steadying and uplifting hand."[4]

Dana, who had taught at the Transcendentalists' Brook Farm colony before turning to journalism, was unfamiliar with soldiers when he first encountered Rawlins; he rated officers as if he were hiring them as reporters for the *New York Tribune.* He said that Rawlins, despite his virtues, was not a first-rate adjutant because "He is too slow, and can't write the English language correctly without a great deal of careful consideration. Indeed, illiterateness is a general characteristic of Grant's staff, and in fact of Grant's generals and regimental officers of all ranks."[5]

Soon after Smith sent Captain Farquhar to question the order sending him to New Castle, one of Grant's aides, Lieutenant Colonel Orville E. Babcock, came galloping to Smith's command post to inform him that "it should have read Cold Harbor instead."[6]

The often brilliant but always contentious "Baldy" Smith apparently had not realized that time was important until he was firmly prodded by Grant. But as he marched and countermarched his divisions, he understood well why the armies were slogging through swamps, going without sleep, testing the enemy here and there. They were wrestling into position for another great struggle on the ground where Lee had driven off McClellan at huge cost in casualties two years before. Smith had been in the thick of it then, commanding a division, before going west and winning Grant's admiration in the Chattanooga campaign.

William Band, a cavalryman with Meade's provost guard, was on familiar ground, too. He wrote to his wife that "we are once mor on the Pencelua. I was in hope that we should never se this place no more. . . . I will not atemp to tell you aney thing of our moove ments it would [take] a loyear to do it. . . . I think we shall loose meny more before we git to richmond ore to crush this rebellion. . . ." Each day, at inconspicuous crossroads, swollen creeks, and along ridges that old soldiers could recognize, the armies' jostling for advantage exploded into nasty local fights.[7]

BOTH COMMANDERS knew that the climax of the campaign and per-haps the war was imminent. For this showdown, they were dredging up reinforcements in increments large and small, wherever they could be found. As one Rebel officer understood it, Grant "needed them, he asked for them, and he got them. He had a right to all he wanted. His original contract so provided; it covered all necessary drafts." It was not quite that simple, but Grant as general of all the Union armies did prevail in his tug-of-war with Ben Butler, who grudgingly sent Smith with his seventeen thousand troops from below the James. Almost two weeks earlier, Washington had already sent 24,700 men to Grant since the campaign began.[8]

Lee knew this from a captured message from Grant to Burnside, which he read while lying ill during the North Anna engagement. At 4:45 a.m. on May 25, he had quickly relayed this ominous news to Jeff Davis. "I understand that all the [Union] forts and posts have been stripped of their garrisons," he added. Every available Federal soldier had been ordered to the front; Norfolk, Fortress Monroe, Washing-ton, and other vital positions were left with only skeleton guard units. "This makes it necessary for us to do likewise," Lee told Davis—"and I have no doubt that your Excellency will do all in your power to meet the present emergency."[9]

Lee, while struggling with Grant's army and his own ailment, was still negotiating through Davis with Beauregard at Petersburg. At one point, he and Beauregard had each suggested that the other leave a holding force on his side of the river and bring the rest of his troops across to combine against the Federals. Beauregard had told Davis, "With regard to re-enforcing General Lee, I shall be most happy to do so whenever you shall judge proper to order it," and Pickett's division and other smaller commands had already been sent. But Lee, facing the Union's most powerful army with his back against the capital, needed more. Unlike many other generals, he had always been known for his restrained language, for not exaggerating the size of enemy forces. When he called a situation an emergency, it was one. Still he had to deal with Beauregard through channels, as with a foreign potentate, as if the James River were an ocean. As the emergency deepened, his patience grew thin. "If Genl Beauregard is in condition to unite with me in any operation against Genl. Grant, I should like to know it, and at what point a combination of the troops could be made most advantageously to him," he told Davis.[10]

On the day of the fight at Haw's Shop, Lee said he hoped to intercept Grant on the Totopotomoy or near Ashland, depending on which way the Union army moved. He would try to confront him "near enough to Richmond for General Beauregard to unite with me if practicable. Should any field nearer to Richmond be more convenient to him, and he will designate it, I will endeavor to deliver battle there." But more haggling was necessary.[11]

The following day, May 29, Beauregard came via Richmond to confer with Lee in his sickroom near Atlee's. No description of the meeting survives; it must have been brief and frosty. The gist of it was that Beauregard told Lee he had only twelve thousand infantry around Petersburg and could spare none. Afterward, with seeming resignation, Lee wrote to Davis, "If Genl Grant advances tomorrow I will engage him with my present force."[12]

As the Federals poked at the Totopotomoy line the next morning, Lee appealed to the Confederate president to send him troops from Richmond's local defenses. "If this army is unable to resist Grant the troops under General Beauregard and in the city will be unable to defend it," he warned. Still the fencing with Beauregard went on, until at 7:30 that evening, Lee's patience broke at last. This time, he wrote directly to Beauregard, in a hand that clearly showed his anger.[13]

"If you cannot determine what troops you can send, the [War] Department cannot. The result of your delay will be disaster. Butler's troops will be with Grant tomorrow."[14]

At the same hour, Lee backed up this message with a similar appeal to Davis: "General Beauregard says the Department must determine what troops to send for him. He gives it all necessary information. The result of this delay will be disaster. Butler's troops (Smith's corps) will be with Grant to-morrow. [Major General Robert F.] Hoke's division, at least, should be with me by light to-morrow."[15]

The word *disaster* stirred Davis to peremptory action. At 10:30, his chief of staff wired Beauregard: "By direction of the President you will send Hoke's division, which you reported ready, immediately to this point by railroad. . . . Move with the greatest expedition, but with as much secrecy as possible."

But Beauregard had apparently made that decision without being ordered. In a message bearing the time of 10:15 p.m., he wrote to Bragg, "General Lee having called on me for re-enforcements, and feeling authorized by the President's letter of 28th instant to send

them, I have ordered Hoke's division to report to him. I will follow
with [Major General Bushrod] Johnson's as soon as enemy's movements in my front will permit."[16]

History has not proven whether Beauregard actually made that
decision on his own, or moved in response to Lee's angry dispatch, or
conceivably received the order and then noted an earlier time on his
reply. Whichever was the case, he was determined not to concede any
deference to Lee.

IN THE WOODS along the Totopotomoy, a lone horseman slipped
through the shadows, watching Union cavalry as it felt around Lee's
right.

This was Franklin Stringfellow, perhaps the most effective of all
Rebel scouts, who risked his life repeatedly by riding in and out of
enemy lines to send fresh intelligence back to Confederate headquarters. The slight, fine-featured Stringfellow had served not only as a
tactical scout in the field but also as an undercover agent slipping in
and out of Washington, sometimes masquerading as a girl. His intelligence career had begun while he was a private in the Fourth Virginia
Cavalry, where Jeb Stuart recognized his brains and boldness and
picked him for duties that would surely have seen him hanged if the
Federals had captured and recognized him. During the Seven Days
battles in this very neighborhood, Stuart had officially praised
Stringfellow's "gallantry and efficiency." Indeed, the Yankees caught
him once during the Gettysburg campaign, but he was exchanged
before his captors realized whom they had.[17]

If the cavalry was the eyes and ears of the army, Stringfellow and
the other unsung scouts were the eyes and ears of the cavalry. They
had made themselves so useful to Lee by the spring of 1864 that in
their defense, he issued a rare reprimand to Stuart. The cavalry general
had enthused about their exploits in a letter to Virginia governor
William Smith, whose kinsman Channing Smith was another of the
scouts. After the governor indiscreetly let some of that letter be published, Lee told Stuart: ". . . I consider the lives of Stringfellow, Channing Smith and others greatly jeopardized. They will be watched for,
and if caught, hardly dealt by. You had better recall them and replace
them by others. . . ." But those scouts were too valuable to be replaced.
Though Union officers searched the Richmond newspapers for every
microscopic hint of possible military significance, and certainly knew

of Stringfellow and his comrades, the Rebel agents survived and became more daring with each campaign.[18]

As the Federals advanced on the morning of Monday, May 30, Stringfellow reined up at Burnt Mill and scrawled a message to Lee. He had watched Sheridan's cavalry moving this way, heard Yankee drums that way, sent men to check this road and that. Young though he was, Stringfellow had the self-confidence of a man who had done this many times before. He offered his own assessment to the venerable general: ". . . although I have no positive proof of the fact, still judging from what I hear and see, I think that General Grant is concentrating a large force on his left, and contemplates a move in this direction very soon." Using the signature "S. Franklin," he wrote, "You will please excuse me for not signing my true name."[19]

Lee knew who "S. Franklin" was, and knew he could trust him. He also had enough information from all along his front to predict almost exactly where Grant would run his lines that day. The Union commander was trying to find an open road to Richmond, and Lee was trying to close off every possibility. How soon he got Stringfellow's message is unknown, but one hour after it was written, Lee himself concurred with it, advising Dick Anderson that "After fortifying this line [the Federals] will probably make another move by their left flank over toward the Chickahominy. This is just a repetition of their former movements." Still eager to deliver battle outside the Richmond fortifications, he added that Grant's move "can only be arrested by striking at once at that part of their force which has crossed the Totopotomoy in General Early's front. . . ."[20]

That part of the Federal force was Gouverneur Warren's Fifth Corps, all of it now below the Totopotomoy on the Union left. That morning it had started west toward Hundley's Corner until it encountered Confederate skirmishers; as the colonel of the Twenty-second Massachusetts officially reported, "The dirty scoundrels had two lines of breast-works at right angles, so that they got a cross-fire upon us." To enfilade this Rebel outpost, Warren's command turned south toward Bethesda Church. By noon, it had picked up a few prisoners, who disclosed that Ewell's (now Early's) corps was down that road, dug in and ready. But the energetic Early, on his first full day as commander of that corps, was not merely sitting and waiting. He ordered his pioneers to cut roads through woods and swamps to enable him to shift to meet the Yankees as they steadily lengthened their lines.[21]

Neither Warren's Fifth Corps nor Burnside's Ninth had met serious

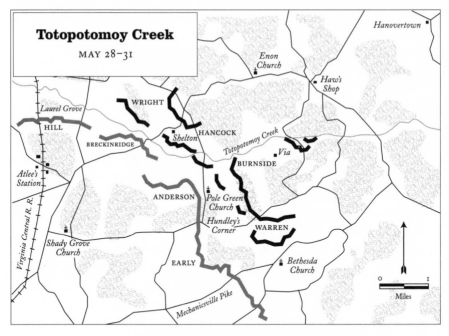

After repeated Federal efforts fail to punch through the Confederate line on the bluffs below the Totopotomoy, Warren's Fifth and Burnside's Ninth Corps swing across the creek to threaten the Confederate right.

resistance as they swung across the Totopotomoy there on the Union left, where Lee's line bent back southeastward. But on the Union right, the Sixth Corps, after tearing up a stretch of the Virginia Central, was delayed for hours by "a swamp and tangle of the very worst character" as it tried to link up with the Second. A footsore soldier in the 110th Ohio wrote that his outfit had been "shifting positions and changing lines, moving hither and thither, forward and back, facing and dressing among the brush and bushes in this Wilderness-looking place." Angry at such slowness, Meade accused Horatio Wright of wasting time to issue rations. Wright protested that he had only "halted to find my whereabouts," adding, "I am mortified to learn . . . that the major-general commanding should suppose that anything short of impossibility should delay me in taking position."[22]

Alongside Wright, Hancock's Second Corps had to fight several sharp skirmishes and artillery duels across the creek valley. Official reports of such actions seldom mentioned civilians, but one of Hancock's aides could not resist telling what happened when a battery of Second Corps artillery set up around the Shelton house, above the Totopotomoy. Several women there refused to leave, even when Hancock's adjutant, Lieutenant Colonel Francis A. Walker, offered them a ride to the rear. They protested that one of their number was too ill to move, and suggested that the Second Corps take another route. "It being not altogether convenient to alter the plans of the Army of the Potomac at so short a notice," Walker told them that "if they valued their lives they would retire." Next he sent the corps surgeon to attend to the allegedly ailing resident. On pronouncing her in fine condition, the doctor got an earful of indignation, and Walker got a letter "in which the opinions of the household concerning the Congress, President, people, and army of the United States were set forth with the utmost distinctness." Declaring that if any of them was killed, their blood would rest upon Walker's soul forever, the women retreated to the cellar when firing started.

Because Union signalmen used the roof as an observation site, the house was targeted and hit repeatedly by Confederate gunners. Cannon of both sides were blazing away when suddenly a house servant, "delirious from fright, and picking up a fire shovelful of live coals from the hearth, rushed out into the yard and threw the coals into one of the gun-limbers, exploding the ammunition it contained. . . ." Fire and splinters from the blast killed two men and blinded others, while "The negress, who was unhurt, ran into the house again as if the devil was after her and nearly scared to death by what she had done." Some soldiers believed the woman's mistress had told her to do it, and suggested that "they should hang her high," but no punishment came of it.[23]

Stubborn Confederate women like the Sheltons knew that hundreds of abandoned houses and plantations had been ransacked, and they hoped their presence would protect their homes from destruction. Some angrily defied the intruders; others, especially when they saw thousands of Union reinforcements marching past, were more submissive. Lyman of Meade's staff thought that poorer Virginians often seemed indifferent, or even opposed to the war, but "bitterness increases in direct ratio to their social position." A well-dressed lady might be more or less courteous, but in her, "hatred will end only with death." Lyman, a learned Boston zoologist, understood this. "There is black everywhere," he wrote, because so many of those women were in mourning for lost husbands or sons. "People of this class are very proud and spirited . . . it is the officers that they supply who give the strong framework to their army. They have the military and irascible nature so often seen among an aristocracy that was once rich and is now poor. . . ."[24]

Rich or poor, "the inhabitants of the country through which we have passed are astounded at such vast multitudes of men," wrote an artillery lieutenant from upstate New York. "They declare that Richmond must be conquered by what they consider such countless numbers." One woman hoped that "it might fall into the Yankees' hands before Saturday night. She, like hundreds of other citizens of the Old Dominion, is heartily sick of the war, and well they may be, because they have been stripped and robbed of everything."[25]

To FIND OUT how many enemy divisions were moving where, both Grant and Lee sent cavalry eastward, beyond the point where Warren's and Early's troops had skirmished near Bethesda Church late on the morning of May 30. Grant was concerned that Lee might come that way and endanger his supply lines from White House, and he wanted to screen Warren's push toward the Confederate right. Lee meant to prevent the Federals' getting around that flank and across the Chickahominy. At about midafternoon—different reports made it anywhere from 1:00 to 4:00 p.m.—these cavalry expeditions collided.

Torbert's Union division, trotting south from Old Church, ran into Calbraith Butler's South Carolina brigade, pushing out from Matadequin Creek. The Matadequin, deep in places, runs roughly parallel to and southeast of the Totopotomoy, flowing into the Pamunkey about six air miles farther downstream. Along its abrupt banks, the cavalrymen clashed for at least three hours.

After the Rebels drove in the pickets of Colonel Thomas C. Devin's brigade, fighting intensified until Torbert ordered up help from Brigadier General Wesley Merritt's U.S. Regular brigade and two of Custer's Michigan regiments. Late in the day, the South Carolinians were joined by horsemen from Brigadier General Pierce M. B. Young's patched-together brigade of mostly Georgia cavalry units. Butler, who had not been with his men in their battle at Haw's Shop, was all over the scene. At one point, he shouted to a squadron, "Men, I have stood it long enough! I wish the enemy driven from that house in the field!" His troopers attacked on foot across an open quarter mile, "making the welkin ring with the old charge shout and yell." They took the house, then burned it because Yankee sharpshooters had been firing from its windows.[26]

This was the first cavalry fight ever witnessed by the correspondent of a Connecticut newspaper who happened to be present. He exulted in "the ring of bugles, the clatter of horses' feet, and clang of out-

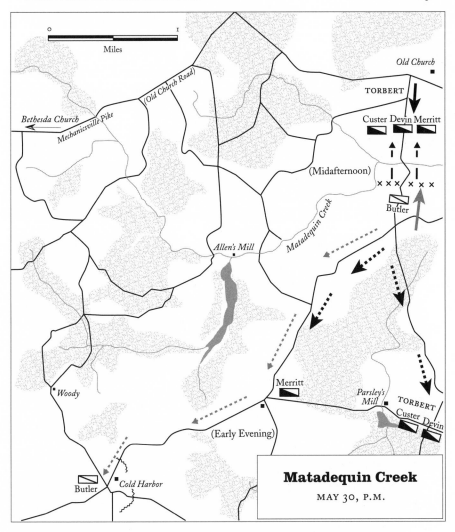

Matadequin Creek

MAY 30, P.M.

After Butler's South Carolina cavalry brigade clashes with Torbert's Union division along Matadequin Creek, the outnumbered Confederates fall back around Cold Harbor. Next day, the Federals push them out of that vital intersection, setting up the major battles of early June.

leaping sabers, the wild shout, the charge, the shock when steel met steel, the rout, the chase, as back across the open fields the chivalrous (?) sons of the Palmetto State fled in their fright, the remounting of dismounted men upon the steeds of fallen comrades to join in the victorious cavalcade, the mingled mass of bleeding dead and dying, friends and foes lying together, calmly gazing into each other's eyes—I shall never forget these—I would not."[27]

Torbert's brigades, unlike Butler's regiments, had brought in horse artillery. With cannon banging away, his dismounted troopers flanked the outnumbered Confederates near dusk and drove them south away from the Matadequin. Some of the Rebels had to swim their horses across, carrying their wounded.[28]

The bruised Confederate horsemen fell back and formed a line facing north just above Cold Harbor. There in the darkness, a contingent of newly arrived Georgians joined them, and corroborated the observation of a South Carolinian who had become a veteran in only two days of Virginia experience: "Cavalry are, on the average, much more liable to panics than infantry; the cause is not far to seek. The excitement of the horse increases that of the man, and vice versa, until both sometimes become mere frantic brutes." Whether this interaction between two species of brute caused that evening's excitement or not, all accounts agree that the equally jaded Yankee cavalry had very little to do with the resulting uproar.

It happened after Butler sent two squadrons of the Twentieth Georgia Battalion to feel out the enemy, up the road toward Old Church, beyond his own pickets. Butler's brigade was just spreading its blankets to bivouac when those outriders met a single volley of gunfire from pickets of the First U.S. Cavalry. "Without a word of warning or report of trouble, we heard the rush of horsemen coming on us like a cyclone from a clear sky," wrote a Carolinian. The troopers who had scouted ahead "came rushing down upon us, in a wild stampede, through tree laps, over fences, ditches and everything in their path." Butler assumed that the Federals must be charging, ordered everyone at hand to block the road, and sent for the Fifth South Carolina to come on the double-quick. When a pistol holstered on the saddle of a loose horse accidentally fired, some of the nearby Carolinians panicked too. In the darkness, several horses plunged into a deep ditch beside the road, crushing men underneath; one trooper remembered "the cries for help and groans, and the fearful shrieks of one broken-backed animal. . . . It was a frightful scene, for the poor victims pulled out from beneath the horses, were literally covered from head to foot with blood, so that they could not have been recognized by their own brothers."

After things settled down, one of the Confederate colonels called the episode "the most inexcusable, unaccountable performance" he had ever known or heard of. A South Carolina trooper told how three or four men were thrown from runaway horses and killed, and next morning others were "hunting up their horses, lost hats and every-thing." Perhaps it was inexcusable, but it was not the first, last, or worst occasion of confusion and chaos, the kind of learning experience that turned green soldiers into veterans to fight another day.[29]

IF NOT FOR the noise of their own melee that afternoon along the Matadequin, those cavalrymen would have wondered at the start-up of heavier gunfire about three miles closer to Richmond. There, near Bethesda Church, Jubal Early was carrying out Lee's wish to foil Grant's latest move by "striking at once." As Grant lengthened his line, each mile of it thinned the overstretched Confederate front. Early saw a chance to stop this menacing extension by attacking War-ren on the eastern flank of the Federal advance. Lee agreed, no doubt hoping that a surprise stroke might even roll up the Federal left and start something as tumultuous as Stonewall Jackson's crowning blow at Chancellorsville. Yet he was aware that ordering such an assault with an inferior force was as chancy as rolling dice.

As the Federal Fifth Corps nudged Lee's right, Warren cautioned one of his division commanders that "I do not wish to crowd them much to-day, but hold on to all we get." On this day, Early would do the crowding. He had stayed ahead of the Fifth Corps by shifting his regiments along those newly cut cross-country passageways to the Mechanicsville Pike, angling across the flank of Warren's advance. Union brigadier general Samuel W. Crawford, at first believing that such fast-moving Confederates were just a cavalry screen, sent a brigade of his Pennsylvania Reserves to brush them away. As this brigade approached Bethesda Church, Early's infantry hit it head-on.[30]

Major General Robert E. Rodes's division, which had led Jackson's attack at Chancellorsville, led this one at Bethesda Church. It drove the Yankee brigade back to the Shady Grove Road, slowing only when well-placed batteries of the First New York Light Artillery opened fire with solid shot, then canister. For anxious minutes, Colonel Charles S. Wainwright, commanding Warren's artillery, saw "things looking very squally for a complete turning of our left. When I went up the road, the reserves had much the appearance of 'the devil take the hind-most.' "[31]

The Confederates could have rolled on if they had quickly followed up their opening rush, Wainwright said. But it took Early perhaps half

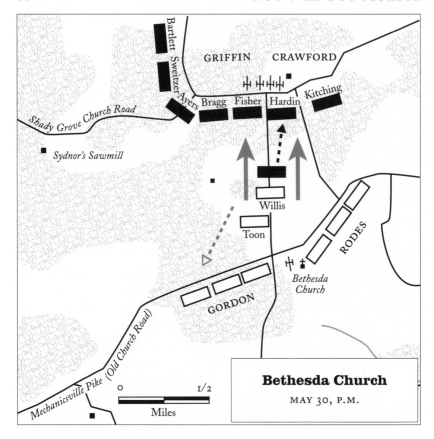

When Warren's Fifth Corps threatens to turn the Confederate right, Early meets it with a costly counterattack. The reinforced Federals turn back the Confederate effort when Anderson's corps fails to support Early.

an hour to recharge the attack by moving forward his own old division, under its new commander, the courageous 26-year-old Brigadier General Stephen Dodson Ramseur. At the same time, Early asked Anderson to send a division to hit the Union position from the flank. All this gave the Federals time to dig in and bring up more artillery, plus at least three more brigades of infantry. At about 6:30, when Early thought Anderson was advancing, he renewed the assault. To spearhead it, Ramseur sent in a brigade commanded by the even younger Colonel Edward Willis of Georgia. In his new role, Willis went forward "in the highest spirits & was determined to win his spurs or die in the attempt."[32]

"The Rebels came to the attack in double lines, exposing themselves with reckless daring," wrote a Pennsylvania chaplain. The Forty-ninth Virginia, which had lost nine color-bearers in the previous month's fighting, led the brigade into line. Suddenly Lieutenant Colonel C. B. Christian realized that the regimental flag was nowhere to be seen. Scanning his ranks, he stopped at a tall, beardless boy from Amherst County. "Orendorf, will you carry the colors?" he asked.[33]

"Yes, Colonel, I will carry them," said Orendorf. "They killed my brother the other day; now damn them let them kill me too." He grabbed the flagstaff and stepped out front.

Christian said the Federal guns had apparently taken the exact range to the woodline where the brigade emerged into an open field. At that moment, he wrote, the waiting Yankees cut loose with "the heaviest and most murderous fire I had ever seen with grape, canister and musketry." The Confederates rushed through this at right-shoulder arms, neither firing nor letting go their usual piercing yell. "Our veterans of a hundred fights knew at a glance that they were marching up to die, rather than to waver," Christian said. "Our line melted away as if by magic."[34]

Union artillery cut down Colonel Willis at the head of his troops. Orendorf took the flag of the Forty-ninth within twenty feet of the Federal line before a cannonball tore him apart. Nearby, Colonel Christian was wounded and captured. One of his soldiers, Buckner Magill Randolph, lost his closest friends in the charge; in his diary, he wrote bitterly that it was "murder for ambition sake." There, Early's flank attack expired.[35]

Charles H. Minnemeyer, of the Eleventh Pennsylvania Reserves, summarized the Union view of the fight more eloquently than any commander's report: ". . . we formd line and pould up rifel pits but they was of a pour Contriving hear the rebels attackkdet us and as we had not support they succeedet in flanking our men and drove them back across a field and into a peas of woods hear the suppord came up and checkt them our men then pould up rifel pits again better one than those before after about one houar the rebels attakdet us again but after a hard fight was repulsed and drove back. . . ."[36]

Early's attack had achieved only its minimum goal, by briefly interrupting the steady Federal slide around the Confederate right. With enough weight to keep up its initial momentum, his effort might have done serious damage. Early blamed Dick Anderson for failing to pitch in; he had asked that Anderson send a division to come at Warren from the other side, by which "I think we could have struck the enemy a severe blow." But eventually, "hearing nothing from Anderson I desisted from the effort to break the enemy's line as it was evident it would be attended with considerable loss and the attack had to be made under great disadvantages. . . . As it is, all we have to regret is the loss of valuable officers and men in Pegram's [Willis's] brigade, which . . . I much deplore."[37]

At 8:00 p.m., Anderson tried to explain to Lee what had happened to his supporting movement: "General Field reports having come upon an intrenched line of the enemy, and owing to that circumstance and the approach of darkness, I have suspended his movement and have drawn my whole line back to the left again. . . ." His corps diary said without elaboration that "Pickett starts to support the movement by going through the breastworks, but soon abandons it. . . ."[38]

Before the Confederates pulled back a fraction of a mile to cover the Mechanicsville Pike, the roar of battle at Bethesda Church prompted Meade to order the Second and Sixth corps to mount attacks along the Totopotomoy line, to prevent Lee from throwing more strength into Early's attack. On the Second Corps front, Hancock's orders for each of his division commanders to "assault at such point of his line as he may deem best" produced uncoordinated thrusts that pushed back Confederate skirmishers along the creek. But Wright was not eager; his Sixth Corps was just moving into place after its struggle through "swamp and tangle" to link up with Hancock, and he had not had time to reconnoiter his front. He told Meade that to follow orders, he would have to risk a night attack. Before this exchange was over, Meade learned that the fighting at Bethesda Church had quieted, and directed all his corps to hold where they were.[39]

Troops of both sides were exhausted; when John O. Casler of the Thirty-third Virginia was tapped for picket duty in front of Early's corps, he pleaded "for God's sake and for the sake of humanity to not leave me on post, for it was impossible for me to keep my eyes open." He was more scared than he had ever been in battle, because the penalty for sleeping on post was "death by a drum-head court-martial," and "I would have rather died a dozen deaths on the field of battle than be disgraced by being shot to death for negligence of duty." But the officer of the guard told him that everyone was in the same condition, so out Casler went. Desperate to stay conscious, he sat in his hole with his chin propped on the muzzle of his upright rifle, so that when he fell asleep his head would drop and jerk him awake. This way, he stayed more or less alert in the rain through "the longest two hours I ever spent in my life."[40]

EARLY'S ATTACK at Bethesda Church had shown Grant how wrong he was to assert that "a battle with [Lee's army] outside of intrenchments cannot be had." This could explain Grant's repetition of the order to General Smith to take his reinforcements from White House to New Castle. At 7:30 p.m., as the firing at Bethesda tapered off, Grant's directions to Smith cited the "possibility of a design on [Lee's] part to get between you and the Army of the Potomac." He said, "Nothing would suit me better," as if he thought of Smith as bait, to tempt Lee into trying something rash. If that happened, Grant would have his long-sought opportunity to deal with the Rebel army in the open, where superior numbers should prevail—or Lee's effort might leave the way clear for a drive straight into Richmond. Positioned at New Castle, Smith's divisions could march in either direction.[41]

Grant was right in assuming that Lee knew of Smith's arrival. Fortunately, the Confederate commander did not have to depend for information on Yankees like the flippant James B. Thompson of the First Pennsylvania Rifles, captured at Bethesda Church. Brought to Lee's headquarters, First Sergeant Thompson was questioned by a colonel who asked him, "Well, Yank, how are things on your side of the line?"

"Looking bright," Thompson recalled saying.

"How many men have you over there?"

"I never counted them."

"Any fool knows that, of course. You didn't count them, but how many do you think there are?"

As listening soldiers laughed, Thompson said, "We don't think; we have generals who think for us."

"Well, just tell me how many *you think* Grant has. You certainly have an opinion."

"Well, in my opinion, I *think* Grant has about four hundred and fifty thousand men and reinforcements coming in every day."

The colonel, who had reddened a bit at Thompson's nonanswers, now joined the laughter. "You'll do," he said. "How long have you been in the service?"

"Over three years."

"Well, ain't you tired?"

"No, I'm only beginning to like it."

Thompson's impudence, which might have provoked summary execution in some other war, earned him no worse treatment than other captives got. Sent to Libby Prison in Richmond, he remembered that "everything [there] was confusion. The citizens were running hither and thither and it seemed to be the general impression that Grant would have possession before forty-eight hours." Union cannon could be heard booming, and "every man who was able to walk had a gun in his hands."[42]

Lee had better sources of intelligence than cheeky prisoners would offer. As the fighting began at Matadequin Creek and Bethesda Church, he had relayed word to Richmond from a scout watching the lower Pamunkey. The message has not survived; it may have been another from Frank Stringfellow. Whoever the scout was, he had gotten close enough to report what Custer and his junior officers were saying: "Butler's fleet" was bringing heavy reinforcements to Grant.[43]

Grant had assured Smith that on the way to New Castle, Sheridan would protect his left flank with two divisions of cavalry. But in advising Smith where other Union commands were posted, Grant misplaced the Fifth Corps by a good mile and a half. That sort of error happened often in this campaign, in both armies. As they issued and followed orders, tracked friendly and enemy movements, officers were still plagued by a problem they had encountered but not solved in this same neighborhood in 1862: maps.

Although the earliest permanent English settlements in the New World were in the Virginia counties along the James River, when the Civil War began, the region was "about as poorly mapped as a section of a civilized country could well be." Inadequate maps had so hampered Lee and Jackson in the Seven Days battles that afterward the Confederate War Department commissioned special survey teams to produce a generally accurate map of Northern Virginia, including the battlefields outside Richmond. But that edition was dated April 26, 1864, and though photographic copies were made, whether they reached Confederate commanders in time for the spring campaign is uncertain.

The Union maps used by McClellan and his generals in 1862 were also full of errors, and little improvement had been made in the interim. Lyman said the result of the mapping preparation for the 1864 offensive was "almost ludicrous! Some places . . . are from one to two miles out of position, and the roads run everywhere *except* where laid down." Many minor roads did not appear at all; the names of churches, roads, and especially plantations, with branches of the same family located at several places on a given sheet, were most confusing. As the Federal army advanced, engineers fanned out on its front and flanks, taking compass readings, calculating distances by the pacing of their horses, and sketching local maps to be pasted together at night and photographed the next day if there was enough sunshine. Union topographer Nathaniel Michler conceded that "however well the only accessible maps might have served the purposes of general knowledge, still they furnish but little of that detailed information so necessary in selecting and ordering the different routes of marching columns, and were too decidedly deficient in accuracy and detail to enable a general to maneuver with certainty his troops in the face of a brave and ever-watchful enemy."[44]

This deficiency would critically affect both armies in the days immediately ahead, as they probed, shifted, and then fought for the country crossroads of Cold Harbor.

5

Hold Cold Harbor at All Hazards

ON THE EVENING of May 29, Union soldiers brought in for questioning one of the Rebels captured in the day's skirmishing along the Totopotomoy. As caricatured by Grant's aide, Horace Porter, this Tar Heel gave Union headquarters a classic show of rustic humor without telling the general-in-chief anything useful. When Grant said in a friendly way, "Oh, you're from North Carolina," the soldier allegedly said, "Yes, and a good deal fa'tha from it jes' now than I'd like to be, God knows."

"Well, where were you taken, and how did you get here?"

"How did I get h'yah? Well, when a man has half a dozen o' them thah reckless and desp'rit dragoons o'yourn lammin' him along the road on a tight run, and wallopin' him with the flats o' thah sabahs, he don't have no trouble gittin' hyah."

After a long, amusing, but fruitless question-and-answer session, Grant gave up trying to extract any valuable intelligence. Before being marched away, the prisoner had his own request:

"Gentlemen, I would like mighty well to see that thah new-fangled weepon o' yourn that shoots like it was a whole platoon. They tell me, you can load it on Sunday and fiah it off all the rest o' the week."[1]

This Rebel rube was not talking about the U.S. rifle-musket, Model 1861, which was the principal weapon of the Civil War. He was thoroughly familiar with it, and the British Enfield Model 1853 that had been bought in great quantities for both armies. These were great advances over the smooth-bore muskets and even flintlocks with which some troops had begun service; rifled barrels extended the effective range of infantry weapons from about two hundred to about five hundred yards, a fact that generals learned only slowly, at a cost of thousands of lives.

But these were muzzle-loading rifles, and many a soldier was shot by the enemy while going through the awkward procedure for reloading the U.S. Model 1861 and the Enfield. The muzzle-loader's optimum rate of fire was only two or three rounds a minute. To shortsighted ordnance officers and generals concerned with logistics, this was enough; they thought faster firing would lead to tremendous waste of ammunition. Then along came breech-loading rifles, which cut down the laborious procedure, but many of these were complicated models that did not hold up in the field. One exception was the Sharps rifle, an accurate and reliable breechloader made famous in action by Berdan's (First U.S.) Sharpshooters. Though much easier to operate than the muzzle-loaders, it was still a single-shot weapon, requiring separate insertion of each cartridge. In striving for a greater rate of fire, the Union army also tried adapting the Colt revolver as a shoulder weapon, but its occasional backflash made it too dangerous to the user.

Quantities of the first efficient breech-loading repeating weapon did not appear in the field until the last year of the war, when new cartridge boxes were issued to certain lucky regiments of Grant's cavalry. Each box contained ten magazines for the highly admired carbine patented in 1860 by Christopher M. Spencer. Each magazine held seven mass-produced copper-rimmed .52-caliber cartridges, each self-contained cartridge combining case, charge, and projectile. The tubular magazine was inserted through a trap in the butt plate, and each shot readied by simply levering the trigger guard and cocking the hammer.

This Spencer repeating carbine was the marvelous weapon that Grant's Carolina prisoner wanted to see. It could not fire all week with one load, but using it, a skilled soldier might get off fourteen rounds a minute. It was the best small arm of the decade; had it been issued to all Union troops early on, the war might have been shortened and thousands of lives saved. Troops were so eager to have a Spencer that they sometimes hoarded their meager pay to buy their own. In Virginia, the first impressive proof of its superiority came on the last day of May and first day of June 1864, around the junction of Cold Harbor.[2]

TENS OF THOUSANDS of men in Grant's and Lee's armies were familiar with that neighborhood as only soldiers can be, for over its uneven, swampy ground they had marched and fought two years earlier.

"There was where my brother was killed," said a man in the
Twenty-first Connecticut, pointing to a worn trench that had been a
skirmish line. "You'll be lucky if you don't see him again before
another sunrise," said a squad mate, and they marched on. Along the
roadside they saw rusty canteens, cartridge boxes, rotting shreds of
uniforms and blankets, reminders of their comrades of 1862. In that
earlier fight here, the second battle of the Seven Days campaign,
Stonewall Jackson, James Longstreet, A. P. Hill, and D. H. Hill had
attacked and driven George McClellan's Federals after a day of delay
and confusion. It was Robert E. Lee's first notable victory, and like so
many to follow, its cost was high. After the battle, those who fought
there were unsure what to call it.[3]

Soldiers often have no idea what to name the great battles they
have been in until long after the guns are silent. Men in different regiments of the same division often give different labels to the same
action, depending on where they have been, whether attacking this
hill or defending that church or creek line. Even in retrospect, Union
and Confederate soldiers, mapmakers, and historians could not agree
on what to call many Civil War battles: what is Bull Run to Yankees is Manassas to Rebels, Fair Oaks is Seven Pines, Antietam is
Sharpsburg.

No other campaign produced such a confusing abundance of battle
names in such a short time as the Seven Days, in the early summer of
1862, when Lee took command of an army for the first time and drove
McClellan away from Richmond. Beginning with Oak Grove, also
known as Henrico, King's School House, French's Farm, or the
Orchards, Lee fought McClellan at Mechanicsville, or Ellerson's Mill,
or Beaver Dam Creek; then at Gaines's Mill, or Chickahominy; Gar-
nett's Farm; Savage's Station; White Oak Swamp, or Glendale, or
Charles City Crossroads, or Frayser's Farm; down the James to
Malvern Hill, or Crew's Farm.

Varied as they are, every one of those designations is easier to
explain than another alternative to Gaines's Mill, a name more
remembered for what happened in 1864 than for the battle in 1862:

Cold Harbor.

Nothing but a mouldering wayside tavern distinguished this
obscure crossroads from a hundred others in war-weary Virginia. The
name hinted no connection with the first families of the Old Dominion, or the nearest farmer, miller, creek, or swamp. Some soldiers
wrote it Coal Harbor, some Cool Arbor. (Theodore Lyman said, "I
can't find which is correct, but choose 'Arbor' because it is prettiest,

and because it is so hideously inappropriate.") No one seemed to know who had named the place, or why. There was no harbor closer than Rocketts Landing, at Richmond. (Pat Devereaux, an erstwhile cannoneer with the Second New York Heavy Artillery, said of arriving at the crossroads, " 'twas no harbor at all, and divil a drop of water to make 'wan wid.") Nor was anything cold to be had there in the muggy days when the war passed through. The most scholarly investigation of the term may have been by the British antiquarian Henry Colley March, who took his research back past Chaucer. "The name Cold Harbour," he wrote, "occurs in England at least one hundred and forty-five times," mostly along ancient roadways. He concluded that it signified "a caravansary, a place of accommodation for travellers where there was no furniture and no provisions but what they brought with them." Some version of this—for example, "an inn that does not provide hot meals"—is now the accepted explanation for the name of the historic crossroads that lies 9.9 miles east-northeast of the Capitol in Richmond.[4]

Grant may never have heard of the place before Sheridan reported it as a checkpoint on his return to the army after his Richmond raid in May 1864. Except for the twists and turns of marching armies, it would have remained as ignored by history as Beattie's Mill, just up the road, or Holt's Corner, just to the south. Instead, it is remembered the way the country junctions of Chancellorsville and Five Forks are remembered. Because five dusty roads came together there, and because it was about halfway between Totopotomoy Creek and the Chickahominy River, both useful anchors for a line of defense, Cold Harbor became what Bruce Catton would call "one of the hard and terrible names of the Civil War, perhaps the most terrible one of all."*[5]

To Grant, this was a new entry on the long list of places in his military education, to go with Monterrey, Molino del Rey, Forts Henry and Donelson, Shiloh, Vicksburg, Chattanooga, the Wilderness, Spotsylvania, and North Anna. But George Meade, like Lee and so many others, had been here before—in 1862, when his brigade was mauled by the Confederates at Gaines's Mill, two days before he was seriously wounded at Glendale. Now both Union commanders realized as clearly as Lee did how important the junction at Cold Harbor would be to Grant's paramount objective in the next critical days. On

---

* Some Virginians, soldiers, and historians called this crossroads Old Cold Harbor, to differentiate it from the next road junction toward Richmond, an even more obscure spot, called New Cold Harbor. The distance between Cold Harbor and New Cold Harbor was just over a mile.

May 29, Grant's chief of staff, John Rawlins, confirmed that "the reduction of Richmond" was the Union commander's original goal, and that "thus far there has been no deviation" from it. "That which we most desire, and what would soonest give us the city, is a battle on something like equal ground, in which I am sure we would defeat and rout the enemy."[6]

At Cold Harbor, they would have their opportunity, for both commanding generals saw that control of the road junction could determine whether Grant succeeded or not. One of the roads swung down from the north, potentially a way to get behind Lee's army and force it to fight outside the Richmond fortifications. One ran in from White House, the Union army's main supply base. Two proceeded south and east across the Chickahominy, toward the James River and Petersburg beyond. And one led indirectly west toward Richmond, Grant's objective when he told President Lincoln, "There will be no turning back."

AFTER TWO DAYS of jabbing to find a weak spot in Lee's Totopotomoy line, on May 31 Grant's corps commanders tried again, but hours of heavy skirmishing convinced them that ramming through would be costly, if not impossible. Confederate gunners made the Union infantry pay for every sortie across the broken, boggy terrain. Meade's chief of staff, Andrew Humphreys, voiced his headquarters' frustration at repeatedly confronting such situations: "As to Lee we are so careful of him that we inquire about him constantly. If for a moment we think he is going away from us, we send out at once, a whole host of people not only to inquire after him, but to feel him and see how he is, and what sort of a place he is in, whether low and swampy or high and dry and open. He has a fancy for tangled, swampy, unhealthy places, which we argue with him about. He is very obstinate."[7]

Wright, on the Union right, reported the Rebels strongly entrenched up a steep slope behind a three-hundred-yard-wide swamp and an abatis of felled treetops. Meade ordered him to attack anyway, but after limited success in the morning, Wright said, "I don't think it advisable to attempt crossing here."[8]

Hancock, once he viewed the heavy Confederate line, told army headquarters that it "cannot be dislodged without a very strong attack." He sent the divisions of Brigadier General Francis C. Barlow and Major General David B. Birney to try, but they had to withdraw after pushing in Rebel skirmishers. One of Birney's Down East soldiers told how his regiment struck the Rebel position, then realized it was out front alone. "Our movement to the rear was executed with great dash," he wrote. "In fact, we nearly dashed our d—n brains out, getting out of this scrape without being gobbled." Back where they started, these soldiers were feeling low: "For several days we had been getting what Paddy gave his drum: hard knocks and nothing to eat." By evening, Hancock concluded that even Barlow's crack division "could not be placed over without a fight, at a great disadvantage" and advised, "I do not propose doing anything more tonight."[9]

Burnside estimated in early afternoon that his main force had moved three-fourths of a mile before confronting the deep enemy works along the crest of the Totopotomoy ridge. But later, he, too, realized that "further advance is impossible without bringing on a general engagement, which I do not understand is contemplated by the order."[10]

Only on the Union left, where Warren's Fifth Corps kept busy skirmishing all night after fighting off Early's attack, did there seem room for further Union movement. When Warren discovered early on May 31 that Confederate pickets had pulled back and uncovered Bethesda Church, he began to pivot his whole corps clockwise around his rightmost division. About two and a half miles beyond his left lay Cold Harbor, held that morning only by Fitzhugh Lee's cavalrymen, anxiously awaiting infantry support.

DESPITE R. E. Lee's desperate appeal for Robert Hoke's division to join him from south of the James "by light tomorrow," the first trainload of Hoke's troops did not depart from near Chester Station, eleven miles south of Richmond, until 5:15 a.m. They were led by Brigadier General Thomas L. Clingman, a former United States senator and Confederate congressman, whose North Carolina brigade was almost sixteen hundred strong. By 9 o'clock, four more trains followed, another was loading, and a seventh was waiting. To reach Cold Harbor via Richmond, Clingman's troops had to cover more than twenty miles by rail and foot. Before they arrived, Lee tried to fill in his lengthening and thinning lines by calling "every available man" into the ranks.

"Gather in all stragglers," he ordered. "Send to the field hospitals and have every man capable of performing the duties of a soldier returned to his command. Send back your inspectors with instructions to see that the wishes of the general commanding are carried out. Let every man fit for duty be present."[11]

Amid this urgent marshaling of forces on both sides, the summoning of reinforcements from as far away as New York and Florida, some of Warren's soldiers were surprised to hear a band strike up in the camp of Crawford's division. As new regiments poured in, there came the incongruous sight of hundreds of healthy veterans marching the other way, toward White House and home. Charles Minnemeyer of the Eleventh Pennsylvania Reserves explained: "Our time is up this day. . . . our men are buerring the dead in front of our rifel pits that was kild the night before. . . . Our divician has bin relievd and stardet back on the roads home. The bras band playing home again and the cullars are flying. . . . the boys are all in good glea. I regread the lose of the rest of our Compney."[12]

These Pennsylvanians were two-year enlistees whose hitch was up, whose last combat had been against Early at Bethesda Church the evening before. Some of the Reserves had reenlisted and were staying, and others would return, but most of the several thousand were glad to be through with soldiering forever. Their departure stripped Crawford's division; two days later, he would take over another. The troops left behind did not resent those leaving, they envied them: "Cheer after cheer went up for the brave boys, and good bye my brave lads, you have well earned your Spread Eagle. Every regiment and Battery as they passed gave them cheers and a good Send off," recalled Avery Harris, another Pennsylvanian, in Brigadier General Lysander Cutler's adjacent division. "We thought just then, that we would like to feel as those brave boys did, and for the same reason, but some of our boys were cruel enough to remind us that, that day for us was fourteen months ahead of us, and that Grant would find enough to do 'till then."[13]

Hoke's Confederates, dispatched from Beauregard's force, were unused to heavy marching like that endured by both armies north of the James. By midafternoon, Clingman's brigade had stretched out as it labored along more than ten miles of road from the Richmond rail station to the front by way of Mechanicsville. About two miles short of Gaines's Mill, nearly four miles west of Cold Harbor, Clingman halted to await further orders. Fitz Lee's cavalry still held the Cold Harbor crossroads without infantry support at 3:15, when he reported Federal cavalry advancing, half a mile out. "I am prepared to dispute their progress," Lee said. But since Clingman's troops were so near, he asked, "Had they not better be ordered on to assist in securing this place?" Clingman had spent three hours resting and closing up his brigade when Hoke instructed him to march to Cold Harbor. When he arrived, gunfire was already crackling.[14]

AFTER DRIVING Confederate horsemen south of Matadequin Creek the day before, Alfred Torbert and George Custer had been sure that Fitz Lee "meditated an attack" on May 31, so they were eager to strike first. Phil Sheridan found them in conference at Custer's headquarters and quickly approved their plan to go at Lee's cavalry holding Cold Harbor from two directions: two of Torbert's brigades would ride directly down the road from Old Church, and the other would head south, then cut back west, "to turn the enemy's right at all hazards, and get in among his led horses." But they did not start until past midafternoon, giving Lee's two brigades time to throw up a light barricade of earth and fence rails about the crossroads. Colonel Thomas C. Devin, assigned to turn Lee's right, was unenthusiastic about his role, and Torbert reported that "it does not appear that a very serious attempt was made to carry out my design" in that direction. But Wesley Merritt's brigade, attacking down the road from Old Church, forced Lee's cavalry back toward its prepared line. Then Custer brought his brigade up to link Merritt and Devin, presenting a broad front to the outnumbered Confederate cavalry.[15]

When fifty-one-year-old Brigadier General Clingman arrived at Cold Harbor, he found Major General Hoke, who had just turned twenty-seven four days earlier, waiting to direct his brigade into place. Clingman's three regiments went in on the left of Fitz Lee's main position; then one of them pushed out a few hundred yards to support dismounted horsemen in a lively firefight. "As this was the most exposed and dangerous part of my line, I remained with it," Clingman wrote. He said the cavalry on his left gave way, then the captain of his infantry on that wing failed to open fire despite three commands to do so. Later, he said, the cavalry on his right also buckled, "alleging that their ammunition had given out." Only then, Clingman explained, did he permit his own troops to fall back. As he did, "a portion of a shell took away the front of my hat and slightly wounded my forehead. Though somewhat stunned for an instant, I was not disabled at all. . . . A few of my command were captured." A neutral observer might say that when Fitz Lee's cavalry fell back in textbook style upon its infantry support, Clingman's newly arrived command forgot the textbook and instead of holding firm, joined the backward movement.[16]

Torbert, rather than sending three brigades abreast against Fitz Lee's stubborn line, had given Merritt permission to swing around Lee's left. Then Devin assailed the other wing, and this pressure from fast-firing Yankees on both flanks forced the Confederates to withdraw or be surrounded. They pulled back through Cold Harbor, then turned about to face the Yankees again in the dusk, perhaps three-quarters of a mile west of the junction. Confronting them, Torbert drew a line that crossed the road to Bethesda Church on the north, arced westward, and crossed the road to Barker's Mill on the south.

But when Sheridan realized that Torbert's command was so far beyond any Union infantry and even from Gregg's cavalry division, he ordered him to withdraw quietly during the night. In uncharacteristic language, Sheridan reported to Meade that "I do not feel able to hold this place [Cold Harbor]. . . . with the heavy odds against me here, I do not think it prudent to hold on."[17]

In the dark, the Union horsemen had trotted all the way back to where they started the day when an urgent directive came from Meade through Sheridan, reversing the order Torbert had just obeyed. According to Torbert, Meade now told Sheridan to "hold on to all he had gained at Cold Harbor at all hazards." He assured him that the Sixth Corps, marching all the way from the right to the extreme left of the Union army, would be there to relieve the cavalry in the morning.

"Will do so if possible," Sheridan replied at 1:00 a.m.

Torbert thus wheeled his division about and shortly before daylight reached the position he had left, all "so quietly that I do not believe the enemy knew that I had, for a time, withdrawn from their front."[18]

DURING THE cavalry fight at Cold Harbor on Tuesday, May 31, the commanders of both armies were thinking the same thing. That road junction represented Grant's last chance to cut between Lee and Richmond, and neither general wanted the Rebels to fall back within the permanent works defending the capital. While Grant was deciding to attack the Confederate right flank at Cold Harbor early the next morning, Lee was planning to attack the Union left flank at the same time and place.

Lee was feeling stronger, although still weakened by his illness, and he moved in his carriage to a new headquarters at Shady Grove

Church. As the guns in the cavalry clash sounded in the distance, he pulled three divisions of Anderson's corps out of his Totopotomoy line and shifted them to Early's right. Their march, completed overnight, put Lee's army on a northwest-to-southeast angle with Hill's corps on the left, Early's corps and Breckinridge's small division holding the center, and Anderson's corps on the right. Hoke's full division would arrive before dawn on June 1 to take over the cavalry lines facing Cold Harbor.

The Rebel cavalry still had no confirmed sighting of Federal infantry on that flank, so Lee quickly saw the chance to switch from tactical defense to offense, for a counterblow heavier and better coordinated than Early's effort at Bethesda Church Monday evening. If he caught the Federals on the move, before their infantry set up at Cold Harbor, he might turn the end of their line, double them back, and take them from the rear. Whatever Lee's own strength or his army's, he was constantly looking for a way to strike, instead of waiting to be struck.[19]

Even earlier, at 10:00 a.m. Tuesday, Meade had told Wright to investigate the roads around Warren's rear, and all day the two of them exchanged messages about the best way to move the Sixth Corps from one end of the main Federal line to the other. After hearing that the first regiments of Confederate infantry had reached Cold Harbor, Meade ordered Wright at 9:45 p.m. to "immediately withdraw your corps from its present position and move to Cold Harbor about two and a half miles east [actually almost three miles south-southeast] of Bethesda Church." Sheridan's cavalry was directed to hold on until the Sixth Corps arrived, Meade said, telling Wright that "it is of the utmost importance you should reach the point as soon after daylight as possible." Although Meade instructed him to march via Haw's Shop and Old Church, he added that "possibly" a shortcut could be found past the church. Still later, he was asking Warren about better roads around the Fifth Corps' rear, concerned that "the enemy will be re-inforced and the cavalry forced back before Wright can get there."[20]

It is not clear why Meade ordered Wright's Sixth Corps to pull out of its battle and picket lines, then march through the night with all its supply trains across the rear area of three other corps, when he could have sent Smith's newly arrived Eighteenth Corps first by a closer, less cluttered route. It is true that Meade himself commanded only the Army of the Potomac, so at that point, strictly speaking, Smith was not his to command. If Grant and Meade had been working as one, Smith's corps would have preceded Wright's, reaching Cold Harbor sooner, in better condition. But not until midmorning Wednesday did Grant place Smith under Meade's command. When Meade ordered Wright to leapfrog from one flank to the other, the Eighteenth Corps was still under Grant's instructions to head for New Castle Ferry. Smith did not get the corrected orders sending him to Cold Harbor until nearly twelve hours after Wright got his—and these, too, came from Grant, not Meade.[21]

"THE MEMORY of that day's march will exist so long as any man, who was in it, continues to live." Years later, survivors of Grant's infantry, soldiers who had made so many prodigious marches that spring that they could hardly count them all, would relive the travails of Wednesday, June 1.[22]

Wright's troops had started before midnight, leaving pickets behind as they withdrew from their end of the main Totopotomoy line. Stumbling in the night along roads that led first this way, then that, they marched through the camps and wagon parks of Hancock's, Burnside's, and Warren's support troops. "The roads [were] ankle deep with dust," wrote Charles H. Berry, of Wright's 110th Ohio, "and yet the 6th Corps veterans, hungry for two days, sleepy for three nights, fatigued with relentless marching by day and by night, all streaming with perspiration, grim and blear eyed, our hair dusted to the whiteness of three score years and ten," pressed on.[23]

Smith's Eighteenth Corps, forced on much of its route to breathe the dust stirred by Wright's thousands of men, animals, and wagons, had not yet learned such stoicism. His troops did not have to wander through the night, but "during the middle of the day the temperature, even in the shade, must have been close up to, if not above, blood heat," a New Englander recalled. Hundreds of men fell out by the roadside; some died of sunstroke. So hard was the march that soldiers seriously believed it covered twenty-five miles, rather than about half that many. And following the baggage train of the Sixth Corps, "the dust was worse, if possible, than the heat." It covered the woods and fields like snow; "I could not see the length of a single company," said a captain of the Twelfth New Hampshire.[24]

The foot soldiers sweated "through a country fetid with putrefying carcasses of animals, the stench from which was sickening and intolerable," yet tolerate it they did. Those dead horses were "Sheridan's milestones"—some were casualties of Rebel gunfire, but many were worn-out Union mounts whose riders had orders to shoot them rather than leave them for the hard-pressed Confederates to rehabilitate. "Dead horses, broken sabres and carbines together with little mounds of earth here and there told more plainly than words the desperate nature of the conflict that had occurred," a New York lieutenant reflected as he neared Cold Harbor.[25]

To make Smith's troops feel worse, as they passed Meade's divisions they had to endure catcalls and shouts of "Hallo! Parlor soldiers!" They put up with these taunts because they came from men who had been through the Wilderness, Spotsylvania, North Anna, and Totopotomoy. "The Army of the Potomac was the nation's idol," admitted W. P. Derby of the Twenty-seventh Massachusetts, in Brigadier General John H. Martindale's division. Many of Meade's veterans "considered the services of other Eastern troops pastime and skirmishing. . . . the strife and carnage attending their engagements seemed to belittle the contests of less pretentious forces. . . . Every field, from the Potomac to the Chickahominy, had drank deep of their life-blood, and though discouraged by frequent and disastrous defeats, they never shrank from meeting the enemy."[26]

Martindale's men, and most of those arriving from below the James, had never seen fighting to equal what had happened the day before around Cold Harbor. They had not learned the hard way what General Gibbon realized as the two armies edged into position to go head-on at each other. "Two things up to this time (May 31) had been well demonstrated," Gibbon wrote. "We had never succeeded in forcing Lee, by battle, from any position he assumed, nor had he succeeded in forcing us from any." So far in this spring campaign, the Union army had penetrated the Confederate line twice, but without decisive effect. "A few hours were all that was necessary to render any position so strong by breastworks that the opposite party was unable to carry it and it became a recognized fact amongst the men that when the enemy had occupied a position six or eight hours ahead of us, it was useless to attempt to take it." Some of the heaviest losses came among new troops, Gibbon wrote, "who had not had sufficient experience in attacking breastworks to enable them to reach the same conclusion as the old soldiers."[27]

As far back as Spotsylvania, Lyman had been impressed by the speed with which the Rebels made rifle pits and piled fence rails, logs, rocks, and sod. "Within one hour," he wrote, "there is a shelter against bullets, high enough to cover a man kneeling, and extending often for a mile or two. When our line advances, there is the line of the enemy, nothing showing but the bayonets, and the battle-flags stuck on top of the work. It is a rule that, when the Rebels halt, the first day gives them a good rifle-pit; the second, a regular infantry parapet with artillery in position; and the third a parapet with an abattis in front and entrenched batteries behind. Sometimes they put this three days' work into the first twenty-four hours."[28]

Since the move south had begun, and especially since the bloody days of Spotsylvania, the Yankees, too, had become diggers. Some of their diaries and letters tell of digging defensive works repeatedly, three or four times a day, at each stop for rest or bivouac. But they were on the offensive, obliged to keep attacking. When Grant reported, "A battle with [the Rebels] outside of intrenchments cannot be had," he considered that apparent fact to be proof of dwindling Southern morale. He had not learned the lessons of May as well as the privates in his own front ranks.

6

The Splendor of Our Victories

LAWRENCE MASSILLON KEITT was a romantic Rebel, a thirty-nine-year-old South Carolinian who as U.S. and Confederate congressman had preached states' rights with furious eloquence. Perhaps because his military experience so far had been in a less than strenuous billet guarding the seaward approaches of Charleston, he seemed just as enthusiastic about war in 1864 as when he had cheered his state's secession in 1860. A Charleston newspaper said while he was posted at Sullivan's Island that Keitt was "panting for a conflict with the Vandal foe." Now he was about to get his wish, leading his Twentieth South Carolina, a regiment more than a thousand strong, on the way to reinforce Lee's army outside Richmond. Arriving in the Confederate capital, he paused to write to his "dear, dear Susie."[1]

Keitt recalled how "full of pleasant remembrances" the same roads north had been when he and Susie were on their way to Europe as newlyweds. "Now coming along I identified each spot. Where the mockingbird sang, catching the [song] of the frogs after the rain . . . passing out some joyous, then some touching tune. . . . Each spot to Richmond conjured up charming memories of the past. I trust that I will be spared to meet you again, and talk them over when this war is over. . . ."

Despite the urgency of his orders to the front, Keitt, as a gentleman of social and political standing, took the time to pay a courtesy call on Jefferson Davis, his former congressional colleague in Washington. He asked Davis to assign his regiment to Brigadier General Joseph B. Kershaw's old South Carolina brigade, and the president gave him a note to Lee endorsing his request. From Davis's office, Keitt proceeded to see ex–U.S. congressman, ex–Confederate general William Smith, now Virginia's governor for the second time. With classic

Southern hospitality, Smith offered to provide a room for Mrs. Keitt when she came to overcrowded Richmond to be near her husband.

The gracious way Keitt was received encouraged his ambition. "If I get through the coming fights, I believe that I shall be promoted," he told his wife. "Every thing is auspicious. Gen'l Lee is seven miles from here, and I am about to go out to him. Perfect confidence is felt here. Gen'l Lee's army is strong, is believed to be as strong as Grant's, and battle is eagerly hoped for. . . . The feeling is prevalent here that peace is at hand. If Lee crushes Grant I think that it is. . . .

"Come to me, *ma belle femme,* as soon as you can."

The next morning, Keitt made his way to the army. He immediately found himself commander of Kershaw's old brigade, because Kershaw had become division commander, and Keitt was senior to the brigade's other colonels. Besides, he noted, the Twentieth South Carolina was "a trifle larger" than the brigade's other five battered regiments and one battalion put together. Indeed, it was the biggest regiment in the Confederate army; as it arrived, some of Kershaw's veterans were so impressed that they called it the "Twentieth Army Corps."

"General Lee is throwing his wisdom over the whole," Keitt reported to his wife. "He has been ill but is better. I believe that Grant will be crushed. . . . I wish that you could see the confidence of the troops. They feel as if led by the hand of Providence. Grant brings his men up only by making them drunk. Those we now take are invariably drunk, and they tell me all are made so, to get them to advance. . . . I think that we shall soon close the war. . . ."[2]

Keitt noted that "the regiments have been cut down very small," but he had not been in the main theater of war long enough for the fact of such losses to dull his eager optimism. A few days more, and he might be as darkly prophetic as Charles Minor Blackford, a Virginia officer at Anderson's headquarters. As Lee turned to meet Grant along the Totopotomoy, Blackford had written that "Grant, it is true, got nearer Richmond by making a detour, but when he got in his present position he was where he could have been at first without seeing a Confederate soldier or losing a man. As it is he has lost fifty thousand men and Lee and his army are before him, full of fight and unconquerable. . . . In one respect only has his campaign been a success: to kill and wound so many of his men required a loss on our part at least one-fourth of his, and he is a hundred times better able to stand it."

With the Wilderness and Spotsylvania fresh in mind, Blackford feared that "We are being conquered by the splendor of our own victories, and Grant accepts defeat with that consolation. . . ." If Blackford had had an accurate count of casualties, he might have been even more gloomy: Grant had lost more than forty thousand at that point, but Lee's losses were nearly half that number, perhaps double Blackford's estimate.

Yet even he thought the Yankees had suffered enough for the moment: "The Federal army is greatly demoralized, and I do not think that Grant will subject them to the test of another general engagement for some time to come."[3]

ON THE NIGHT of May 31, only hours after Lawrence Keitt reported for duty, he moved his South Carolinians into position as the rightmost brigade of Kershaw's division. To their right was Clingman's brigade of Hoke's division; between them ran a ravine with a small stream bordered by a swampy thicket. Anderson had ordered Kershaw and Hoke to advance in the morning on Cold Harbor—Kershaw guiding south-southeast along the road from Beulah Church, while Hoke would head northeast, along the road from New Cold Harbor. Anderson wanted them to push ahead "to find out positively what is in front of me."[4]

What was there was Torbert's division of Sheridan's cavalry, in the line it had abandoned, then reoccupied between dusk and dawn. Some of the "weary and disgusted" Union horsemen were busy improving the rifle pits they had dug earlier, but many had lain down to doze in the rear, the bridles of their mounts hooked to their arms. They collapsed from exhaustion, trying to sleep despite knowing that they were well beyond the main Union army; the only support anywhere close was a brigade of Gregg's cavalry division, on its way from Old Church.

The Federal horsemen at Cold Harbor were still without infantry support because both Wright's Sixth and Smith's Eighteenth Corps were having problems on the way. When Meade ordered Wright at 9:45 the previous evening to move "immediately" and reach Cold Harbor "as soon after daylight as possible," he had not considered how long it would take merely to pull a corps of infantry out of line and assemble it in the dark. The first of three Sixth Corps divisions did not set out until after midnight. Repeatedly, couriers from Sheridan appeared along the road, urging Wright to hurry. But Wright's last brigade did not start its long, dusty march until 4:30 a.m. And it was midmorning before Smith, at New Castle, finally got corrected orders to head for Cold Harbor.

Anderson's artillery commander, Brigadier General E. Porter Alexander, saw that until Federal infantry arrived on the Confederate right flank, "Luck seemed to be on our side & a great opportunity was offered us. We had all the time we needed to work our own sweet will upon Sheridan, & if we had once gobbled him the other corps, in their scattered condition, should have been easy prey."[5]

By 5:00 a.m., the tired Union cavalrymen were stirring to the smell of boiling coffee. Minutes later, gunfire jerked them wide awake. While they rushed to the line, pack mules brayed and kicked, scattering mess gear and baggage. Captain Theophilus F. Rodenbough, commanding the Second U.S. Cavalry, remembered how "Suddenly, jackasses, mules, and contrabands made for the rear, encountering on the way the corps commander [Sheridan] and staff, who only by turning into a convenient farm-yard escaped the deluge."

At the center of the Union line facing Kershaw, six hundred cavalrymen of Merritt's brigade crouched in their rifle pits, with timber to their front and rear, a clearing on their left and a bog on their right. According to Rodenbough, four of Merritt's regiments were still armed with Sharps breechloaders; only one, the First New York, had received Spencer repeaters. The fast-firing Yankees turned back the first Rebel rush, then waited tensely for perhaps two hours before hearing more scattered shots from beyond the timber.

There, the lead elements of Kershaw's division were milling about, reorganizing to advance again. At about 8:00 a.m., the Federals heard "a compact mass of infantry" moving through the timber. Then they were surprised to see a Confederate officer emerge from the woods, riding a superb iron-gray charger.[6]

The mounted man was Keitt, out front, with his brigade coming on in column behind him. As some of Kershaw's veterans recalled, "Every man in ranks knew he was being led by one of the most gifted and gallant men in the South." Keitt pranced ahead "like a knight of old . . . and looked the embodiment of the true chevalier that he was." But he was a novice at this. His advance had begun only after delay and confusion; "his pressing orders to find the enemy only added perplexity to his other difficulties." And never before in the whole war had Kershaw's brigade been led into battle by a commander on horseback, waving his sword—"a fine target for the sharpshooters."[7]

On the South Carolinians came, with the Georgia brigades of

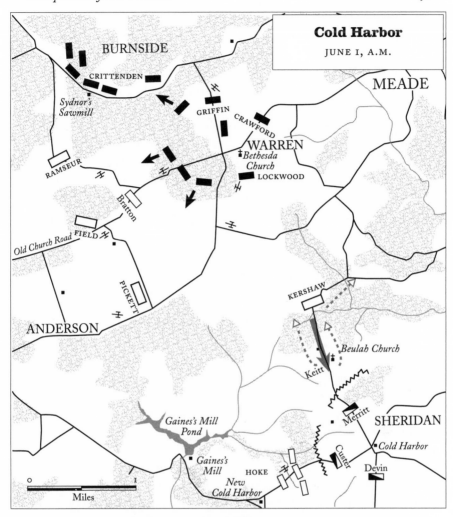

Cold Harbor

JUNE 1, A.M.

BURNSIDE

CRITTENDEN

MEADE

Sydnor's
Sawmill

GRIFFIN

CRAWFORD

WARREN

*Bethesda
Church*

RAMSEUR

LOCKWOOD

Bratton

Old Church Road FIELD

PICKETT

ANDERSON

KERSHAW

Beulah Church

Keitt

Gaines's Mill
Pond

Merritt

SHERIDAN

*Gaines's
Mill*

HOKE

Custer

Cold Harbor

Devin

*New
Cold Harbor*

o   I

Miles

*Keitt's South Carolinians lead the Confederate charge against Sheridan's cav-
alry holding Cold Harbor. Keitt is killed and the attack repulsed as Hoke fails to
cooperate. Meanwhile Warren expands his position around Bethesda Church.*

Brigadier Generals Goode Bryan and William T. Wofford in support.
As they approached, Federal officers shouted Sheridan's order from
trench to trench: "Hold at all costs!" Expecting a close and sustained
fight, cavalrymen armed with Sharps and Spencers had also piled pis-
tols and ammunition beside their holes. Peering through the timber,
they could see Confederate bayonets flashing in the morning sun.
"Howly Mother! here they come wid sabers on fut!" hollered a little
Irish corporal in the Second U.S.

There was a sputter of fire as Union skirmishers did their job and fell back. Then the Confederates shifted to double-quick step and charged, letting loose the Rebel yell. At that, "a sheet of flame came from the cavalry line, and for three or four minutes the din was deafening," said Rodenbough. "The repeating carbines raked the flank of the hostile column while the Sharps single-loaders kept up a steady rattle." Amid the excitement, a cavalry band struck up "Rally 'Round the Flag, Boys"—"one of the most inspiring moments of my life," wrote Lieutenant Isaac Dunkelberger of the First U.S.[8]

Keitt, trying to rally his troops, was shot through the liver. Seeing this, the men around him "went to pieces in abject rout." An artillery officer in support said, "I have never seen any body of troops in such a condition of utter demoralization; they actually groveled upon the ground and attempted to burrow under each other in holes and depressions. . . . We actually spurred our horses upon them and seemed to hear their very bones crack, but it did no good; if compelled to wriggle out of one hole they wriggled into another."[9]

The Rebel spearhead got no help at all on its right, where Hoke's division had hardly budged. Thus the defending Yankees could focus their fire on the Twentieth South Carolina, and when it broke, the smaller veteran regiments alongside were forced to give way. "The whole thing was over in less than five minutes," said Rodenbough. "The enemy, surprised, stunned, and demoralized, withdrew more quickly than they came, leaving their dead and wounded."

The heavy firing had set the woods afire; after the Rebels pulled back, Captain Charles McK. Leoser of the Second U.S. came out of his line to save "a young gentleman without any top to his head" from burning. He asked the Confederate "what had induced his people to do so foolhardy a thing as to attempt to carry that position." "Oh!" said the dying soldier, "we thought there were only a few cavalry up here."[10]

Lawrence Keitt had thought the same, and in those few minutes, he became "a martyr to the inexorable laws of the army rank"—and to inexperience, and perhaps to vanity.[11]

He was not left on the field, but brought back into Confederate hands. As his men carried him in, a friend from Anderson's headquarters stopped them and gave him a draught of whiskey. Keitt, faint but conscious, smiled and whispered, "Such is the fate of war." After a doctor administered more whiskey and morphine, Keitt was taken on a litter three miles to the rear, to a crowded farmhouse hospital. There he died the next morning.[12]

Porter Alexander maintained that "the reason why we did not destroy Sheridan was solely & entirely because he had magazine guns." Both Confederate attacks that morning, he wrote, "were repulsed by the fire of the breech-loaders from the breastworks." But Captain Rodenbough, in the midst of the Federal line, said that only some of Sheridan's troopers had Spencer "magazine guns," while others had single-shot breechloaders. As demonstrated by the rustic Carolinian questioned by Grant, and by Alexander's impression afterward, the presence of the repeaters in Yankee hands played on the imagination of Rebel soldiers, and had a genuine morale effect. Later on June 1, some Confederates surrendered after mistakenly thinking they were facing seven-shot repeaters because the advancing Yankees did not have bayonets fixed.[13]

However great its impact on the minds and bodies of Rebel troops, the Spencer carbine alone did not decide that morning's fight. Kershaw had contributed by appointing his own old brigade to lead the way, with the untried Keitt in command and the erstwhile garrison troops of the Twentieth South Carolina in front. Inexplicably, Hoke failed to advance alongside Kershaw (according to Lee's chief of artillery, Brigadier General William N. Pendleton, the Union position in Hoke's front "was, after careful reconnaissance, deemed too strong to attack"). And Anderson failed as corps commander by not coordinating the operation, lashing Hoke into action. For all those reasons, Lee's hope of turning the Union flank was frustrated. The spot where Keitt fell was as far as Anderson's corps advanced that Wednesday.[14]

When the seasoned regiments accompanying Keitt pulled back, they spontaneously broke out bayonets and started to dig in, piling the earth with their tin drinking cups to provide skimpy protection. Soon the whole command, without being ordered, was entrenching where it had halted. Then Anderson sent instructions to close gaps, and the impromptu trenches became Kershaw's main line of resistance. Alexander ran his guns up to sight across terrain ideal for defending artillery. "It was a country generally flat, with many small clearings, & thin woods, & scattered pines," he wrote. "No long ranges, but favorable to cross fires & smooth bore ricochet firing—I put in position every gun I had." Because the line there was fairly straight, Alexander told his artillerymen that where possible, they should set up ahead of the breastworks to create better angles of fire. Colonel John W. Henagan, who had commanded Kershaw's old brigade before the arrival of the Twentieth South Carolina, took over again after Keitt fell. He settled his troops into Kershaw's division front alongside Bryan and Wofford.[15]

Beyond Kershaw's right, Hoke's division had done almost nothing

that morning. Clingman began the day by actually withdrawing his
left about two hundred yards to what Hoke thought a better position.
Clingman said that before the attack, he had asked the colonel of
Keitt's nearest regiment about closing the gap where the swampy
ravine ran between them, but the South Carolinian declined. Through
this ravine drained one of half a dozen creeks that fed Gaines's
millpond. Three of those streamlets flowed westward from near the
Federal lines into the developing Rebel front; the southernmost of the
three ran in the thickly grown ravine between Hoke and Kershaw.

Clingman said that despite orders, he was about to extend his line
leftward when he was told that soon another South Carolina brigade,
under Brigadier General Johnson Hagood, would come up to cover
the gap—which it did, only to pull out on Hoke's orders, reopening
the gap in early afternoon. Clingman tied in on his right with
Brigadier General Alfred H. Colquitt's Georgians, who linked with
Brigadier General James G. Martin's North Carolinians on the Confederate army's far right. There, Martin pushed back Sheridan's skirmishers before entrenching along a ridge that stretched south of the
road between the two Cold Harbors. All of these extemporaneous
trenches, adjustments, links, and failures to link would matter in the
hours ahead.[16]

HORATIO WRIGHT trotted into Sheridan's position at Cold Harbor
at 9:00 a.m., after what Meade's chief of staff called "a night march of
more than fifteen miles, through a strange country covered with an
intricate network of ill-defined roads." True as it was, that description
did not mention the heat, the dust, and the fact that the march was
through the rear area of three other Union corps. Wright appeared at
nine o'clock, but his Sixth Corps was still strung out behind; when the
Vermont brigade led the tired infantry in, Custer's brigade band
greeted it with "Hail Columbia." Not until midafternoon did the last
of Wright's troops fill in the lines that Sheridan's cavalry gratefully
vacated.[17]

The Eighteenth Corps began arriving about that time, after eating
the dust of the Sixth along the road from Old Church. To start the
day, Smith's men had tramped to and from New Castle Ferry—"For
some reason we got on the wrong road and marched twelve miles for
nothing"—and their spirits were hardly boosted by not knowing why.
Hundreds had fallen out by the road until provost guards prodded
them to their feet to shamble on.[18]

On the way, Smith got orders from Meade to follow the Sixth Corps in and form on its right, holding a line from Bethesda Church to Cold Harbor while preparing to attack. By then, Smith's force was less than ten thousand strong; realizing that reaching as far as Bethesda Church would stretch it across nearly three miles, Smith decided that he could follow only the second part of the orders; as his brigades came up, he positioned them to attack. By late afternoon, the Sixth and Eighteenth corps were both in line of battle, ready to throw most of their weight against two Confederate divisions.

AFTER THE Southerners' morning attempt to retake Cold Harbor failed, Lee had ordered Breckinridge to pull out of his place farther up the line and bolster the Confederate right. But jousting with Federal forces held Breckinridge in place for hours. Captain T. C. Morton of the Twenty-sixth Virginia Battalion said that there his company found itself "the centre of the most furious cannonading we had ever before experienced." Among his casualties was a man detailed to the rear to cook breakfast, who was returning to the front toting a kettle of cornbread and beef. When the shelling commenced, he ran for the trenches, his hungry comrades watching. Just before he reached safety, a shell exploded in front of him. When the smoke cleared, one of the soldiers spoke sadly for the rest: "Lor', boys, just look, Joe Flint is all mixed up with our breakfast, and it aint fit for nothing!"

Morton's outfit did picket duty to hold off the Federals while Breckinridge fell back to straighten the defensive line. The captain of the adjacent company said he had "the same damn orders," adding, "We'll all be in hell or Boston before tomorrow night." Then, he said, Lee would report that his army had had a skirmish, "and only lost about two hundred killed and missing. That's all of us, you know, but we aren't hardly worth counting down here among all these men." The firing held up when a man from each side walked out between the lines carrying a white rag on a stick, to swap Virginia tobacco for Rio coffee. Soon afterward, the Federals pushed the defending pickets back; Morton suspected that the Yankees had initiated the swap to get a closer look at how thinly the Rebel front was held.[19]

Lee, already expecting the Union Eighteenth Corps to appear at Cold Harbor, learned during the morning that the Sixth Corps had disappeared from his left. Desperate to block the fast-developing Union threat to turn his line and drive across the Chickahominy into Richmond, he again sought help from below the James.

At 12:45 p.m., he sent a dispatch to Beauregard, trying this time to play on the Creole general's well-known vanity. First, Lee acknowledged the danger of losing the vital communications between Richmond and Petersburg if Beauregard's force was stripped too thin. But, he asked, "as two-thirds of Butler's force has joined Grant can you not leave sufficient guard to move with the balance of your command to north side of James River and take command of right wing of army?" In late afternoon, he tried again. And once again, this time correctly, Beauregard said that he could not comply unless Butler sent the rest of his force to join Grant, or President Davis decided to abandon the rail line between Richmond and Petersburg.[20]

Not yet fully recovered, Lee realized that he must move closer to oversee what was coming. Late in the day, he transferred his headquarters from Shady Grove Church to a spot by the road just west of New Cold Harbor, below Gaines's millpond. His army was now on a line running northwest to southeast, with Hill's corps on the left, Early in the center, and Anderson on the right. Grant's army faced him with Hancock on its right, Burnside in reserve behind him, Warren next, then Smith and Wright.

While the heavy infantry corps were shifting southward, cavalry was off on both flanks of the armies. After holding Cold Harbor in the morning, Sheridan's fatigued troopers went into camp well behind the front, around Parsley's Mill. But Fitz Lee's division was actively screening the ground between the Confederate right and the Chickahominy. At the other end of the lines, Union brigadier general James H. Wilson's division had been destroying the railroads and bridges north of Richmond to cut off Confederate access to the Shenandoah Valley and Fredericksburg. Between Ashland and Hanover Court House, it drove through a force of Confederate horsemen under Pierce Young before being attacked by Tom Rosser's brigade of Wade Hampton's cavalry division. Charge and countercharge went on until late evening, when the Yankees pulled back past the court house.[21]

This partly uncovered the Federal right, where Hancock now held the end of the main Union line, so he ordered brisk skirmishing to stay in touch with any Confederate moves. Aggressive jabs by both armies dented the line here and there, delaying Breckinridge's departure to strengthen the Confederate right, and keeping troops on both sides in a high state of watchfulness. During this action, Brigadier General Joseph Finegan's brigade (three Florida battalions that had traveled farther than any other reinforcements summoned by Lee, plus fewer than three hundred Floridians of the wounded Brigadier General

Edward A. Perry's devastated command) was noticed for the first time since reaching the front. Colonel George S. Patton, heading one of Breckinridge's brigades alongside, complained that Finegan had failed to cooperate in a local advance. But the Florida troops would soon make up for any early shortcomings.[22]

At the southern end of the line, Lee had shifted from the morning's counteroffensive to the afternoon's purely defensive stance. There, the Confederates still faced two Union corps. And though Anderson commanded four divisions, two of them—Pickett and Major General Charles W. Field—were farther up the line; only Kershaw and Hoke were close at hand. They were busy throwing up breastworks and positioning cannon to greet six Federal divisions under Brigadier Generals John H. Martindale, William T. H. Brooks, and Charles Devens, Jr., of Smith's Eighteenth Corps, and James B. Ricketts, David A. Russell, and Thomas H. Neill of Wright's Sixth Corps.

The Smith-Wright line started at a point between Beulah Church and Woody's house, about a mile north-northwest of Cold Harbor; curved gently down to cross the Cold Harbor–New Cold Harbor road, almost exactly halfway between the two; then refused on the Union left to face southward, ending astride the road from Cold Harbor to Barker's Mill. At each end, the Union force in this sector bent back away from Anderson's Confederate breastworks, which ran south-southeast from Walnut Grove Church Road before making a jog due south at the swampy creek between Kershaw and Hoke. Then the Rebel line resumed its original course, to end along a low, irregular north-south rise known as Turkey Ridge, leading to a hardly distinguishable eminence called Turkey Hill.

Lee knew this "classic ground." Nearby, on June 1 two years earlier, he had taken command of the Army of Northern Virginia. A few days after that, he had won his first clear victory here in the battle of Gaines's Mill, or, as some would call it, First Cold Harbor. It had been a close, seesaw affair, with the position of the forces almost reversed— Lee swinging his force from east and north against McClellan, whose grand army straddled the Chickahominy. Lee had not been familiar with the neighborhood, and his maps were much poorer than the ones Confederate topographers had produced for 1864. He was on the offensive-defensive then, he and his generals were unused to one another, and he had a hard time coordinating his attack. It stretched into a five-hour series of piecemeal assaults, repeatedly turned back by the Federals until John B. Hood's Texas brigade led the first breakthrough late in the day.

Lee's victory was the most expensive of the bloody Seven Days; in the stand-up fight, his army suffered nearly nine thousand casualties in driving McClellan south of the Chickahominy toward Malvern Hill. But it had saved Richmond, and enemy infantry had not come within ten miles of the Confederate capital again until this June, two years later. Now half a dozen more great battles in the East were history, and Lee's soldiers were doing less and less stand-up fighting. The road from the Rapidan through the Wilderness, Spotsylvania Court House, the North Anna, the Totopotomoy, and Bethesda Church was stained with proof of the good sense of building breastworks instead of charging them.

7

You Cannot Conceive the Horror

Soon after converting to infantry duty, back up the road near the South Anna River, one of the heavy artillerymen brought down from Washington as Union reinforcements had hanged himself. A. Jackson Crossley, an engineer at Meade's headquarters, told a friend that the poor soul had been "in low spirits—he had not the moral courage to face the music but was brave enough to string himself."

Crossley could sympathize. "These heavy artillery men have been awfully deceived," he wrote. "They were enlisted as they supposed to garrison forts only, to have no field service but Genl Grant has got them out here acting as Infantry and a sicker set of fellows you never saw. They thought to lay around Washington and them places but they are now out here doing Infantry duty."

Out of the Washington area defenses, Grant had summoned eight New York heavy artillery regiments, plus others from Pennsylvania, Connecticut, Massachusetts, Maine, and Vermont, assigning them to infantry brigades throughout the Army of the Potomac. "They are bringing everything in the field now," wrote Crossley. "This army is stronger to day than when it crossed the Rapidan in regard to numbers but we have lost some good men that will not be replaced in a hurry."[1]

Just before the Heavy regiments were ordered south, Brigadier General A. P. Howe had inspected them thoroughly at their forts in the Washington defenses. He rated the Second Connecticut as only "fair" in artillery and infantry drill, but that was superior to most of the other Heavy units inspected. Detachments of the Second New York, for example, were found "very ordinary" to "deficient" in artillery drill, and in infantry "wants improving much" to "very deficient." Howe gave the Seventh New York similar grades, and found the Ninth New York "in point of discipline and drill (both in artillery and infantry)" the least efficient of all those in the capital's defenses. Yet, because these artillery regiments were full and their men were fresh, they would be given leading roles in the assaults just ahead.[2]

On Wednesday afternoon, June 1, the erstwhile cannoneers of the Second Connecticut Heavies dragged into Cold Harbor with the Sixth Corps, then hurried into line of attack for the first time as infantrymen. Then they waited. On any other day, the waiting might have been a more unnerving experience, but now they were "drugged, as it were, with utter fatigue," so deadened from marching and want of sleep that they could hardly take in the meaning of the bustle around them, even after artillery opened from both sides. They had been foot soldiers for less than two weeks; the order yanking them out of their relative luxury in the forts about the capital had come on May 17, and they had reached the army at the end of the Spotsylvania campaign on May 20. Their only casualties so far had been in a skirmish on the North Anna.

Now, as part of Emory Upton's brigade in Brigadier General David A. Russell's division, they trudged into the lines at Cold Harbor to await the arrival of the Eighteenth Corps, coming on behind them. For the last few miles of their march, they had repeatedly given way on the road to ambulances loaded with wounded cavalrymen. They understood that serious combat was imminent, and, commanded by the twenty-four-year-old Upton, they were sure to be in it. Upton had been a famous fighter since his bout with a future South Carolina artilleryman when both were West Point cadets during the prewar debate over secession. Wounded at First Bull Run, he had returned to duty and risen from lieutenant to brigade command before being hit again at Spotsylvania. For his performance there, Grant promoted him to brigadier general on the spot. One of the Connecticut cannoneers said that on meeting Upton, "it was love at first sight. His coolness in fight, his kindness, his military judgment & vigor, his freedom from bluster & fuss & his upright conduct & good habits, make him the perfectest soldier I have ever seen."[3]

The colonel of the Second Connecticut Heavies was Elisha Strong Kellogg, a square-built forty-year-old former sailor said to have been jailed once in a foreign port for assaulting a man who insulted the American flag. In 1862, he had fought over these same acres of Virginia as a major of artillery. On this day, said one of his men, "he was fully impressed with a sense of what was before us." Kellogg knelt to draw arrows in the dust, showing his officers how to advance against the waiting Rebels. His untried regiment, some eighteen hundred men strong, was cast in much the same role that the Twentieth South Carolina had played in Lee's army that morning. The Heavies would lead Upton's brigade on the right of the Cold Harbor road, forming the first three lines of attack while the remaining four regiments, depleted by constant campaigning, would make up the fourth line.

Kellogg reminded his men how those others had kidded the Heavies as a "band-box" regiment. "Now," he said, "we are called on to show what we can do at fighting."[4]

At about five o'clock, the Sixth Corps started forward with the Eighteenth Corps on its right. Within minutes, the advancing line of battle melted into disorder as different brigades and divisions stepped out ahead or fell behind. Nor was there a clear objective in front of them. The terrain was confusing; although the advancing troops realized they were marching slightly uphill, there was no definite high ground except toward the southern end of the front. The angles of the Confederates' ad hoc line, thrown up when they fell back from their morning attack, were even more confusing; along one stretch, the Federals could see rifle pits across a broad plowed field, but at other points there seemed to be nothing more ominous than an uneven tree line, in some places as close as three hundred yards, in others fourteen hundred yards away.

Captain James Deane, of the Heavies' Company L, told how "we rose up, dressed our ranks, and started in" with Colonel Kellogg out front. The lines advanced "straight as if we were parading in a review," but that did not last long. As firing broke out, a big sergeant came running back from the left without his musket, warning, begging the Heavies not to keep on. Deane whacked him with the flat of his sword and the sergeant lay down to hide as the Heavies left him behind. A salvo from Rebel pickets broke up the regiment's first rank, but the following lines pushed across the picket posts into the timber and reached a low ridge. Fragments from Union artillery firing overhead hit several of Deane's troops as they neared what they thought were the main Confederate defenses.[5]

Kellogg led the way, cheering, his face streaked with blood from a scratch wound in the cheek. To that point, the regiment had charged "with a force and impetus which would have carried it over [the Rebel line] like Niagara but for an impassable obstruction"—a hasty abatis, a thicket of pine saplings felled with interlacing branches toward the attackers. This barrier was some seventy feet in depth, but the Confederates had left two paths through it, each wide enough for four men abreast. As the Heavies crowded into these openings, there burst "a sheet of flame, sudden as lightning, red as blood, and so near that it seemed to singe the men's faces . . . and the ground and trees behind our line was ploughed and riddled with a thousand balls that just missed the heads of our men." Two volleys knocked down several of the Connecticut troops, but most of the defenders' Minié balls whined high. The Heavies thought they could have taken the breastworks but for a sudden "fire which no human valor could withstand" from their left. "The air was filled with sulphurous smoke, and the shrieks and howls of more than two hundred and fifty mangled men rose above the yells of triumphant rebels and the roar of their musketry."

Seeing his regiment disintegrate under this flanking fire, Kellogg shouted, "About face!"—and toppled dead across the breastworks, shot in the cheek, in the arm, and finally just above the ear.

"Wild and blind with wounds, bruises, noise, smoke, and conflicting orders, the men staggered in every direction," wrote the Heavies' historian. Some died "upon the very top of the rebel parapet, where they were completely riddled with bullets—others wandering off into the woods on the right and front, to find their way to death by starvation at Andersonville, or never to be heard of again."[6]

A glancing bullet struck Captain Deane in the forehead, plowing a three-inch furrow under the skin. He rolled behind a tree for cover, got a handkerchief from a following soldier, and tied it about his head to slow the bleeding. Taking a swig of cold coffee from the man's canteen, he rose to his feet and was promptly nicked twice more. He finally realized that with a ball stuck in his scalp, he had better withdraw while he could. Back where he started, he came upon a skulker stealing hardtack from the regiment's discarded packs, and kicked him away. Then he wandered in the falling darkness until he found a Sixth Corps hospital behind the lines.[7]

Under murderous fire, General Upton ordered the Heavies to lie down where they stood, to hold what they had taken without risking further destruction. Kellogg and fifty-two others in the regiment were killed outright, and another 333 were counted wounded or missing; most of the latter died on the field. To the Heavies, their sacrifice at first seemed useless, simply a bloody repulse. The regimental chaplain, Winthrop Phelps, wrote, "You cannot conceive the horror & awfulness of a battle. I never wish to *hear* another much less *see* it. I went out to see this but found myself in such danger I soon fled. . . . Pray for me. I cannot write—am not in a fit state of mind. . . ."[8]

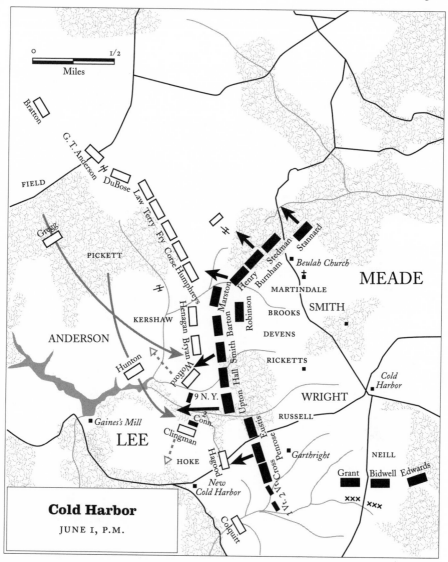

Smith's Eighteenth Corps, arriving from below the James, joins Wright to
strike Anderson's line in late afternoon. The attack penetrates along the
ravine between Kershaw's and Hoke's divisions. Field and Pickett send
brigades to help seal the breach.

But after the shock of their terrible baptism of fire, the Heavies
would realize that they had led the only notable penetration achieved
by the Federals that evening. Upton's brigade, the right element of
Russell's division, with Benjamin Smith's brigade of Ricketts's division
alongside, had driven into the first line of Confederate works, captur-

ing several hundred defenders. The route of their success was that marshy creek bottom, the much-discussed but still-unplugged gap between Hoke's and Kershaw's Rebel divisions. The Union Sixth Maryland and 138th Pennsylvania led Smith's brigade, and the terrain pulled them without apparent plan into the opening. There the thickets in the ravine concealed Upton's right and Smith's left as they advanced. This allowed them to move unseen between Wofford's brigade of Kershaw's division and Clingman's brigade of Hoke's division. Thus flanked, both Rebel brigades broke to the rear.[9]

Confederates would argue for years over who was responsible for this embarrassment. The official diary of Anderson's corps implied that Clingman collapsed first: "Clingman's brigade gives way. Wofford's on his left, being flanked, does the same. The Fifty-third Georgia on Wofford's left, ditto."[10] As Clingman told it, his brigade was fooled three times as the Yankee attack developed. After hugging the ground under a heavy artillery concentration, he heard "a heavy discharge of musketry" in Kershaw's direction just as the first Federals came within rifle range. According to Clingman, he assumed that the enemy had merely feinted that way, "whereas, in fact [Wofford's] brigade fled precipitately from the field after discharging their muskets." The Federals moved closer, Clingman thinking at first that they were friendly troops. As they came within a hundred yards, he realized his mistake and his men opened fire, gradually turning back the Yankees. He called "Cease fire!" to let the smoke lift; it was so thick that his troops did not see "a large column of the enemy" moving through the ravine and angling into their front. "We did not from our position behind our hastily made earthworks, observe the low ground in front and to the left," Clingman wrote. His aide, Captain Fred R. Blake, stood to see what was happening and suddenly yelled, " 'Here they are, as thick as they can be!' "

There they were, within a few paces, a heavy column marching at quick step, "about thirty men in front . . . closed in mass very compactly." They wore new blue uniforms, Clingman said, and some captured later said "they were fresh troops that had been in garrison and had not previously been engaged, and had expressed great confidence that they would march into Richmond."[11]

Clingman said he shouted, "Aim low and aim well!" and his men cut loose at nearly point-blank range. Just then "a tall and uncommonly fine looking officer in the front rank of the enemy's column, hearing the order and looking me directly in the face, though he changed countenance for a moment, took off his cap and waving it about his head, cheered his men in words which I could not catch. Just as he had placed his hat back on his head . . . a soldier immediately on my right discharged his musket and the ball entered the upper part of his forehead, and he fell backward staggering the two men behind him." So died Colonel Kellogg.*12

The attacking troops, "either acting under orders, or from panic, lay down," Clingman wrote. "Nothing could have been more unfortunate for them." The defenders kept firing, reloading, and firing into "the thick, dark mass." After his men poured fifteen or twenty rounds apiece into the Federals, they let up. According to him, perhaps a tenth of the Union troops rose and tried to escape, providing target practice for the defenders as they ran.

The Rebels let go a cheer at their seeming victory. Only then, Clingman wrote, an hour after he believed Wofford's brigade had "abandoned the field," did more concealed Union troops charge from the ravine against his left and rear. "The odds in such a struggle were so great, and our men fell so fast," that Clingman ordered them to withdraw and form a new line perpendicular to the one abandoned. Later, he said, with support from Colquitt's Georgia brigade, his regiments counterattacked and retook their original position. According to Clingman, they gave it up reluctantly that night under orders from Hoke to make way for reinforcements from Pickett's division.13

Colquitt, who had been transferred from the Army of Northern Virginia under a cloud after his faulty performance at Chancellorsville, was eager to redeem himself with Lee. He sent his Nineteenth, Twenty-seventh, and Twenty-eighth Georgia dashing about 150 yards across an open field into the line vacated by Clingman. Captain John Keely, leading the brigade's skirmishers, said they lost forty-six men getting to the trench, but then marched along it, cleaning out the Federals. As the major of the 106th New York, in Ricketts's division, offered his sword to Keely in surrender, a Georgian six feet away raised his rifle to shoot him. Keely knocked the barrel of the man's weapon upward with his own sword, and the shot sang overhead. The relieved Yankee thanked Keely and offered him a drink of whiskey

---

* Charles J. Calrow wrote that the fresh troops faced by Clingman were the Ninth New York Heavy Artillery, two battalions of which were assigned to the second and third attack lines of Smith's brigade. He based his belief on Upton's report that after the Second Connecticut's initial charge was stopped, "Opposite the right of the regiment the works were carried," and a captured North Carolina major (obviously of Clingman's brigade) "informed me that their flank had been turned." However, it is unlikely that Clingman was describing the Ninth New York, since official records show none of its officers killed in this action. (Charles J. Calrow, "Cold Harbor," p. 124½; OR I 36, pt. 1:174, 671.)

from his canteen. The two officers became "as good friends as if we belonged in the same regiment," Keely wrote, until he sent the major to the rear as a prisoner.[14]

Clingman's self-serving postwar account of Wednesday evening's fight was a more elaborate version of a letter that he wrote to the editor of the *Richmond Whig* while the outcome at Cold Harbor was still in doubt. At that time, he said that "no Brigade from any State in this war, or any other war, ever acted better than did mine under such circumstances." He was angrily critical of Wofford's brigade (which he did not name in his published accounts, then or later). "A brigade from another State than my own, stationed on our left," gave way, he said. He maintained that his own brigade retook its line, "but the position of the Brigade on my own left remained in the possession of the enemy, without any attempt ever being made to retake it." Citing his brigade's heavy losses in the preceding three weeks, he said four-fifths of them were "sustained solely because its flanks have been left unprotected by the troops which should have been there."[15]

Though Wofford left no official explanation of his brigade's actions on June 1, his Georgia soldiers and his division commander were frank in admitting what had happened. Captain Charles Sanders, of Cobb's Legion, told his sister that he had such a painfully blistered heel that he hobbled about the defensive works that afternoon with one boot on and one boot off. When the Yankees charged, he said, he "was busy as a bee loading guns and giving out the cartridges to the men in front so that they might fire rapidly," and during the intervals "the men [were] laughing how many they had killed." But then, from the neglected ravine—"it was a great oversight on our part. . . . all at once a perfect shower of bullets came from behind." With troops in blue charging from both directions, the Legion was ordered to retreat. "I always thought I could run pretty fast," Sanders wrote. "But I didn't know until then how fast I could run. . . . I wish I had a picture of myself as I looked when I came out of that place with my old boot hanging to me."[16]

In the Fifty-third Georgia alongside Wofford, Arthur B. Simms admitted that on being flanked, "we ran off in very great disorder and never rallied in an hour or two." The enemy made nothing of the defenders' confusion—"I think they must not have known it," Simms wrote, adding, "If Grant had known what he might have done by following up the small advantage in our line, I think he could have inflicted quite a heavy loss upon us."[17]

Kershaw wrote that after Hoke pulled Hagood's brigade out of line between their divisions without informing him, "the enemy finding a vacancy on Hoke's left, came in through a ravine and made his appearance in rear of Wofford's right flank, and bore down on him in heavy force. Wofford's Brigade was dispersed almost immediately, and two regts of Bryan's Brigade [to its left] were curled back." The Second and Third South Carolina of Kershaw's old brigade, now under Colonel Henagan, soon charged at the double-quick and threw the enemy out of Bryan's lines "at the point of the bayonet," Kershaw said. "This was the most dashing affair that I witnessed during the war."[18]

But Kershaw sketched a map showing that at nightfall the Yankees still held their wedge into his division's right, where Wofford's position was bent back at about a forty-five-degree angle, facing into the ravine. Through that gap, the enemy might pour enough troops to roll up Lee's whole line in both directions. Realizing the emergency, at 10:00 p.m. Anderson sent a dispatch to Lee saying, "Re-enforcements are necessary to hold this position." He had already ordered Brigadier General Eppa Hunton's brigade from Pickett's division and Brigadier General John Gregg's brigade from Field's division to reinforce Hoke and Kershaw. But in the meantime, he said, his works were broken: "The enemy having possession of our lines on the right, they must either be expelled or the present line abandoned. There is still some firing, and the enemy will undoubtedly renew the attack at daylight."[19]

Marching his troops through this confusion, Hunton came up on Hoke's left in early morning, retaking almost the same line that Clingman had held when the Yankee attack started. But Gregg, rather than pushing forward to the works originally defended by Wofford, extended Wofford's angled line to the right, reaching to connect with Hunton across the ravine. And had it not been for the heroic crew of a lone cannon at the shoulder of that angle, the whole Confederate position on Wofford's side of the ravine might have crumbled, with disastrous results.

Lieutenant Robert Falligant, of Colonel Henry C. Cabell's artillery battalion, went ahead in the dark to scout a position for his Napoleon twelve-pounder. His superiors advised him not to tell his troops what they were getting into, but Falligant knew these Georgians better, told them the truth, and called for volunteers. Every man of his crew stepped forward with a shout, and Alex Campbell, sergeant of another Napoleon, begged to go along as gunner. He did, and Falligant ran the gun along with the infantry rushing to hold the angle, "coming into battery and fighting fiercely whenever the enemy seemed to be holding the brigade in check, and limbering up and moving forward with it while it was advancing."

When a new wave of Federals opened fire at close range from the ravine, its first volley knocked down all of Falligant's horses. The Yankees pushed to take the gun, but the crew swung it into their faces, "belching fire like a volcano." Sergeant Campbell stood waving his hat in the air and shouting over the din, "Ready! Fire! Ready! Fire!" as fast as the men could load and reload. Falligant yelled at him not to be so reckless, but Campbell said, "Lieutenant, the bullet ain't molded to kill me!" At a lull, he saw a wounded Federal writhing in pain before the line and rushed out to bring him in. The Union attackers saw what was happening and held their fire until he was safe beside his gun. Campbell was hardly back in action when a Yankee bullet struck him in mid-shout. His crew hesitated to fire over his wounded body, but he raised himself and shouted, "Give 'em hell, boys! Don't mind me!" and died as the gun blasted away above him.

The infantry alongside rallied, and after the "furious little fight," won time to dig in around Falligant's gun. That was as far as the defenders advanced to restore Wofford's line—"nor was there at any time a Confederate infantry soldier to the right of this piece [toward the ravine], nor a spadeful of earth, except the little traverse we threw up to protect the right of the gun," wrote battalion adjutant Robert Stiles. "I have no hesitation in saying that in all my experience as a soldier I never witnessed more gallant action than this of Lieutenant Falligant and his dauntless cannoneers. . . ."[20]

Marching troops about through thickets and gullies in the darkness is a harrowing operation under the best conditions; bringing up reinforcements into the Confederate lines that night was far riskier because muskets and cannon were still banging away, and skittish defenders who had been surprised by attacks from flank and rear were primed to fire at unidentified sounds and silhouettes. Deep into the night, local commanders, at regimental and even company levels, made repeated efforts to retake lost ground. Union general Upton reported that the Second Connecticut Heavies kept fighting in the first line of Rebel defenses until 3:00 a.m., when the defenders fell back to a second line. Rather than withdrawing to their point of departure, the Yankees stayed where their attack halted, in some places holding and reversing that first line of Confederate works, in others digging in within fifty yards of the hastily strengthened Rebel positions.[21]

The most enthusiastic diggers on the Southern side must have been the survivors of Keitt's battered regiment. William Meade Dame, a private in the Richmond Howitzers nearby, noted that before being so rudely repulsed by the Yankee cavalry that morning, the South Carolinians had "seen nothing of war except the siege of a Fort, and their idea of the chief duty of a soldier was—to get as much earth between [them] and the enemy as possible." Moving onto line that night, they saw the skimpy bank of earth put up by the rest of Kershaw's men, about two feet thick and three feet high, and "were perfectly aghast." They started throwing dirt, until by morning they had a wall in places eight feet high and six to eight feet thick. "Of course," Dame wrote, "they couldn't shoot over it, except at the sky; perhaps they thought that *anything blue* would do to shoot at and the sky was blue." When the cannoneers protested that they were "supported by Infantry that could not fire a shot," Kershaw ordered the great wall shoveled down, but before this was done, the Yankees attacked. Some of the Twentieth fought bravely, standing to fire from boxes or logs, but as Dame remembered it, the regiment was later turned into "a sapping and mining corps."[22]

Dick Anderson's worst fears did not materialize on the night of June 1 because Federal commanders could not take advantage of the opportunity before them. They were just as confused as Anderson, neither ready nor willing to throw more force into a black hole of uncertainty. At 7:45, Union general Ricketts, who had attacked Kershaw, reported, "I have the honor to announce the complete success of my advance of this evening. I have driven the enemy from their works, and now occupy them." But soon afterward, corps commanders Wright and Baldy Smith were telling Meade that they were unsure whether their troops could hold what they had gained, and anxious about possible counterattacks. Captured Rebels helped the Confederate cause by telling Wright that "all Longstreet's [Anderson's] corps is here, and the rest of the army is moving down . . . in very large force." From this, Wright concluded that "My position is not secure." Smith, low on ammunition, said that he had reported his situation, and "must leave it to the general commanding to determine as to how long I can hold this line if vigorously attacked."[23]

.   .   .

George Meade was not in a mood to hear contradictory reports. The tension of battle always made him touchy, even when he could see with his own eyes that things were going according to plan. Confusion, darkness, the too-familiar feeling of disconnection from his troops, made matters worse. The morning's fighting had been an unqualified success, securing the Federal hold on Cold Harbor. It was clear later that the most critical point on the battlefield that Wednesday evening was where the Federals drove between Kershaw and Hoke. All four of Meade's center divisions—Russell, Ricketts, Devens, and Brooks—had moved their positions forward, in places as much as three-quarters of a mile, but nowhere did they break through Lee's main line of resistance. While that was happening, Meade, like Lee, was also trying to keep up with other potentially serious clashes up and down the long front between the armies. And even limited success was costly; although 3,700 fresh Union reinforcements arrived that day, another 2,800 or more men, far from fresh, were added to Meade's casualty list.[24]

Again, the toll was heavy among Federal field officers. On the Eighteenth Corps front, Colonel Jeremiah C. Drake was cut down leading Devens's advance brigade. And alongside in Brooks's division, Lieutenant Colonel George E. Marshall of the Fortieth Massachusetts in effect committed suicide in his fury at an unfair suggestion that he had not done his duty. The Fortieth had charged once, fallen back under withering fire from its flank, then re-formed and charged again, to be "repulsed with terrible slaughter." The brigade commander, Colonel Guy V. Henry, remembered as "an intrepid young West Pointer of magnetic presence and merciless discipline," had ridden back and forth, driving his men on. "At last," as one of his captains embellished it, "with a smile of cool defiance, [Henry] leaped his horse over the enemy's works, and as the dying steed lay struggling on the parapet, its rider coolly standing in his stirrups emptied his revolver in the very faces of the awestruck foe."[25]

Henry's leadership, which won him a Medal of Honor, was as remarkable as his luck in surviving, but it could take his troops no farther. As they lay beneath the storm of bullets, Henry turned on Marshall, criticizing his handling of the Fortieth. "This enraged Marshall, who seized the regimental colors, and advancing several paces in front of the men . . . planted them in the ground and commenced to stride deliberately back and forth." At once, the Confederates focused their fire on him; his soldiers screamed and begged him to lie down, but he refused. In moments, he was hit. "Turning as he was struck, he bounded to the rear, cleared a line of men with a jump, and with a groan fell, and instantly expired." His regiment held what it had taken. Colonel Henry said in his official report only that his losses included "the lieutenant-colonels commanding the Fortieth Massachusetts, Ninety-second New York, and Twenty-first Connecticut Volunteers, and many other valuable officers and men killed or mortally wounded."*[26]

As early as midafternoon, Meade had reacted to Lee's morning effort to turn the Union left by ordering Hancock to bring his Second Corps from the far right to the far left. Five hours later, Hancock had just started pulling his regiments out, advising Meade that "The withdrawal will take some time, as our line is very complicated and very close to the enemy." Meade, who deeply admired Hancock for his courageous performances at Gettysburg and Spotsylvania, told him, "You must make every exertion to move promptly and reach Cold Harbor as soon as possible. . . . Every confidence is felt that your gallant corps of veterans will move with vigor and endure the necessary fatigue. You will pass by my headquarters and I should like to see you as you pass."[27]

Before Hancock started his march, his officers had spotted Confederates moving to his right, and he prepared to attack to forestall any enemy effort there. But sharp clashes between skirmishers showed Hancock that A. P. Hill's Rebels were strengthening their already formidable line before him, so he dropped any plan to advance. On Burnside's front, a Confederate column drove in Major General Thomas L. Crittenden's division in early evening before Colonel John F. Hartranft sent reinforcements who turned it back. Soon afterward, another Rebel force struck Hartranft's flank, but it also was repelled.[28]

At some point in these actions on the Rebel left, guns of the Third Company Richmond Howitzers, supporting A. P. Hill's corps, took aim at Yankees sheltering around Pole Green Church. William S. White, manning one of the cannon, was a member of that church, and in his diary he recorded the painful result of the barrage: ". . . as the

---

* Marshall's friends honored him after his father went to Virginia in 1866 to retrieve his body. At a public burial in Fitchburg, Massachusetts, Governor Alexander H. Bullock paid tribute to the fallen colonel and added, "The battle of Cold Harbor was so barren of any appreciable advantage, that I would inscribe on the headstone of every Union soldier who laid down his life there, for his epitaph of renown, that he fought and died [only] in obedience to orders, and for the sake of his example." (Charles A. Currier, "Recollections of Service," p. 103a n.)

sound of men's voices rose above the din and confusion-ensanguined strife, a stream of fire rises from the roof of that old time-honored house of worship, the church of my ancestors, the church of Samuel Davies . . . perhaps the oldest Presbyterian church in Virginia—set on fire by a shot from my own gun."*[29]

The Confederate thrusts at that end of the lines were diversionary actions, Lee's efforts to keep Meade busy while he bolstered his own right. Meade was busy enough without such diversions. Warren's Fifth Corps demanded much of his attention. In peculiarly conditional language, he had told Warren that "it is very desirable" that the Fifth Corps join the attack by the Sixth and Eighteenth—"unless in your judgment it is impracticable." Almost as tentatively, Warren ordered Brigadier General Henry H. Lockwood to advance his division and "take part in the action [with Wright] if opportunity offers." But the rambling roads to and from Cold Harbor combined with the army's erratic maps to take Lockwood out of the action and end his career with the Army of the Potomac.[30]

Warren was nearly as snappish that day as his commanding general. Normally, his bearing was that of a "thoughtful, modest scholar" who had taught mathematics at West Point. He showed no "vanity in look or speech," but wore "an habitual and noticeably grave expression"— except when laughing at one of the limericks in a little volume he carried with him. A headquarters officer wrote that "He would repeat them at almost every meal . . . with wonder that they did not seem nearly so amusing to others as they did to him." But on this Wednesday, Warren's artillery chief, Colonel Wainwright, said the general was "as ugly and cross-grained as he could be. . . . One would suppose that a man in his position would be ashamed to show that kind of temper. . . . He has pitched into his staff officers most fearfully, cursing them up and down as no man has a right to do, and as I wonder that they allow."[31]

Warren informed Meade that "in some unaccountable way, [Lockwood] took his whole division, without my knowing it, away from the left of the line of battle, and turned up at dark 2 miles in my rear, and I have not yet got him back." Apparently Lockwood had used an unfamiliar road that ran eastward before turning south parallel to the front; it is doubtful, however, that his whole division was ever two miles behind the main line. Some of his troops reported passing

---

* The Reverend Samuel Davies was a famed crusader for religious freedom and founder of the College of New Jersey (later Princeton University). His ideas and oratory inspired Patrick Henry, who was born at Studley, just over two miles northeast of Pole Green Church.

Grant, Meade, and their staffs as they sat on pews under the trees outside Bethesda Church, where Warren also spent most of the day. Later, these troops advanced into brisk fighting along the skirmish lines. But Warren, furious, did not wait for Lockwood's explanation of what had happened. "All this time the firing should have guided [Lockwood] at least," Warren told Meade. "He is too incompetent, and too high rank leaves no subordinate place for him. I earnestly beg that he may be at once relieved from duty with this army." Meade complied immediately.[32]

Dealing with all this, Meade was already in "one of his irascible fits" when Baldy Smith's trusty courier, Captain Farquhar, arrived at headquarters. Farquhar told Meade that Smith, who had had to leave White House without his supply train, "found his situation precarious," was almost out of ammunition and short on transportation.

"Then, why in Hell did he come at all for?" roared the general.

As one of his staff officers noted, such an oath was rare for Meade. But by that hour, he had to realize that he had just missed the chance for a major breakthrough. He had succeeded in bringing six divisions against the enemy's two, a matchup that fit the rules of war. But he had marched Wright's three of those divisions through dust and darkness, without time for rest or food, so that they reached the line of departure leg-weary and shaky from hunger. The other three, Baldy Smith's, unused to hard marching, were mistakenly sent on their hot, useless trek to and from New Castle, and arrived just as exhausted. Before these divisions reached Cold Harbor, their movements made clear to Lee what the Yankees were up to, and when they obligingly did it, they were fully expected. In addition, Meade sent the attack across ground that had not been adequately scouted, so that once the advance began, the unfamiliar terrain controlled the Federal approach to the irregular Confederate works more than did the vaguely drawn attack order. Furthermore, lack of reconnaissance effectively took Martindale's and Neill's divisions on the north and south wings of Smith and Wright out of the operation, because they held back to guard against nonexistent Rebel threats to the flanks.[33]

Determined to make the best of what he had gained, Meade sent orders for Smith and Wright to resume their attack Thursday morning—"with your whole force, and as vigorous as possible." When Smith responded, Meade's temper shot up again; there had never been an excess of affection between them.

"I have endeavored to represent to you my condition," Smith wrote. He was dangerously short of ammunition, and had asked Wright for about 100,000 rounds; under the circumstances, he declared, "an attack would be simply preposterous."[34]

IN A BROTHERHOOD of soldiers where blasphemy often greeted unpleasant news from front or rear, it still took something special to bring on such an "irascible fit" as Meade flew into that night. Though Smith's response to Meade was justified, the way he expressed it was plain insubordination.

If that was not enough, atop the frustrations of the day's fighting, the ground for Meade's outburst may have been laid by arrival of the latest newspapers from the North. Even when the Union army was in serious action, the papers often reached headquarters with remarkable speed, by rail from New York or Philadelphia to the ferry across the Susquehanna, by rail again to Washington or Baltimore, then by boat down the Potomac or Chesapeake to whichever supply point was in current use.[35]

On Monday, May 30, the day of the fights at Bethesda Church and Matadequin Creek, the *New York Times* printed Secretary Stanton's two-day-old communiqué on the army's crossing of the Pamunkey, and William Swinton's report on its departure from the North Anna—which informed readers that "General Grant has as little idea as you can imagine of butting his head against prepared works. . . ." Neither account mentioned Meade's name. By then, Meade was used to being ignored in news stories, but this edition also carried an editorial of specific interest to the generals in Virginia.

It did not mention Meade, either. It was all praise for Grant and "the marvelous skill with which he has maneuvered the army." The march south was achieved by force of arms, of course, "but chiefly by force of intellect he has driven Lee from the all but impregnable positions that he had prepared on the road to Richmond." The conception that Grant was "merely a hard fighter—that his style was simply that of concentrating great masses of men, hurling them upon the enemy or his works, and achieving success by what is called 'pounding' "— that idea had been disproven in the past four weeks. By following Grant's May campaign, the tribute concluded, "We have been enabled very clearly to discover, not only the blaze of musketry and the march of columns, but the flashing of genius and the triumphs of intellect."[36]

That editorial could hardly have been more perfectly phrased to inflame Meade. By then, any word of praise for Grant seemed to Meade a word of personal criticism of the publicly nonexistent commander of the Army of the Potomac; to attribute any asset to Grant—intellect, for example—was to suggest its absence in Meade. Whether he read that particular *Times* editorial is unstated, but that he and his wife read and felt every item of war coverage within reach is borne out in their almost daily correspondence, and every Northern paper was still trumpeting Grant, Grant, Grant. That evening, while Meade's Sixth and Eighteenth Corps were struggling before the Rebel lines, he somehow found time to write to Margaret again.

He often tried to relate his own role to that of classic soldiers, to give his experiences some perspective by comparing them to the battles of history. Now he told Margaret that the Union army must drive the Confederates into the fixed defenses of Richmond, "and then will begin the tedious process of a grand siege like that of Sebastopol" in the Crimean War, only a decade earlier. The siege of Richmond, he predicted, "will last as long [349 days] unless we can get hold of their rail roads & cut off their supplies; then they must come out and fight." Though he said again that "I don't like to write about Grant & the public," as usual he could not resist commenting on what he had recently read. His train of thought would later seem prescient:

"The papers are giving Grant all the credit of what they call success. I hope they will remember this if anything goes wrong."[37]

8

Richmond Dead in Front

"EVERY ONE FELT that this was to be the final struggle. No further flanking marches were possible. Richmond was dead in front. No further wheeling of corps from right to left by the rear; no further dusty marches possible on that line, even 'if it took all summer.'" So wrote Lieutenant Colonel Martin T. McMahon, adjutant of Wright's Sixth Corps, reflecting what "every one" in the Union high command felt early on Thursday, June 2.[1]

Within the city "dead in front," John B. Jones, a clerk in the Confederate War Department, had no such intimate knowledge of Yankee intentions. He judged the imminence of what he repeatedly called "the GREAT BATTLE" by the sound of cannon, rising and falling with the ever-closer clashes to the east. Richmonders had become expert at estimating the distance and direction of gunfire; they had been threatened many times before. After three years of war, the rumble of guns was not as alarming as it had been in 1862, when Union gunboats probed up the James and McClellan's army pressed within hearing of Richmond's church bells. Then, many Confederate congressmen and bureaucrats had fled by railroad and canal boat—the *Richmond Whig* alleged that "to protect the stampeders from the snakes and bullfrogs that abound along the line of the canal," headquarters had "detailed a regiment of ladies to march in advance of the ranks, and clear the towpath of the pirates." In the months since, cavalry raiders had struck twice into the city's defenses, and now Butler's army was ensconced to the south as Grant came closer.[2]

A Rebel deserter told Meade's intelligence chief, Colonel George H. Sharpe, about "the cessation of all business in Richmond . . . the closing of stores, shops, schools and the Government departments, that all the men might be spared." He exaggerated. Those Confederates were organized into defense battalions by place of work, one battalion each from the Tredegar Iron Works, the Arsenal, and the Armory, and one of white-collar clerks from the scattered government departments. They had mobilized against the sudden menace of Sheridan's raid in May, kept their muskets handy as Grant's much greater threat came closer, and now stood ready in the extensive works guarding the city. Still, Jones told his diary, "Every one is confident of success, since Beauregard and Lee command." Citizens were able to laugh when Northern newspapers filtered into town quoting one of Stanton's communiqués: "A woman reports that a meeting was held yesterday, while she was in Richmond, to see whether the City should be surrendered or burnt. The Mayor [Joseph C. Mayo] advocated surrender, and was put into Castle Thunder" political prison. Except for the militia called to the city's defense, most Richmonders went about their lives as they had learned to do during lesser disturbances of their peace.[3]

They were encouraged in this by "Ivanhoe," the *Examiner's* correspondent at the front, who heard from citizens in the countryside that it was the Yankee soldiers who were "much demoralized," believing their army had lost sixty thousand men so far in the campaign. The news was so bad for Union troop morale, Ivanhoe reported, that they were not permitted to read papers from the North. He concluded that after the Federals had taken so much punishment, "I cannot think Grant has any intention of attacking us. He expects, doubtless, to set down and dig up to Richmond. On his new front near this point he is intrenching."[4]

Jeb Stuart's recent death, at his brother-in-law's home on Grace Street, had saddened the city. After a ceremony at St. James's Episcopal Church, his funeral cortege had proceeded through the streets to Hollywood Cemetery, but there were no crowds, no regimental escort, and no music, because the honor guard and the bands were in the fortifications outside town. That made the occasion somehow sadder than Stonewall Jackson's funeral a year earlier, when thousands watched a mile-long procession, and "the city [was] one house of mourning, the stores closed & crape hanging from each door & window." Before and after that, thousands of honored officers and anonymous privates had been trundled through the streets to graves in Hollywood Cemetery, "that fast growing city of the dead." But by now, Richmond did not linger over its mourning. It honored Stuart by giving his name to a new hospital in what had been the quarters of the mobilized City Battalion, a place "for the reception and care of the wounded now arriving and expected to arrive in Richmond from the battle fields below."[5]

At that point, eight hundred Union wounded were in the capital's other hospitals. On one day some 200 prisoners were marched in, the next day 275, the next 707, the officers sent to Libby Prison, the enlisted men to Crews's tobacco factory. To make room for more, and to guard against any prison uprising, eleven hundred Yankees captured earlier were shipped south to Danville and on to Andersonville. Some of the new prisoners were New York Zouaves, "hard looking, dirty, begrimed, gaunt, sun-browned, and hungry-looking, as though they could steal anything, from a needle to an omnibus"—gaudily uniformed, but otherwise little different from more than 150,000 other soldiers of both sides in the lines outside the capital.[6]

In the mayor's police court, "Seven vagabond negro women caught together in a house of ill fame, on Fifteenth street, near the dock, were ordered to be whipped, and most of them committed to jail, for going at large." Two days later, "Nine Negroes were ordered to be thrashed for being in and constituting an unlawful assembly." The old tradition of corporal punishment had long been an incentive for slaves to flee northward; now the nearness of the Union army inspired hundreds more to leave, some to become Federal soldiers. Clement Barksdale, of Halifax County in southside Virginia, offered a five-hundred-dollar reward for the capture of four runaway servants. "As they left without provocation," his advertisement said, it was believed they were trying to join Yankee cavalry raiding the Richmond & Danville Railroad. Colonel C. E. Thorburn, of Powhatan County, just west of the capital, posted a five-hundred-dollar reward each for the return of eight departed slaves. Among them, he said, were Caesar and his wife, Ellen, who "when she is not at her work . . . is very much given to whistling and singing." But the enemy's approach apparently eased an earlier rash of petty crime in Richmond: According to the *Examiner*, "Thieving among the negroes [has] been made rare within the last two or three weeks by an order which has consigned the most abandoned of them to labor on the fortifications."[7]

Month after month, there had been dispiriting changes in what pre-war Richmond considered business as usual. Refugees, job-seekers, speculators, loose women, wartime opportunists of every stripe, crowded the capital. Inflation and shortages were so severe that civilians there drew the sympathy of soldiers who knew the hardships of campaigning. During the battles at Cold Harbor, the Confederate Congress could, and did, pass a bill increasing its own pay by 100 percent. But civilians could not manage their personal economics so adroitly. On June 1, while Anderson's corps was in desperate combat, Charles Minor Blackford took a timely holiday from its headquarters to visit state attorney general John Randolph Tucker's family in Richmond. Mrs. Tucker told him "she had seventeen persons in the white family and ten in the black, making twenty-seven in all to feed besides an innumerable host of straggling connections who find a square meal under their hospitable roof." Bacon was now $10 a pound and flour $350 a barrel. "How vast must be the suffering in Richmond," Blackford wondered, "not merely amongst the poor . . . but amongst the class that is generally the happiest, those who have neither poverty nor riches." The Tuckers were among the luckier Richmonders; Blackford could not speak for the less fortunate, like the women who had rioted for bread a year earlier. In the interim, things had only gotten worse.[8]

For Jefferson Davis, who worried himself sick over bread riots, restive governors, and trivia that should have been handled by third-level clerks, the approach of the Union army was a concern of proper presidential magnitude. In one way, he seemed to welcome having the war so close at hand. Seventeen years after winning fame as colonel of the First Mississippi Regiment at Monterrey and Buena Vista, he still found comfort in the clear tangibles of weapons and tactics, and the frank talk of career soldiers. Now, as the enemy came nearer, he could ride out occasionally to confer with the professional he admired above all, Robert E. Lee. From Lee he heard the details of plans and possibilities on the battlefield, and with him he may have discussed a factor in Grant's decision-making that could not be diagrammed on a map: politics—Northern politics.

In Baltimore, delegates were arriving for the convention of the National Union party, where Lincoln's nomination for a second term was scheduled within the week. Frémont was being nominated by the radicals to oppose the president on one political flank, and the Peace Democrats were about to offer McClellan on the other. Newspapers in the North, read within days in Richmond, were full of praise for Grant, but alongside the praise ran columns of agate type listing the casualties of his overland campaign. The word *butcher* was not prominent in the papers, but it was beginning to be heard in the barrooms of New York and Boston. In Washington, Secretary of the Navy Gideon Welles wrote in his diary, "Great confidence is felt in Grant, but the immense slaughter of our brave men chills and sickens us all. The hospitals are crowded with the thousands of mutilated and dying heroes who have poured out their blood for the Union cause."[9]

Elsewhere in Virginia, the Union offensives designed to supplement Meade's advance—Sigel's in the Shenandoah Valley and Butler's south of the James—had been frustrated. This allowed the transfer of Breckinridge, Pickett, and Hoke to reinforce Lee against the grand attack that politics had made inevitable. For Grant to pull away from Lee at this juncture, or to cross the James and invest Richmond from below, would be to many a sign of failure by Lincoln's personally chosen general-in-chief.

Grant's aide Horace Porter acknowledged this, writing that "people would be impatient at the prospect of an apparently indefinite continuation of operations." The war was costing the Federal government nearly $4 million a day, and there were still rumors that if it dragged on, Britain and France would recognize the Confederate government. In sum, Porter said, "Delays are usually dangerous, and there was at present too much at stake to admit of further loss of time in ending the war, if it could be avoided." Except for politics, wrote a historian of the Twenty-first Connecticut, "the battles we now describe would never have been fought. . . . It was still possible, however, that Lee might be overcome by a coup de main, and to this final attempt at crushing his foe Grant now resolutely advanced."[10]

ON WEDNESDAY evening, at his headquarters in the Via house, just south of Totopotomoy Creek, Grant sat to enjoy a shipment of oysters brought up from White House. Though he disdained personal glitter, he lived well; one of the U.S. Engineers nearby told of reading "that General Grant fares the same as his men and that he makes no display but I am here at Head Qtrs and see all this. Genl Grant, Meade & staffs could not be better or fare better in the best Hotel in the North than they do here in the field, and to see the show that the staff & escort makes you could think at a distance it was a Regiment of cavalry."[11]

As Grant ate his oysters and exchanged messages with Meade, discussing their next move, he kept returning to something that had happened on the road earlier in the day. Riding with his staff, he had come upon a teamster whose wagon was stuck in a swampy spot; the man was beating his horses in the face with the butt of his whip and swearing "with a volubility calculated to give a sulphurous odor to all the surrounding atmosphere."

Spurring toward him, Grant shouted, "What does this conduct mean, you scoundrel? Stop beating those horses!"

The teamster whacked a horse again and said to the general, "Well, who's drivin' this team anyhow—you or me?"

Shaking his fist in the man's face, Grant cried, "I'll show you, you infernal villain," and ordered an escort officer to have the teamster bound to a tree for six hours as punishment.[12]

Still smoldering hours later, Grant returned to his customary calm as he dictated dispatches, confirming his decision to advance Thursday morning. He hated the sight of blood; more than once on the battlefield, he had turned away in distress from the sight of mangled horses. Yet, as generals must, he managed a stoic front when he issued orders that he knew would send hundreds of soldiers to their deaths.

During Wednesday evening, Grant agreed with Meade to give more aggressive orders to Hancock's Second Corps. At 8:30 p.m., Hancock had notified Meade that he was withdrawing from the Union right, and by eleven o'clock, two of his three divisions were on the march toward the southern end of the line. On arrival there, instead of merely reinforcing Wright's Sixth Corps, Hancock was now to "at once attack the enemy, endeavoring to turn his right flank and interpose between him and the Chickahominy." Hancock's arrival was predicted for 6:00 or 7:00 a.m. If at that time it seemed better for him to support Wright's attack, that was approved in advance; in any case, his force "should be brought to bear against the enemy as promptly and vigorously as possible."[13]

Winfield Scott Hancock, leader and inspiration of Meade's most dependable corps, looked his part—much the way "Old Fuss and Feathers" Scott had looked as a young hero a decade after the War of 1812, when Hancock was named for him in Montgomery Square, Pennsylvania. After graduation from West Point, Hancock had served as a lieutenant under Scott in Mexico. At a time when physiognomy was in fashion, John Gibbon saw the forty-year-old Hancock on first meeting as "a tall, soldierly man, with light-brown hair and a military heavy jaw; and . . . the massive features and the heavy folds round the eye that often mark a man of ability." Morris Schaff, one of Meade's junior aides, said Hancock was "very handsome, striking-looking . . . the military type . . . looked and moved grandly. . . . authority was in his open face, which, when times were storming, became the mirror of his bold heart."[14]

By June 1864, Hancock had been superb as a division commander at Chancellorsville, and in leading the Second Corps at Gettysburg and Spotsylvania. At the height of the struggle in the Wilderness, excited stragglers came back saying that Hancock was fleeing the enemy. Told this, Grant turned the stick he was whittling, said "I don't believe it," and kept whittling. The severe thigh wound that Hancock suffered at Gettysburg was open again when he rejoined the army on the Rapidan, and it troubled him throughout the campaign. Somehow, in all the blood and turmoil, he always wore a clean white shirt, said Lyman. "Where he gets them, nobody knows."[15]

Under Hancock, the Second Corps had earned the reputation of standing when others fell, of charging where others held back. But it was just as susceptible to mistaken orders and misleading maps as the meanest rabble of shirkers. In shifting Hancock from right to left of the army, Meade once again specified movement by roads that strayed from where he thought they ran. Once again, he issued virtually impossible orders—for a major command to attack without rest after marching all night through blackness and confusion. This time, he tried to help by sending along an engineer officer as guide, but that turned out to make things worse.

This officer, Captain William H. Paine, undertook to save Hancock's corps time and energy by leading one division on a shortcut by a woods road. After following the road deep into the forest, the troops felt it narrow until it became just a path in the darkness. Finally, the wheels of the division's guns hung up between the trees. Hancock's adjutant, Francis Walker, recalled the experience with some restraint: "much confusion arose throughout the column, and the troops became mixed to a degree which made it difficult to straighten them out again. The night had been intensely hot and breathless, and the long march through roads deep with dust, which rose in suffocating clouds as it was stirred by thousands of feet of men and horses and by the wheels of the artillery, had been trying almost beyond the limits of endurance."[16]

The first contingent of Hancock's corps did not find the right road and reach Cold Harbor until after 6:00 a.m., thoroughly fagged. The rest were still on the way, "having considerably opened out during the night." After conferring with Wright, Hancock advised Meade that the Second Corps should form to the left of the Sixth, on the army's southern flank. Wright thought that two divisions abreast would reach to "the high ground" of Turkey Hill, thus "virtually controlling the ground between it and the Chickahominy." However, said Hancock, it would be hours before his corps was ready to attack; twelve regiments left behind on picket had not started until 2:00 a.m., and "there was a good deal of straggling, owing to extreme fatigue of the men and dusty roads."[17]

This wiped out any possibility of a morning attack. At 1:30 Thursday afternoon, Meade ordered the operation postponed until 5:00 p.m., adding that "Such examinations and arrangements as are necessary will be made immediately." Then, a half hour after Meade rescheduled the attack for five o'clock, Grant wrote to him that in view of the lack of preparation, the heat, and the fatigue of Hancock's troops, "I think it advisable to postpone assault until early tomorrow morning. All changes of position already ordered should be completed today, and a good night's rest given the men, preparatory to an assault at, say, 4.30 in the morning."

Meade followed this with a circular order for commanders to "employ the interim in making examination of the ground on their fronts and perfecting their arrangements for an assault." In relaying this word downward, Hancock ordered that "unless the enemy attack us, the time will be devoted to rest," and division commanders "will examine the ground well and have the proper points of attack selected."[18]

As Hancock's exhausted troops moved into their new line, they had to contend with stubborn Confederate skirmishers. Grabbing a few prisoners, they were surprised to find that these were Breckinridge's men. The day before, when Hancock got his orders to pull out from the Union right, he was sparring there with Breckinridge, in fact delaying the Rebel general's departure toward the Chickahominy. Now, after Hancock's laborious all-night march, here was Breckinridge again. And shortly after this discovery, further skirmishing brought in captives from Hill's Confederate corps, which had also been in Hancock's front when he departed the far end of the line.

MEADE AND LEE had sent troops on another race, this one to the southern flank of their armies—Meade to attack the gap between the existing line and the Chickahominy, Lee to seal it. Again, Lee's men had won.

Luck, which often favored Lee, played a part. He had ordered Breckinridge to the right early Wednesday, but after skirmishing all day, Breckinridge had not marched until after 10:00 p.m. His men were so tired after the constant action along the line that they took a break each half hour on the road. And Breckinridge, like Hancock, was hindered by a staff officer trying to help. This was Major H. B. McClellan, a cavalryman assigned as his guide, who had no map and no close knowledge of the country. In his well-meaning ignorance, he took Breckinridge's light division on a route that delayed it still further.

Lee awoke Thursday expecting to greet Breckinridge about the same time he expected to hear the Federals resume their attack on his lines. Neither happened. Though Lee was still sickly, he set out on Traveller to find the missing command. At Mechanicsville, more than four miles up the road, he came upon Breckinridge and his troops having breakfast. Breckinridge, a forty-three-year-old former U.S. congressman, senator, vice president, and 1860 candidate for president, had never served under Lee before. Appointed a brigadier general in late 1861, he had fought in the West and the Shenandoah Valley before bringing his two brigades to reinforce the army outside Richmond. Lee apparently said nothing critical to him at Mechanicsville, at least not within earshot of others. But Breckinridge did not dally longer over breakfast.

Later, Lee sent for Major McClellan, who reported to the headquarters tent "with a sinking heart." Lee ran his finger along a map and said evenly, "Major, this is the road to Cold Harbor." McClellan answered, "Yes, General, I know it now." No further words were spoken. "That quiet reproof sunk deeper and cut more deeply than words of violent vituperation would have done," McClellan recalled.[19]

About the time Lee put Breckinridge back on the road, he had learned that Hancock's troops facing Hill's corps had pulled out. This could only mean that Meade was committing more strength to his imminent attack at the other end of the line. At this, Lee ordered Hill with two of his three divisions, under Brigadier General William Mahone and Major General Cadmus M. Wilcox, to head south immediately. Hill left Henry Heth's division with Early on the northern flank.

Marching along closer roads, along interior lines, Lee's reinforcements won their race and were waiting when Hancock probed their positions Thursday afternoon. Had Hancock's men not been slowed and confused by their nighttime detour into the woods, they might have been in condition to attack that morning. And because Breckinridge was delayed, these Yankees would have found Lee's right flank and the way to Richmond sparsely defended. But Lee's luck held.

To improve it, he gave Jubal Early permission to attack if he saw a chance on the Union right, where there was likely to be confusion as Burnside re-formed after Hancock's departure. This confusion was assured by Meade's order for Burnside to swing back into Warren's rear, facing north to protect that flank of the army, and for Warren to close on Smith, contracting his front to free troops as a reserve. All the while, Warren was to cooperate with Smith, Wright, and Hancock by attacking when they did, and Burnside was to be ready to cooperate however needed. Postponement of the Union attack excused them from trying to carry out all of these instructions at once, which was fortunate for them, because Early seldom passed up an opportunity to take the offensive.[20]

At the end of the race to the southern end of the front, Hill moved Breckinridge in beside Hoke, and put Wilcox's division on the far right, closest to the Chickahominy. Mahone was behind them in reserve. Facing this extension of the Confederate line, Hancock placed John Gibbon's division beside Wright's Sixth Corps and put Francis Barlow's on the Union extreme left, with David Birney in support. These newly positioned commands immediately began grappling to take favorable ground for the coming showdown.

THERE IS no closer student of topography than the trudging infantryman, who remembers ridges and valleys where the casual traveler sees nothing more notable than gently rolling terrain. The foot soldier, lugging food, shelter, and the tools of his trade, feels every slightest slope. On the march, he unconsciously picks out every ravine and thicket that might provide cover. As soldiers rise in rank, their vision broadens; lieutenants look for copses and fence lines that might conceal fifty men, while generals peer at maps to decide what lies beyond range of their binoculars. Some of the greatest blunders in warfare come when generals ignore what junior officers could tell them, when there is a fatal gap between the commander's ambitious view and the private's personal acquaintance with the ground underfoot.

Lee had made mistakes, but few of that kind. He had spent decades as an engineer, and as a captain under Winfield Scott in 1847, he had brilliantly scouted the way to Mexico City. As army commander, he still concerned himself with specific details of terrain. On June 2, he was worried that the Federals would control Turkey Hill. It was no more a hill than the rest of the gentle ridge that he had fortified, but it overlooked the fields and swamps between the existing lines and the Chickahominy.

Beyond that ridge, Sheridan's horsemen had been probing toward the Chickahominy bridges, pressing to find out what Confederates, if any, were posted on that flank. Rebel artillery blasted them; one solid shot cut in half the First Maine Cavalry's chaplain, the Reverend George W. Bartlett. As soon as this skirmish was over, the preacher's comrades buried him, and that night auctioned off his horse and effects among them. The regimental historian acknowledged, "In the cool pursuits of civil life, to read of such a proceeding thrills one with horror, but in the bustle and exigencies of active service, it was looked on as a matter of course, and the men turned from the tears at his grave and in his memory, to the curiosity of the auction sale, and then to the round of duties, with tender reverence, but with no thought of undue haste or any impropriety."[21]

As soon as Breckinridge and Hill were in place, Lee ordered them to take the higher ground toward Turkey Hill. About the time a heavy rain shower began in late afternoon, Breckinridge's guns laid down preparatory fire. Then his two brigades and two from Wilcox's division, under Brigadier General James H. Lane and Colonel Thomas J. Simmons, charged the ridge and drove the Yankees off after a brisk fight. In the attack, Lane was seriously wounded at the head of his North Carolina troops. Taking that end of the ridge gave Lee's artillery a clear field of fire all the way to the Chickahominy.[22]

As Breckinridge's infantrymen settled in, frighteningly accurate rounds from Yankee sharpshooters kept their heads down. "A hat put on a ramrod and raised a little would be perforated in a jiffy," wrote T. C. Morton. Taking a quick peek, Morton saw a heavy column of men in blue moving through the timber. Peeking again, he spotted the puff of smoke from a sharpshooter's weapon, and ducked before the ball arrived. Calling up his best marksman, he pointed out the enemy sharpshooter, and the next time the Yankee stepped out from behind his tree, the marksman fired. Thinking that had taken care of the problem, Morton raised his head to look the other way, "when instantly I felt a shock, like a red-hot iron had pierced my brain. I experienced a great jar, saw a thousand stars, and then all was blank, and I saw no more of that fight." But he survived his glancing wound, to remember it a quarter of a century later.[23]

The Yankees who had occupied Turkey Ridge were not used to being driven. Their brigade commander was Colonel Nelson A. Miles, who years later would get the Medal of Honor for his bravery in 1863 at Chancellorsville. And Miles's commander was the twenty-nine-year-old Barlow, one of Grant's most aggressive generals. Unlike Hancock, his corps commander, Barlow didn't look the part of square-jawed leader. Indeed, to Lyman, he looked like "a highly independent mounted newsboy," wearing a checked shirt, an old blue kepi, a big cavalry saber, and a "familiar sarcastic smile."

Barlow, a Harvard-educated lawyer, had enlisted when war began as a private without a day of military experience. Before being badly wounded at Antietam, he had risen to brigade command. Returning to service, he was shot again at Gettysburg, temporarily paralyzed, and left for dead on the field until being taken to a safe place by Confederates. After ten months in hospitals, Barlow came back to command a division before the Wilderness campaign began. His wife, Arabella, whom he had married the day after he enlisted, was serving as a nurse in the hospital at Fredericksburg when casualties came flooding in.* By the time Barlow's division reached Cold Harbor, it was known as an outfit that "for fine fighting cannot be exceeded in the army."[24]

Thus, when Hancock got Barlow's dispatch of 5:00 p.m. Thursday, after his front-line troops had lost their game of king of the hill with the Confederates, he took his concerns seriously. The Rebel skirmish line was very strong, Barlow reported, and "much higher and more commanding than ours." Southern artillery had been throwing canister across his lines; he grossly underestimated its weight, saying, "They certainly have two and possibly more guns." By dawn Friday, four battalions of Hill's cannon would face Hancock's corps—up to sixty guns when at full strength, including one battalion of nine Napoleons, seven Parrott ten-pounders, and a three-inch rifle on Turkey Ridge. Everything considered, Barlow said, "I cannot move my line of battle farther forward." Coming from him, such a cautionary report should have made an impression on higher headquarters. But neither his words nor Gibbon's earlier, similarly pessimistic message would affect Grant's determination to attack in the morning. Neither would Jubal Early's attack Thursday afternoon on the far right of the Union lines.[25]

EARLY SENT three divisions, under Major Generals Robert E. Rodes, John B. Gordon, and Henry Heth, to swing around Bethesda Church and hit the Yankees in the midst of what Union generals hoped would be an orderly withdrawal. Burnside and his staff were about to have a late lunch on a tablecloth spread in a field where the Seventh Rhode Island and other regiments of Brigadier General Robert B. Potter's

---

* Mrs. Barlow died of typhus on July 27, 1864; her grieving husband took leave and traveled abroad until returning to the army three days before Appomattox. (*Harper's Weekly*, 13 August 1864.)

division had stacked arms to rest. "Suddenly, there was a spiteful rattle of musketry" from a thicket close by. Generals sprang for their horses, troops ran for their rifles, and teamsters crowded wagons onto the roads, "lashing their mules furiously, and turned the air blue with their oaths." The Rebels came on in a triple line, shaking Yankee nerves with their shrill "Yi, yi, yi!" After fleeing in surprise with the rest of the Federals around him, Burnside turned back to steady his troops. "Well, they didn't quite catch me," he told them with a smile as he steered his horse past the Brooklyn Zouaves, whose bright uniforms had drawn much of the attackers' attention.[26]

As an old man, Captain William S. Long, of Heth's Forty-fourth North Carolina, told his son of charging that day with Confederate artillery firing overhead and hurriedly unlimbered Yankee guns spewing canister into his company: ". . . each second brings a belching forth of death and you hear the dull thud so often spoken of as a bullet strikes the yielding body of a comrade—a sound like the striking of a base ball on a catchers glove. Sometimes [it] brings forth an exclamation of surprise, horror, pain, anger, exultation, fury. You see the fire as the flash leaves the muzzle of the gun. You hear the swish of the shrapnel, the hum of the minie, the plunge of grape, groan of the wounded, the agonizing shriek of terror & pain from the mortally wounded."

But the Rebels charged on, with Long yelling, "Give 'em hell, boys!" And hell it was: "That field was a mass of yelling shrieking demons wild with pain, thirst, anger and excitement as we rushed, raged, swore, cried, laughed & laughed, raged, yelled, cried, & swore," he wrote. "The earth shook. The dirt flew, as the grape, shell, canister & bullets crashed, tore, whistled, shrieked and plunged through flesh & earth."

As Early's attackers kept going, suddenly Long saw a Yankee close at hand raise his rifle, saw "the spiteful flash" as it fired. "The earth opened, every thing looked red, then black, & a sensation of a great weight was upon me, dragging me down, down, down." He told of awaking in darkness. Around him he heard the calls of other men lying wounded. He slept again, then was awakened by another soldier, his cousin, who gave him water and brandy (and was killed twelve days later). After lying another day and night on the field, Long was brought in by friendly troops.[27]

The attack turned both of Burnside's flanks, driving his corps and the right end of Warren's back about half a mile. Rebel skirmishers reached as far as the Via house, Grant's headquarters the night before,

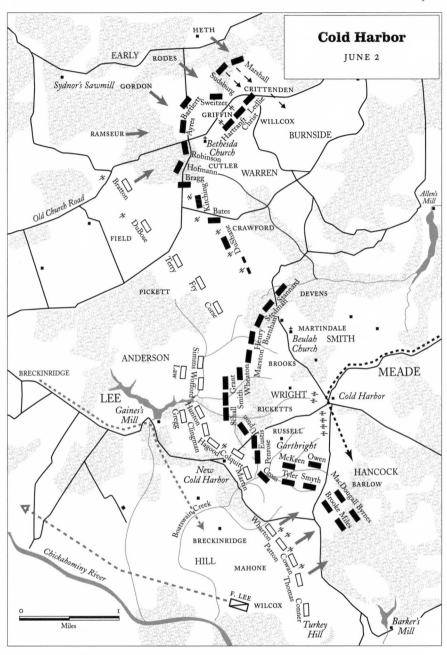

Cold Harbor

JUNE 2

Early attacks the Union right, driving Burnside and Warren back toward Bethesda Church. Hancock's corps arrives after a forced march from the north end of the line, and wrestles for control of high ground to the south.

and cut the Union telegraph line. Early's assault forced both Burnside and Warren onto the defensive, into digging earthworks rather than carrying out their orders to consolidate the Union army's position.

Many of the Federals had reacted to the sudden attack as Burnside did, skedaddling to escape capture before standing to fight. Among them were troops nicknamed "the Fairies" of Company K, 118th Pennsylvania. They were "boys in years, light in weight, small in stature, [with] lithe forms, quick active ways, smooth faces and ever-smiling countenances. . . ." Posted as pickets, they fell back, but as they fled they grabbed up extra muskets discarded by others. When they reached their regiment, they turned and lined up with their comrades. There they had fun propping their weapons and firing from both shoulders, one of them shouting, "Fire by battery!" each time they blazed away. After this display of spirit, the Fairies were called the "Jackass Battery" instead.[28]

By early Thursday evening, Warren told Meade that "I hardly know what you would like to have us do under the circumstances. The enemy now have the breast-works we built when we had our fight night before last and we hold their [previous] position." Along those works, the Federals finally held, stiffened by the "magnificent fighting" of U.S. Regulars in Brigadier General Romeyn B. Ayres's brigade. Early's attack ground down in the gathering dusk; Brigadier General George Doles, whose Georgia brigade had spearheaded Stonewall Jackson's attack at Chancellorsville, was killed by a sharpshooter as he adjusted his line about three-fourths of a mile north of Bethesda Church. The offensive had bent back the Union right so that for almost a mile beyond the church, Burnside's and part of Warren's corps now faced more north than west.[29]

As a last defiant jab against Early's attack, Brigadier General Charles Griffin sent Battery B of the Fourth U.S. Light Artillery out to silence Rebel guns that were spraying canister at his division near the church. Pointing, Griffin told the gunnery officer, "James. . . . I would like to see that battery silenced." Lieutenant James Stewart said unhesitatingly, "I will shut it up, sir."

With that, his battery took off, "every driver lying forward on his horse, whipping and yelling; every Gunner and Cannoneer hanging on for life to the guard-rods of the limber-chests, and bounding six inches high from the springless seats as the huge wheels flew over the ruts; a long trail of dust streaming behind, and the very earth made to smoke and tremble under the fierce tramp of the flying steeds! Speed was everything. . . ."

Rebel fire knocked down ten or eleven of Stewart's men before they could unlimber and load. After they opened fire, the smoke from their guns hung low so that after the first few rounds they could not see the enemy, but "could hear his canister rattling among our guns and wheels like big hailstones, or whizzing past our heads, or whirring through the grass and bushes." Stewart's gunners kept their pieces aligned with the tracks made by the first recoil, and continued firing until the Rebel canister slackened. When the smoke lifted, the Confederate guns stood unmanned in the field.[30]

With the telegraph wire broken between corps and army headquarters, Warren sent Major Washington A. Roebling to advise Meade that "I will do my best when morning comes." In reply, Meade said that whatever the situation, Warren and Burnside should both attack with the rest of the army at 4:30 a.m. He added what may have been the most specific instructions issued by his headquarters to any command about how to carry out the morning assault: "If the enemy should appear to be in strongest force on our left, and your attack should in consequence prove successful, you will follow it up, closing in upon them toward our left. If, on the contrary, the attack on the left should be successful, it will be followed up, moving toward our right." The same orders were dispatched to Burnside. Significantly, there is no record that Meade reemphasized his earlier order for commanders to use the hours between for "examination of the ground in their fronts and perfecting their arrangements for an assault."[31]

HOWEVER PERFECT or imperfect the arrangements, every man in both armies knew the grand assault was next. Six days of wrestling into place for it had cost thousands of casualties; as Meade would say, "In this country I must fight a battle to reconnoitre a position." Each preliminary clash—at Haw's Shop, along the Totopotomoy, on the Matadequin, twice at Bethesda Church, and twice at Cold Harbor— had been impressive enough to stand in history as a separate battle if it had happened at some other time and place of the war. As May faded into June, the escalating skirmishes had come as rumbles of threatening storm, the battles like a series of advancing lightning strikes. Now the thunderhead was about to burst.[32]

Confederate brigadier general Evander McIvor Law said he was "as well satisfied that [the attack] would come at dawn the next morning as if I had seen General Meade's order directing it." He had been sent with his own and Brigadier General George T. Anderson's brigade of

Field's division to cover the gap between Kershaw and Hoke, where the Federals had punched through on Wednesday. He saw immediately that "under such assaults as we had sustained at Spotsylvania our line would be broken" if the Yankees struck again there where Wofford's line angled back.

Though no major action took place on this sector of the front on Thursday, there was constant skirmishing, and sharpshooters kept reconnaissance by both sides at a minimum. "The enemy is improving his ditch, and we annoy him as much as possible," wrote a lieutenant in the Twenty-third Georgia. After waiting till dark, General Law himself went out with a hatchet and two staff officers, driving a series of stakes where he wanted his troops to dig in. This new line curved across the base of the angle, to "throw the marshy ground in our front and give us a clear sweep across it with our fire from the slope on the other side." When Law's men moved in, that put four brigades shoulder-to-shoulder between Wofford's and Clingman's earlier positions, facing a shallow horseshoe-shaped dent where the dangerous gap had been.[33]

With that, the shifting and shoving for position was done. The two armies were poised for an all-out test of strength, along a front of almost six miles between the Totopotomoy and the Chickahominy, from a mile north-northeast of Bethesda Church to a mile and three-quarters south of the Cold Harbor crossroads.

Early commanded on the Confederate left, with the divisions of Heth, Rodes, and Gordon abreast where they held up after Thursday evening's attack, and Ramseur on their right. Anderson held the center of Lee's front with Field, Pickett, Kershaw, and Hoke. The northern part of Anderson's front was lightly manned; Field and Pickett had sent brigades to bolster the place where the Federals broke through on Wednesday. Along this thinly defended sector, Anderson was counting heavily on artillery sited by Porter Alexander. On the Rebel right, Hill was in charge, with Breckinridge and Wilcox on line and Mahone in reserve behind them. The heaviest mass of both Confederates and Yankees was there near the southern end of the front, where the Confederates had reinforced and extended the Kershaw-Hoke line and Lee accurately expected the Federals to try to smash between his flank and the Chickahominy. Confederate cavalry and home guards from Richmond watched the bottomlands from the Chickahominy to the James.

From end to end, Lee's front made a wobbly crescent, its concave side toward the Union line. Within that long, shallow curve there were two smaller arcs, one before Field and Pickett, another across the ravine where Law redrew the line during the night. Other creeks and gullies ran through the lines, offering tempting avenues of approach; some branched parallel to the defenders' works, making obstacles to attackers and places for troops to hide. These natural features and the seemingly minor irregularities in the Confederate line would be crucial when morning came.

Meade had made his headquarters about three-fourths of a mile northeast of Cold Harbor, on the road to Old Church. On his far right, Burnside's Ninth Corps was bent back above Bethesda Church, with the divisions of Potter and Orlando B. Willcox on line and Crittenden in support. Warren's Fifth Corps stretched from Bethesda Church across the Federal center, with the divisions of Griffin, Cutler, and Crawford on line. The three-quarter-mile gap between Crawford's left and Baldy Smith's corps was covered only by pickets. Smith's Eighteenth, Wright's Sixth, and Hancock's Second Corps formed a compact arc with its outer face toward the Rebels, running from just above Beulah Church south toward Turkey Hill, beside the Barker's Mill road. Right to left, Smith placed the divisions of Devens, Martindale, and Brooks, and Wright positioned Neill, Ricketts, and Russell. Hancock was on the Union's far left, with Gibbon and Barlow on line and Birney in support.

A newcomer to the Yankee army might have looked out across the lines before night fell that Thursday and wondered where all Lee's Rebels had gone. Lyman, who had been with Meade since the previous autumn, had a better understanding of the situation. By June, he said, soldiers had learned to dig in at every halt, then to build themselves a parapet, preferably in a tree line, hidden, but with a wide field of fire. In front of this line pickets entrenched, not merely to fire and skedaddle, but to fight, with good supports. And behind the main line were concealed batteries of artillery. Yet what would a soldier see on approaching an army thus deployed? "The answer is one word," wrote Lyman—"nothing!"

A signal officer might climb a tree and make out a streak of fresh earth, or a battle flag, or an enemy officer galloping across an opening. Such evidence called for a reconnaissance: skirmishers would move out, a little artillery duel would begin, a few musket shots sputter in the front, and then the officer in charge would push troops ahead to feel out the main line. Sometimes a whole brigade, sent to straighten the line and bring back the skirmishers, would provoke an unplanned battle. After hours of such "desultory but destructive" work along a front of several miles, there might still be no clear picture of what lay ahead. Over here the opposing pickets might be pressed back, but over there the probe might have gotten nowhere near the defending line. Meanwhile, and most ominously, "the enemy's general has leisure to strengthen and reinforce the most exposed parts of his front. These parts, although best prepared to resist an assault, are precisely those most likely to be assaulted, because they are the only ones which have been determined by reconnaissance."[34]

Lyman was nicely describing what the Federals faced at Cold Harbor, except that their actual situation was even more difficult. Lee's troops were world-champion diggers by then, skillful self-taught military engineers. At places in their line, they had had only hours to entrench, but at others they had a day, even two days. They had created not one main line of resistance, but two and in places three, following the uneven terrain, snaking in and out of gullies and clumps of woods, from the ridges near the Totopotomoy to the swamps along the Chickahominy. Given time, they laid head logs atop their earthworks, with firing holes and crevices in between, and cut thickets of saplings to make defensive abatis. They placed their cannon not just behind their main line but also in works projecting forward, sited to fire across the front of attacking forces. They cut roads through the woods and laid bridges over ravines to feed ammunition to their artillery. By dawn on Friday, June 3, most of the Confederates would be more thoroughly dug in and ready than on any morning since the spring campaign began.

The veterans in Grant's army fully understood this. They might look out toward Richmond and see, as Lyman said, "nothing," and Thursday afternoon, their visibility was limited further by the cooling downpour that turned the dust to mud. But they knew what those splashes of raw earth and occasional spats of musketry across the way meant, as certainly as if they stood within the very lines of the Confederates. They had seen that kind of nothing before. They knew as well as staff officers did that all the maneuvering was over, and "Richmond was dead in front." Here and there, as they improved their rifle pits, they and the Confederates alike had unearthed the barely buried bones of unidentified soldiers who had fallen there two years earlier.[35]

That evening, in a tapering drizzle, Grant's aide Horace Porter picked his way through the troops of a front-line brigade to deliver final orders for the morning assault. He noticed that many soldiers, who usually wore their coats day and night, in sun and rain, now had them off, and seemed to be making repairs to them. "This exhibition of tailoring seemed rather peculiar at such a moment," he thought. Then he could see that they were not sewing up rips. They were being calmly realistic, writing their names and addresses on slips of paper and pinning these to the backs of their coats, "so that their dead bodies might be recognized upon the field, and their fate made known to their families at home."

"Such courage is more than heroic," wrote Porter. "It is sublime."[36]

9

It Was Not War, It Was Murder

BEFORE DAWN, a foggy mist hung over the quiet bottomlands of the Totopotomoy and the Chickahominy, hugging the winding gullies that cut between the breastworks of the armies. Near Bethesda Church, James Madison Stone, of the Twenty-first Massachusetts, walked out to where Federal guns had silenced a Rebel battery when the Ninth Corps rallied the previous evening. As the sky behind the Yankee lines began to pale, he found dead horses, broken caissons, and a few human bodies strewn about.

In the faint light, Stone thought he saw one of those bodies barely lift a hand. It was "a live Johnny," lying flat on his back, his eyes gazing upward into the fog. Stone leaned to ask if he was badly wounded.

"Yes," whispered the Rebel. "I guess it is all up with me." He apparently had been shot in the spine; all but his hands seemed to be paralyzed. Stone asked if he could do anything for him.

"Yes," he said. "I wish you would turn me over on to my side so I can see the sun rise."

This Stone did, and then found a canteen and went to fetch water. When he came back a few minutes later, the wounded Confederate was dead. "He had fallen asleep," Stone wrote, "to awake, I trust, to a more glorious sunrise than that early sunrise of June 3d, 1864."[1]

Nearly five miles south, George Gracey of the Second New York Heavy Artillery was awake well before daybreak, eager and proud of the honor bestowed upon him by General Hancock himself. Gracey was one of the Union army's most eloquent buglers: "There was music in every sound he made," wrote a drummer boy who was his companion. "I have seen officers of other commands stop and listen when the little Swiss was trumpeting the calls." Hancock had picked Gracey to provide inspiration at the army's moment of greatest need—to sound the charge when the Second Corps joined the Sixth and Eighteenth to attack Lee's lines at dawn.[2]

Just behind the Union line, cannoneers of the Eleventh New York Light Battery ate breakfast in darkness, admittedly "loath to go into action." To their front, they could hear but not see infantrymen stirring, the familiar click and rattle of ramrods against rifle barrels as weapons were loaded, very few human voices as men stowed haversacks and strapped on cartridge boxes and swords. As the light rose ever so slowly, they gradually made out moving figures. Some of these slipped silently through the wet woods, obviously slackers getting away to safety before the battle began. Riders passed by; then orderlies and servants came back leading horses, which meant field officers were preparing to go in with their regiments on foot. Peering out toward the west, the artillerymen thought the Rebel works seemed deserted; "not a man was to be seen behind them."[3]

ACROSS THE LINES, Confederates in Captain William F. Dement's First Maryland Battery, dug in beside Breckinridge's command, had sent their horses to the rear hours earlier to clear their post for action. In the night, Yankee artillery fired on them "quite lively," but the Maryland gunners held back, not replying, saving ammunition for the morning. When the Yankee shelling died away, the Marylanders had kept on piling dirt until they could shovel no more. Totally unnecessarily, they had asked infantrymen in rifle pits alongside to "call us if anything should happen." Then they had spread their blankets in the mud, dropped, and tried to sleep, ignoring a ripple of skirmish fire "too tame and distant to disturb our slumber."[4]

To the left of the Maryland battery, the rainstorm had broadened the headwaters swamp of Boatswain Creek, which ran west into the Confederate lines and then swung south into the Chickahominy. George Patton, commanding one of Breckinridge's two Virginia brigades, felt that his troops should not have to sleep in such a bog, so he had pulled most of them away onto slightly higher ground, leaving their breastworks manned only by pickets. Concerned at their resulting "exposed and weak condition," officers of the Twenty-second Virginia sent a lieutenant to appeal to Breckinridge, but in the muddy darkness he could not find the general, so the line stayed as it was.[5]

About a hundred yards back of Breckinridge's works stood a farmhouse surrounded by trees, and in a gentle swale behind it, nearly four hundred infantrymen of the Second Maryland Battalion had made camp. Before they lay down, their commander, Captain J. Parran Crane, made a speech about how Marylanders had helped Lee to victory here two years earlier, and soon they would be called on to uphold the Old Line State's reputation on the very same ground. Without entrenching or pitching tents, the troops wrapped themselves in their blankets, hugging their rifles to keep them dry, and tried to sleep.[6]

Another couple of hundred yards from the front, back of the Second Maryland, Joe Finegan's Florida brigade was dug in with Mahone's division, the only command that Lee was able to hold back for emergencies. Finegan's recently arrived troops had put up with the usual kidding from Lee's hardened soldiers when they came to Virginia. But these were piney-woods types, not well fed, spick-and-span garrison troops like some of the others who came as reinforcements. One of the Florida veterans with whom they merged to make a single brigade said, "Here was a hard-looking lot of soldiers. They were all smoked from the lightwood knots and had not washed or worn it off yet. . . . most of them with bed quilts instead of blankets." And a captain of Mahone's Richmond Grays said Finegan's command was mostly "very young, half grown men, and not very healthy & strong looking. . . . To look at these men would convince one that they was a pitiful, sorrowful looking crowd. That they were here and did not know for what purpose."[7]

Left and right, Union and Confederate, soldiers in the trenches and gun pits knew very well why they were waiting for dawn that Friday, and because they did, they got very little rest during the night. Evander Law's Alabamians had not slept at all. The brigade had spent the night digging, fortifying the position that Law had staked out toward the ravine between Hoke and Kershaw. General Hoke had left orders for Clingman's and Hunton's brigades, still in trenches where the Confederates had finally held on Wednesday night, to pull back into the new line before daylight. According to Hunton, he was supposed to retire on hearing from Clingman, so neither brigade would be dangerously exposed during the withdrawal. But as dawn approached, he had heard nothing. When he sent to query Clingman, he found that the Carolinian had "vacated the line and retired without notifying me, leaving our whole front open to the enemy." The angry Hunton managed to reposition his brigade between Clingman and Wofford before the sun rose.[8]

In Law's Fifteenth Alabama, Colonel William C. Oates was at last satisfied with his regiment's new works. Before sunup, he sent details to a spring for water. Just as they returned, Oates heard a volley in the woods ahead. Major A. A. Lowther, commanding the regimental pickets, came running up the ravine. Then came Oates's skirmishers, under Captain Noah B. Feagin, racing back from the abandoned line and climbing into the earthworks. And behind them came a column of soldiers in blue, seemingly ten lines deep, carrying their rifles at trail arms and shouting "Huzzah! Huzzah!"

At that instant, Oates realized that while laboring during the night, his men had put their weapons aside; not a rifle in his main line was loaded. He screamed for his troops to load while his officers took up axes and stood to the works.[9]

WHEN GEORGE GRACEY'S bugle sounded the Union charge, its notes did not carry far in the thick, wet atmosphere. Many Union troops would admit that the attack order "was not received with much hilarity." There was even some hooting at officers when it was first issued, until the men realized that those officers were going to lead from out front. But a few needed more than a bugle call to start them that morning. John Gibbon, riding through his division at first light, was amazed to find "one whole brigade, including its commander [Brigadier General Joshua T. Owen], still sound asleep." Gibbon, furious, soon got it moving, and later would dismiss Owen for this and other failings.[10]

In fits and starts, with delays here and there, the Federal line started to move within minutes of 4:30 a.m. Very few of the soldiers in it recalled anything like the parade-ground spectacles so vivid in reminiscences of Fredericksburg and Gettysburg. Harvey Clark, of the Twenty-fifth Massachusetts, maintained that when the Eighteenth Corps started forward, he was on high ground and looked out to the Sixth Corps on the left and the Second beyond it to the south. "This was a grand sight," he said. "I do not know how many thousand were massed in line." But the terrain, the vegetation, and the layout of the Confederate lines quickly threw formations out of order, conspiring with the vagueness of the Union battle orders to prevent coordination among the advancing corps. Before the first Federals reached Lee's works, the grand attack had broken into a series of essentially separate operations.[11]

Fred Mather, of the Seventh New York Heavy Artillery, was so fatigued after days of unaccustomed labor as a foot soldier that he had not stirred when his regiment rose and moved out in the darkness. He awoke under a tree, and dimly saw someone he called "a darky," who pointed and said, "Dey's down dar in the edge of the woods." Mather hurried to find his company, apologized to his captain, James Kennedy, and fell in with his comrades as they started forward.

"It was beyond the gray in the morning, but not quite sun-up," Mather wrote, "when we moved through the thin strip of woods, and, coming into the open, saw the enemy's works, and with a hearty cheer we charged them."[12]

Just as in the Union attack on Wednesday, a brigade commander had chosen artillerymen brought in as infantry reinforcements to lead his assault. The Seventh New York Heavies had left the defenses of Washington on May 15. In their first contact with the Rebels at Spotsylvania, they had retreated under fire until their colonel rallied them by shouting, "Men, don't let the news of this break go back to Albany!" There and on the Totopotomoy, they had taken enough casualties to understand the seriousness of their role this day: because they had come sixteen hundred strong, they were out in front of Hancock's advance, the southernmost infantry corps on the Union line.

Hancock formed his corps for attack with Barlow's and Gibbon's divisions leading and Birney's in support. Barlow put the brigades of Colonels John R. Brooke and Nelson Miles in his first line. Gibbon, to his right, chose Brigadier General Robert O. Tyler's and Colonel Thomas A. Smyth's brigades to lead his advance. The Seventh New York Heavies, with Colonel Lewis O. Morris in command, stepped out in front of Brooke's brigade, Barlow's division.

At one moment, no one was visible in Breckinridge's Confederate works, which took in a sunken farm road angling across the low ridge. At the next moment, there appeared a line of slouch hats, and then a long flash of gunpowder. Three times between the woodline and the road cut, the Rebels shot down the Heavies' color-bearer. Each time, another soldier picked up the flag and kept going. A shell burst near Mather; a fragment broke the scabbard of his sword; at the same time, something hit his left hip, knocking him over. A mere bruise, he thought, getting back to his feet and pushing on. He was so keyed up that the air "seemed buoyant" around him. But that air was full of Minié balls and canister, swishing through the New Yorkers' line like bird shot through a flock of ducks. Just before the Rebel works was a steep bank, and then "we were on them."

As Mather told it years later, the Heavies saw white handkerchiefs and thought the shock of their attack had persuaded the Confederates in front of them to give up. Then "a reb rose up and fired into our color-guard, dropped his musket, threw up his hands and said, 'I sur-

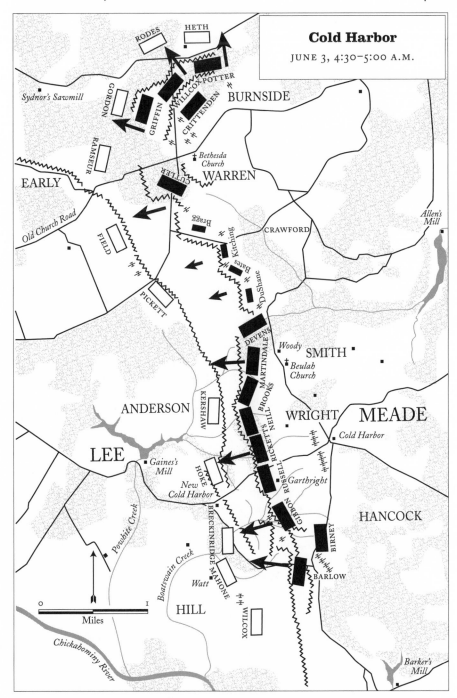

Cold Harbor

JUNE 3, 4:30–5:00 A.M.

*Following Grant's order to attack all along the line from above Bethesda
Church to below Cold Harbor, all five Union corps move out at daybreak
against Lee's entrenched Confederates.*

render.' The Color-sergeant thrust the steel lance on the color-staff into his open mouth, and, with a reference to his canine ancestry, said, 'You spoke too late.'"

Colonel Brooke fell, badly wounded, as he brought the rest of his brigade forward. Colonel Orlando H. Morris of the Sixty-sixth New York took over the brigade and almost immediately dropped with a mortal wound; he was replaced by the Heavies' Colonel Lewis Morris, who would survive this melee only to be killed the next day. After what Brooke described as "terrific fighting," most of the Confederates in that part of the line fled, but many dodged into "rat holes," as their bombproofs were called, and the Federals started digging them out as prisoners.[13]

Captain Kennedy jumped onto the artillery redoubt and tried to turn one of the brass guns against the retreating Rebels. As he did, a man aimed his musket up from a hole, but, Mather said, "a shot from my revolver changed his mind." Another Rebel tried the same thing, and was quickly bayoneted by a Union sergeant. With help, Kennedy swung the gun, but before he could load it, the Confederates had fallen back on their second line, turned about, and opened heavy fire on the attackers. Mather was picking Rebels out of rat holes when he heard the order to charge again. But as he tried to get his men back into line, "the enemy charged us, and in our broken form we could not resist them."

"What was to be done?" one of the recently converted artillerymen asked himself. "We had lost all semblance of organization—a veritable mob with no means to turn the captured guns upon the enemy. In this dilemma, each man decided that question for himself. Green soldiers though we were, our short experience had taught us to know just when to run, and run we did. . . ."[14]

Nelson Miles's brigade, the left arm of Barlow's attack, charged with the newly assigned Fifth New Hampshire, the 183rd Pennsylvania, and the Second New York Heavy Artillery in front. They fought their way past skirmishers, crossing the Barker's Mill road that runs south from Cold Harbor. Yards short of the main defensive line, slashing fire halted Miles's lead regiments, and the attackers dug in as best they could under pounding by cannon and muskets. Colonel Richard Byrnes was killed as his Irish Brigade came on in support; Captain James Fleming of the Twenty-eighth Massachusetts reported that "our men fell in heaps" before reeling back "badly used."[15]

A Federal gunner, watching from behind where Barlow's men had started, saw them go over the Rebel earthworks cheering. But he was dismayed that "there in our front lay, sat, and stood, the second line, the supports"—Birney's division. Why, he asked himself, "did they not go forward and make good the victory? They did not." Why they did not is one of the unanswered questions of the struggle. Hancock's headquarters record offered no explanation, stating only that "We might have held on in Barlow's front had Birney's division moved promptly to its support, which was not done—great delay occurring on Birney's part or that of his subordinates."[16]

Hancock's other assault division, under John Gibbon, was delayed first by the slowness of Owen's brigade in getting organized. Then, before the division reached the enemy works, its battle line was "cut in two by a deep, impassable swamp, which widened as we advanced toward the enemy." Here, perhaps more than at any point on the long line, casual reconnaissance cost Meade's army grievously. Neither good soldier Gibbon, nor Hancock and Meade and Grant above him, nor the brigadiers and colonels below him, seem to have realized that this barrier lay across part of his front.[17]

In Smyth's brigade, on Gibbon's left, Charles D. Page of the Fourteenth Connecticut told how nearby troops took more than an hour to "pierce the jungle" before their final assault got under way. Then they crawled over a fence and met a terrific volley as they started up the ridge. "For a time it was alive with fire," Page wrote. "The men were dropping, wounded, all along the line. To reach the enemy the men were obliged to pass through a jungle very thick and tangled and almost impenetrable." When they got within sixty to one hundred yards of the defensive line, Smyth reported, his ranks "had become so thinned and the fire from the enemy's artillery and musketry was so destructive that the men were compelled to halt" and seek shelter.[18]

One of the first bursts of Rebel fire severely wounded General Tyler, whose brigade led Gibbon's right. The Eighth New York Heavy Artillery drove ahead past him. Its colonel, Peter A. Porter, died a few yards from the Confederate line; as Gibbon reported, Porter was "surrounded by the dead of his regiment, which, although new to the work, fought like veterans." The swamp diverted Colonel John E. McMahon of the 164th New York and part of his regiment away from the rest of Tyler's brigade. Pushing on, McMahon led his men onto the Confederate breastworks, cheering alongside his flag, until he fell. Gibbon reported that McMahon "expired in the enemy's hands, losing his colors with honor," though others said he collapsed against a tree when shot, and was hit by two or three more bullets before his body was recovered from between the lines. Colonel H. Boyd

McKeen, bringing his brigade on behind Tyler, was killed and succeeded by Colonel Frank A. Haskell of the Thirty-sixth Wisconsin,
who was almost immediately hit and carried off, mortally wounded.[19]

While such men were striving and dying, the hapless Owen made
the mistake that would end his army career. He deployed his brigade
into line too soon, disobeying Gibbon's orders to push on in column to
support Smyth.[20]

Gibbon and Barlow had what seemed at first the good fortune to
attack one of the softest spots in Lee's long line, the half-mile between
Hoke's and Wilcox's divisions, defended by John Breckinridge's light-
weight command. But it was also the only sector where Lee had
placed a reserve to deal with any breakthrough.

A VOLLEY of musketry by the pickets woke J. W. F. Hatton of the
Confederate First Maryland Battery as he lay in the mud beside his
cannon. He threw off his blanket and shouted, "To your guns, boys—
bring up canister! They're charging!" Infantrymen near the gun position were popping off rounds, then reloading before the Yankees came
into range, making sure their powder was dry. All was confusion.
Rebel pickets and skirmishers were racing back to the lines. Behind
them, left and right, Hatton saw "a blue mass of humanity, shouting,
firing, with officers directing them with drawn swords, with the 'Stars
and Stripes' waving over their ranks. . . ."

For the moment, the Maryland cannoneers were only "nervous
spectators," unable to fire because of the retreating Confederates
before them. Hatton stepped on top of the breastworks and waved his
cap back and forth in his right hand for the incoming pickets to see.
They understood him and divided as they ran back, leaving a lane
before the battery. Hatton jumped down, aimed his gun out the lane,
and cried, "Fire!"—and later claimed that his was the first Confederate cannon to open on the charging Yankees that morning. As soon as
the pickets were in, the whole Rebel line blazed away. The Federal
ranks "were being thinned, but on they rushed, whooping and firing."
Aiming his cannon low, Hatton made his shots ricochet into the
oncoming Yankees rather than sail over their heads. The attackers
swerved away, toward works held only by riflemen. Swinging the trail
of his piece, Hatton followed them with fire, throwing a wall of canister across the front of the friendly infantry.

He recalled "the bursting of shells, the popping of muskets, the
deafening roar of artillery, the rattling of arms, the whizzing of bullets,

the shrieks of the wounded and the moaning of the dying"—and yet despite this "pandemonium that can not be described nor forgotten," some Confederates just behind the defensive ridge did not realize yet that the great battle had begun.[21]

In the hollow near the farmhouse back of Breckinridge's line, many men of the Second Maryland Battalion were still asleep when the familiar racket of skirmishing on the lines grew louder. One soldier had risen and was just tying up his gear when he looked east toward the front and saw in the mist what he thought was a heavy line of Confederates running back. Another crowd of troops followed, clustering around the house. The soldier did not know who they were until they opened fire on the unprepared Marylanders, killing a few before they could roll out of their blankets. Still some of the Rebels thought these were friendly skirmishers who had fallen back and mistaken the Second Maryland for enemy infantry. Then someone made out "the gridiron"—the name many Confederates had given to the U.S. flag—carried by Barlow's Yankees.

They had driven in Patton's pickets and broken through the center of his line, capturing four guns of Captain William H. Caskie's Virginia battery in furious point-blank fighting. Some Rebels nearby maintained that Breckinridge's "whole line fled panic stricken," and that Patton's brigade *broke and ran away.*" But John K. Thompson, commander of the Twenty-second Virginia, insisted later that "no part of our division ran away," and one New Yorker in the Seventh Heavy later declared that "the charge of misbehavior imputed to the occupants of that salient is unjust and untrue; for if any body of troops ever got a warm reception we did. The enemy bravely stood their ground, not waiting for us to come over their works, but meeting us on the parapet. They contested every inch. . . . Clubbed muskets, bayonets, and swords got in their deadly work."

Thompson said that from the Rebel command post, he and Patton could not see the Yankees in the mist until they were angling past within a hundred yards. According to him, Patton let the attackers rush by and sent his adjutant to rouse the Floridians and Marylanders in reserve.[22]

Veterans of the Twenty-sixth Virginia asserted that their regiment briefly stood firm on one shoulder of the salient. "All knew that our line could not hold out against such hosts of the enemy as was converging on us, but the chance to kill Yankees was fine," recalled C. W. Humphreys. He said that the regiment's color-bearer, Chap Woodram, emptied his revolver into the oncoming Federals, then

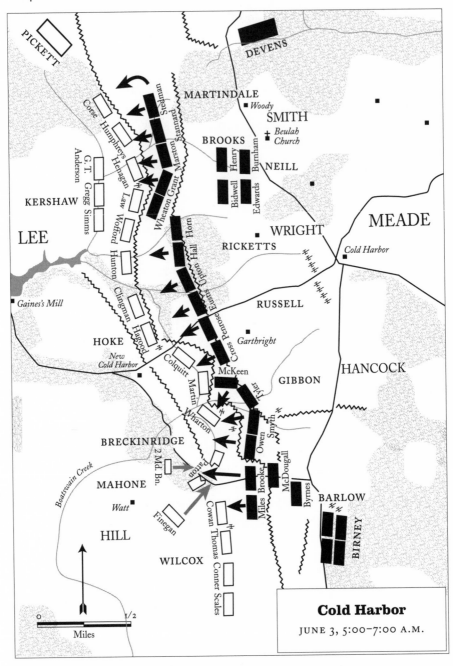

Cold Harbor

JUNE 3, 5:00–7:00 A.M.

The heaviest Union assault is at the southern end of the front, where Barlow's division of Hancock's corps breaks through, only to be driven back by a counterattack from Finegan's Florida brigade and one Maryland battalion.

furled his flag and used its staff as a spear. About to stab another attacker, he was shot dead, and the memoirist's brother, C. B. Humphreys, grabbed the flag, only to have it jerked away by four Yankees.* He watched them pass it back, hand to hand, until he was disarmed and ordered to the Federal rear.[23]

Hatton, the Maryland artilleryman, was sure that just then the battle and perhaps the war "hung by a thread," that "failure here meant the defeat of the whole army. The tension was great, and a few moments would decide the issue." The Yankees' success caused "a momentary paralyzation" that broke when Buck Weems, a high private in the Second Maryland, waved his big straw hat and yelled, "There they are, let's charge 'm!" Captain John W. Torsch joined in, shouting, "I see the gridiron, boys! Let's at them!" Lieutenant James S. Franklin drew his sword and started forward, roaring, "Come on!"

No one gave a battalion order, and there was no time to fall into formation. "We must every man of us at the same moment [have] recognized the United States flag," wrote John Goldsborough White, and "a hundred of us must have yelled in one breath, 'It's the Yankees!'" In a loose bunch, the Marylanders charged the Yankees around the house at a full run. They kept going and drove the surprised attackers out of the main line, where Lieutenant Charles B. Wise took over one of the disputed guns and poured canister after the fleeing enemy.[24]

Just back of the Marylanders, Finegan's Florida troops had seen Breckinridge's men retreating, "running over us like a bunch of Texas steers, stampeded the worst sort." One of Finegan's admirers said that the rollicking Irishman jumped to his horse and "went slashing to and fro ahead of his men," calling them into line. David Lang, Finegan's senior colonel, stood on the regiment's hastily thrown breastworks and shouted, "Charge, boys, charge!"[25]

Captain Council Bryan of the Fifth Florida wrote that as soon as the retreating Virginians passed to the rear, Finegan's men "poured two volleys into the advancing droves of yankees then jumped the breastworks and charged them—Five to one but each one a hero." They came within fifty yards of the Federals, who "halt, waver—and run." The Florida troops let go "one more volley and Breckinridge's breastworks so ingloriously lost are ours—the breastworks recaptured

---

* Corporal Terrance Begley of the Seventh New York Heavy Artillery was awarded the Medal of Honor for capturing the defenders' colors. He was killed at Petersburg before receiving the honor.

and the battle won. . . . The new troops fought like 'tigers' and we feel proud of them." Fifteen minutes later, the Federals rose from where they had taken cover to try one last charge, which got nowhere.[26]

Ever since that morning, Maryland and Florida historians have disagreed over who deserves more praise for the countercharge that stopped Barlow's attack. Finegan's was by far the heavier force, but as early as 1879, a Marylander asserted that "the whole credit of the recapture of the Confederate works on the morning of June 3d, 1864, as far as actual fighting effected it, belongs to the Second Maryland, Finnegan's brigade contributing no more to the result than the moral support of its presence." A modern Florida historian says the Second Maryland hurried "to support the embattled Floridians," clearly implying that the Floridians charged first.

But what one Marylander recorded in his diary that day made it seem a tie: "Yanks break through our line a little to our left and front," wrote James W. Thomas. "The line in rear of us charge. No order given us but a majority of the battalion can not be restrained and rush in with them. This causes a little confusion, but the charge is successful and we retake the trenches. The battalion is pretty well mixed up. . . ."[27]

The credit matters less than the result: the Rebel reserves threw back Barlow's attackers, retaking Breckinridge's works and the captured guns. Barlow's division suffered crushing losses; the surviving Yankees sought shelter on the field, diving into abandoned picket holes, squeezing into wrinkles in the ground, many literally within a stone's throw of the restored line. But at that point, less than half an hour after the Union offensive had begun, Captain Bryan had no way of knowing whether the battle was over, either there or anywhere else up the line. Neither did Grant nor Meade, nor Lee, nor any of the corps commanders North or South. Too much had happened, was still happening, and no one could see it all.

To HANCOCK's right, Horatio Wright put all three of his Sixth Corps divisions—Russell, Ricketts, and Neill—into broad lines of battle, two to four ranks deep. They advanced soon after 4:30, against the same stretch of front they had failed to take on Wednesday evening. Since then, the defenses there had been strengthened by Lee's shifting of brigades and Law's creation of the new trench line reaching toward the bloody ravine between Kershaw's and Hoke's divisions, plus another two nights and a day of digging. Wright's generals understood what this lapse of time meant, and none of them was eager to try there again.

Law watched the Yankees charge over the old line, manned only by skirmishers. The attackers, thinking this was a breakthrough, let out a cheer and rushed into the boggy ground below. "Line followed line until the space inclosed by the old salient became a mass of writhing humanity, upon which our artillery and musketry played with cruel effect," Law wrote. The irrepressible Lieutenant Falligant of Callaway's Georgia battery worked his Napoleon furiously at the heel of the horseshoe. Law, looking on from the slope behind, was afraid his riflemen were firing so fast that they would run out of cartridges. He ran forward to the trenches, where his men were confidently laughing and joking as they blazed away. There he could see more plainly "the terrible havoc made in the ranks of the assaulting column."

In front of the Fifteenth Alabama, the Yankees had come within about thirty strides when Oates ordered his single artillery piece to cut loose with double charges of canister. So close were the oncoming troops that the flame from the muzzle of the cannon shot right into their ranks. After a minute or two of this, the Federals pulled back, only to try again forty minutes later. This effort, aimed at the Fourth Alabama, broke against what Oates called "the most destructive fire I ever saw." The Alabamians threw up a wall of seemingly automatic fire—as fast as they emptied their single-shooters, they passed them back to Bryan's Georgians, who reloaded and handed them forward. Oates said, "I could see the dust fog out of a man's clothing in two or three places at once where as many balls would strike him at the same moment. In two minutes not a man of them was standing. All who were not shot down had lain down for protection."[28]

On Hoke's front, before Colquitt's brigade, a correspondent reported that he had "never seen as many dead in one place." Russell's Yankees "came up to the butchery splendidly, and our men like shooting them so well, that they say as long as they can get ammunition and something to eat, they will stand in breastworks and let Grant bring up the whole Yankee nation."[29]

A bullet nicked General Law above the eye, making him one of the few ranking Confederate casualties on a day that was devastating to brigadiers and colonels in the Union army. Law had vivid memories of dead Yankees stacked up before the railroad cut at Second Manassas and the stone wall at Fredericksburg, but he had never imagined anything like this morning at Cold Harbor. "It was not war," he wrote, "it was murder."[30]

Emory Upton, whose brigade had taken heavy casualties cracking the first Confederate line in the previous effort, covered this day in a single sentence of his otherwise detailed campaign report: "June 3rd, another assault was ordered, but, being deemed impracticable along our front, was not made." In letters home, he would say much more. Major Henry R. Dalton, adjutant of Russell's division, wrote that "another advance was ordered and attempted along the whole line; but little ground was gained, however, and other works were immediately thrown up under sharp and deadly musketry fire."[31]

Not one of Wright's divisions got as far as the main Confederate trenches—they met "frontal fire, enfilading fire from the right and from the left, musketry, and artillery, and it was more than this already shaken corps, or any flesh and blood, could endure. Where the line stopped, it stayed, and dug in or died."[32]

Frank Wheaton was the only one of Wright's brigadiers who included in his report even the pro forma line that the troops of his brigade "advanced with spirit." They carried what Wheaton called "the first and imperfect line of rifle pits"—the original works beside the ravine, now abandoned by the Confederates. But in trying to take "the second line"—Law's repositioned main line—"they were repulsed with great loss." Brigadier General Lewis A. Grant, heading the Vermont Brigade in Neill's division, moved his troops up to relieve Wheaton's battered command. After he was stopped cold, two of his regiments were left needlessly exposed. He asked permission to withdraw them, leaving a skirmish line, but permission was refused. Grant, thinking of his men's lives, moved them anyway.[33]

BALDY SMITH, whose Eighteenth Corps had been resupplied with ammunition by Warren, pushed off promptly at 4:30 a.m. He formed each of his two attacking divisions in a column of massed brigades, rather than in broad battle lines like those sent forward by Hancock and Wright. This was meant to create a dense battering ram, so that if the leading brigades penetrated the defensive works, those following could rush through to exploit the success. Smith held back Devens's badly damaged division, facing it off to the right, not attacking but securing the long stretch between his and Warren's corps. Martindale's division, which had suffered least in the earlier fighting, would lead the right column of Smith's assault, with Brooks on the left.

Martindale had orders to attack along the northernmost of the three roughly parallel ravines that run west into Gaines's millpond. But just short of Kershaw's Confederate works, that ravine split into two branches, one of them angling across Martindale's line of march. As the right end of Martindale's column slashed its way through that obstacle, it unintentionally turned away from its original course. "The fire at this time was exceedingly severe," Martindale reported. "My columns had their bayonets fixed and pieces uncapped. They were met by a storm of grape, canister, and musket-balls, not only in front but especially on my right flank. . . ."

To deal with this, Martindale split the head of his division, sending three regiments off in one direction and the rest in the other. This spread his force into line, rather than column, and it typified the way in which unscouted terrain and irregular Rebel works soon had the Federals trying to advance at different angles up and down the front.[34]

"We started with a yell," recalled Clark of the Twenty-fifth Massachusetts. "The first we saw was a line of men shoulder to shoulder waist high above their works, then a solid sheet of fire, and such a shower of shell and bullets. It is hard to describe the sensation I had. It was like being alone in the midst of a whirlwind and was obliged to stop. Before I could realize what was best to do, I was lying flat on the ground."[35]

Some of the fire that razed Martindale's division erupted from Henagan's Confederate brigade, including the Twentieth South Carolina, which had learned from its disastrous introduction to war less than forty-eight hours earlier. The South Carolinians waited, resting their rifles on the breastworks, sighting in, as Martindale's troops came on. Then they cut loose at once, volley after volley. The first line of attackers "reeled and attempted to fly the field, but were met by the next column, which halted the retreating troops with the bayonet, butts of guns, and officer's sword, until the greater number were turned to the second assault." The defenders reloaded, and when they opened against this second effort, there were "men falling on top of men, rear rank pushing forward the first rank, only to be swept away like chaff." Smoke settled over the field, punctuated by muzzle flashes as a third line of assault mingled with the first two, and then, beneath the smoke, the defenders could see the ground covered with bodies.[36]

At that point, Baldy Smith, overseeing Martindale's advance, ordered him to hold up until Brooks's division got moving on his left. But Martindale thought renewed defensive fire on his left meant Brooks was attacking, and realized that his men had to do something or lie there and passively die. He ordered them to assault again, and they made three more efforts, getting within fifty yards of the main Rebel works.

Colonel Griffin A. Stedman, Jr., waved his brigade on, wielding an iron ramrod as a sword. "The men bent down as they pushed forward, as if trying, as they were, to breast a tempest," and they fell "half a platoon almost at a time, like grain before the reaper." Captain Thomas Barker of the Twelfth New Hampshire thought that troops lying beneath the defensive fire were shirking and yelled at Captain Edwin E. Bedee to drive them up into line. Bedee ran among the fallen men, kicking and poking with his sword, until he realized that "nothing but the judgment tramp of the Almighty would ever bring those men upon their feet again." Barker, while the bullets were still flying, "declared with an oath that he would not take his regiment into another such charge, if Jesus Christ himself should order it." Finally, Martindale saw that "it was impossible for any body of men to do more." The survivors fell back a few yards and tried to hide.[37]

Clark lay beneath the smoke, surrounded by dead and wounded comrades. No one could move without drawing fire, he wrote; "their men remained in full view above the works, watching for any movement we might make to get away." He lay for what seemed a long time, until a voice from the rear told the regiment's survivors to work their way back slowly so the Rebels would not notice their moving. Flat on his belly, Clark eased himself away from the defensive works a few inches at a time. Eventually he backed into a brush patch, but could not stand up to go over it, so he pushed himself into it feet first, still flat. When he felt he was out of sight, he realized his feet were in the face of Frank Barrett, who had slept beside him the last night, on fence rails that kept them up out of the mud. Barrett had waked that morning "pale and trembling, would not make any conversation," Clark recalled. "I thought then he felt something would happen to him." Now Barrett was lying head down, his body exposed on top of the brush, his premonition fulfilled by a Minié ball in the right temple. "I knew he had a watch and some money, but did not dare expose myself to get it," Clark wrote. He worked his way through the brush, then rose to his hands and knees and crept back to low ground.[38]

Brooks's division, the other column of Smith's attack, had guided along the left side of the ravine. But after driving the Rebels from their first line of rifle pits, these attackers came under fire "too murderous for any troops long to sustain." Brigadier General Gilman Marston, commanding one of Brooks's brigades, reported that "the ground was swept with canister and rifle-bullets until it was literally covered with the slain." Seeing this, Smith told Brooks to halt his division and seek cover until the devastating barrage let up.

His order came after the fact: as Marston said, "When it was apparent that further effort would only result in useless slaughter, the men returned, a portion to the partial cover of the embankment from which the enemy had been driven, and the rest to the shelter of the wood through which they had advanced." The Confederate fire kept on until Smith advised Meade that "My troops are very much cut up, and I have no hopes of being able to carry the works in my front unless a movement of the Sixth Corps on my left may relieve at least one of my flanks from this galling fire."[39]

THE UNION high command apparently expected little from the Ninth and Fifth Corps on Friday, and that is what it got. The role of Burnside and Warren was to keep the Confederates busy at their end of the front so Lee could not shift more strength to meet the main attack to the south. Burnside's first tactical objective was to reclaim the ground that Early had taken the previous evening; Warren was stretched so thin that he could not mount a serious offensive. But their orders were just as firm and simple as those issued to Smith, Wright, and Hancock—to attack the enemy in their front. And to the soldiers involved, those clashes were just as important and deadly as others down the line.

On Burnside's right, he sent Colonel John I. Curtin's brigade of Potter's division ahead at daybreak, pushing through a brushy swamp, driving in Confederate pickets hiding in a farmhouse and outbuildings, and reaching close to the Shady Grove Road. These troops called up artillery that knocked out one Confederate battery and chased away another. Burnside reported that although resistance was "very determined," he had captured the Confederates' first line and was reforming to assault their main works. But nothing further came of this limited opening success.[40]

On Burnside's left, Colonel John F. Hartranft's brigade of Willcox's division started later. It took a line of Rebel rifle pits, then stopped and dug in under heavy enfilading fire that made it impossible to bring up artillery support. That was as far as Willcox advanced.[41]

Warren tried to cooperate, advancing Griffin's division with orders to make contact on its right with Burnside. From their first step, Griffin's skirmishers took steady fire that soon drove them to shelter in a belt of woods. Later, Warren told headquarters that he had forced the enemy back on the Shady Grove Road but that he had only a single line of troops and could not keep on without reinforcements. He suggested taking troops from his left to strengthen further effort on his right. Instead, Meade urged him to attack on his left, to halt flanking fire that was holding up the advance of Smith's Eighteenth Corps.[42]

Facing that thinly manned stretch between Warren and Smith, Joseph W. Eggleston of Lamkin's Virginia battery considered himself "entirely free from danger" when he stood on the works and "plainly counted fourteen columns" coming toward the Confederate lines farther south. The Yankees surged forward with "great gallantry," he said, "only to be slaughtered by thousands." He watched "line after line melt away and the field was almost in a moment practically covered with dead and wounded. . . . The first line seemed to have come nearer than any subsequent one. Toward the last the men began to falter and mounted officers were seen plainly trying to drive them in hopeless attack. The lines seemed to wave like wheat in a breeze, then dissolve, with the men gathering in bunches and being shot down."

Eventually Confederate commanders in that sector ordered their infantry to stop firing. Men in the trenches beckoned to Federal officers on the field to "drive them in," to bring their troops into the lines as prisoners rather than risk further slaughter. When they did not respond, "a deadly fire was poured into their ranks and few escaped."[43]

Hundreds, thousands of Union soldiers, dead and wounded, lay within rifle range of the Confederate works. Many others, unhurt, tried to make themselves invisible, unwilling to risk running back under vicious Rebel sharpshooting. "It was almost impossible to move and live, the lifting of a head or hand being a signal for volleys of musketry." Soldiers lying surrounded by fallen comrades pulled the dead bodies close, to hide behind them. Some of the survivors dared to stumble into the defensive lines and surrender; a few who tried this were shot by Union troops behind them before they reached safety as prisoners.[44]

Law, after watching what happened at the center of the attack, said it gave "a fair picture of the results along the entire line—a grand advance, a desperate struggle, a bloody and crushing repulse." But that was easier to see from the Confederate works than from Union headquarters.[45]

10

A Simple and Absolute Impossibility

WHEN HIS RELUCTANT army started ahead in the faint dawn, Meade moved up to Wright's command post, the Kelly family's house at Cold Harbor. Wright himself had gone forward to oversee the Sixth Corps' advance. There behind the center of his main attacking force, Meade and his staff tried to keep up with what was happening, to find out what all the rumbling cannon meant. Though the front was less than a mile west, the guns sounded far away, and nowhere around the crossroads and its decrepit farmhouse was there a high, clear place to watch the battle unfold. Lyman, who stuck close to Meade, said, "There has been no fight of which I have seen so little as this. The woods were so placed that the sound, even, of the musketry, was much kept away, and the fighting, though near us, was completely shut from view. All the warfare for us was an occasional roundshot, or shell, that would come about us from the Rebel batteries."[1]

Thus deprived of personal observation, Meade could only wait for word from his generals.

The first came from Hancock, and it was encouraging: before 5:15 a.m., Barlow had pierced the enemy's works, taking colors and guns. Meade relayed this to Grant, brightening expectations at both headquarters. But only fifteen minutes later, he advised Grant that Barlow could not hold what he had taken, had pulled back a short distance, and was "about attacking again." He still had not heard from Smith or Wright. A half hour after that, Hancock said his men were "very close to the enemy, under a crest, but seem unable to carry it." Birney, in support, had moved his division into the trenches from which Barlow and Gibbon advanced. But at this point, those two did not think they could use more troops "with any great certainty of success," and Hancock told Meade, "I shall await your orders, but express the opinion that if the first dash of an assault fails, other attempts are not apt to succeed better."

Meade did not want to hear this kind of caution from his favorite corps commander. Indeed, from what followed, it seems that he misunderstood what Hancock was saying. He replied as if Hancock had said he was preparing another assault. "Your dispatch received," Meade wrote. "You will make the attack and support it well, so that in the event of being successful, the advantage gained can be held. If unsuccessful report at once."

Before seven o'clock, Meade heard from Wright that the Sixth Corps had taken the Confederate skirmish line in its sector and Smith's Eighteenth had advanced just as far but was retiring. Smith himself was still unheard from. Though Meade, not Grant, was issuing orders directly to the corps, this mix of pessimistic and only tentatively favorable reports made him hesitate. He had told Hancock to attack again, despite what that sturdy general had advised. Should he order Wright and Smith to press on? By now, he had learned to be exceedingly careful in such situations. He wanted to be sure he was not alone in making decisions that could be costly, both in men's lives and in generals' reputations. At 7:00 a.m., he told Grant, "I should be glad to have your views as to the continuance of these attacks, if unsuccessful."[2]

Grant immediately replied: "The moment it becomes certain that an assault cannot succeed, suspend the offensive, but when one does succeed push it vigorously, and if necessary pile in troops at the successful point from wherever they can be taken. I shall go to where you are in the course of an hour."[3]

His advice was so obvious that it might have applied to every attacking force in the history of warfare. In essence, it told Meade to use his own judgment. As Meade read Grant's dispatch, he had to consider each word with care, and one of them stood out among the others: Grant sanctioned calling off the offensive the moment it became *certain* that further attacks could not succeed. And who had to decide whether and when it was certain? The commanding general of the Army of the Potomac.

Meade would go to his grave still bitter over the maneuvering against him after Gettysburg by politicians and some of his own generals, who accused him of preparing to retreat before the battle was joined. Now he was unwilling to take the chance of more such damage to his place in history.

At 7:40, Meade told Hancock that "No orders have been sent you suspending or rescinding the original order to attack." He recounted the exchange of messages about whether Gibbon had attacked, and whether Barlow was attacking again. "I desire every effort be made to carry the enemy's works," he declared. And then he passed some accountability downward, as he had sought to share it upward with his query to Grant. "Of course if this is deemed impracticable, after trial, the attack should be suspended," he told Hancock, "but the responsibility for this must be on your judgment. I cannot give more decided orders."[4]

Hancock assured him that both Barlow and Gibbon had attacked on schedule at 4:30, and if the guns on their flanks could be silenced, they would go in again. "Our troops hold advanced ground—only awaiting the decision of the question whether any additional assaults are wise. I will let you know soon what is my judgment.

"I consider that the assault failed long since, but I volunteered the statement that we would cling to the advanced positions gained, so that, if any successes were gained by other corps on our right, we would feel ready to try it again, as we would feel that additional chances had arisen."

Meade would not let up. He sent Hancock two dispatches from Wright, who had said he could carry the Rebel works if he was supported by attacks by Hancock and Smith. "It is of greatest importance that no effort should be spared to succeed," said Meade. "Wright and Smith are both going to try again, and unless you consider it hopeless I would like you to do the same."

Hancock, who was far enough forward to see the situation, tried again to make Meade understand what he was saying. "Some of my dispatches cannot have reached" army headquarters, he said. His lead divisions had attacked, retired a short distance, and were awaiting further orders. "An assault can be promptly repeated if desired, but division commanders do not speak encouragingly of the prospect of success since the original attacks failed." Without underlining their names, Hancock was letting Meade know that even the offensive-minded Barlow and Gibbon balked at attacking again. "Unless success has been gained in other points, I do not advise persistence here," he said.[5]

The Union corps commanders made sure that responsibility, thus potentially blame, was distributed laterally as well as up and down the chain of command. As early as six o'clock, Warren had advised Meade that "I cannot well advance unless those on my right or left succeed in doing so." Smith, in reporting that his troops were "very much cut up," said he had "no hope of being able to carry the works in my front unless a movement of the Sixth Corps on my left may relieve at least one of my flanks from this galling fire." Wright asserted that he had ordered an attack by his center, but that "my flanks cannot move without a corresponding movement of the corps on my right and left. . . . I may be pardoned for suggesting that the important attack for our success is by the Eighteenth Corps." At eight o'clock, he added that his Sixth Corps was "a good deal in advance" of both the Second and Eighteenth, "and the reason why General Smith thinks that I am not moving with him is that he is behind me."[6]

Meade, from where he sat at Cold Harbor, was unable to referee among these contentions. At 6:35, he had ordered Hancock to renew his attack. At 8:00 a.m., he ordered Wright and Smith to try again without regard to the corps alongside. At 8:15, he tried to encourage Wright by saying, "There is not the slightest idea that the 6th Corps is not doing what it always has done nobly and well. It is a question of judgment as to the timing of assaults which between the three corps may involve delay and failure. Push on & when you think time to stop report." At 8:45, he gave similar instructions to Warren: "You must not wait for simultaneous attacks, but push forward your assaults."[7]

Smith, who had been at the front overseeing his corps' attack, told Meade that Martindale's division was too badly cut up to go in again, and Brooks had only about five regiments in condition to make another effort. Nevertheless, Smith said, "I will do whatever can be done, or attempt whatever may be ordered." (After the battle, however, he wrote that "later in the day," he got a verbal order from Meade to try again, "and that order I refused to obey." No mention of such a verbal exchange appears in the published Official Records.)[8]

Meade's orders to resume the offensive caused hardly a man to stir on the Union left, where the worst of the morning's terrible casualties were suffered. Toward the right, Warren reported that he had pushed the enemy back along the Shady Grove Church Road, but could not keep on without reinforcements. "I am not waiting for anybody, but putting in whenever I can judiciously," he said.[9]

The 10:00 a.m. message from Meade to Warren, urging him to try to relieve pressure on Smith, proved once again either the erroneous character of Meade's battle map or his own constant misreading of it. "Your movement, as far as you can control it, should be toward the left or southeasterly, keeping up a connection and cooperating with

Smith," Meade wrote. But he meant southwesterly; to move southeast, Warren would have marched directly away from his front, as the cashiered Lockwood had mistakenly done. Meade told Warren that he could not send reinforcements because "all the corps here [are] fully engaged endeavoring to break through the enemy's line, as yet without success, but not without hope of ultimate success." A half hour later, he reversed this decision, answering Warren's request by sending him Birney's division of Hancock's corps, a force that might have turned the day into a Union celebration if it had followed through in support of Barlow's opening attack.[10]

Whether Meade's willingness to shift Birney away from Hancock meant that by 10:30 he realized that his main offensive had failed is not clear. By then, the sporadic blasts of action that followed the din of the first assault had settled into a steady rumble of gunfire. Yet Meade maintained that he—or perhaps he meant to speak only for his nearby corps commanders—was still "not without hope of ultimate success." He was still urging his generals on, although turning his attention to the northern half of the front. Not only did he reinforce Warren; he urged Burnside to keep pushing "as long as there is any chance of success," and he ordered James Wilson's cavalry division to help Burnside by attacking Lee's left flank from the rear.[11]

A gap had developed between Burnside's corps and Wilson's division, which was assigned to screen the Union right toward the Pamunkey while Sheridan's other two cavalry divisions watched the southern end of the front, toward the Chickahominy and the James. Now Wilson was slowed by a collection of thoroughly fatigued troops under Colonel Louis P. di Cesnola, reinforcements that had attached themselves to the cavalry division as they approached the combat zone from Port Royal. Wilson was not happy with this addition, which he described to Meade as "about 1,400 infantry that are efficient, 1,200 or 1,500 disarmed stragglers, an indifferent force of dismounted cavalry regiments, and about 1,000 good cavalry." He seemed relieved to report that he had dropped Cesnola's force on Burnside's right, extending it toward the Totopotomoy. Then, when he set out to get at Lee's left rear as ordered, he smacked into Wade Hampton's Confederate cavalry near Haw's Shop.[12]

By late morning, Meade was beginning to realize that Hancock had been correct when he said that "if the first dash of an assault fails, other attempts are not apt to succeed better." The all-out offensive against Lee's right, the climax of Grant's overland campaign, had failed before the sun cleared the treetops. And while this hard fact took hours to penetrate the headquarters of Meade and Grant, their soldiers understood it from the moment the opening wave crested and fell back from the Confederate works. That moment came at different minutes by the clock, depending on which corps, division, brigade, or regiment was involved, on whether or not it struck a swamp or ravine or abatis before the defenders opened fire. But from beyond Turkey Hill on the south to beyond Bethesda Church on the north, it came quickly.

ALMOST A MILE west of the front, listening at his headquarters near Gaines's Mill, the usually imperturbable Lee was at least as worried as Meade. He had more to lose—more than a battle, more than a reputation; this morning could cost the Confederacy its capital, even the war. And he had less to fight it with, by then fewer than half as many troops as Meade. He heard "the grand roar of the battle coming upon the stillness of the early dawn" the same way the veteran artilleryman Porter Alexander described it, as "the whole strength of both armies . . . being put forth against each other, at once, more completely than ever before or afterward."[13]

Lee heard the crashing exchange when Barlow broke through Breckinridge, when the Floridians and Marylanders counterattacked, and when Kershaw turned back Martindale. From left and right he heard the boom of Falligant's Napoleon, more than four hundred other cannon, and the rattle of thousands of rifles. Occasionally, a stray shell sailed over the fight and exploded near his command post, and exuberant cheers sifted back between bursts of gunfire. But he could not be sure what it all meant, except that the Federals obviously had attacked everywhere at once, and might break through anywhere along his thin line.

He had no reserve left, and without knowing what was happening where, he could not risk pulling troops out of one sector to reinforce another. His men had to throw back the enemy's grand attack where they stood and knelt in their trenches. The noise rose from one direction, fell and rose again in the other, as if the attacks were coming in waves. Lee sent riders off to each of his commanders.

Minutes, then half an hour, went by before couriers galloped back from the right half of the Confederate front, the closest sector, where the fighting had been fiercest. There, A. P. Hill had invited Lee's aide to look out across the line. Sweeping his arm toward fields strewn with bodies in blue, Hill said, "Tell General Lee it is the same all along my front." Robert Hoke sent word that the dead and dying covered the ground before his works but that he had not lost a single soldier. The Yankees had pierced Breckinridge's line, but the Floridians and Marylanders had driven them out. Dick Anderson's headquarters reported that by eight o'clock, fourteen assaults had come against Kershaw's sector, all of them repulsed with severe enemy losses. This must have meant fourteen efforts by a series of battle lines that dropped under fire, then rose and dropped repeatedly until they dared not rise again. Lee heard such reports from every sector, but he could not afford to believe that the grand assault had already peaked and receded; he had to assume that another attack, and another, was coming.[14]

Lee needed men. He dispatched an urgent circular order for his commanders to push to the front every soldier on extra duty, every spare teamster and clerk. He ordered cooked food to be brought forward in wagons so troops would not stray away to prepare their own. "Men must not be sent to the rear upon any pretext whatever," he said, unless disabled or on specific business.

Thinking of Breckinridge's fight for Turkey Hill on Thursday and the temporary enemy breakthrough at dawn, he was particularly concerned about that general's sector. He sent a dispatch reminding Breckinridge of elementary matters: to keep his command resupplied with ammunition without waiting for it to be exhausted, to send inspectors back to press every man to the front, to keep ordnance wagons within reach, to be sure his brigade commanders knew his position. At ten o'clock, he told Breckinridge that he had heard that some of his breastworks were too high, which would cause defenders to fire over the heads of the oncoming enemy. Either the works should be lowered or fire steps should be built, Lee said. As a postscript, as if he realized that Breckinridge might be insulted by such basic instructions, he thanked him for "the gallant manner in which your command has maintained its position."[15]

BEHIND LEE, the city of Richmond had come awake in the predawn dimness to the loudest cannonade ever heard from the many battles on the outskirts. Concussion from shell blasts was still rattling windows there at eleven o'clock, when Postmaster General John H. Reagan of Texas appeared at Lee's headquarters to find out what was happening. Riding from the capital with Judges W. H. Lyons and John A. Meredith, he found the general at his tent at the Gaines's Mill farm, attended by a single orderly.

Reagan had fought Indians out west and had served in Richmond since the day it became the Confederate capital, so he was familiar with the noise of battle, but he had never heard anything like this. He asked whether the artillery was especially active.

"Yes," Lee told him, "more than usual on both sides," but "that does not do much harm here." Then, beneath and between the boom of cannon, came the rippling sound of musketry. "It is that that kills men," Lee said, waving toward the front. At that moment, Grant's troops were assaulting Confederate lines at three places, with columns of troops six to eight deep, he added. Reagan wanted to know what reserve he had, in case the enemy broke through.

"Not a regiment," said the general, biting off each word. "That has been my condition since the fighting commenced on the Rappahannock. If I shorten my lines to provide a reserve, he will turn me; if I weaken my lines to provide a reserve, he will break them."

While he had the ear of a cabinet member, Lee took the opportunity to make clear that his army was thin not only in numbers. His soldiers had to march and fight without rest; their meager and monotonous rations included no vegetables; they had to dig in the woods for roots and wild grape buds, and these did not come close to meeting their needs. Some soldiers were suffering from scurvy. Lee asked Reagan to see the stubborn commissary general, Lucius B. Northrop, and urge him to send the troops potatoes and onions.

Reagan agreed, but he had more to say. He was as concerned for the commanding general as for his soldiers—not because Lee had been ill, but because he might have been foolhardy. Reports of his conduct at the Wilderness and Spotsylvania had high-ranking civilians worried that he was exposing himself too much in battle. Judges Lyons and Meredith had noticed that he made his headquarters in the open, rather than in the cover of nearby trees. Couldn't he do his duty just as well from farther back?

Lee told them that when shells began to fall too close, he had ordered scattered quartermaster, commissary, medical, and ordnance wagons back under shelter of the woods. But he needed to be near the front. "I have as good generals as any commander ever had, and I know it," said Lee, "but still it is well for me to know the position of our lines." For example, he said, in forming his present front, he had directed that the right should cover Turkey Hill, from which artillery could sight over the Chickahominy lowlands. But this was not done, so on Thursday afternoon, he had to order Breckinridge to retake the hill, "an assault which cost us a good many men."

Reagan headed back to the capital, impressed that though Lee "was situated in the midst of a great battle, he was calm and self-possessed, with no evidence of excitement," thinking only of his men's needs and of defending the capital.[16]

As the postmaster general left, Lee dispatched a message to President Davis: "So far every attack of the enemy has been repulsed." But he was still desperate for reinforcements, and again he looked south of the James. His men had taken prisoners from the Union Eighteenth Corps, which confirmed that Grant had weakened Butler's force there to strengthen his attack at Cold Harbor. Lee sent this evidence to Davis, saying, "No time should be lost if reinforcements can be had." Davis promptly ordered another brigade sent to Lee despite Beauregard's protest that this would mean abandoning some of his lines. But that brigade would not depart Beauregard's command until early the next day.[17]

BEFORE REAGAN visited Lee and his single orderly, Grant had joined Meade at Sixth Corps headquarters at Cold Harbor. Among those watching was the correspondent William Swinton, whose eavesdropping had angered Grant early in the campaign. Now, wrote Swinton, "The fate of the day was like the aspect of the heavens above—mingled light and shade, a clear issue nowhere. . . . Would the assault be renewed?" He saw no answer in Grant's "face of stone—a Sphinx face."

Swinton thought that "nothing . . . could be more striking than the contrast presented by the two commanders, as they stood in consultation on that bare hill, with their faces turned Richmond-ward." Grant, shorter, slightly stooped in the shoulders, with his sunken eyes and reserved, impassive expression, stood beside the tall, nervous, emphatic Meade, whose complexion seemed "as of antique parchment."

The generals' tone, Meade's tension and Grant's apparent lack of it, said to those watching that the conversation was indecisive. Grant broke it off by suddenly mounting his horse and riding toward the front to see corps commanders Hancock and Wright. His senior aide, Comstock, went to consult with Smith and inspect his front. When Grant returned, said Swinton, "it was plain there would be no renewal of the battle, for we all rode leisurely back to the old camp occupied the night before."[18]

That was about noon. At 12:30, Grant lifted responsibility off Meade's shoulders.

"The opinion of corps commanders not being sanguine of success in case an assault is ordered, you may direct a suspension of further advance for the present," he wrote.

"Hold our most advanced positions, and strengthen them. Whilst on the defensive our lines may be contracted from the right if practicable. Reconnaissances should be made in front of every corps, and advances made to advantageous positions by regular approaches," which meant digging zigzag trenches toward the defensive works.

Grant said that it was necessary to hold all of Lee's force in place to aid the Shenandoah Valley offensive by Major General David Hunter, who had replaced Sigel and was marching south. And to do this, it was better to keep Lee's army outside the Richmond fortifications rather than inside, where they could defend the city with fewer troops. Finally, Grant instructed that "Wright and Hancock should be ready to assault in case the enemy should break through General Smith's lines, and all should be ready to resist an assault."[19]

An hour after Grant's message, Meade issued a circular order that "For the present all further operations will be suspended."

As if to remind the staff officers who had read Grant's message that he himself still commanded the army, Meade reworded the general-in-chief's orders: "Corps commanders will at once intrench the positions they now hold, including their advanced positions, and will cause reconnaissances to be made with a view to moving against the enemy's works by regular approaches from the advanced positions now held. Should the enemy assume the offensive and succeed in breaking through any point of our line, the corps commanders nearest the assaulted point will throw their whole force upon the enemy's column, making the attack."[20]

Thus the generals declared the climax of the battle and the campaign to be officially over. But along the lines fighting went on, because the armies were so close to each other that they could not let go. Mortars, and cannon set up as mortars, lobbed shells onto the trenches and the supply camps and command posts beyond. Sharpshooters climbed trees to look for unsuspecting targets at gaps in the opposing works. In between, thousands of Union soldiers held the ground they had taken, embracing it as closely as possible.

SINCE THAT morning, men who were there and historians to the present day have differed among themselves over whether Meade's soldiers would not, or simply could not, obey his repeated orders to resume the attack. The survivors of the attacking regiments lay among their dead and wounded comrades, most within shouting distance of the watchful defenders. Hiding behind stumps and in any slightest depression of ground, they used bayonets, spoons, and fingernails, trying to scrape their way deeper into the earth. In the jumble of blue-clad bodies, anyone seeming to be unhurt was likely to be picked off by the Rebels. A badly mangled man of the Twelfth New Hampshire "was seen to forever end his sufferings, that he could no longer endure, by deliberately cutting his throat with a jackknife." The idea that soldiers in such a fix might rise in broad daylight and advance in the gunsights of eager expert marksmen could issue only from the minds of others far back of the lines. Meade, insulated as he was from the sight and sound of battle, had told his army to press on. But somewhere between him and the men cowering on the field, those orders lost their way.[21]

Swinton later wrote that Meade's orders to renew the attack were issued through corps commanders to their subordinates, "and from them descended through the wonted channels; but no men stirred, and the immobile lines pronounced a verdict, silent, yet emphatic, against further slaughter." However, there is serious doubt about how far the army commander's orders proceeded on the normal course from corps to division, through brigade and regiment, to the men trapped between the lines.[22]

Hancock reported that "The major general commanding was anxious that I should renew the attempt, if practicable, but I did not consider it wise to make another assault, if the matter was left to my judgment." As Meade had told him at 7:40 a.m., it was left to his judgment, and so Hancock did not order another attack.[23]

Colonel Clinton D. MacDougall reported that his brigade of Barlow's division could not carry the Rebel works, but held its position before them for three and a half hours, until it was flailed by canister from the front and both flanks. At that, "the Brigade broke & fell back in confusion. . . . All efforts to rally them were without effect—that is the large proportion of them."[24]

The outspoken Baldy Smith was the only ranking officer who, by his own account, actually refused to obey an attack order, so presumably that one never went further down the chain of command in his corps. Some other commanders, at levels high and low, were not so blunt in their official reports, but they left little doubt about their response to what they considered an impossible order. They did not refuse; they simply did not obey. In most cases, the order never reached troops in the forward regiments. Merely delivering it down the chain, to where men lay pinned flat by Rebel riflemen, was too dangerous.

Wright's adjutant, Martin McMahon, wrote later that the series of messages in which corps commanders said they could not move unless their neighbors moved "necessarily caused mystification at headquarters." The resulting order for each corps to advance without regard to those alongside was "understood to be from Lieutenant General Grant," McMahon said—although it was signed by Meade.[25]

This understanding seems to contradict Meade's own assertion, in a letter to his wife, that "I had immediate and entire command on the field all day, the Lieutenant General honoring the field with his presence only about one hour in the middle of the day." That was the hour when Grant rode to the front and talked to the corps commanders, just before noon. But at 7:00 a.m., Grant had notified Meade that he was coming to him "in the course of an hour," and according to Swinton, an apparent eyewitness, the two were together at Wright's Cold Harbor headquarters as of 8:00 a.m., conferring at length before Grant set out on his reconnaissance. The Official Records show no dispatches at all between Grant and Meade from 7:00 a.m. until Grant's 12:30 permission to suspend the attack. Obviously, while the two were together, they talked rather than exchanging messages. And while they were together, Meade was issuing orders to renew the offensive.[26]

That fact helps clarify the question of who was pressing the attack—Grant or Meade. Meade issued the orders, but during those hours he was discussing the situation with Grant, and surely made no serious decision against Grant's advice. Thus McMahon and others had good reason for "understanding" that the orders came from the general-in-chief.

As Sixth Corps adjutant, working between army headquarters and the front-line regiments, McMahon was able to take in what happened as clearly as anyone. "Unity of action, so necessary to success, could certainly not be expected" from orders directing each corps to advance independently, he wrote. "The attack was made here and there by the advance of troops that had retired for shelter, and by merely opening fire from troops that had already reached obstacles which they could not surpass; and the corps commanders duly reported that the attack had been made and had failed."

When the order for a general assault all along the line came to corps headquarters a third time, said McMahon, it "was transmitted to the division headquarters, and to the brigades and the regiments without comment. To move that army farther, except by regular approaches, was a simple and absolute impossibility, known to be such by every officer and man of the three corps engaged. The order was obeyed by simply renewing the fire from the men as they lay in position."[27]

As on almost every other detail, there was disagreement over how long that morning's assault lasted. That evening, Swinton wrote that "into ten mortal minutes this morning was crowded an age of action. Ten minutes of the figment men call time, and yet that scant space decided a battle!" Some who were there said it took twenty minutes, some said thirty, some said an hour, some said all morning. The Confederates waiting in their works, except those who had seen the fury of Barlow's assault, could not understand that the worst of it was over so quickly. "It may seem incredible," wrote a Georgian with Colquitt's brigade. "I wouldn't believe it if I had not seen it, that we could kill so many hundreds with so slight a loss. After the enemy commence the charge they don't fire. . . .

"The troops we fought belonged to a great many different commands. Most of them were troops who have been doing duty about Washington, Alexandria and Baltimore. Many of them were heavy artillerists, and all the 'city officers,' 'stay at home soldiers' and skulkers in the army. Grant's policy of fighting makes it necessary that we should have relief in loading and firing."[28]

The written testimony of how this could happen lies in the messages from Union corps commanders, each insisting that he could not press on unless the corps beside him advanced, too. As McMahon said, those messages "caused mystification at headquarters," no doubt because they came from usually reliable generals. They were not merely excuses, efforts to pass responsibility for failure to the next commander on line. They were accurate statements of the situation.

Because the Confederate front made a long, slight crescent, outreaching the Union lines at both ends, it drew the assaulting forces apart as they advanced. To go at the defenses directly ahead, the attacking corps and divisions had to angle away from the commands alongside, like spokes of a wheel whose hub was somewhere east of Cold Harbor. As they continued, this opened wider and wider gaps between them. By the time they charged the Rebels, each command was slashed by cannon and musket fire not only from straight ahead but also from one or both of its open flanks.

This situation was repeated on a smaller scale at what the Confederates expected to be the most critical point of defense. There the concave front was drawn intentionally—the horseshoe that General Law created when he repositioned the line above the ravine the Yankees had penetrated earlier. There the Rebels cut up the attackers with merciless fire from three sides.

Confederate artillery, some pieces boldly sited in gun pits jutting out from the main defensive works, took advantage of the curving line to fire across the front and into the flanks of the advancing Federals. And the skillful way the defenders used each ridge, creek, and clump of trees made irregularities that were not imposing to the eye confusing and deadly to the attackers.

To attack such a formidable defense "all along the line," without detailed reconnaissance, without specific objectives, and without a follow-up plan, was an act of colossal misjudgment. By the time Grant called off the attack, that was clear to every general and every private. They understood what had happened, and after belatedly inspecting the field, the generals understood how. Now, some in outrage, some in puzzlement, some in shame, they tried to understand why. But to soldiers deepening their trenches and clutching the earth between the lines, the first question was whether they would survive.

The killing was far from over.

11

All a Weary, Long Mistake

SOMETIME AFTER the Florida brigade drove the Yankees out of the Confederate works on Friday morning, Joe Finegan encountered Jubal Early back of the lines. "General," said Early, "allow me to congratulate you, sir; your brigade has made quite a reputation. . . ."

"Beg pardon, Jinneril," said the Rebel from Ireland. "You are mistaken. They are only sustaining it, sor."[1]

Finegan was easily caricatured: short, dapper, flourishing his native brogue, a jaunty man who often crossed the line between convivial and bibulous. In this case, he had something to strut about. His men's performance in action was much better than their bumpkin appearance when they joined the Army of Northern Virginia. "If they did have on bed-quilts and homespun jackets, they made a reputation here that morning that proved they were as good as the best we had in our army," wrote one of the veteran Floridians who was already with Lee when the newcomers arrived.[2]

Now the Confederates looked out over fields where "men lay in places like hogs in a pen—some side by side, across each other, some two deep, while others with their legs lying across the head and body of their dead comrades." Occasionally there was a cry for help, or a white handkerchief waved by a hiding survivor who wanted to surrender rather than be shot in the back trying to escape to his own lines. During a lull, a squad of defenders took a chance on running out to bring in a handful of captives. The prisoners' faces "were red, streaked with perspiration, dirt and powder, and the Rebs behind with bayonet set, urging them to the rear," wrote artilleryman Hatton. "A prisoner was an unchallenged passport to the rear, and there were many to covet the opportunity."[3]

Finegan's men were keeping an eye on soldiers of Barlow's and Gibbon's Union divisions who had taken cover in the holes that Confederate pickets left when the Federals advanced at first light. Some of these Yankees had managed to scoop out new rifle pits less than a hundred yards from the defenders' main breastworks. While surviving attackers were hiding from Rebel riflemen along most of the front, the fact that Breckinridge's original breastworks bulged slightly outward now put Finegan's Confederates under harassing fire from three sides. The Yankees there, crouched on the field among their wounded and dead comrades, were in a vengeful mood. Though pinned down in holes and behind stumps, they had the advantage of aiming upward at the defenders along the ridge, while the Confederates had to stand in their trenches to fire down at them. When the Federals shot away a Rebel flag above the works, they dared the defenders to raise their "rag" again. Occasionally the Yankees shouted out a command, as if they were about to charge again, which brought Confederate heads popping up like targets in a shooting gallery.[4]

By 10:00 a.m., the frustrated attackers had had five hours to recover from the shock of their repulse and dig in. About that time, as Meade was still prodding Union generals to continue their attack, Finegan decided that his Floridians had to retake the picket line before them.

Finegan was not up with his men in the recaptured works, where they were sweltering without water because they had left their gear behind when they rousted out to charge the Yankees at dawn. Messages from his command post to the regiments were passed by word of mouth or handed from man to man. When the order came forward for company commanders to detail every fifth man for a skirmish line to take back the picket holes, the troops could hardly believe it. Then came another order, naming Major Pickens Bird to command this effort, then another saying that at Bird's order, company officers would see that the designated men moved out as skirmishers.

A few minutes later, Bird's command rang out above the background of gunfire: "Attention skirmishers! Forward march!"

Lieutenant Henry W. Long of the Ninth Florida recalled that "It [was] self evident that obeying that fool hardy order, by whom issued is not known, would result in certain death," so many of those supposed to go forward stayed put. When those in Captain Robert D. Harrison's company failed to move, the captain jumped onto the breastworks, waving his sword to inspire them. A sharpshooter's bullet promptly knocked him down. Major Bird started forward, leading his skirmish line; he advanced hardly thirty steps before he was struck by fire from the picket holes and the main Union line. Captain James Tucker leaped forward and ran to Bird. As he lifted him in his arms, he too was shot. Lieutenant Ben Lane went over the works and picked up Bird; returning with him, the lieutenant was hit and mortally wounded.

Bird and Tucker lay in a shallow trench beneath the glowering sun until the firing let up. Then Sergeant Peter N. Bryan and two other soldiers crawled out and dragged them into the works a few feet at a time. That night, litter-bearers carrying them back for medical help had to drop the stretchers and lie flat beneath bursts of Yankee fire. Bird died in Richmond within days, and Tucker was disabled for further service. Finegan's order to retake the picket line had produced nothing but more casualties.[5]

THIS BRIEF flare-up was part of the continuing rumble of cannon and sputtering of muskets, one fracas among many, each hardly noticed by other troops up and down the front. Neither Grant nor Lee mentioned it in reporting the morning's fighting. But surely Grant had some idea of the scale of his army's losses, if not the numbers, by the time he reported to Washington at 2:00 p.m.:

> We assaulted at 4:30 a.m. this morning, driving the enemy within his intrenchments at all points, but without gaining any decisive advantage. Our troops now occupy a position close to the enemy, some places within 50 yards, and are intrenching. Our loss was not heavy, nor do I suppose the enemy to have lost heavily. We captured over 300 prisoners, mostly from Breckinridge's command.[6]

In fact, the Army of the Potomac had lost about seven thousand men in the ill-fated attack, roughly five times more than the Army of Northern Virginia, which lost fewer than fifteen hundred that morning. Considering this, Lee's 1:00 p.m. report to Davis was a model of restraint:

> ... So far every attack of the enemy has been repulsed. His assaults began early this morning, and continued until about 9 o'clock. The only impression made on our line was at a salient of Gen Breckenridge's position, where the enemy broke through and captured front of a battalion. He was immediately driven out

with severe loss by Gen Finnegan's brigade & the Md. Battalion, and the line restored. . . .[7]

Still, casualties mounted, a handful in a skirmish over a line of picket holes, a few when a well-placed mortar shell plunged into the rear ranks, and one after another picked off by sharpshooters of both sides.

In the afternoon, Jeff Davis and his military adviser, General Braxton Bragg, rode out to see Lee. So did Colonel Josiah Gorgas, Confederate chief of ordnance, and assorted other officials from Richmond. Gorgas and those with him "had scant time for observation," he wrote, because rounds from Union sharpshooters about seven hundred yards away were whistling closer and closer. He was impressed by the Confederates' triple line of breastworks—they "have acquired quite a respect for this sort of entrenchment, and work like beavers when they take up a new position. They began the war with a contempt for the spade, but now thoroughly believe in it."

When Gorgas found Lee and Davis close to the front, the general cautioned him not to go near the lines, because with his blue cape he might be shot by either side. Lee said he would prefer that Gorgas survive and send him more ammunition. Gorgas promised him a Whitworth gun, and later kept his promise. He said Lee and the president were "in excellent spirits, and agreed that the Yankees' loss that morning must have been enormous."[8]

THE SHARPSHOOTING that made Gorgas so nervous also disconcerted veteran troops long familiar with less personal killing by mass attacks and artillery bombardments. At Cold Harbor, where the lines were so close together and so many targets lay in between, the particular skill and temperament of the trained sniper may have been more intensively employed and more feared than anywhere else in the war. Artilleryman Robert Stiles wrote that "the regular sharpshooter often seemed to me little better than a human tiger lying in wait for blood." David Geer of the Florida brigade thought more kindly of the sharpshooters: "If you held up your hand you could get a furlough."[9]

Some of the marksman's deadliness depended on his choice of weapons. The renowned Berdan's Sharpshooters used Sharps breech-loading rifles; to join that regiment, an applicant allegedly had to place ten consecutive shots within a five-inch bull's-eye at two hundred yards. In trained hands, the .45-caliber Whitworth rifle reputedly could put twenty rounds in a thirty-one-inch bull's-eye at eleven hundred yards. A few specially made target rifles, with heavy barrels and telescopic sights, weighed from twenty-five to thirty pounds and were even more accurate.[10]

Resting the muzzle of his weapon on something solid like a fork cut from a sapling, the sharpshooter would fix his sights on a chosen spot in the enemy line. Often he aimed at a narrow gap in the opposing works, or a hole where an artillery gunner had to lean to sight his piece. Holding a steady bead on that spot, the shooter waited until a face appeared at the hole or a body darkened the gap, then squeezed off a round. At first, soldiers in the works had no thought of getting hit at such long ranges. Then, after seeing some unwary comrade's brains blown out, they kept their heads low and stayed away from those gaps, digging deeper down and farther back, honeycombing the surface with trenches and traverses.

Especially accurate sharpshooters could be such a threat that a whole battery opened fire to silence a single marksman. On Kershaw's front, Lieutenant D. J. Griffith of the Fifteenth Alabama took ten men creeping into the underbrush to watch an enemy position while another Rebel waved a blanket at an exposed place to draw the fire of a bothersome sniper. Spotting the Federal in a tall gum tree, the detail slipped closer and sighted in at him. "No sooner had his gun flashed than ten rifles rang out in answer and the fellow fell headlong to the ground. . . . Beating the air with his hands and feet, grasping at everything within sight or reach . . . at last he strikes the earth, and with a terrible rebound in the soft spongy needles Mr. 'Yank' lies still. . . ."[11]

LATE IN the afternoon, Joe Finegan ordered another attempt to push skirmishers out ahead of the front retaken by his brigade. The Yankees had reversed and strengthened the defenders' original picket line, keeping the Floridians under pesky fire from the field as well as from the main Federal works. For the troops involved, that made this second effort ordered by Finegan just as suicidal as the one that had failed in the morning. This time, most of the skirmishers came from the Second Florida, a regiment worn down to company size by heavy losses at and after Gettysburg.

Captain C. Seton Fleming, still nursing two wounds from the Wilderness, commanded this skeleton regiment. He protested Finegan's order, but it was repeated. When his men heard it, they balked, some "remonstrating against it as an egregious folly coming from a greenhorn." Fleming sent a note, passed hand to hand down the trench line, to the commander of the Eighth Florida, asking how his troops felt about going out. The Eighth was no more eager than the Second, but it "would go if called upon."

Fleming had been wounded while trying to rescue a wounded soldier at Williamsburg in 1862, captured, and exchanged in time for Second Manassas. Now, at twenty-five, he was strict but popular with his troops, beloved for what they had been through together. He called on that affection as he stood on the works and made a little speech, saying he was ordered to go and was going, and asking them to follow. He said that this was very likely the last order he would ever give them. As he did, one of his men called out, telling him to get down, he was too exposed. Fleming said that didn't matter, it was only a difference of a few moments. He handed his heirloom watch, his pocketbook, and his personal papers to a regimental surgeon, a friend of his family. Then he drew his sword, said, "Goodbye, boys," and stepped out toward the enemy.

He fell when he had barely started, thirty or forty yards ahead of the works. So did most of the men who went with him. Fire from the Yankees was so furious that those who survived and fell back could not bring in their captain's body.[12]

To Fleming's men, the operation seemed a useless sacrifice, but they could not see the whole thing. On the Floridians' right, Breckinridge's Virginians had also pushed out, with their general watching. He had ridden up with his teenage son, both sitting their horses within view of Yankee snipers. Teasingly, Breckinridge said to the boy, "Look out there, Cabell, that fellow came pretty near getting you that time!" Seconds later, the general's horse reared and toppled, its leg broken by a cannonball. Breckinridge fell to the ground, then managed to rise. Stroking the horse's neck until the animal was calm, he drew his pistol and shot it. Later he reported that "a satisfactory line of skirmishers has been established." The bruises he suffered in the fall would keep him out of the saddle for a few days, during which Brigadier General Gabriel C. Wharton would command his division.[13]

BETWEEN SUCH bloody morning and evening excursions, the tactical situation up and down the front had reversed itself. Except on its far right, the grand Union offensive had turned into a defensive excavation project, with picks, shovels, and bayonets as busy as cannon and muskets. By the time Meade issued his 1:30 order halting further offensive action, the all-out attack had already ground down in fields strewn with Federal casualties.

On the Union right, Burnside had sent a brigade to try to turn the flank of Henry Heth's Confederate division, but it was forced back by scorching artillery fire. Heth mounted a local counterattack, and Burnside was trying to organize another effort when he got Meade's order to desist. "I think it was fortunate we were not allowed to advance," he reported.[14]

Farther to Burnside's right, James Wilson's cavalry got around behind Heth's flank after clashing with Confederate horsemen at Haw's Shop. But his effort came to nothing, and he backed off before getting a wishful late-evening message from Meade that urged him to keep going. Wilson's venture made so little impression on Jubal Early that Early suspected the cavalry probing that end of his line might have been friendly riders, throwing a few shells at Heth's position by mistake.[15]

When Meade queried his corps commanders about prospects for the following day, Warren, Baldy Smith, Wright, and Hancock all were pessimistic. Warren said that with Birney's borrowed division filling out his line, he could hold his own, but he had reservations about his right, left, and center. Smith said he was "intrenching myself as rapidly as possible," but "I can only say that what I failed to do today—namely to carry the enemy's works on my front by columns of assault . . . I would hardly dare to recommend tomorrow with my diminished force." Wright said that "the result of an attack would in my judgment be doubtful," especially without adequate reconnaissance, which was impossible under the circumstances. Hancock said Gibbon's front brigade had fought off one counterattack (a Rebel effort to push out a picket line) but that he expected others and "would feel more secure if I had some reserve. . . ."[16]

At about 6:00 p.m., Meade dispatched Colonel Lyman to find out whether Warren could contract his line enough to let Birney's division return to Hancock. Lyman found Birney, "with his usual thin, Puritanic face, very calmly eating tapioca pudding as a finish to his frugal dinner." But he had trouble finding Warren, who had, his staff said, "ridden out along the lines."

"Confound that expression!" wrote Lyman. It conjured the "delightful vision of a line of two miles or so of breastworks with the infantry safely crouched behind, and you perched on a horse, riding down, taking the chance of stray shot, canister, and minie balls, looking for a general who probably is not there." When eventually he found Warren, he wished he hadn't. He looked "care-worn," Lyman said: "Almost all officers grow soon callous in the service . . . unaffected by the suffering they see. But Warren feels it a great deal," and he showed it.

He told Lyman, "For thirty days now, it has been one funeral procession, past me; and it is too much! To-day I saw a man burying a comrade, and, within half an hour, he himself was brought in and buried beside him. The men need some rest. . . ."[17]

About the same time, a mile southwest of Warren's headquarters, Yankee skirmishers pushed against the thin lines held by Confederate general Pickett. According to Pickett's wife, Sally, who often lent unlikely eloquence to her husband's published correspondence, he made time to write her about the long day past. He recalled how Lee had once been nicknamed "Old Ace of Spades" because of his belief in building breastworks. That morning, Grant had assaulted six miles of Lee's works, and "The whole Confederate line poured a stream of fire, and thousands of Grant's soldiers have gone to reenforce the army of the dead.

"Oh, this is all a weary, long mistake," said Pickett, who still mourned the devastation of his division eleven months earlier at Gettysburg. "May the merciful and true God wield power to end it ere another day passes!"[18]

BY 8:45 P.M., Lee was able to report to Richmond what had happened in each sector of the line—that the enemy had been "repulsed without difficulty. . . . met with great steadiness and repulsed in every instance. . . . repulsed with loss," everywhere except temporarily on Breckinridge's front. Summing up, Lee said, "Our loss to-day has been small, and our success, under the blessing of God, all that we could expect."[19]

He had won the day, but he did not know yet whether he had won the battle. In less than a month, his troops had inflicted roughly as many casualties on Grant's force as Lee had men in his whole army when the campaign began at the Rapidan. Yet the Federals were still there in front of him, nine miles from the Capitol in Richmond, and they still outnumbered the Confederates facing them by about two to one. Grant and Meade still had the power, in numbers and guns, to mount another major attack. Whether their soldiers, or the generals themselves, still had the will to try it was another matter.

By the calendar, only eight days had passed since Grant had confi-

Heading South.
U. S. Grant, at left, obscures George Meade as he leans to inspect a map during a council of war at Massaponax Church.
(LIBRARY OF CONGRESS)

On the March.
Artist-correspondent Edwin Forbes caught the dogged attitude of Union troops as they trudged south, some carrying foraged hams and chickens, others drying laundry on their rifles and bayonets.
(LIBRARY OF CONGRESS)

George G. Meade.
The victor of Gettysburg was unhappy about Grant's decision to make his headquarters in the field with the Army of the Potomac, and his face showed it.
(NATIONAL ARCHIVES)

U. S. Grant.
The new Union general-in-chief still looked determined at Cold Harbor, after the Confederates had fought off his monthlong series of assaults.
(NATIONAL ARCHIVES)

Robert E. Lee.
By 1864, the Confederate leader had aged drastically since the first year of war. He was plagued by illness during the spring campaign.
(LIBRARY OF CONGRESS)

Yankees Could Dig, Too.
One of Grant's key mistakes was ordering his infantry to delay above Haw's Shop, rather than pushing past Lee immediately after crossing the Pamunkey River.
(FORBES. LIBRARY OF CONGRESS)

Winfield Scott Hancock
(LIBRARY OF CONGRESS)

Gouverneur K. Warren
(LIBRARY OF CONGRESS)

Horatio Wright
(NATIONAL ARCHIVES)

Ambrose E. Burnside
(LIBRARY OF CONGRESS)

William F. "Baldy" Smith
(NATIONAL ARCHIVES)

Lee Loses Patience.
*After repeated pleas for Beauregard to send
reinforcements from below the James, Lee
warned of disaster after learning that Grant
was bringing troops from that front.*
(BATTLES AND LEADERS)

Gul J G Beauregard
Hancocks House —

At Lees 7½ P. M. 30 May '64

If you cannot ~~determine~~ what troops be you
can spare the Dept cannot — The result ~~will
be disaster~~ of you delay will be disaster —
Butlers troops will be with Grant tomorrow

2 7/3 40 Ofp

R E Lee

Richard H. Anderson
(LIBRARY OF CONGRESS)

Jubal Early
(U.S. ARMY MILITARY
HISTORY INSTITUTE)

A. P. Hill (NATIONAL ARCHIVES)

The Bucktail's Last Shot.
*This sharpshooter of the famous "Bucktails"
(13th Pennsylvania Reserves), picked off at
Bethesda Church on May 30, might have gone
home with his regiment the next day.*
(FORBES. LIBRARY OF CONGRESS)

Sheridan (NATIONAL ARCHIVES)   *Keitt* (MUSEUM OF THE CONFEDERACY)

The Cavalry Holds.
*Union horsemen under Philip Sheridan defended Cold
Harbor against a June 1 attack led by South Carolinian
Lawrence Keitt, killed in his first serious combat.*

Sixth Corps Attacks.
*After a long, hot approach march, Wright's Union troops
pierced the Confederate lines late on June 1, but could not
follow through.*
(FORBES. LIBRARY OF CONGRESS)

Richmond Howitzers.
*William L. Sheppard, who
became Virginia's foremost
genre painter, caught men
and horses of the famous
Confederate artillery battalion at the peak of action.*
(NATIONAL ARCHIVES)

"Now Show What We
Can Do."
*Colonel Elisha Kellogg,
leading his 2nd
Connecticut Heavy
Artillery, fell before the
Confederate works.*
(LITCHFIELD HISTORICAL
SOCIETY)

Cold Harbor Tavern   June 3rd
                                            1864

Cold Harbor.
Thousands died in the struggle over this
undistinguished old crossroads, critical because
it controlled movement in five directions.
(FORBES. LIBRARY OF CONGRESS)

(BATTLES AND LEADERS)

Death from the Sky.
ABOVE: *Union mortars and Confederate cannon rigged as mortars dropped high-angle fire behind each other's lines.*
BELOW: *Troops like these in Hancock's sector tried to protect themselves from such fire by building earthen roofs for their works.*

(FORBES. LIBRARY OF CONGRESS)

(ALFRED WAUD. LIBRARY OF CONGRESS)

The Grand Climax.
Francis Barlow's division crashes into the Confederate lines on June 3, penetrating the sector held by Virginians under former U.S. vice president John Breckinridge.

Breckinridge (LIBRARY OF CONGRESS)

Floridians Plug the Hole. *Joseph Finegan's brigade, along with a smaller Maryland unit, counterattacked to drive the Federals out. Later, Capt. Seton Fleming knew he was going to his death when ordered to retake Finegan's picket lines.*

Finegan
(LIBRARY OF CONGRESS)

Fleming
(MUSEUM OF THE CONFEDERACY)

The Union Spearhead.
*General Hancock (seated) and his division
commanders (left to right)—Barlow,
David Birney, and John Gibbon—still
seemed to swagger, even after their terrible
losses in the assault.*
(NATIONAL ARCHIVES)

Looking for a Friend.
Troops could not find and bury fallen comrades until four days after the climactic fight, when Grant and Lee finally worked out a brief cease-fire.
(BATTLES AND LEADERS)

Moving On.
Grant, on horseback at left center, and Hancock, seated nursing his old Gettysburg wound, were sketched by William Waud as they watched the Second Corps cross the James on June 14.
(LIBRARY OF CONGRESS)

The Wages of War.
Shortly after Appomattox, workmen and soldiers
retrieved the remains of hundreds of soldiers on the
Cold Harbor battlefield.
(LIBRARY OF CONGRESS)

dently advised Washington that "Lee's army is really whipped. The prisoners we take now show it, and the action of his army shows it unmistakably." From that day on the North Anna to Cold Harbor, Lee's army had shown Grant that his optimism was expensively premature. Indeed, by now the feeling of being "really whipped" was more true of Grant's men than of Lee's. As Lyman observed, "The best officers and men are liable, by their greater gallantry, to be first disabled; and, of those that are left, the best become demoralized by the failures, and the loss of good leaders; so that, very soon, the men will no longer charge entrenchments and will only go forward when driven by their officers."[20]

Some Confederates maintained that Union troops going into the grand assault that morning had called on external help to bolster their inner will. Kinloch Falconer, an adjutant serving with the Army of Tennessee, quoted an official dispatch from Richmond saying that the Federal assault had been "renewed several times with fresh troops, many of whom, it is said, were drunk." This apparently was based on reports from front-line troops, like those from Finegan's brigade: U. H. Hane wrote that "Many of the Yankees had whisky in their canteens"; Captain Council Bryan said "the Yankees had plenty whiskey aboard, some of them were staggering along and nearly fell over the breastworks," and Colonel David Lang added that some of the captives were "under the majic influence of old rye." A correspondent in the Forty-fourth Alabama told of capturing a lieutenant colonel from Massachusetts who was "considerably intoxicated, in fact all the prisoners had liquor in their canteens." The same was heard from the Second Maryland Battalion.[21]

Many Federals did indeed take on whiskey as they headed into the fight, knowing that they might not survive. Edward Pendleton, of the Twenty-seventh Massachusetts in Martindale's division, wrote that "we had large rations of whiskey given out" during Thursday night's rainfall, and Union soldiers' diaries often tell of welcome rations of rum. The idea that the Yankees had to be drunk to attack as they did was more acceptable to the defenders than the possibility that they were brave enough to do it sober. And finding alcohol on a few Federals could stir stories that they all had to be bolstered by artificial means, rumors comparable to the one saying that Meade used black soldiers in the attack.[22]

Several Confederate accounts make this assertion, for example the history of Kershaw's command: "Negro troops were huddled together and forced to the charge by white troops—the poor, deluded, unfortunate beings plied with liquor until all their sensibilities were so deadened that death had no horrors." It is likely that individual black soldiers, teamsters, cooks, and orderlies employed by Union officers did appear at the front, but not in organized units. Meade's army still had only Ferrero's two brigades of U.S. Colored Troops, and on that Friday one of these was camped on the ruined plantation of the famed pro-slavery agitator Edmund Ruffin, near the Pamunkey River, while the other was with the supply trains back of Cold Harbor.[23]

As DUSK DEEPENED, Grant's staff officers gravitated to the general's tent to talk about bloody Friday and the days ahead. By then, in that company, Grant was more realistic than in the afternoon, when he had reported to Washington, "Our loss was not heavy."

"I regret this assault more than any one I have ever ordered," he admitted to the colonels and generals around him that evening. "I regarded it as a stern necessity, and believed that it would bring compensating results; but, as it has proved, no advantages have been gained sufficient to justify the heavy losses suffered."

He tried to rationalize what had happened by looking back at his western experience: His early assault on Vicksburg, he said, was not successful, either, but it had taught his troops that they could not take that Confederate stronghold without laying siege. The frustrated attack there was "the means of making them work cheerfully and patiently afterward in the trenches, and of capturing the place with but little more loss of life." Without that learning experience, the men would still have believed that they could take the city "by making a dash upon it which might have saved them many months of arduous labor, sickness and fatigue."[24]

If anyone present dared suggest that Grant had just tried precisely that kind of unrealistic dash at Cold Harbor, it was not noted by Horace Porter, the aide who reported the conversation. Nor did anyone say, at least in Grant's presence, that if he considered this day's attack another instructive failure like the one at Vicksburg, the price of the lesson had been exorbitant. No one had to.

That night, Union troops were busy between the lines, but the possibility that the morning's frustration might make them dig "cheerfully" could exist only in Grant's imagination. Pioneers came up with axes and shovels to build breastworks, try to straighten the front, and run connections between forward regiments and the rear. Musicians and ambulance corpsmen rustled about in the dark, groping to find men crying for help. The slightest noise, a cracked twig, might bring a shot from the enemy works so close ahead. Pleas for water came out of the gloom. Officers with orders for the morrow crawled about trying to find their way from one headquarters to another. "It was well nigh impossible to take a step without treading upon some human being, either alive or dead," wrote a soldier in the Twenty-first Connecticut.[25]

Behind the Confederate lines, one artilleryman counted ninety bullet holes through a pup tent used by Callaway's Georgia battery. Callaway himself, though several times wounded, did not leave the field; his clothes looked "as if he had been dragged through a briar patch." His field glasses were smashed and the trigger guard of his pistol shot away. The bronze Napoleons of one Virginia battery "looked as if they had smallpox, from the striking and splaying of leaden balls against them." In another battery, a gun was put out of action when every spoke of both wheels was hit by enemy fire.[26]

Wrapped in darkness, some soldiers softened toward enemies they had tried to kill in daylight under the gaze of their officers. "Calls all night long could be heard coming from the wounded and dying," wrote a South Carolinian; "one could not sleep for the sickening sound 'Water' ever sounding and echoing in his ears. Ever and anon a heartrending wail as coming from some lost spirit disturbed the hushed stillness of the night." Here and there, Southerners unable to stand the pitiable cries of victims close at hand slipped out to bring wounded Federals to safety. In the rifle pits ahead of the Maryland battalion, two Confederates and two Yankees had dived into the same hole at the same time. Small-arms fire was too hot for them to raise their heads to go either way. Rather than grappling in hand-to-hand combat, they agreed that whichever army held that portion of the line at nightfall could claim the other pair as prisoners. When Rebel skirmishers took the pits after dark, the Marylanders brought the Federals in as their personal captives. James Thomas, who set down this incident in his diary, also told a tale of two opposing soldiers trapped in the same hole who played cards until dark, when the Confederate claimed the Yankee loser as his prisoner.[27]

Since early in the war, killed, wounded, and captured enemy soldiers had been a major source of resupply for sparsely outfitted Confederates. As long as sharpshooters could see a target, Rebels did not risk venturing onto the field of Cold Harbor to strip Union casualties of coats, boots, weapons, and greenbacks. A Georgia officer wrote that when nearby Confederates were told not to waste ammunition by firing so much, one soldier complained that if they let up, "the Yanks would come and get all the forage—that is would rob the dead Yankees of all that was valuable which our speculative friend was unwilling to see done." Despite the firing from both sides, the temptation was strong, and after dark, Tom Paysinger, of the Third South Carolina, set out from his lines. He had been detailed earlier as a scout, so those who watched him suggested that he could have been searching for intelligence as well as for booty. Creeping across the field, he rifled the pockets of fallen Yankees until one of the bodies that seemed dead raised up and shouted, "You d—n grave robber, take that!"—and let go a shot at close range. The slug hit Paysinger in the thigh, crippling him for months.[28]

Repeatedly, shots by nervous pickets and local efforts to reestablish picket lines set off firefights that flared into booming exchanges, lighting the night. Troops on both sides later mistakenly reported these as serious offensives by the enemy. Henry Bird, with the Twelfth Virginia in Mahone's division, wrote to his beloved that one Yankee attack on Friday evening lasted forty-five minutes, involved fifty thousand rifles, and was thrown back with fifteen thousand Union casualties against fewer than a hundred Confederate losses. Lyman, somewhat more realistic, described one of the scrapes as "a fierce attack" by the Rebels. In repulsing it, soldiers of Gibbon's division showed a spark of spirit that was rare along the Federal line that night. "Come on!" they shouted. "Come on! Bring up some more Johnnies! You haven't got enough!"[29]

Lyman thought that nothing could convey grim tenacity of purpose better than "the picture of these two hosts, after a bloody and nearly continuous struggle of thirty days, thus lying down to sleep, with their hands almost on each other's throats! Possibly it has no parallel in history. So ended the great attack at Cool Arbor."

Some Union officers still wanted to believe that the day was a series of unsuccessful blows by both sides, indeed that the Federals had a marginal advantage because they had moved their lines closer to the enemy. But others realized that they had lost many times more soldiers than the Confederates, and the conclusion was inescapable. As Lyman wrote, "We gained nothing save a knowledge of their position and the proof of the unflinching bravery of our soldiers."[30]

That fact had taken longer to sink in at headquarters than on the battlefield. There, between the lines, one of the Union soldiers whose bodies were recovered by their comrades had scrawled a final entry in his blood-smeared pocket diary: "June 3, Cold Harbor. I was killed."[31]

12

You Kneed Not to Be Oneasy

THE UNPREDICTABILITY with which death carried off one soldier and spared the next moved Charles M. Miller of the Richmond Howitzers to take out an insurance policy: on the field of Cold Harbor, he had himself baptized from a rusty tin cup by the Reverend William Page, an Episcopal priest. Perhaps as a result, he would live on past Appomattox. Others sought more tangible protection, deepening their holes and creating bombproofs against missiles falling from the sky.[1]

As Federal infantry and pioneers edged their trenches forward under cover of darkness, Yankees manning little Coehorn mortars spent the night adjusting their range. The Coehorns, weighing 296 pounds complete, were portable by four men, so they could be set up anywhere close behind the lines. When Saturday morning came, one of them "opened upon us with mathematical precision and deadly slaughter," wrote a soldier of the Florida brigade. By then, Confederate troops could tell when mortar fire was coming their way. They could hear the *poof* when the stubby tube sent its missile aloft, a rounder sound than the report of standard artillery weapons. They could watch the seventeen-pound shell rise—in daytime, "it would look like a rubber ball going through the air," and at night "like a small ball of fire."

The Yankees "could elevate those short pieces just a little toward us from straight up, and drop those old death-dealing shells almost in on our ditches," wrote another Floridian. If the fuse was cut a little too long, he said, the shell would bury itself, then burst, making a hole in the sandy soil as much as waist-deep and three or four feet across. If it burst above ground, it threw slashing fragments for yards about. "The boys called them 'Demoralizers.' And they were demoralizers, too! For a man to sit behind a bank of earth and hear one of these old mortars belch, look up and see the shell going up toward the skies until out of sight, knowing that it was going to come down and perhaps burst in the air just above the ground and the instruments of death send hither and thither over a line of helpless men—such surely was demoralizing."[2]

Mortar rounds might drop in at any time, and so might artillery shells from either side, fired from cannon whose trails were lowered into ditches, thus raising the muzzles for a high angle of fire. This field expedient had been used earlier in the war by Confederates trying unsuccessfully to knock down Union observation balloons. Plunging fire was effective against entrenched troops, and so was used much more as the armies edged closer to each other. It motivated harddigging soldiers to start laying logs and earth above their trenches for overhead protection. Cramped in their works, unable to lie down to sleep, to walk out or stand erect, men lived through "night alarms, day attacks, hunger, thirst, supreme weariness, squalor, vermin, filth, disgusting odors everywhere." As the sun climbed, sharpshooters of both armies were back at their trade. They struck at such extreme ranges that sometimes troops heard a thud and looked up to see a comrade fall, but never heard the shot.

Amid this kind of tension, a Richmond Howitzers ambulance corpsman who was fondly nicknamed "the Old Doctor" suddenly announced that he was going to the spring for water. His friends argued against it, but he insisted, so they loaded him with their canteens. When one urged him at least to take a covered route, he said, "I can't do it, Adjutant. It is dirty; a gentleman can't walk in it, sir." Striding upright, he made it to the spring and had started back when his mates saw him stumble, but he regained his balance and returned to the works. Handing his captain a cup of water, he apologized for spilling part of it; a sniper's round had cut off the upper joint of his thumb. Then he apologized to the adjutant for disregarding his warning, but repeated that a gentleman simply could not walk in "those filthy, abominable covered ways."[3]

WHILE MEN in the lines were trying to preserve their souls, their bodies, and tiny scraps of dignity, those who could find a quiet moment were trying to put what had happened into perspective. In conversation, in their diaries, and in letters to friends and family, they tried to make sense of it. Whether they expressed anger or pride, optimism or foreboding, depended not only on which army they served in, but very much on which commander they served under. Every soldier, except Lee and Grant, could point to someone above.

Arthur Simms was an aide to his brother, Colonel James P. Simms, who had taken over Bryan's Georgia brigade late Thursday. He wrote to his sister that "Our troops are in excellent spirits and perfectly confident. They want no easier task than to whip the Yankees when they have works to fight behind. Grant I think has displayed but very poor Generalship thus far. . . . He will never take Richmond with his present force and if he continues to fight as he has been fighting, it will not take Gen. Lee's army thirty days longer to destroy his whole force. . . . He will get his troops so demoralized that they will not fight at all after awhile."[4]

William Brotherton of the Twenty-third North Carolina told his family, "I have bin shot threw my clothes in three differance places sceince this fight commence I was shot threw the side into my shirt and the owther side was shot two and also in my pants But never tech the skin so that is anuf on that I will tell you we are slaying the yanks like flys. I think we will gain the day we are in Brest works and still fortifying ever day we give them A complete whipin yestoday. . . . you kneed not to be oneasy About our side I think grant will get A complete whippin. I think this fight will close the war. . . ."[5]

Such thoughts might have been expected from any Confederate soldier after that gory Friday. But at Cold Harbor, as at no other battle except perhaps Fredericksburg, the letters of many Union troops conveyed gloom and bitterness, and the bitterest words came from officers whose units had suffered most.

Emory Upton, with whose brigade the Second Connecticut Heavy Artillery had charged to near-destruction on June 1, would confine his official report of the Friday action to a single cold sentence. But in writing to his sister, he let himself go: "I am disgusted with the generalship displayed. Our men have, in many instances, been foolishly and wantonly sacrificed. Assault after assault has been ordered upon the enemy's intrenchments, when they knew nothing about the strength or position of the enemy. Thousands of lives might have been spared by the exercise of a little skill; but, as it is, the courage of the poor men is expected to obviate all difficulties. I must confess that, so long as I see such incompetency, there is no grade in the army to which I do not aspire." The next day, still anguishing, he wrote that the June 1 assault had been "murderous," that "Some of our corps commanders are not fit to be corporals. Lazy and indolent, they will not even ride along their lines; yet, without hesitancy, they will order us to attack the enemy, no matter what their position or numbers."[6]

General Wilson would write that "there can be no doubt that the real fighting men of the army held the views which Upton expressed." In this outburst, Upton did not name the general or generals with whom he was so disgusted. Those above him included Russell, Wright, Meade, and Grant, and he may have meant all four, but his assertion that he was qualified for any rank, however high, suggested that he was aiming beyond his own division.[7]

"I would give a great deal to know if this mode of attacking works is Grant's or Meade's idea," Warren's artillery chief, Colonel Wainwright, mused in his diary. "The orders come to us from Meade, but I cannot think it is his, having the opinion I have of his ability as a general." The follow-up order for each corps to attack without coordinating with its neighbors "looked as if the commander, whoever he is, had either lost his head entirely, or wanted to shift responsibility off his own shoulders," Wainwright wrote. The newspapers constantly credited Grant for successes, but "here we see nothing of General Grant; I hardly hear his name mentioned. . . . Whoever is responsible for this extended mode of attack [all along the line] is getting no military credit, nor the love of the men who are about used up by it."[8]

Whenever criticism turned toward Meade, loyal Pennsylvanians were there for support. One of his staff officers, James Biddle, wrote to his wife that what the newspapers were reporting was "preposterous," because they "represent Lee's army as demoralized & in full retreat for Richmond. . . . The rebel army fight desperately, and have contested heroically every inch of ground. They have fallen back, because they have been outflanked, but in no case has it been a disorderly retreat with our army on their heels. . . . The stories in the papers about Grant's doings are perfectly preposterous. They speak of his riding along the lines night and day, personally superintending the operations of the Army. He does nothing of the kind, he leaves everything to Genl Meade, whom I consider as far superior as a general. . . . Genl Meade's only fault is his irritability, which does not affect him as a general, but only exasperates the unfortunates who are so unlucky as to be the cause of his ire. He was in a very bad humor yesterday."[9]

But Biddle was wrong to brush off the idea that Meade's irritability might affect his generalship. He told his wife that during Friday's fight Meade had been annoyed by the fact that two of his staff officers were away from headquarters without his specific approval, so when they returned, he sent them on a meaningless and perhaps dangerous inspection mission. Meade also had ordered his entire staff to be mounted and ready to ride out with him at 4:30 a.m. Saturday, for no apparent purpose. He already had a standing order for them to be ready every morning at daylight, Biddle said, adding, "I get up and dress myself, but I do not dare to eat my breakfast before eight or nine o'clock." The angry disposition of the commanding general of the Army of the Potomac affected his relations with his subordinates, sometimes crushing any enthusiasm to carry out his orders. It also, importantly, affected his relations with the general-in-chief, not in face-to-face conversation, but in the frustration that ground away inside Meade.[10]

WHEN NIGHT FELL, both sides threw out more pickets than usual to guard against surprise and encroachment where the lines ran so close together. John Haley of the Seventeenth Maine was among them, and said that "such dodging and ducking was enough to throw one all out of joint. The enemy seemed to be everywhere, and we didn't know which way to turn. Sometime after dark we were ordered in and told to report to our regiment, an almighty indefinite order, for we had no more idea of its whereabouts than we did as to when Queen Victoria last pared her corns."[11]

Between midnight and dawn on Saturday, Jubal Early drew his Confederate corps back from the lines above Bethesda Church to which he had driven Burnside's troops on Thursday. Extended that way, he would have been vulnerable if the Federals had mounted a flank attack stronger and more determined than the nighttime gesture made by Wilson's Federal cavalry. Resettled in the works they had left on Thursday, Early's troops now faced generally northeast rather than southeast, still connecting with Anderson's corps on their right. At the same time, Lee transferred Heth's division from Early's sector to rejoin A. P. Hill's corps. Farther right, Confederate engineers laid pontoons at one Chickahominy crossing and hastened work on another close behind the front, to be ready in case the Federals tried to get at Richmond between the Chickahominy and the James.[12]

Even before learning that Early had pulled back, Meade was continuing to strengthen the Union army at the southern end of the front. At 7:15 a.m., he had issued orders for Birney's division to return to Hancock's corps, for Warren to swing back along Matadequin Creek, and for Burnside to withdraw behind Cold Harbor, "prepared to move in support of any part of the line that may require it." Then, when he heard that Burnside's and Warren's pickets had found Early's lines empty, Meade changed these orders, causing temporary confusion when he bypassed his chief of staff, General Andrew Humphreys.[13]

He was thinking now of defense, not offense. The Fiftieth New York Engineers were busy building artillery emplacements and lashing together about three hundred gabions—cylinders made of saplings and filled with earth—and rolling them into place, mostly in front of Hancock. Meade warned that Early's move was "either to mass for an attack somewhere on us, or they are withdrawing beyond the Chickahominy. . . . we had better get ready for receiving attack as soon as possible." When the confusion with Humphreys was cleared up, Burnside moved south into the gap between Warren and Smith that was created by Birney's departure. This shortened the main Union line by nearly a mile on the north, leaving Warren with an unguarded stretch between that flank and Wilson's cavalry.[14]

Late Saturday morning, while these shifts were being organized, Meade and a cluster of staff officers went calling on the corps commanders closest at hand. He started with Hancock, where conversation was limited by the roar of a nearby battery. In that sector, where the struggle had been fiercest, Union artillery fought heavy but inconsequential duels in late morning and early afternoon against the cannon massed on Lee's right.[15]

From Hancock's command post, Meade moved on to see Wright briefly, and then to Smith. There he found a headquarters tent much grander than his own, and was invited to a champagne lunch that "quite astonished" his staff. Whether these visitors were agog at Smith's luxury or offended by such ostentation is not known. But Meade voiced no objection; he stayed on past mealtime, talking and smoking with his host, while occasionally a Rebel round shot crashed through the trees or ricocheted across the field in front.

Lyman, an inquisitive scientist in civilian life, was fascinated by the way those artillery shells went "hoppity-hop." As he waited for Meade, he noted that from the proper angle, potential victims could see the rounds coming and going, watch them pass "with a great *whish*, hit the ground, make a great hop, and so go skip, skip, skip, till they get exhausted, and then—*flouf*—raising a puff of sand." That, he reasoned, was why round shot were more dangerous than conical shells, "which strike perhaps once, vault into the air with a noise like a catherine's wheel, topple over and over, and drop without further trouble."

After several hours, General Burnside appeared at Smith's tent, probably in search of Meade, and this broke up the luncheon party. Smith, and perhaps others present, had held a grudge against Burnside since his disastrous generalship at Fredericksburg eighteen months earlier. Thus, according to Lyman, "they don't speak now"—a situation hardly helpful to coordinating an army in combat. But, he said, as the generals went their separate ways, "we enjoyed the military icicle in great perfection!"[16]

BACK OF GIBBON's lines, beyond the reach of sharpshooters, assistant surgeon John G. Perry of the Twentieth Massachusetts stopped work briefly, exhausted, to let his wife know that he was still all right: "I have not had a moment to write for nearly a week. It has been fight, fight, fight, and every day the hospital is again filled. For four days now we have been operating upon the men wounded in one battle, which lasted only about two hours, but the wounds were more serious than those from former engagements. I am heartsick over it all. . . ."[17]

Perry's was by no means the most damaged regiment in the two major attacks on Lee's lines. It lost only nine killed and twenty-six wounded, hardly enough to keep him as busy as he described. In raw numbers, the huge converted heavy artillery regiments suffered most—the Seventh New York lost 418 and the Eighth New York 505 in the first two weeks of June. Those totals included many missing, left on the field, who would later be found dead. By Saturday, when Perry wrote to his wife, he and his colleagues were treating wounded from throughout Hancock's corps, which lost 3,510 men in those two weeks.[18]

Thomas A. McParlin, chief surgeon of the Army of the Potomac, reported that a total of 2,125 casualties were brought into field hospitals Wednesday, June 1, most of them from Wright's Sixth and Smith's Eighteenth Corps. On Thursday evening, after Meade ordered up a full issue of rations from White House, the army's emptied supply wagons were turned over to the medical service for use as additional ambulances. Some 2,107 casualties were brought in that day. As Friday morning's great assault was tapering off, McParlin dispatched a wagon train carrying 2,177 patients to White House. Later Friday, the army's hospitals received another 2,980, mostly from Hancock's Second

Corps. McParlin estimated then that eleven hundred Union soldiers were left on the field because they were "completely covered by the enemy's sharpshooters."

By this spring of 1864, the Federal medical service was thoroughly organized. More than three years of experience, enormous resources, and the tangible support of civilian groups such as the Sanitary and Christian commissions had overcome the tragic shortcomings of early campaigns. At Cold Harbor, Baldy Smith's corps had arrived from south of the James without its supply, ordnance, and medical trains, but Warren, Wright, and Burnside were so well stocked that they were able to share with him. Still, Smith had no ample ambulance service, which often meant "2 or 3 soldiers leaving the ranks with each severely wounded man, and forgetting to return, while the roads and woods were lined with stragglers. . . ."[19]

Though White House was more than fourteen miles from the front, some of the walking wounded preferred making the trip on foot rather than being jostled and bruised in transit aboard springless supply wagons. Proper ambulances, rigged for at least a modicum of comfort, were reserved for the seriously wounded, of whom there were thousands. But William H. Reed, a nurse at White House, told of patients "being violently tossed from side to side, of having one of the four who occupy the vehicle together thrown bodily, perhaps, upon a gaping wound; of being tortured, and racked, and jolted, when each jarring of the ambulance is enough to make the sympathetic brain burst with agony. How often have I stood on the step behind, and heard the cry, 'O God, release me from this agony!' and then some poor stump would be jolted from its place and be brought smartly up against the wooden framework of the wagon, while tears would gather in the eyes and roll down over furrowed cheeks. And then some poor fellow would take a suspender and tie it to the wagon top, in order to break the effect of the jolting ambulance, as it careened from side to side. . . . And yet, as a class, these ambulance drivers were humane men. . . ."[20]

At White House, a depot hospital of about a hundred tents had already been set up by June 1. It stretched three-fourths of a mile along a flat spot by the Pamunkey, below the ruins of the plantation house that had belonged to Martha Washington before descending to the cavalryman Rooney Lee and being burned by the Yankees in 1862. In the first two weeks of June, 13,656 wounded and sick troops would be loaded aboard vessels that were still bringing supplies and reinforcements to Grant. Though about a thousand casualties departed each day, the hospital tents were continually full. An Ohio chaplain wrote that many soldiers had to lie in the sun or in ambulances for hours, waiting for surgeons to dress wounds infested with maggots. Some of the overloaded boats were outfitted as hospital ships, but most were freight vessels, their decks bedded with straw. Some wounded went directly on board from ambulances, without stopping to be admitted at the depot hospital. Crowded with ailing soldiers, a steady stream of these vessels headed down the Pamunkey and York, then up the Chesapeake and Potomac to general hospitals in and around Washington.[21]

For civilians in the Union capital, the sight of those casualties was the truest evidence of what was happening at Cold Harbor. Secretary Stanton's censorship and delay of the news kept timely details from other cabinet members as well as from the general public. On Saturday, as delegates to the Baltimore political convention bustled through Washington, Secretary of the Navy Gideon Welles wrote, "There has been continued fighting, though represented as not very important. Still there is heavy loss, but we are becoming accustomed to the sacrifice. Grant has not great regard for human life."[22]

No matter how well organized, the Union medical service could not ease the pounding of primitive transportation over roads jammed and rutted by unceasing army traffic. And back at Cold Harbor, the most efficient ambulance corps could not save casualties caught between the lines as long as expert marksmen kept them in their sights. Dr. McParlin, who had estimated on Friday that 1,100 were left on the field, reported that 1,701 were brought in on Saturday, and hundreds more still lay suffering. Virtually all of those rescued were pulled off during the hours of darkness. A few brave soldiers risked digging shallow trenches out to the wounded in daytime, for protection as they dragged comrades to safety. More lives could have been saved by asking to retrieve the wounded under a white flag of temporary truce, but this could be done only on orders from above, and no such orders were forthcoming.[23]

The number of wounded sent from Union field hospitals to the rear peaked on Saturday, when 544 wagons and ambulances headed to White House carrying 2,794 wounded and 161 sick Yankees. In the days following, the proportion of sick to wounded soared upward, causing McParlin to appeal to Meade for improved rations and sanitation. In thirty-two days since the crossing of the Rapidan, no vegetables had been issued, he said—and the army "has now reached a region of country notoriously miasmatic and unhealthy." The troops were using surface water "saturated with organic matter. . . . The ground around many camps is strewn with dead and decomposing horses and mules, and with the hides and offal of slaughtered beef cattle." Very few regiments had provided sinks (latrines), so "their excreta are deposited upon hill sides to be washed from thence into the streams." Thus sickness, especially diarrhea, was raging.

McParlin told Meade that vegetables should be "among the very first supplies brought up." He reminded him of what had happened to the Union army on the same ground in 1862: "Chickahominy fever may be in a great measure prevented, but when it has once occurred its subjects are lost to the army so far as this campaign is concerned." The vague, dreaded "fever," which may have been anything from malaria to dysentery to scurvy, had been talked about so much that it seemed to play on Union troops' minds as much as specific illnesses did on their physical health. "We are now near the sickly swamps of the Chicahominy, where the army of general McClellan, two years ago, had its repeated encounters with the enemy," wrote a soldier of the 120th New York. "The rays of the sun poured down upon us with unsparing fierceness, the water was poor, and sickness began to tell upon our ranks." Meade reacted quickly to McParlin's requests; quantities of vegetables arrived at White House, but most of the perishables were served in the hospitals there because the wagons going forward were loaded with marching rations.[24]

ASIDE FROM wounded Union soldiers, some of the wagon trains heading for White House carried Rebel prisoners taken in the first days of June. In the other direction, the Yankees captured by Lee's men slogged on foot to Belle Isle, Libby, and other improvised prisons in Richmond. George W. Bagby, capital correspondent for a string of Southern newspapers, described the prisoners brought from Cold Harbor as "the most hardened, beastly brutes the eye ever beheld—old in years and older in iniquity . . . these devils would have burnt our houses, cut our throats, ravished our women and murdered our babies . . . without a thought of remorse." Bagby was a fluent propagandist for the Confederate cause, and, like many civilians, he was verbally harsher toward the enemy than the soldiers who did the fighting. One of the Federal "devils" he described was disappointed when he arrived in Richmond, looking around and saying, "Wal! This is a darned sorry lookin' place to fight so much for."[25]

By then, it was. Although the city had suffered no structural damage from the repeated Union offensives that came so close, hunger had
made many of its citizens look sorry indeed. Jeff Davis had regretfully
sent his cat, "the companion of my nightly vigils in the interests of
Southern Independence," to friends out of the city because he could
no longer feed it. Commissary General Northrop was saying that Lee
must defeat Grant before more Union reinforcements arrived, "or we
are gone." Northrop feared that the Federals would destroy the railroads north and northwest of the capital—the Richmond, Fredericksburg & Potomac and the Virginia Central, the latter feeding the city
from the Shenandoah Valley. Indeed, Grant would soon give renewed
attention to that crucial line. But even as Northrop worried, supplies
to Lee's troops briefly improved over previous weeks because as the
enemy came closer, food from the countryside was transferred directly
from incoming trains to wagons headed for the front. That bypassed
Richmond's commissary warehouses, controlled by the argumenta-
tive, red tape–bound Northrop. Fat Nassau bacon, green onions, sugar,
and coffee made their way to the troops, who were so grateful that
some commands voluntarily sent provisions back to needy civilians in
Richmond.[26]

Lee himself had just been through the only major battle that his
Army of Northern Virginia had ever fought without his direct supervision. He had chosen to defend the Totopotomoy-Chickahominy
line, recognizing the importance of Turkey Hill, and had saved the day
by placing his only reserve where it was most needed. He had sent
a few orders directly to subordinates in the front lines, as when he
warned John Breckinridge, former vice president of the United States,
that his breastworks were too high. But Hill, Anderson, Early, and
officers down to regimental level had made tactical decisions on the
field while their commanding general was back at his tent nearly a
mile behind the fighting, just as blind to what was happening minute
by minute as was Meade across the lines.

Though Lee's illness had sapped his strength, his health was almost
back to normal, and he had abandoned the borrowed carriage to
remount his faithful Traveller. Now his spirits were up, too: his Friday
evening report that "our success, under the blessing of God, [was] all
that we could expect," was remarkably exultant, for him. His words
were restrained in victory because self-congratulation was alien to
him, but also because he understood the remaining situation better
than anyone. As the Federals neared Richmond, he had written to his

invalid wife in the capital, urging her to leave for some safer refuge. On Saturday, he wrote again, telling her, "It is evident that great danger is impending over us, & therefore those not required to meet it, or who might be overwhelmed by it should it fall upon us, should get out of harm's way in time." But Mrs. Lee was housebound, and her faith in her husband and his men was unshakable; in the first year of war, she had refugeed from place to place, and now she refused to move again.[27]

The general's own assessment of what could happen was based on more than faith. He knew how close the issue had been when the Federals made their temporary breakthrough, and he had some concept of how grossly they still outnumbered his army. He did not know what Grant and Meade would try next, but he knew that whatever it was, he would need still more troops to meet it.

GRANT REALIZED that he had just suffered the worst defeat of his career, and by his own example, he made Friday's battle a forbidden subject in his presence. After he admitted regretting the assault more than any he had ever ordered, "The matter was seldom referred to again in conversation," wrote his admiring aide, Horace Porter. "General Grant, with his usual habit of mind, bent all his energies toward consummating his plans for the future."[28]

Captain Charles Francis Adams, Jr., of the First Massachusetts Cavalry, grandson and great-grandson of presidents, watched the general-in-chief daily as an officer of the provost guard. "He has evidently been thinking hard," Adams wrote on Saturday. "Formerly he always had a disengaged expression in his face; lately he has had an intent, abstracted look . . . puffing at his cigar and whittling at small sticks. . . . In fact as he gets down near Richmond and approaches the solution of his problem, he has need to keep up a devil of thinking. . . . He always is repulsed when he attacks their works, and so are they when they attack him." Adams thought that the obvious best move would be to cross the James River and take Richmond from the rear, but "Grant seems to hesitate to do this and to desire to approach by this side."

This did not affect Adams's belief that Grant would eventually take Richmond—he thought he operated "on the apparent principle of trying everything, but leaving nothing untried." Adams was foresighted, predicting that wherever the campaign led, "the rebellion will feel the entire strength of the Government exerted to the utmost," and that no matter how Grant took Richmond, doing so would essentially destroy Lee's army, for "they will never again fight as they now do, when once that is lost." But the general-in-chief would not see that prediction come true for months to come. He must have been glad at the moment to shift his mind to responsibilities far beyond Cold Harbor—to Georgia, where Sherman was pushing toward Atlanta, and to the Shenandoah Valley, where Hunter was burning homes and barns as he marched south.[29]

Amid these concerns, Grant was so irritated by Confederate artillery on Saturday evening that he wrote to Meade saying, "It would be well to retaliate by opening every battery that bears upon them at 12:00 or 1:00 tonight. It will have the effect to wake up the whole of the enemy's camp and keep them on the watch until daylight." Meade replied that while this would keep the Rebels awake, their certain reply would keep his own army awake, and, besides, would interfere with the trenching forward that he had ordered. Grant seemed to shrug, answering that he had only wanted to repay the bothersome Confederates, and if doing so would hinder operations, Meade could forget it. But instead of forgetting it, Meade issued a circular order for each corps commander to do just what Grant had suggested, "if in his judgment it will not, by a retaliating fire from the enemy, cause as great annoyance and loss to our troops as to theirs, and if it will not interfere with the advance of the regular approaches ordered for tonight."[30]

Once again, Meade had demonstrated, at least to himself, that he and not Grant commanded the Army of the Potomac. And once again, he had passed responsibility to his corps commanders, this time to decide whether or not the artillery should vent the general-in-chief's frustration on the Rebels. After Hancock, Smith, and Wright exchanged messages, they decided that the army would rather try to get some sleep instead.

13

Like a Scene in an Opera

"My previous high estimate of Gen. Grant has been maintained and heightened by what has occurred in the remarkable campaign he is now conducting. . . ." So said Abraham Lincoln in his message to a New York political gathering on Friday, June 3, the day Grant's army was thrown back at Cold Harbor.[1]

The president spoke those words of support before news reached Washington about what had happened: Grant's first report on Friday, with the assurance that "Our loss was not heavy," was not sent until 2:00 p.m., and Charles Dana's message from Grant's headquarters to Secretary of War Stanton, on which the first official communiqué was based, did not reach Washington until 8:50 a.m. Saturday. In it, Dana said that Grant figured his Friday losses at about three thousand, less than half the actual figure. But even if Lincoln had been unaware of Friday's defeat when he restated his admiration for Grant, by that time he did know about the repulse of the Union attack on Wednesday: Dana's reports on that action had arrived Thursday evening.

Throughout the spring campaign, in his public utterances, the president had refused to mourn the mounting casualties. With Republicans heading for their nominating convention in Baltimore, he had good political reason to keep up the appearance of optimism. But ordinary soldiers of the Army of the Potomac did not depend on either Grant or Dana for news of what had happened around them, and politics was a minor factor in their opinions about their generals. The first wave of their reaction to such a defeat was all emotion, in conversation and in letters home. Then, in the next hours and days, those less painfully involved could be more analytical, and some tried to find out what had gone on in the minds of the commanders responsible. When put together, an insight here and a disclosure there would eventually explain what seemed to many soldiers, then and later, a reckless waste of life.

Captain Adams wrote that the Army of the Potomac had "literally marched in blood & agony from the Rapidan to the James. All of this fighting has been unsuccessful fighting—hard, brutal, barren pounding." Yet Adams had "great faith" in Grant, feeling that "he takes hold of his work as one having confidence in himself & not the least afraid of his adversary; he is bold & takes great risk, thus inspiring confidence in his army. . . ."[2]

Discerning though Adams was, his cool view was that of a headquarters officer, not a front-line private. He could hardly have felt so certain about the army's morale if he had read what David Coon, of the Thirty-sixth Wisconsin in Gibbon's division, told his daughter: ". . . no words that I can write can give you an idea of it. How would you feel to see your father lying in a ditch behind a bank of earth all day, with rebel bullets flying over his head, so that his life was in danger if he should raise on his feet, without a chance to get anything to eat . . . [then] running across an open field towards a rebel battery with rebel bullets, grape and canister, flying like hail, and men falling killed and wounded all about him, and finally . . . ordered to fall on our faces so that the storm could pass over us, and then be obliged to lie in that position until covered by the darkness of night so that we could get away, and then start on a forced march in the night without any chance to get any supper, and so weak that he could scarcely walk . . . to see him lie down in the dirt, and if allowed to stop for a few minutes, so exhausted as to fall asleep. . . . My dear daughter, your father may be lying dead on the field of battle and you may not know it. . . ."

The next day, Coon wrote to his son: "You complained of being tired, and no doubt do get so. I used to, but find that after all I knew but little about what the word meant until lately. . . . We now lie right in the hot sun behind our works, with bullets whistling over us. This morning one of our company was wounded and a man of another killed by the same shot from a sharp-shooter while attending a call of nature." (One Federal cannoneer said that among infantrymen, there was "an unwritten code of honor that forbade the shooting of men" at such moments, but "these sharpshooting brutes were constantly violating that rule. I hated sharpshooters, both Confederate and Union . . . and I was always glad to see them killed.")[3]

Between 1861 and 1865, countless soldier letters told the folks at
home that their sons and husbands were seeing gruesome sights but
were thus far unharmed. They advised wives about planting potatoes
and selling horses, and cautioned daughters against going to dancing
parties. Never would so many Union soldiers put aside this mask of
good cheer as they did huddling in their holes to write home from
Cold Harbor.

Adams understood generals better than he did lowly infantrymen
like Coon. "One can see that [Grant] believed in incessant fighting &
marching as producing necessary results not only on his own army but
on the enemy," he wrote. "If his army is fought & worked out &
exhausted & needs rest, it is not only likely that the enemy, with his
smaller numbers, is even more so, & so the moment of greatest
exhaustion becomes that of the greatest effort."

Adams was reading Grant's mind more clearly than many who have
tried from a greater distance. He guessed that the general's chances of
taking Richmond were three out of five, but that to do it, he would
have to cross the James and cut off Richmond and Lee from the south.
In repeating this prediction, he was far from alone: private soldiers
were saying the same thing, and Burnside's corps took prisoners who
said such talk was current among Confederate soldiers. Those on the
Union side were particularly motivated to move on: "The memories of
the Chickahominy are not pleasant to this Army," wrote Adams. "It is
not pleasant to be butted head foremost against such works of such an
enemy, & finally, we are already weary of that wretched, God & man
forsaken country of sand fields & pine barrens."[4]

General Wilson, who had come east considering Meade to be
"weak, timid and almost puerile," and later would write extensively
about the war, made a point of stopping at Meade's and Grant's headquarters when his cavalry was being shifted about. Meade, he recalled,
strode up and down, flicking his boot tops with his riding whip. He
was cordial, complimenting Wilson for his division's performance on
the army's flank. Yet he seemed on his guard; he was conscious of Wilson's long association with Grant and Smith.[5]

"Wilson," Meade asked, "when is Grant going to take Richmond?"

"Whenever the generals and troops in this theater all work together
to that end," Wilson replied.

He was surprised by the way Meade had emphasized the name
Grant, giving the impression that "it was Grant's special contract and
not that of his subordinates and their forces, as well." To Wilson, it
meant that Meade did not think any honors had been won so far that

were worth claiming, so "he was apparently willing Grant should have all the credit, along with all the responsibility."

Riding on to Grant's headquarters, Wilson tried to calibrate the degree of unhappiness he found there—"a different feeling, if not one of despondency." Grant was not downcast, but openly disappointed "at his failure to overwhelm Lee, and especially at the failure of his subordinates to whom the details of carrying his general orders into effect were left, to select proper points, form proper plans of attack, and, above all, to provide carefully for the contingency of success." This last meant having a support force poised to exploit any break-through.

"What is the matter with this army?" asked Grant.

"It will take too long to explain," Wilson replied, "but I can tell you how to cure it. Give Parker a tomahawk, a supply of commissary whiskey and a scalping knife and send him out with orders to bring in the scalps of general officers." Captain Ely S. Parker, Grant's adjutant, was a Seneca Indian.[6]

Grant was just then realizing, Wilson said, that "his general orders, instead of being elaborated and conscientiously carried into effect, as they should have been, were far too frequently transmitted to those below literally, without any special explanation whatever, and that the inevitable result would be to place the responsibility upon him." Wilson said that Grant's chief of staff, John Rawlins, and Dana, among others, agreed with this version. But both of them held Grant himself responsible for "the policy, if not the practice" of making head-on attacks against "entrenched and almost impregnable positions."

The next day, Rawlins and Dana visited Wilson and disclosed more about what went on inside Grant's headquarters. The sudden arrival of Warren interrupted this conversation; "he was far from happy or hopeful," Wilson recalled. After Warren rode on, Rawlins and Dana voiced admiration for Grant's steadfastness, but both of them spoke against "a certain baleful influence which had finally become paramount" within Grant's staff. Rawlins, his face "already pale and wan with disease, grew white with rage while he denounced the influence of Colonel Comstock."* The engineer officer, Rawlins said, "having won Grant's confidence, was now leading him and his army to ruin by senselessly advocating the direct attack, and driving it home by the deadly reiteration of 'Smash 'em up! Smash 'em up!' "[7]

---

* Rawlins died of tuberculosis in 1869, five months after President Grant appointed him secretary of war.

Rawlins's furious denunciation of Cyrus Comstock exposed the rivalry within Grant's staff, which had worsened as casualties rose and strong personalities asserted themselves. Rawlins, Grant's fellow townsman from Galena, had been close beside him for almost three years of war, and had become his intimate adviser as well as defender against the bottle, the latter an unofficial duty at which he apparently succeeded throughout the spring campaign. At one point, Grant called Rawlins "the most nearly indispensable" officer on his staff. Comstock had been with Grant only a year, but his service in the siege of Vicksburg had lifted him in the general's opinion as an expert on all engineering matters, especially on assaulting strongly defended positions.

Rawlins and Dana told Wilson that Comstock's repeated urging to "Smash 'em up!" "embodied the pernicious idea which had taken possession of Grant and done all the mischief." Rawlins said it was "almost impossible to neutralize [Comstock's] influence." The two men implored Wilson to rejoin Grant's staff, where he had served as engineer and inspector general before moving east and becoming a cavalry commander. But Wilson, then the junior brigadier in the army, reminded them that while he was willing, he could not transfer without orders from above. He could only promise his support, while urging Rawlins to stand firm "as he had always done in the great emergencies of Grant's life."[8]

LEE, WITH HIS skeleton staff, did not have to worry about infighting at his headquarters. But on Sunday, June 5, even as Grant's troops dug their way toward his works, he got news that would soon diminish his overstretched army. In the Shenandoah Valley, Union general Hunter was driving south. Responding to calls for help, Lee told Davis that the only force he could send to the Valley was Breckinridge's thin division. He was pulling back those two brigades, worn down to about 2,100 men, and fitting Mahone's division into the Cold Harbor line to replace them. Lee was reluctant to let go of even Breckinridge's small force, because he was still unsure what Grant would do next.[9]

From the start of the spring campaign, the Union commander had hoped to catch the Confederates out of their works for a stand-up battle that would favor the heavier force, but Lee stubbornly refused to cooperate. Assuming that Grant would not simply go away after paying so much to come so far, the Union commander still had four possibilities: to keep inching toward Lee's present lines and try another head-on rush from close quarters; to swing back to his right, moving to cut the Virginia Central and drive on Richmond from the north; to cross the Chickahominy on the Union left and go at Richmond between that river and the James; and to cross the James to join Butler and besiege the Rebel capital from the south. Lee's only realistic option was to wait and watch for Grant to commit himself one way or another.

According to Comstock, Grant had spoken on Saturday of ordering another direct assault. But even Comstock was not enthusiastic; he had urged that the whole army march north to destroy Richmond's supply lines from the Shenandoah Valley, temporarily abandoning the base at White House if necessary. Meade, however, thought the cavalry could do that job while the army stayed where it was. "I don't think so, in any reasonable time," Comstock wrote in his diary, "and it seems to me that we are marking time here."[10]

Sunday morning, Meade's corps commanders sent reports of minimal progress toward Lee's works by "regular approaches." Hancock's men had pushed forward "some 15 or 20 yards." One of Wright's divisions had moved "about 40 yards," the others hardly at all. Warren said, "I was unable to make any advance during the night." Smith and Burnside were quibbling over the latest rearrangement of lines, Smith complaining testily and Burnside half apologizing for bothering him, so they gave little attention to digging.[11]

"The siege operations progress very slowly," wrote Charles Wainwright—"so slowly, indeed, that their progress is invisible." The Federal works were extending faster and farther backward, one trench behind another, than ahead toward the enemy. One Confederate who looked over the Union digs after the battle "was surprised to see what a short distance they were from ours, and how enormous and elaborate they looked in comparison. . . . At some points it really seems as if the Federal army had anticipated attack from every point, except the skies, and fortified against them all." Meade may not have expected much forward progress by digging, but the tactic served to hold Lee in place while Grant was making up his mind.[12]

Sometime that Sunday, Grant did. He wrote to Chief of Staff Halleck in Washington:

A full survey of all the ground satisfies me that it would not be practicable to hold a line northeast of Richmond that would protect the Fredericksburg railroad, to enable us to use it for supply-

ing the army. To do so would give us a long vulnerable line of
road to protect, exhausting much of our strength in guarding it,
and would leave open to the enemy all of his lines of communication on the south side of the James.

This suggests that he had considered, then eliminated the option of
extending the army to the right to go at Richmond from the north.
Grant continued:

My idea from the start had been to beat Lee's army, if possible,
north of Richmond, then, after destroying his lines of communication north of the James river, to transfer the army to the south
side and besiege Lee in Richmond, or follow him south if he
should retreat. I now find, after more than thirty days of trial,
that the enemy deems it of the first importance to run no risks
with the armies they now have. They act purely on the defensive,
behind breastworks, or feebly on the offensive immediately in
front of them, and where in case of repulse they can instantly
retire behind them. Without a greater sacrifice of human life
than I am willing to make, all cannot be accomplished that I had
designed outside of the city.

Grant thus admitted defeat of his major objective, to beat Lee's
army north of Richmond—blaming it not on his own strategy, but on
the Confederates' unwillingness to abandon their trenches and fight
on his terms. Therefore, he said, he would stay essentially where he
was while sending cavalry to destroy the Virginia Central for twenty-
five or thirty miles beyond Beaver Dam, near the northwest corner of
Hanover County. Then, he said,

I will move the army to the south side of James River, either by
crossing the Chickahominy and marching near to City Point, or
by going to the mouth of the Chickahominy on north side and
crossing there. To provide for this last and most probable contingency six or more ferry-boats of the largest class ought to be
immediately provided. Once on the south side of the James
River I can cut off all sources of supply to the enemy, except what
is furnished by the [James River & Kanawha] canal. If Hunter
succeeds in reaching Lynchburg, that [the canal] will be lost to
him also. . . .[13]

Grant ended this pivotal dispatch by asserting once again that he would beat Lee if only the Confederates would come out and fight. "The feeling of the two armies now seems to be that the rebels can protect themselves only by strong intrenchments," he wrote, "while our army is not only confident of protecting itself without intrenchments, but that it can beat and drive the enemy wherever and whenever he can be found without this protection." Night and day, his troops were demonstrating that they were not nearly as sure as their commander stated: engineers, cannoneers, and infantrymen were building fortifications even deeper than the Confederate works that had repelled them, in some stretches twelve or fourteen layers front to back.[14]

Soon after notifying Washington of his plans, Grant gave Meade instructions for a cavalry expedition more ambitious than the one he had described to Halleck. Sheridan was to break up the Virginia Central all the way to Charlottesville, then work along its branches toward Staunton and Lynchburg. "It is desirable that every rail on the road destroyed should be so bent or twisted as to make it impossible to repair the road without supplying new rails," Grant said. After that, Sheridan and Hunter would join forces and march together back to the Army of the Potomac. By then, between them, they would have destroyed Richmond's main supply line from the Rebel granary in the Valley.[15]

Dana had advised Washington that the necessity of cutting those railroads "will probably detain us here some days." Anticipating this delay, Meade moved to shorten and solidify the Union army's position as Sheridan prepared to take two of its three cavalry divisions away. Warren would pull back Sunday night into reserve behind Cold Harbor, and Burnside would create a new front south of Bethesda Church, facing north along a line reaching to Matadequin Creek. Smith would adjust his right to link with Burnside's changed position. On the left, Birney's division would extend Hancock's front farther toward the Chickahominy. Wilson's cavalry division would stay with the army, one brigade picketing from Burnside's right to the Pamunkey and another from Hancock's left along the Chickahominy.[16]

At nine o'clock Sunday evening, after ordering these shifts, Meade wrote to his beloved Margaret. "The sound of the artillery and musketry has just died away . . . ," he said. "I don't believe the history of the world can afford a parallel to the protracted and severe fighting which this army has sustained for the past thirty days." He believed that what had happened should prove that he had been right in not assaulting Lee's fortified positions the previous year at Williamsport (after Gettysburg) and Mine Run (along the Rapidan). "In every instance that we have attacked the enemy in an entrenched position we have failed," he wrote, "except in the case of Hancock's attack at Spottsylvania, which was a surprise discreditable to the enemy. So, likewise, whenever the enemy has attacked us in position, he has been repulsed.

"I think Grant has had his eyes opened, and is willing to admit now that Virginia and Lee's army is not Tennessee and Bragg's army. Whether the people will ever realize this fact remains to be seen."[17]

GENERAL GIBBON would write that those days in the trenches, when troops were "unable to obey a call of nature or to stand erect without forming targets for hostile bullets, and subjected to the heat and dust of midsummer, which soon produced sickness and vermin," were "the most trying period of a most trying campaign." While the Union army rearranged itself, officers in the works could hear the gradually weakening cries of soldiers still lying helpless between the lines. While the sun beat down, vultures circled and swooped low above the battlefield. A Rebel officer wrote that "The stench from the dead between our lines and theirs was sickening. It was so nauseating that it was almost unendurable; but we had the advantage, in that the wind carried it away from us to them."[18]

At 1:00 p.m. Sunday, Hancock had appealed to Meade: "Can any arrangement be made by which the wounded in front of Barlow can be removed?"

Meade was exquisitely aware of the protocol involved in such a situation. A day earlier, he had approved the dishonorable dismissal of Lieutenant Colonel M. C. Murphy of the 170th New York for sending a white flag to the enemy lines on the North Anna without permission from higher authority. Thus Meade forwarded Hancock's question to Grant: "Is it possible to ask, under flag of truce, for permission to remove the wounded now lying between our lines, and which the enemy's sharpshooters prevent me bringing off?"[19]

Grant answered that "A flag might be sent out proposing to suspend firing where the wounded are, until each party got their own. I have no objection to such a course." But Meade was not about to order this in his own name. He told Grant that "Any communication by flag of truce will have to come from you, as the enemy do not recognize me as in command whilst you are present."*[20]

Grant thus wrote to Lee:

It is reported to me that there are wounded men, probably of both armies, now lying exposed and suffering between the lines occupied respectively by the two armies. Humanity would dictate that some provision should be made to provide against such hardships. I would propose, therefore, that hereafter when no battle is raging, either party be authorized to send to any point between the pickets or skirmish lines, unarmed men bearing litters to pick up their dead or wounded without being fired on by the other party. Any other method equally fair to both parties you may propose for meeting the end desired, will be accepted by me.[21]

The wording of Grant's letter—"It is reported to me"—sounds as if he had been busy with larger matters and therefore had not realized until then that those wounded men had been lying helpless for more than two days. To deliver the letter, Meade called Lyman into his headquarters at 3:00 p.m. Lying on his cot with his boots cocked on the headboard, speaking casually, "as if asking for a piece of bread and butter," he said, "Lyman, I want you to take this letter from General Grant and take it by a flag of truce, to the enemy's lines. General Hancock will tell you where you can carry it out."

Lyman wrote that until then, his idea of flags of truce had been "chiefly medieval . . . associated with a herald wearing a tabard." But he accepted the order as if he had been running such errands since childhood, and promptly donned "store clothes"—sash, white gloves, and "all other possible finery." He could not find a bugler to blow the call to parley, so he set out with a cavalry sergeant and found Hancock, "reposing on *his* cot." Hancock told him that things were too hot to

---

* Colonel Oates of the Fifteenth Alabama wrote that on June 4, "A white flag was displayed and firing was suspended. A Union officer came half-way and met a Confederate staff officer, with a request from Major-General Augur for an armistice for six hours with permission to bury the dead. It was sent to General Lee, who returned it, saying that he did not know General Augur as Commander of the Army of the Potomac." Augur was not part of Meade's army; he was commander of the Union Twenty-second Corps, in the defenses of Washington. He would have been concerned for the Cold Harbor casualties because so many were in the heavy artillery regiments he had sent to the front, but he had no authority to ask for such a truce, and the author finds no mention of this incident in the Official Records. (William C. Oates, *The War Between the Union and the Confederacy*, p. 367.)

take the flag out just there, that he should try someplace farther to the left. The general assigned his own aide, Major William G. Mitchell, to accompany Lyman. They ripped up a pillowcase—a rare luxury in an army in combat, but apparently not around Hancock, who still insisted on that fresh white shirt each day. They tacked this makeshift flag to a staff, and Colonel Charles E. Hapgood of the Fifth New Hampshire found some whiskey to create good will with the Rebels. Then the delegation rode toward the left behind Barlow's lines, with Hapgood as guide.

As they started forward near Nelson Miles's brigade headquarters, another officer asked, "Do you know where you are going? There have been two field officers killed just here." Hapgood, who had a bullet hole through his hat, one through his trousers, and another through his scabbard, said jovially, "Yes *sir!* I *do* know where I am going. There's some bullets comes through here; but *none to hurt.*" They moved from one patch of woods to another, past a field bordered by trees infested by sharpshooters. Reaching the picket line along the road toward Barker's Mill, they shouted their mission to the Rebels less than two hundred yards away, and eventually a Confederate officer ordered his men to stop firing.

With the sergeant waving the white flag, the Federals walked out past the pickets and met a Rebel greeting party. To Lyman, it all "looked exactly like a scene in an opera," with the sun setting and two officers in gray standing before perhaps twenty of "the most gipsy-looking fellows imaginable." Lyman and Mitchell introduced themselves to Major Thomas Wooten of the Eighteenth North Carolina, and they agreed to call a cease-fire along that half mile of front while the parley went on. Then they waited while a Confederate messenger tried to find General Lee, who was away from his headquarters.

Amid the "positively frightful" aroma of dead cavalry horses, they sat and had a friendly chat with Wooten, whom Mitchell described as "a good fellow." Lyman later wrote that "I am free to confess that the bearing of the few Rebel officers I have met is superior to the average of our own." They were earnest and slightly reserved, which he attributed to the hardships they and their homes had suffered, and to "a sense of ruin if their cause fails. We attack, and our people live in plenty, with no one to make them afraid; it makes a great difference. . . ." Mitchell reported that the Confederates "all expressed themselves as extremely desirous that the war should terminate. I think the hard knocks we have given them this campaign has a little sickened them of the 'Yanks.' "

While they waited and evening fell, an artillery salvo ripped into Hancock's corps headquarters, where Mitchell otherwise would have been. Taking their example from the parley group, nearby pickets of the two sides decided to declare their own truce, and climbed out of their holes to talk and swap until officers ordered them back. Soon afterward, a squall of musket fire swept too close across no-man's-land until those officers ran out to stop it. Not until about 11:00 p.m. did a Rebel lieutenant bring word that the Federal party need not wait longer, that Lee would send his response via the pickets. When Lyman got back to Meade's headquarters, the general said, "I thought perhaps the Rebs had gobbled you up."[22]

Lee's reply, when it came, said that he feared the arrangement proposed by Grant would "lead to misunderstanding and difficulty." Instead, he suggested that whenever either side wanted to bring off its dead or wounded, it should send a flag of truce, "as is customary." As far as circumstances allow, he said, "It will always give me pleasure to comply with such a request."[23]

Neither Lee nor Grant had to say what both men knew—that by long tradition, sending out a white flag to ask permission to collect casualties was an admission of defeat. That is why soldiers who did so without authority risked drastic punishment, though they intended an act of mercy. That is why Lee, who had very few wounded men between the lines, insisted on proper protocol. And that is why Grant, when he sent another message Monday morning, June 6, seemed to misunderstand what Lee had said.

The Union commander told Lee that he would order men immediately, "as you propose," to bring in casualties, and would allow the Confederates to do the same. He suggested that this be done between noon and 3:00 p.m., adding, "I will direct all parties going out to bear a white flag, and not to attempt to go beyond where we have dead and wounded, and not beyond or on ground occupied by your troops."[24]

Lee promptly responded, saying, "I . . . regret to find that I did not make myself understood." He had not consented to removing casualties as Grant proposed; he meant that "when either party desire such permission it shall be asked for by flag of truce in the usual way. Until I receive a proposition from you on the subject to which I can accede with propriety, I have directed any parties you may send under white flags as mentioned in your letter to be turned back."[25]

This was hairsplitting, but the distinction was serious. To Lee, what was "customary" and "usual" did not mean merely permitting colonels and captains to show white flags and retrieve casualties in their sectors. It called for the commanding general of one army to send a formal request by flag of truce to the commanding general of the opposing army, asking for permission to bring in the dead and wounded. To Grant, that meant conceding what every soldier in both armies could see but had not yet been absorbed in Washington and beyond: that he had been decisively beaten in the climactic battle of the bloody spring offensive, his first campaign as general-in-chief.

At 4:50 Monday afternoon, Major Mitchell put out a flag and passed to Major Wooten another message from Grant. This time, Grant gave in, saying, "The knowledge that wounded men are suffering from want of attention, between the two armies, compels me to ask a suspension of hostilities for sufficient time to collect them, say two hours." Whatever time Lee suggested would be acceptable, and the Confederates would be allowed the same privilege.[26]

This letter reached Lee at 7:00 p.m., when he wrote to Grant that he regretted that it was too late to give orders to allow collection of casualties by daylight. Nevertheless, "in order that the suffering of the wounded may not be further protracted," he had ordered that it be allowed between 8:00 and 10:00 p.m. At that time, Confederate pickets were drawn back and a few rescue parties went out from Lee's lines. Union pickets, not notified of any truce, captured eight North Carolinians who were looking for the body of their colonel. They were later released on Grant's orders.

But once again, the slowness of communications across the lines, in falling darkness, up and down the chain of command, was costly to the stricken. Lee's message got to Hancock too late, at 10:45, three-quarters of an hour after the period specified, and reached Grant's headquarters between 11:00 p.m. and midnight. Through another night, a few individual Yankees crept out, trying to find and drag in wounded comrades, but most of the suffering still lay untended. With each hour, the cries for help became fainter and fewer.[27]

GRANT, WHEN he called off the great Union offensive at midday Friday, had told Meade that he wanted to hold the entire Rebel army in place so Lee could not detach troops to oppose Hunter's march up the Shenandoah Valley. But the way the Federals shortened their front and repositioned their corps on Sunday encouraged Lee to make a decision that a less assured general would not have considered.

On Monday morning, Lee heard that Hunter had routed W. E. "Grumble" Jones's skimpy Confederate force at Piedmont, near Port

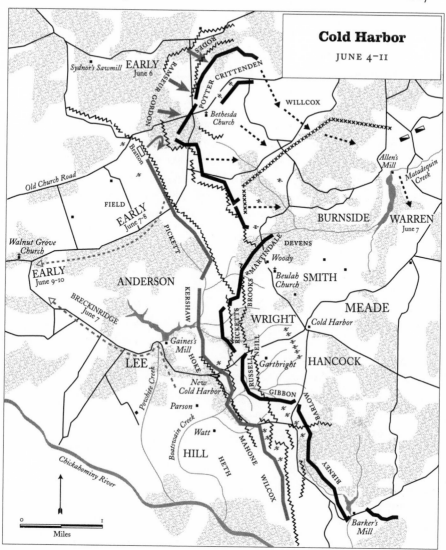

Cold Harbor

JUNE 4–11

Troops under Hancock, Wright, and Smith inch forward, digging into no-man's-land strewn with Union bodies. Warren and Burnside, pressed by Early, pull back into a tighter defensive position. Early then withdraws into Confederate reserve while Breckinridge departs for the Shenandoah Valley.

Republic in the Valley, killing Jones, capturing about a thousand Rebels, and moving on toward Staunton. Slashing and burning, the Federals were threatening to cross the Blue Ridge and march on the important rail and supply point of Lynchburg. At the same time, Lee heard that Union troops had disappeared from Early's front and Anderson's left.

The new Federal line bent back away from Kershaw's position, near the center of the long line, and then turned farther back toward Allen's Mill. Testing it, General Field had sent out patrols from his division at dawn and found the previous Union works abandoned. A little later, Early's skirmishers pressed all the way down in front of Pickett and Field without striking any force more substantial than pickets. Early wanted to keep going, and wished he had cavalry available to scout ahead; he had not heard from Wade Hampton for two days.[28]

Though Lee was still concerned that the Federals might be throwing their weight across the Chickahominy, their new lines looked to him like a purely defensive arrangement. Thus, late Monday morning, he was less reluctant to send help against Hunter. He wrote to Davis that "some good officer should be sent into the valley at once to take command there and collect all the forces, regulars, locals and reserves, and endeavor to drive the enemy out." He nominated Breckinridge, who was still resting in Richmond but should be back in the saddle soon. "It is apparent that if Grant cannot be successfully resisted here we cannot hold the Valley," he said, though "if he is defeated it can be recovered. But unless a sufficient force can be had in that country to restrain the movements of the enemy, he will do us great evil. . . ." In the afternoon, Lee added that Breckinridge, who had defeated Sigel in the Valley, could "do a great deal personally in rallying the troops & people" there.[29]

Early, he reported, was trying to press the Union flank, but "the nature of the country & the labyrinth of fortifications made by the enemy" slowed him down. And in words that mirrored what Grant had written to Washington a day earlier, Lee told Davis, "I shall make every effort to strike him, but fear that his usual precautions will prevent unless I undertake to assault his fortifications which I desire to avoid if possible."[30]

MEADE, AFTER rearranging his lines, asked his corps commanders Monday morning to report what progress they had made during the night and what they thought of making another attack. The responses by now were predictable: a few yards of movement here, none there, and unanimous advice against further assaults.

The generals usually most eager for a fight now opposed one for more than strictly tactical reasons. Before replying to Meade, Hancock questioned his division commanders. Francis Barlow, with much of his badly damaged division still on the field, told him, "The men feel just at present a great horror and dread of attacking earth works again, and the unusual loss of officers which leaves my regiments in command of lieutenants, and brigades in command of inexperienced officers, leaves us in a very unfavorable condition for such enterprises." John Gibbon said he was "decidedly against the practicability of such an assault," his men "a good deal exhausted, which, I presume, in a measure, is the case with the whole army."[31]

Hancock accordingly told Meade that "I am averse to an assault, simply because my men have been so constantly out at the front, lying in the trenches all the time for three days, and are so fatigued that I fear they have not the dash necessary to carry them through the obstacles of a second line. They have lost the officers who have been accustomed to lead them, and . . . the obstacles are materially greater than they were on the first day." Nevertheless, he added, "Whatever may be the orders they will be cheerfully obeyed and faithfully executed."[32]

Wright reported that his division commanders all thought another attack impracticable, and Smith said such an effort should not be undertaken unless supporting artillery could be placed on the line now abandoned by Burnside, an obvious impossibility. Though there was constant picket sparring, sharpshooting, and artillery dueling, the only gestures of offensive action on Monday would come from the Rebel side.

The ever-active Early pushed Dodson Ramseur's division south against Burnside, bringing up cannon and driving in skirmishers shielding Robert Potter's and Thomas Crittenden's Union divisions. The Rebels called off this forced reconnaissance at dusk, allowing the Federals to solidify their line along the road toward Allen's Mill. Farther south, a smaller Confederate probe was turned back by Barlow's men.[33]

MEADE, THOUGH he bared his inner self in letters to his wife, was usually cautious about disclosing any plans that might be of interest to the enemy. If his letters to Philadelphia had been intercepted by Rebel agents, they would not have told Lee anything useful about what the

Union army was going to do next. But, proper though he was about risking operational secrets, Meade seemed unaware that information about the state of mind of senior officers could also be highly valuable intelligence.

Late that Monday, he apparently had seen another batch of Northern newspapers, still trumpeting Grant's triumphs. Among the latest was the *New York Times,* with another provocative editorial about the superiority of the general-in-chief's strategy against Richmond. It maintained that "The old personal jealousies and different gradations of loyalty, which used to prevail among the corps commanders, and make it almost impossible to secure concert of action, no longer exist. Absolute devotion to the cause and perfect singleness of purpose actuate the present leaders. . . . now, for the first time, are seen a complete unity of spirit and a perfect discipline, not only among the led, but among the leaders, indispensable to the full efficiency of an army. . . ." These words were written before the disjointed assault of June 3; how Meade felt if he read them afterward is easy to imagine.[34]

"Do not be deceived about the situation of affairs by the foolish despatches in the papers," he told his wife. "Be not over-elated by reported successes, nor over-depressed by exaggerated rumors of failures. Up to this time our success has consisted only of compelling the enemy to draw in towards Richmond; our failure has been that we have not been able to overcome, destroy or bag his army.

"His success has been in preventing us from doing the above, and in heading us off every time we have tried to get around him. In the meantime, both sides have suffered great losses. . . . The great struggle has yet to come off in the vicinity of Richmond."[35]

14

Killing Without Any Battle

FROM THE POCKMARKED field close in front of Kershaw's Confederate division, a fallen Yankee pleaded for help. His cries went on as shells crashed into the Rebel lines from artillery behind Baldy Smith's Federal corps. At last, Captain Edward S. McCarthy of the Richmond Howitzers stood and said, "Boys, I can't stand this. I don't order any of you to accompany me; but, as I can't manage him alone, I call for one volunteer to go with me and bring in that poor fellow."

Several men started to rush out with their battery commander, but Sergeant T. D. Moncure brushed them back. "You can't go, boys," he said. "I am chief of this piece." He and the captain went over the works, picked up the Yankee, and brought him to safety—too late. He was dead when they laid him down.

Soon afterward, Porter Alexander, commanding Anderson's corps artillery, called for an observer to adjust the fire of several Rebel howitzers tilted up to operate as mortars. Instead of detailing someone else, McCarthy himself stood on the works to watch the impact of the falling shells. Within minutes, a sharpshooter's round ended his life, adding one more casualty to the days of early June that Navy Secretary Gideon Welles called "killing without any battle."[1]

Captain McCarthy, a romantic figure in a grubby, unromantic campaign, was admired by his men. In Richmond, he was mourned as if he had been a general, in contrast to the wagonloads of ordinary soldiers trundled to common graves without ceremony. Robert Stiles, who wrote of McCarthy's final days, also told how his own brother, nicknamed "Skipper," almost met his end in the constant eruptions of gunfire between the trenches at Cold Harbor.

Skipper Stiles was an ex-sailor, and he had such a remarkable tenor voice that all conversation in the camp hushed when he sang. In almost the same spot where McCarthy was killed, he was shot in the temple and thought to be dead. But when his friends bent over him, he said, "If you fellows will stand back and give me some air, I'll get up!" He did, and refused help as he walked to a field hospital. There doctors succeeded in extracting the bullet and a piece of his felt hat from deep in his skull. But the wound, or perhaps the operation, blinded him. As Robert wrote, "While in utter darkness he sang most of the time, and I remember our dear mother was troubled by a fancy that, like a mockingbird she once had that went blind in a railroad train, he might sing himself to death." But the indomitable Skipper kept singing, and later recovered his sight in one eye.[2]

So the killing and maiming went on, day after day, with the wails of the wounded fading, while at last the opposing generals worked out the problem of simple communication between headquarters barely two miles apart.

AT 10:30 A.M. Tuesday, June 7, Grant wrote again to Lee, explaining that the Confederate commander's note setting the hours of truce had arrived too late to allow collecting casualties Monday evening. He said he regretted that "all my efforts for alleviating the sufferings of wounded men left upon the battle-field have been rendered nugatory." Major Mitchell passed this message across the lines at 11:50, and at 2:00 p.m. Lee responded, saying that he was "willing, if you desire it, to devote the hours between 6 and 8 this afternoon to accomplish that object." But Grant did not receive this note until 5:30, which he said was too late to start the truce at 6:00. Nevertheless, he told Lee, "I will avail myself of your offer at the earliest possible moment, which I hope will not be much after that hour."[3]

Finally—after most of the wounded soldiers remaining between the lines had lain untended for four and a half days—formal recovery efforts began. Federals as well as Confederates thought this delay was scandalous. Colonel Francis Walker, adjutant of Hancock's corps, which had suffered so grievously in Friday's attack, later spoke for tens of thousands of Federal soldiers in placing the blame squarely where it belonged:

"If it be asked why so simple a duty of humanity as the rescue of the wounded and burial of the dead had been thus neglected, it is answered that it was due to an unnecessary scruple on the part of the Union commander in chief. Grant delayed sending a flag of truce to

General Lee for this purpose because it would amount to an admission that he had been beaten on the 3d of June. It now seems incredible that he should for a moment have supposed that any other view could be taken of that action. But even if it were so, this was a very poor way of rewarding his soldiers who had fallen in the attack, or of encouraging their comrades to take similar risks."[4]

Asa W. Bartlett of the Twelfth New Hampshire wrote: "That the wounded were thus allowed to remain in suffering helplessness upon the field day after day, unless sooner rescued by their pitying comrades, was because of such a shameful and criminal negligence as no common words can fully and justly characterize. . . . For ordering the charge, or ever allowing it to be made at the time and place it was, there may perhaps be found, among all the surrounding circumstances, some show of excuse, if not of justification; but for permitting wounded heroes of that charge to suffer and die as they did, one must search in vain for either. . . ."[5]

IN ANNOUNCING the truce, Meade's headquarters warned each corps commander that only medical officers and stretcher bearers would be allowed on the field: "No other officers or men will be permitted to leave the lines, and no intercourse of any kind will be held with the enemy." The order was ignored by the troops, and officers made only a gesture toward enforcing it.[6]

Up from their rifle pits and bombproofs, soldiers rose in early evening to search for missing friends and face the hard duty of burying the dead. Work parties tied kerchiefs across their faces, but this did nothing to lessen the overwhelming smell. The number of Yankee casualties far outnumbered the Confederates, and the number of dead far outnumbered the handful still living. Many whose wounds would have been nonfatal had died for lack of treatment, food, and water. Flies and vultures, so pestiferous when the sun was high, disappeared at dusk, and searchers lit lanterns to find their friends. The soldiers who had sewn their names to their coats on Thursday evening had been prescient: many of the bodies on the field were unrecognizable—black and swollen, bursting the buttons off their tunics, so ripened by the sun that they could not be lifted whole. Hundreds were simply covered with soil shoveled onto them where they lay. Others were taken to mass graves.

Around a hole where ten Federal bodies were placed side by side, soldiers from both armies paused to swap newspapers, tobacco, coffee, and rumors and to drink from shared canteens. When a Rebel asked who would be the next president of the Union, one Yankee said, "Waal, I am in favor of Old Abe." The Rebel shot back, "He's a damned Abolitionist!" and the Yankee responded by whacking him between the eyes, starting a brawl that officers had to break up.[7]

Drummer boy Delavan Miller told the tale of a New York City soldier, believed dead, who was gathered up and dropped beside an open trench. The fall seemed to wake him, and he feebly asked, "What's going on, boys?" An upstate sergeant in the work detail told him, "We were going to bury you, Shorty." The wounded man came fully alive and flared: "Not if I know myself! Get me a cup of coffee and I'll be all right; I won't be buried by that country clodhopper."

The drummer boy was sentimental about his comrades, and after Cold Harbor there was much to be sentimental about. In his memoir of the war, Miller would include a poem entitled "A Truce," which said in part:

> *Let us bury our dead:*
> *Since we may not of vantage or victory prate;*
> *   And our army, so grand in the onslaught of late,*
> *All crippled has shrunk to its trenches instead,*
> *   For the carnage was great;*
> *Let us bury our dead.[8]*

During the truce, Union chaplain Winthrop Phelps sat behind the lines, writing to his wife at home. He was despondent at having to deal with so many letters addressed to men of the Second Connecticut Heavies, soldiers who would never answer another mail call. "It is a miserable life to live," he wrote. "In opening the letters of the killed I read those from mothers, widows and lovers, all hoping the dear ones will be spared. I write upon [them] that he was killed, & send back, to their sorrow of course. . . ."[9]

Captain Oliver Wendell Holmes, Jr., an aide to General Wright, felt just as low. He had been wounded three times in earlier battles, doing more than his duty as a front-line officer, and had been thinking all year of quitting the war. Cold Harbor made up his mind. Holmes wrote to his mother, "I started in this thing a boy I am now a man and I have been coming to the conclusion for the last six months that my duty has changed." He confessed the kind of uncertainty that has worried many a soldier on the edge of battle, a concern that had grown in him in the past few days: "I can do a disagreeable thing or face a great danger coolly enough when I *know* it is a duty—but a doubt demoralizes me as it does any nervous man—and now I honestly think the duty of fighting has ceased for me. . . ." Within six weeks, he was at home in Boston. He would live another seven decades, dying at the age of ninety-four, after thirty years as a justice of the U.S. Supreme Court.[10]

A Confederate cannon fired a blank round to signal the end of the truce, and troops on both sides shouted to one another, "Get back in your holes, boys!" So ended the only extended break in the daylong, nightlong sounds of digging, picket firing, and artillery sparring.

TUESDAY MORNING, General Barlow had reported that after pressing his regular approaches all night "as vigorously as possible," one side of his division had advanced six yards, the other four. "Only 1 man can work at a time," he explained, "and last night the flashes of the lightning constantly revealed the positions of the working party to the enemy, and enabled them to interrupt the work by their fire. . . ."

"The mine is being pushed," Barlow added. He and Hancock apparently were thinking of a coup de main like that attempted by Union troops a few weeks later outside Petersburg. Neither of them described the effort, but Gilbert Thompson, a topographical engineer with Hancock's corps, confided to his journal that "A portion of the [engineer] Battn attached to the 2d corps was engaged in running a mine up to the enemy's battery occupying the crest and overlooking Gaines Mill. The army moved before the mine was completed." One of Barlow's soldiers in the Irish Brigade, Daniel Chisholm of the 116th Pennsylvania, wrote home that "I think charging is played out now after this, it will have to be done by undermining their works and sieging. Our men have dug under their works now some place along here so they say."[11]

To tunnel and plant a mine beneath the Confederate works would have made sense, considering the closeness of Barlow's lines to the enemy and the lack of enthusiasm among his troops for another stand-up charge. The opportunity was so obvious that there was talk of it on the Southern side, too. A soldier in the Eighth Alabama, with Mahone's division, wrote, "If Mr. U. S. [Grant] could undermine us, he would certainly do so. Perhaps some of those fine mornings he intends to blow us all up! Wonder what kind of sensation that will be; certainly a novel one. He has admirably succeeded in blowing up the Yankee nation; will he succeed in blowing up some Rebs also?"[12]

THE WORK at the front proceeded yard by yard, in places only foot by foot. But far to the rear, both armies were covering miles as they shifted toward the final phase of the Cold Harbor campaign.

Starting before dawn that Tuesday, Phil Sheridan had taken eight thousand Yankee horsemen clattering back across the Pamunkey River. These were Torbert's and Gregg's divisions, setting out on Grant's plan to cut Richmond's supply lines north of the James River, then connect with Hunter after he had swept the Shenandoah Valley. Wilson's cavalry division stayed behind to keep watch on both flanks of the Union army.

At the same time, two of the four infantry divisions in Warren's reorganized corps trudged south to extend the Union front to the Chickahominy, picketing the bank downstream to Dispatch Station. When they arrived at the river, they secured the bridges and reported unidentified Confederates already dug in and waiting on the other side. Grant ordered his force not to try to cross, but to hold the bridges to prevent the Rebels from attacking. A Yankee artillery captain on the Chickahominy wrote that the Rebels were zeroing in a five-inch railroad gun, which they had run out on the Richmond & York River line. A day later, one of its shells killed three Federals and wounded four as they sat quietly eating supper.[13]

Despite the continual firing, behind the lines there was a feeling that the worst was over—a situation that cheered some but could not lift others gloomy over lost comrades and the prospect of soon joining them. The first sutlers to appear since the campaign reached the Peninsula were welcomed behind the Union lines. Two of them, in an open buggy loaded with tobacco, were so busy winding through entrenchments that they unknowingly got too close to the front. A sudden burst from Rebel marksmen killed one of the men and wounded their horse. The other man managed to turn the buggy, but the frantic horse crashed the whole rig into a trench. Soldiers watching first scrambled after the spilled tobacco, then lifted out the driver and his dead companion and shot the horse.[14]

At Warren's headquarters, another sutler drove up from White House, bringing "quite a little batch of stores for the officers," including butter, ale, and champagne. But Charles Wainwright said that the corps commander was in a state of deep depression. Warren "will not move," he wrote. "He appears to have sunk into a sort of lethargic sulk, sleeps a great part of the time, and says nothing to anyone. I think at times that these fits of his must be the result of a sort of insanity; indeed, that is perhaps the most charitable way of accounting for them."[15]

By repositioning the Fifth and Ninth Corps on the wings of his army, Meade had drawn into a compact and defensible horseshoe, with a supply corridor running back to White House. But along the center of this front, Hancock, Wright, and Smith were so interlocked with the enemy that neither side could advance or retreat. To a Union artilleryman there, it seemed that "now the whole army is under ground. Line after line of trenches are dug nightly. Gaines will hardly know his farm, & 10,000 darkies could not make the ground fit for cultivation in two years. . . . The two armies are so near each other, the men can converse from their rifle pits. Each side is so strongly entrenched, that it seems impossible to do anything but look at each other."[16]

The revised Union front was meant to hold off Lee until Sheridan returned, bringing Hunter's command with him, and Grant began his major move across the James. To prepare for that operation, Grant dispatched Cyrus Comstock and Horace Porter south of the river to consult with General Butler and plan the march route.[17]

At the northern end of the front, Confederates of Jubal Early's corps and Pickett's division pressed hard against Burnside as he tried to solidify his new line. Lee, confident that the latest Federal deployment was strictly defensive, now felt free to send Breckinridge's two brigades west to the Shenandoah Valley, under temporary command of General Wharton.

FOR A WHILE after the burial truce, there seemed a sense of relief along the lines, as if two hours of conversation had reminded soldiers of the fraternal feeling they shared with the men beyond the tangled abatis. Through the night and into the morning, there was less firing than on the days before. Here and there, troops shouted across the works to declare their own unofficial truce to trade delicacies. Pickets along the Chickahominy dropped fishing lines into the river at opposite ends of the bridges, within easy rifle range of one another. In the Thirteenth Massachusetts, little Stevie Warren lay in his tent playing his fife until his comrades "were all sick of it," while John Hill and

Henry Vining established a barbershop upon a stone and a stump, charging a nickel for a shave and a dime for a haircut. After becoming reluctantly familiar with the Mattaponi, the North Anna, and the Pamunkey, now they dug and lived beneath Turkey Hill and along the dreaded Chickahominy.[18]

"Had we been muskrats, frogs, or water Snakes or blood Suckers we might have had some Sport in those murky waters of the Chickahominy," recalled Avery Harris of the 143rd Pennsylvania, "but being neither, nor yet ducks or geese, we were denied the luxury of that liquid element, tho I think a few did try it, and when they came out they had to have the bloodsuckers scraped from them. The water was blacker than old Tea Pond. They issued that delightful beverage of whiskey and Quinine to us here." Harris set down those memories of life on the Chickahominy years later. In the field in 1864, when soldiers could forget the struggle to survive, their minds inevitably turned homeward.[19]

"My Dear Parents," wrote James P. Coburn of the 141st Pennsylvania. "This morning we have killed & issued our daily ration of beef & I am off duty for the remainder of the day unless we move. It takes about 30 oxen a day to supply the whole Division. . . . You may think it odd that we consider the siege of Richmond commenced while our line is from 8 to 12 miles from the city."

He tried to depict the army's situation in terms better understandable to his family on the upper Susquehanna, along the Pennsylvania–New York border: "Suppose that the Rebel capital was Owego [N.Y.] & we had driven the enemy from the Eastern part of Penna. Suppose that our right wing rested at Apalacon Corners [modern Apalachin], on the [Susquehanna] river & our left at Nichols [N.Y.] then suppose that every range of hills, Mutton Hill, Bush Hill, Dunham Hill, Waits Hill, Pitcher & Corbin Hill, &c were all held & well fortified by the enemy then perhaps you can understand something more about it."[20]

Before the war, most soldiers in both armies had been small farmers, and though on leaving home they had had to turn over the management of their domestic affairs to the women who stayed behind, many felt that the women still needed expert advice. South Carolinian John Cumming wrote to his wife Carrie that ". . . I am glad to here that the crop looks verry well I hope it will continue so if Jeff is not sick you had better have him plowed a little to keepe him Jentle, if the little coalt looks bad and aint shedded off get some one to examine it and see if it has lice and have it gave medicine, the negros must ride

Nancy before fall to get her Jentle before she goes in the fields. Have the peas planted as soon as possible it is now time they was planted to come early write to me how the string peas potatoes shugar milet and every thing looks write to your mother to have the mill made to grinde your millit, have the cow pens moved as fast as they are manured and have as many slips planted as you can do the best you can. . . .

"My Dear wife I would be verry glad to see you and the children but I cannot so I will have to poot up with it. . . . tell the children howdy for me. . . . may God protect us all and spare our lives to see each other again. . . ."[21]

15

A Nice Friendly Chat

BEHIND THE FEDERAL lines on Wednesday morning, June 8, a wave of rough laughter ran from one regimental camp to another. Heralded by a bugler and drummers beating the "Rogue's March," a particularly homely mule plodded past tents and campfires, carrying a civilian facing to the rear, wearing signs front and back proclaiming him "Libeler of the Press." For hours the little parade wound on, amid jeers from thousands of soldiers. "He was howled at," said one private, "and the wish to tear him limb from limb and strew him over the ground was fiercely expressed" in every corps.[1]

The butt of the fun was Edward Cropsey, correspondent for the *Philadelphia Inquirer*, whose work was reprinted widely in other newspapers. He had offended Meade in print, and now he was paying for his sin.

On or before that Tuesday, the *Inquirer* of June 2 had arrived at army headquarters. It was Meade's friendly hometown newspaper, and after his victory at Gettysburg, he was Pennsylvania's greatest hero. He read the *Inquirer* closely and expected to find compliments there. In this issue, he was pleased at first to see a dispatch that seemed a flattering description of his role in the current campaign. "Grant plans and exercises a supervisory control," it said, "but to Meade belongs everything of detail. He is entitled to great credit for the magnificent movements of the army. . . . In battle he puts troops into action and controls their movements; in a word, he commands the army. . . ."

But it went on: "History will record, but newspapers cannot, that on one eventful night during the present campaign GRANT'S presence saved the army and the nation, too; not that General MEADE was on the point to commit a blunder unwittingly, but his devotion to his country made him loth to risk her last army on what he deemed a chance. GRANT assumed the responsibility and we are still ON TO RICHMOND."[2]

Meade boiled over. He sent a mounted guard to arrest Cropsey, who had returned to the army from Washington. He demanded to know where the reporter had gotten such a story.

Cropsey said he had heard that at the Wilderness, Meade had urged Grant to fall back across the Rapidan. "It was the talk of the camp," said the correspondent.

"It was a base and wicked lie," the general declared. He told Cropsey that he would make an example of him that would not only deter other journalists from committing such offenses but would also "give publicity to his lie and the truth."

Cropsey did not name his source then, but later evidence pointed to Grant's promoter, Illinois congressman Elihu Washburne. He had spread the camp rumor in Washington, perhaps to diminish any possible rival to the general-in-chief. As one of Meade's biographers wrote, "However the story originated, every man knew it next day, one soldier declaring that he had heard it fifty times."[3]

Meade consulted Provost Marshal Marsena Patrick about what to do with Cropsey. The humiliating sentence, to parade the correspondent through the camps and then banish him from the army, apparently was Patrick's idea. Meade said that Grant was present as he wrote out the order for punishment, and the general-in-chief approved it, "although he said he knew the offender, and that his family was a respectable one in Illinois."[4]

If any soldier in Meade's command somehow had not heard the rumor or read Cropsey's dispatch, the general's order corrected that situation. It said that Cropsey (repeatedly misspelled "Crapsey") had published "a libelous statement on the commanding general of the army calculated to impair the confidence of the army in their commanding officer," a report that "he has acknowledged to have been false, and based on some idle camp rumor."[5]

Meade informed his wife that "the sentence was carried out much to the delight of the whole army, for the race of newspaper correspondents is universally despised by the soldiers." Then, after it was done, he said, "I learned to my surprise that this malicious falsehood had been circulated all over the country."[6]

It was true that Cropsey's dispatch had been printed in newspapers other than the *Inquirer*, but in the end the rumor revived by the correspondent's vaguely worded paragraph did much less damage to Meade than did his own angry response. Back in Washington, Cropsey and his colleagues of the press agreed not even to mention Meade's name in future dispatches unless in connection with a defeat. Whitelaw Reid, then of the *Cincinnati Gazette,* wrote an unpublished Washington dispatch saying that Meade was "as leprous with moral cowardice as the brute that kicks a helpless cripple on the street." Reid said that the truth of the rumor was well understood in Washington, and "some of the highest officers of the Government firmly believe it."[7]

High officials may have believed it, but publicly they denied it. Dana wrote to Stanton that the report of Meade's having "counseled retreat" was "entirely untrue. He has not shown any weakness of the sort since moving from Culpeper, nor once intimated a doubt as to the successful issue of the campaign." Stanton instructed Dana to tell Meade that "the lying report alluded to in your telegram was not even for a moment believed by the President or myself. We have the most perfect confidence in him. He could not wish a more exalted estimation of his ability, his firmness, and every quality of a commanding general than is entertained for him."[8]

This came from a secretary of war whose own communiqués seldom noted the accomplishments of any Union general in Virginia other than Grant. Indeed, since the campaign had begun, Stanton's news management had set the pattern for the press boycott of Meade, and under the circumstances, his professing an "exalted estimation" of the general seemed pure hypocrisy. The correspondents' pledge to ignore Meade held for about six months. Some of the general's admirers thought that the blackout might have cost him the presidency— that if Meade had been publicized as the eventually victorious commander, he, rather than Grant, might have proceeded to the White House.

POLITICS WAS much on the minds of both politicians and generals, because on the same day that Cropsey was paraded through the army, Lincoln was renominated. Robert J. Breckinridge of Kentucky was temporary president of the Union party convention at Baltimore's Front Street Theatre. "Great applause" greeted his hard-line opening speech, which reminded listeners of his feelings toward his nephew, the Confederate general. "No Government has ever built upon imperishable foundations, which foundations were not laid in the blood of traitors," he said. "It is a fearful truth, but we had as well avow it at once . . . every lick you strike, and every rebel you kill, every battle you win, dreadful as it is to do it, you are adding, it may be a year, it may be ten years, it may be a century, it may be ten centuries to the life of the Government and the freedom of your children."[9]

The only convention contest was over the vice-presidential candidate; in it, Lincoln's choice of former senator Andrew Johnson, military governor of Tennessee, prevailed over the incumbent, Hannibal Hamlin of Maine, and Daniel Dickinson of New York. Despite the preconvention efforts of radical Republicans, Lincoln's own nomination was expected to be unanimous, but it was not quite: before the gathering roared approval of a motion to nominate him by acclamation, the Missouri delegation had followed instructions from home and cast its twenty-two votes for Ulysses S. Grant.

Those instructions from Missouri had been issued long before Grant and Meade arrived outside Richmond. Realization of what had happened at Cold Harbor within the week was trickling only slowly into Washington, Baltimore, and homes across the North. The day after the peak of battle, Senator Lafayette S. Foster of Massachusetts had the barest misleading fraction of the truth from official communiqués when he wrote to his wife from the Senate floor: "Genl Grant had a fight yesterday with Lee—he drove Lee's army within their intrenchments, but gained no decided advantage—We lost some three thousand in killed & wounded—loss of the enemy not known."[10]

On the day when the convention met, the *New York Times* carried the most detailed contemporary account of the June 3 fight, an exemplary piece of deadline reporting filed by William Swinton at ten o'clock on the evening of the battle. But the *Times*'s headlines and even the opening of Swinton's 6,500-word narrative softened the hard facts of the conflict.

Judged by its severity, that fight should be called a battle, Swinton said, but in perspective "it is perhaps, hardly more than a grand reconnaissance—a reconnaissance, however, which has cost us not less than *five or six thousand* killed and wounded."* The object of the attack was to force Lee's Chickahominy line, said Swinton, but the result was merely to feel it instead, and to conclude that "any victory that could here be won must cost too much in its purchase." Thus, he predicted, "there will be *no renewal of the assault on the lines of the Chickahominy*," because Grant's eyes had already turned toward "lines and combinations more bold than any yet essayed."[11]

---

* See Appendix 2, page 277.

Swinton's dispatch was as accurate and fair as any one reporter could have made it under the circumstances, gathering details from weary, defeated officers and writing by candlelight in a tent behind the lines. But in an army whose generals were bitter with frustration, one paragraph of his article got him into the same kind of trouble that Cropsey had faced a few days earlier.

Swinton obviously had done his interviewing in the Second, Sixth, and Eighteenth corps, where the fighting was fiercest, and had not spent time with officers farther north. "Operations along the fronts of Warren and Burnside were of an importance quite subordinate to that of operations on the left," Swinton wrote, correctly. "No results were achieved except the carrying of the line of rifle-pits occupied by the rebel skirmishers. The Fifth and Ninth Corps nowhere struck the enemy's main work. Burnside kept up a furious cannonade for some hours; but it was nothing—*vox et preterea nihil* [sound and fury signifying nothing]. From the tenor of one of Burnside's morning dispatches, it was at one time hoped that he would be able to turn the enemy's left; but this hope also was doomed to disappointment."[12]

When the usually modest and genial Burnside read this, his first impulse was to order Swinton seized and placed before a firing squad. He wrote to Meade that the offending paragraph was "plainly a libel upon the Ninth Corps, as well as upon myself." He said that two small divisions of his corps had lost more than a thousand men during the assault, establishing themselves close to the enemy line, ready to attack again.

"I beg that this man immediately receive the justice which was so justly meted out to another libeller of the press a day or two since, or that I be permitted to arrest and punish him myself," Burnside said. Remembering the official warning to Swinton after he was caught eavesdropping on Grant, Burnside added, "This is not his first offense."[13]

Cooler heads prevailed, perhaps belatedly realizing that Meade had overreacted against Cropsey. Instead of executing or humiliating Swinton, Grant ordered him out of the army's lines, and he spent much of the next few months writing propaganda about the war for the Republican presidential campaign.[14]

IN SUBSTANCE, these wrangles with the press amounted to very little, but they testified to the touchy egos of ranking generals, to their hope of controlling what the nation learned about the campaign, and possibly to the guilt they felt after such a defeat. Grant himself did not want to talk about what had happened at Cold Harbor, and he disclosed almost nothing about what came next. His actions said more than his few words about the battle; the realignment of the Union front spoke of defense, not attack, and his sending away two-thirds of his cavalry meant that he would not need it right away. And up to this point, Lee read Grant's actions correctly.

On Wednesday, Jeff Davis left Richmond and came out to see Lee again. They rode along the lines, inspecting the ground where the fighting had been fiercest and where it might move next. Looking out toward the Chickahominy, and beyond it the James, the president said, "The indications are that Grant despairing of a direct attack is now seeking to embarrass you by flank movements." This was not a startling suggestion, since Grant had repeatedly tried to do that after each unsuccessful attack since crossing the Rapidan. Now he had tried assaulting again, and his overland campaign had crashed to a halt against Lee's army before the Chickahominy. Not even Grant was likely to order another such head-on attack against those troops in those works. The question at hand was not whether he would move to the flank; steadily and incrementally, he was already doing it every day, and newspapers North and South were dropping hints of something more dramatic.[15]

Wade Hampton had informed Lee early on Wednesday that Sheridan and two divisions of cavalry, with artillery, a wagon train, and a herd of beef, had camped the previous night at Aylett's on the Mattaponi River. Lee ordered Hampton to take his own division and one other to chase Sheridan and turn him back. Hampton sent for Fitz Lee's division, then patrolling the Chickahominy flank of the army, to follow as he started toward Ashland. That left the Confederate army facing Grant and Meade with the skimpiest of cavalry screens—one brigade under Brigadier General John R. Chambliss on its north flank and a mixed force under Rooney Lee on the south—to watch Grant as he prepared his next move.[16]

Otherwise, that Wednesday was a day of more minor shifts, sharpshooting, digging, and waiting, as soldiers tried to read the minds of commanders both enemy and friendly. What was happening in Baltimore, 140 miles away, seemed far removed, in a different world from the reality of the front. Henry H. Hopkins, chaplain of the 120th New York in Birney's division, wrote of the "unnatural lull to night in the firing: for more than one hour not a gun has broken the stillness of the night. The hateful clamor has been kept up so constantly that I am

almost disturbed by the unwonted calm." Soldiers of his regiment
were stuck in the front lines; "I despise myself in their presence and
wonder that they can tolerate me abiding as I do in comparative
safety...."

Hoping to boost the folks at home, Hopkins wrote that "There is
no despondency or faltering here. From Genl. Grant to the drummer
boys there is one faith and expectation. We don't care for political conventions. Blood is flowing every day for the country's life. Shall it be
for naught in the bitter end or shall we succeed is the only issue
here...."[17]

AT 7:40 WEDNESDAY evening, Grant told Meade that "to prepare
for the withdrawal of the army from its present position, which will
take place in a few days," he should mark off a fallback line from the
army's right to its left and partly fortify it. "To perfectly cover such a
withdrawal," two of Warren's divisions, with help from other corps,
would occupy that line when the move began.[18]

The wording of Grant's message sounded as if he were informing
Meade of the planned withdrawal for the first time. The likely move
had been discussed in the ranks of both armies for days; soldiers had
written to their wives predicting it, and had even sent letters to their
hometown newspapers speculating about it. Writing to a Rochester
paper, Lieutenant George Breck of the First New York Light Artillery
had said: "It seems to be the general impression among the troops,
that military operations are to be transferred to the James River, but it
is next to impossible to ascertain with any degree of positiveness, what
is transpiring in the army, outside of one's own immediate command.... There has probably never been a campaign when so little
was known [of] what was going on on the field, or what movements
were likely to take place, outside of the commanding General. Corps
commanders have been kept in the dark, absolutely so, very frequently
as to the main designs and plans of the General commander. It has
been a matter of almost as great conjecture to them at times as to what
general army movements meant, as to subordinate officers.

"Perhaps," wrote the lieutenant, as if the thought had just dawned
upon him, "Perhaps the success that has attended this campaign is due
in a measure to the secrecy with which it has been carried on by Grant
and Meade."[19]

If Grant had had his way, even such uninformed speculation would
not have been permitted. According to Horace Porter, the general-in-

chief had "acted with his usual secrecy in regard to important move-ments, and had spoken of his detailed plans to only a few officers upon whose reticence he could rely implicitly, and whom he was compelled to take into his secret in order to make the necessary preparations." Leakage and speculation were inevitable, but his front-line troops, as well as the enemy, were still unsure of exactly when he would move, and whether he would stop at the James or cross it.[20]

Lee, sensing that the Federals were about to make yet another withdrawal from their right, issued orders at 8:00 p.m. Wednesday for Pickett to attack an hour before Thursday daybreak "under certain contingencies." This assault would aim at the angle where Burnside's front bent back from that of Smith's Eighteenth Corps. Lee hoped to strike while the Yankees were pulling away, which would at least con-fuse and delay their movement, and might break into Smith's rear, opening the way for a more ambitious offensive. Orders went to Ker-shaw and to John Gregg, then commanding Field's division, to be ready to follow Pickett "and support him with your whole strength and vigor" in "a sudden and disastrous blow to the enemy." But when pickets detected no Union pullback during the night, the attack was called off.[21]

Thursday, June 9, dawned warm and pleasant; along part of the front, troops were enjoying an informal, unauthorized truce with the enemy across the lines. Clarke Baum, of the Fiftieth New York Engi-neers, explained how such things happened: "The Rebs and our men got tired shooting and *stopped* without any arrangement between them. . . . one of our men exposed his hat on a ramrod above the works, the Rebs did not shoot, by and by he exposed his head a little; then a Reb showed his, no shooting—then one exposed a little more, then the other a little more & so on till both stood up in full view of the other and then others tried it without any trouble, then they began to talk backwards & forwards and then on both sides began to get up on the works & then to walk out toward the others works and so on until they were having a nice friendly chat. Men all left their guns in the pits and met as friends (some say shaking hands and drinking together but that I dont know about) and were laying down on the top of the works"—until the Union officer of the day appeared.

This colonel rode along the front line, something that would have been "certain death" at any other time, then dismounted and strode out between the armies. He commanded troops of both sides to return to their works or he would order the second Federal line to open fire. When they were back in their holes, they hollered to one another, "Watch out, Yanks, I'm going to shoot," and "Take care there, Johnnie, your head's in the way of my bullet," as they resumed their target-shooting.[22]

There was a sense of fun, spiced by fear, in the ordinary soldiers' defiance of authority. S. H. Walkup of the Forty-eighth North Carolina, in Heth's division, told of what happened when a gun fired to end a spontaneous truce in his front. Men of both armies set off "like frogs when a snake is after them or sheep strike for home when dogs or wolves pursue them . . . some half clad, clothes in hand, some with breakfast half-eaten. Some laughingly & others with consternation in their faces." But in front of the Twenty-fifth Massachusetts, in Martindale's division, soldiers rose that Thursday morning to join their comrades and enemies in what had become the routine of "firing all day to keep up appearances."[23]

The resulting casualties were real, but not all were authentic. Union cannoneer Frank Wilkeson recalled how a pale infantryman limped back to his battery suffering from a foot wound. Wilkeson took pity on him and asked for permission to escort him back to the corps hospital. There, a surgeon knocked the soldier out with chloroform and removed his boot—to find black powder marks where a bullet had penetrated the foot. "The cowardly whelp!" the surgeon growled, proceeding to saw off the sleeping soldier's leg below the knee. Waiting for the patient to wake up, watching the pile of other men's amputated limbs grow beside the operating table, Wilkeson mused that "the utter contempt of the surgeons, their change from careful handling to almost brutality, when they discovered the wound was self-inflicted, was bracing to me." Later, he "rammed home the ammunition in gun No. 1 with vim."[24]

AFTER JUBAL EARLY's men prodded Burnside's line on the Union right again early Thursday, Lee was satisfied that there was no immediate threat from that direction. Thus, that evening, he withdrew Early's corps from the front line into position behind Anderson's left. Anderson covered part of the line that Early vacated by retrieving the brigades he had detached to reinforce against the previous week's Union attacks. These shifts gave Lee a ready reserve, with Early placed to move to either flank or to support the main line against an unlikely assault.[25]

Lee was waiting, watching for any hint of the next Union move. If he had heard just then from a spy across the lines, he would have been certain that such a move was imminent, but still unsure when and where it would come. Meade ordered his troops to draw another two days' rations, which would make four days' worth as of Friday morning, and ordered corps commanders to stop all informal communication across the lines. The most specific confirmation of what was coming was Grant's order that henceforth all reinforcements would be directed to City Point, on the south side of the James, rather than to White House. But that message was sent upward, from Grant's headquarters to Washington, not downward to Union corps commanders.[26]

By Friday morning, June 10, engineers and work parties from Hancock's and Wright's corps were well started on the rear trench line ordered by Grant. Meade pulled Warren's two reserve divisions back toward Bottom's Bridge on the Chickahominy. Lee's cavalry jabbed at the Union right, but discovered nothing that would give away Grant's plans. The Confederate commander was concerned about what Sheridan was up to. Nothing had happened to change his earlier belief that Sheridan's cavalry expedition was headed to join Hunter, but he warned Richmond that it might turn south to cross the James above Richmond and try to cut the rail line from the capital to Danville.[27]

As SHERIDAN's troopers rode west, they rehearsed the scorched-earth tactics that they would later apply on Grant's orders to clean out the Shenandoah Valley. Foraging parties swept each side of the Union column, taking "everything edible for man or beast, operating over strips of country for miles wide." Captain William Hyndman of the Fourth Pennsylvania Cavalry admitted that "There were rather rough deeds perpetrated by us in Virginia at this time," but he said they were done "out of sheer necessity." Poor people along the cavalry's route already were short of provisions, he said, "and we thus gave them fair prospects of a famine. . . . We came down upon them like swarms of locusts, eating up the very seed for their next harvests."

Angered by this, the few Confederate men left in the countryside waged guerrilla warfare, hovering about the Yankees' flanks, picking off stray foragers. Hyndman wrote that "It was no uncommon sight to see our dead comrades suspended conspicuously from the limbs of trees along our line of march, and labelled 'Such will be the fate of every forager caught!' But . . . these scarecrows, horrible and revolting as they were, only whetted the operations of our men, giving to their movements sometimes a slight coloring of vengeance."[28]

Lee was unaware of these depredations as he wrote to Richmond of his concern about Sheridan's mission. And since he had no late report of the Yankee column's movement, he did not know that Wade Hampton was about to overtake the Federal cavalry near the Louisa County village of Trevilian Station, on the Virginia Central about twenty-five miles east of Charlottesville.

There on Saturday morning, June 11, Hampton ordered his two divisions to join and strike Sheridan's advancing troopers at the crossroads of Clayton's Store, northeast of Trevilian. As Hampton's lead brigades collided with Torbert's Federals, he got word that George Custer had driven his Michigan brigade between Hampton's and Fitz Lee's divisions. Custer captured Hampton's wagons and some eight hundred horses before the Rebel general turned on him and took back his losses, plus several hundred Yankee prisoners and Custer's headquarters wagon. But Custer held on to Trevilian Station and blocked Fitz Lee from joining Hampton until midday Sunday, June 12. On that day, Sheridan made the mistake of throwing a full-scale attack against Hampton's entrenched division, suffering so many casualties that he called off his expedition and headed back to the Army of the Potomac.

Hampton had scored a clear victory in blocking Sheridan's operation. But meanwhile Union general Hunter, strengthened by General George Crook's force from the mountains of western Virginia, had marched into Lexington, burning the Virginia Military Institute and the homes of conspicuous Confederates. Breckinridge had retaken command of his light division heading in that direction, but together with the Rebels already there, this was not enough to stop the Yankee advance toward Lynchburg. When Breckinridge reported en route, General Bragg in Richmond endorsed his message by saying, "It seems to me very important that this force of the enemy should be expelled from the Valley. If it could be crushed, Washington would be open to the few we might then employ."[29]

Without comment, Davis passed this on to Lee, who agreed in principle with the idea; it reminded him of Stonewall Jackson's 1862 Valley campaign, which had diverted Union strength from McClellan's operations against Richmond. But in this case, the more important result might be the diversion of Confederates protecting Richmond. "The only difficulty with me is the means," Lee said. "It would take one corps of this army." However, he would take the chance, "if it is deemed prudent to hazard the defense of Richmond." He said, "I think this is what the enemy would desire," then went on almost wistfully: "A victory over General Grant would also relieve our difficulties. . . . Think he is strengthening his defense to withdraw a portion of his force, and with the other move to the James River. To attack him here I must assault a very strong line of intrenchments and run great risk to the safety of the army."[30]

Lee understood correctly that Grant was deepening his works to cover a withdrawal, but he suspected that Grant would move in two stages rather than one. He also thought that Grant wanted him to whittle away the Army of Northern Virginia by detaching forces to deal with Hunter and Sheridan. Grant actually wanted the opposite, to hold Lee's whole force in place while Sheridan and Hunter destroyed the railroads and the main Union army moved across the James. In the event, Lee's sending away important elements from the Richmond front served Grant better than what the Union commander had planned.[31]

That Sunday, Braxton Bragg again urged an emergency Confederate expedition to the Valley. "It seems to me a pressing necessity to send at least 6,000 good troops to reenforce Breckinridge," he told Davis. After this, and after seriously pondering the risk of such a drastic decision, Lee decided to order Jubal Early to take his corps to the Valley, defeat Hunter, and march north down the Shenandoah to threaten Washington. That might relieve Union pressure on Richmond, but it would leave Lee without almost a third of his infantry and two-thirds of his cavalry in the critical hours when Grant started his strategic move to the James.[32]

16

The Heavens Hung in Black

OCCASIONALLY, AS they rested from digging yet another trench to connect with the one they had dug the day before, soldiers lay half-dozing, listening to the capricious gunfire close overhead. "These bullets," mused Wilbur Fisk of the Second Vermont, "have a peculiar sound. Some of them come with a sharp 'clit,' like striking a cabbage leaf with a whip lash, others come with a sort of screech, very much such as you would get by treading on a cat's tail." Others sounded to him like a huge bumblebee, then like a heavy sledgehammer striking a tree. And between these buzzes, thuds, and screeches, soldiers writing home were often charmed to hear birds carry on their sweet songs, as if the racket of war were no more than a breeze stirring the branches above. Such musing was a way for soldiers to put out of mind, for a moment, newly departed comrades with whom they had spent the most memorable time of their lives.[1]

In the days after the defeat at Cold Harbor, Federal commanders stopped calling for routine morning reports of strength on hand. Colonel Joshua L. Chamberlain, who had commanded the Twentieth Maine, told why: "When we asked explanation our superiors answered—confidentially, lest it seem disloyal: 'Because the country would not stand it, if they knew.'"[2]

But, gradually, the country did know. Stanton had laundered and delayed the news, and Grant tried to pretend that what had happened was just another bump on the road south. But they could not hide the casualty lists that ran in column after column, reaching into counties from Maryland to Maine to Minnesota. Boatloads of the wounded and dead crowded the hospitals and mortuaries of Washington. The smell from embalming shops there was so depressing that capital newspapers complained that the undertakers were spreading pestilence and ruining the business of restaurants. The cemetery at the Soldiers' Home was more than full, and acres of new graves covered the hills of the Arlington plantation that Lee had abandoned when he went south to war.

That summer, Union morale slumped lower than after the defeats at First or Second Bull Run, lower than after Fredericksburg or Chancellorsville. Noah Brooks, Lincoln's closest newspaper friend, wrote that "those days will appear to be the darkest of the many dark days through which passed the friends and lovers of the Federal Union. The earlier years of the war, it is true, had been full of grief, despondency, and even agony; but the darkness that settled upon us in the summer of 1864 was the more difficult to be endured because of its unexpectedness. The hopes so buoyantly entertained by our people when Grant opened his campaign in Virginia had been dashed.

"No joyful tidings came from the Army now; a deadly calm prevailed where had so lately resounded the shouts of victory. In every department of the Government there was a manifest feeling of discouragement. . . ."[3]

Swinton believed that "there was at this time great danger of a collapse of the war"—that if better news had not come from other battlefields, it would have been impossible to rebuild the Army of the Potomac, "which, shaken in its structure, its valor quenched in blood, and thousands of its ablest officers killed and wounded, was the Army of the Potomac no more."[4]

The mood within the Union was so low that many citizens were willing to believe a published story that Lincoln had issued a proclamation announcing the failure of Grant's campaign. The fake report in two New York newspapers said the president was calling for a day of "fasting, humiliation and prayer" and a draft of 400,000 more men for the army. In reaction, Stanton shut down the *World* and the *Journal of Commerce* until the hoax was traced to Joseph Howard, Jr., and Francis A. Mallison, frustrated journalists who had used stolen Associated Press stationery to falsify the report in hopes of making profits on the gold market. They were arrested and spent several months in Fort Lafayette prison.[5]

In mid-June, Lincoln spoke in Philadelphia at a Sanitary Fair raising funds to help the troops. "War, at the best, is terrible," he said, "and this war of ours, in its magnitude and in its duration, is one of the most terrible." Sadly, he admitted that "it has carried mourning to almost every home, until it can almost be said that the 'heavens are hung in black.' " But he vowed that the war would end only when the

Union was restored—and "I say we are going through on this line if it takes three years more."[6]

Such a speech could hardly cheer the North. The soldiers and the country wanted to understand why the grand hopes of spring had been so brutally dashed. In conversation and letters during the temporary leisure of stationary warfare, officers fought and refought the Cold Harbor campaign, laying down arguments that historians would still be dissecting in the twenty-first century.

GRANT WAS the only one of the three principal commanders at Cold Harbor who made his case in print after the war. Though he would explain himself more fully than either Lee (who died in 1870) or Meade (1872), he never disclosed the details of his decision-making or his consultations with Meade and his other generals. In a fifty-one-page official report of his time as general-in-chief, Grant would devote barely more than a page to the time between crossing the Pamunkey and marching to the James—sixteen days when his army suffered about fourteen thousand casualties. He gave only three sentences to the attack in which most of those losses took place: "On the 3d of June we again assaulted the enemy's works in the hope of driving him from his position. In this attempt our loss was heavy, while that of the enemy, I have reason to believe, was comparatively light. It was the only general attack made from the Rapidan to the James which did not inflict upon the enemy losses to compensate for our own losses."[7]

In his two-volume, 1,231-page memoirs, completed when he was dying of cancer in 1885, Grant would cover the same period in sixteen pages. That included three on the exchange with Lee over retrieving casualties, and only four on the climactic and controversial attack of June 3. Near death, when his political career was long past, his summing up was brief but frank: "I have always regretted that the last assault at Cold Harbor was ever made. . . . no advantage whatever was gained to compensate for the heavy loss we sustained. Indeed, the advantages other than those of relative losses, were on the Confederate side."[8]

The two fundamental questions about Cold Harbor were why, under all the circumstances, the general-in-chief had ordered the final frontal attack against Lee, and why that attack, once ordered, was carried out so disastrously.

Only Grant and Meade had the final answers, but others had first-hand evidence and strong opinions. The most authoritative, presented during and after the campaign, came from Federal officers who were there. Southerners were glad to stand aside from the long-running debate, contributing only an occasional comment about specifics, for no one seriously argued over who had won the battle of Cold Harbor, only why.

Grant's most fervent justifiers were those in his headquarters retinue, not troops of the line or commanders of his corps, divisions, and brigades. Charles Dana would write that Cold Harbor "has been exaggerated into one of the bloodiest disasters of history, a reckless, useless waste of human life. It was nothing of the kind. The outlook warranted the effort." Breaking Lee's lines would have meant "his destruction and the collapse of the rebellion," and "if Grant had won, who would have thought of the losses?" But Grant did not win, and so "when we lay at Cold Harbor . . . the principal topic of conversation was the losses of the army. The discussion has never ceased," Dana wrote thirty-three years after Appomattox. He conceded that many accused Grant of "butchery" in the campaign. But he maintained that in the war's first three years, the campaigns headed by McDowell, McClellan, Pope, Burnside, Hooker, and Meade combined had cost more Union casualties than Grant lost in the eleven months from the Rapidan to Appomattox Court House.[9]

Horace Porter wrote that the critics who condemned Grant's hammering tactics "were found principally among the stay-at-homes, and especially the men who sympathized with the enemy." Not so. It was Lewis Bissell, an ordinary soldier of the Second Connecticut Heavies, who declared in a letter home that "They can never get us to make another charge. We don't care where they put us the men will not do it." He was one among many.[10]

And it was Baldy Smith, the corps commander who had been farthest forward with his troops on June 3, who asserted years later that the concept of that assault—"an attack along the whole line—is denounced by the standard writers on the art of war, and belongs to the first period in history after man had ceased to fight in unorganized masses. Giving up the few advantages belonging to the assailants, it increases largely the chances of successful defense, and would never be adopted by a trained general, except perhaps under certain peculiar conditions, where also the attacking force had an overwhelming superiority in numbers."[11]

Although Grant had earlier considered Smith to lead the Army of the Potomac, Baldy's frank criticism of his seniors, specifically Meade and Butler, would soon provoke the general-in-chief to relieve him of field command. But Smith's criticism was usually well founded.

John C. Ropes, who had never been a soldier but whom Captain Adams considered the best military historian of his time, wrote one of the most caustic studies of Grant's tactics. "It is difficult to find any justification for the battle of Cold Harbor," he concluded. That struggle "is in truth the most terrible instance which this terrible campaign affords of the folly of fighting with no reasonable chance of success and with a dead certainty of a heavy loss." By the time Grant crossed the Pamunkey, he should have had enough of assaults and sought a position in which Lee would have to attack him, for example by pushing quickly south to the Chickahominy. "But in fact nothing of the sort seems to have entered Grant's head," Ropes asserted. "His only idea seems to have been . . . to find out as soon as he could where Lee's intrenchments were, and then to assault them."[12]

Theodore Lyman, the most perceptive chronicler of events at either headquarters, came closest to explaining why Grant ordered the attack. The blunder was not "the outcome of a headstrong belief in brute combat," Lyman wrote. "Rather may it be called a subjective mistake. Because [Grant's] teeth were as firmly set as ever, he supposed that the nerves of other people were still well strung. His want of imagination rendered it difficult for him to understand the condition of his soldiers, or to measure the spirit of his enemy."[13]

Grant had disclosed this "want of imagination" a week before he ordered the final assault at Cold Harbor, when he advised Washington that "Lee's army is really whipped. The prisoners we take now show it, and the action of his army shows it unmistakably." As Ropes said, Grant had arrived from the West "ignorant, grossly ignorant" of his own army's history, "thinking that it only needs to be fought thoroughly to destroy its formidable antagonist." Grant's impression that Confederate morale was broken recalled a maxim that he had often stated to his aides—that "there comes a time in every hard-fought battle, when both armies are nearly or quite exhausted, and it seems impossible for either to do more; this he believed the turning-point; whichever after first renews the fight, is sure to win."[14]

When Grant crossed the Pamunkey thinking that the Rebels before him were already "whipped," he saw it as that turning point, a chance to end it all quickly, and he did very much as Ropes said: he looked for Lee's lines, determined to attack them. The Union army was suffering, but Grant believed the Confederates were suffering more. He would be first to renew the fight, and so, he believed, he was sure to win.

Grant badly misunderstood the enemy, from Robert E. Lee down to the leanest Alabama rifleman. That helps explain why he ordered the final assault at Cold Harbor. He also misunderstood his own army, from George G. Meade down to the weariest Massachusetts private. That helps explain why the assault failed so miserably.

MEADE'S FRIEND John Gibbon, a relentless and studious professional soldier, wrote that Meade "seemed at times perfectly beside himself with passion at some real or imaginary slight he considered had been put upon him." And his "peculiar position" as commander of an army in the constant presence of his general-in-chief produced such slights, real or imaginary, every day.

"The relations between two officers so placed is entirely different from those which exist between an army commander and the commanders of his corps," Gibbon said. "In the latter case, all know that the army commander gives his orders and from them there is no appeal. But in the other case, whilst all the details of projected operations are left to the army commander he cannot help but feel that they are under the immediate supervision of another and he must necessarily be shackled and sensible of the fact that he is deprived of that independence and untrammeled authority so necessary to every army commander.

"In consequence therefore, the arrangement is one condemned in all war-like operations, where *one poor* commander is declared to be better than *two good* ones. With the best and most patriotic intentions on the part of both, clashings are almost certain to occur and here was evidently one which with a *single* commander would never have occurred."[15]

That was the root of the Union army's command problems throughout the spring campaign. Gibbon's assertion is so obviously true, especially in hindsight, that it could stand as a warning for any command relationship, from squad to army group, in any war. In Virginia, Grant did not know the Army of the Potomac intimately enough to give detailed orders as if he were the only general in charge. And Meade did not feel deep personal responsibility for managing operations that Grant had broadly planned. Ropes wrote that "It was for one of them to order what the other was to do, and as the other did only what the first had ordered, many things were ordered which could not be done, and many things were done which ought not to have been ordered." And because of Meade's sensitive pride, repeatedly reinjured by Secretary Stanton's manipulation of the news from Virginia, the awkward situation was never more costly than at Cold Harbor.[16]

As we have seen, Meade seemed to look ahead when he wrote to his wife on June 1, saying, "The papers are giving Grant all the credit of what they call successes; I hope they will remember this if anything goes wrong." On June 9, after the first full newspaper reports of the Cold Harbor fight had reached the field, he told her, "I fully enter into all your feelings of annoyance at the manner in which I have been treated, but I do not see that I can do anything but bear patiently till it pleases God to let the truth be known and matters set right. . . . Now, to tell the truth, [Grant] has greatly disappointed me, and since this campaign I really begin to think I am something of a general."

He resented Grant's "want of delicacy of feeling & sensibility. . . . I dont suppose he has the slightest appreciation of the position he has placed me in & probably is not conscious that in all his dispatches of the operations of this army which he knows has been handled by me he has only once and then accidentally mentioned my name, so that the future historian when collecting official documents to compile a truthful record, would absolutely not know from any evidence (in Grant's dispatches) that I was even present with the army. Now I feel sure if I was to tell this to Grant he would be amazed himself."[17]

Grant could read the Northern newspapers as well as Meade; he was bound to see that he was getting all the credit and Meade was hardly mentioned. He could have advised Halleck, or Stanton, or both, to remember that Meade still commanded the Army of the Potomac. It is possible that Grant was so focused on operations near and far that the unfairness of Stanton's communiqués never occurred to him. It is also possible that he enjoyed the publicity as long as it was favorable, and that he was privately pleased by suggestions that he might become president. If he had political ambitions, or if others like Washburne and Stanton had ambitions for him, there was no reason for them to boost Meade in public opinion. Meanwhile, newspaper reports of the campaign still trumpeted Grant, Grant, Grant, and each day Meade became more unhappy about it.

Few students of the campaign have given full weight to Baldy Smith's postwar account as evidence of Meade's frame of mind at Cold Harbor. On June 5, Meade had gone to Smith's headquarters to explain how he was going to fill the thin stretch of line between the Eighteenth Corps and the Fifth on its right. Smith wrote that in that conversation, he bluntly asked Meade "how he came to give such an order for battle as that of the 2d." According to Smith, Meade replied "that he had worked out every plan for every move from the crossing of the Rapidan onward, that the papers were full of the doings of *Grant's* army, and that he was tired of it, and was determined to let General Grant plan his own battles.

"I have no knowledge of the facts," Smith wrote, "but have always supposed that General Grant's order was to attack the enemy at 4:30 a.m. of the 3d, leaving the details to his subordinate."[18]

Smith's account of that conversation was published years after Meade's death. But it supports what is obvious from the documentary record and the opinions of Charles Dana, Generals Wilson, Rawlins, and Gibbon, and analysts like Ropes and Calrow: Grant left the details to Meade, and Meade left the details to Grant.[19]

More than once on the way from the Rapidan, Grant had issued movement orders that spelled out which roads and bridges each corps would take, and in what sequence. At Cold Harbor, Meade had given exhaustive attention to how Warren and Burnside would accommodate their lines to each other, and to much pettier matters. But in the thirty-plus hours after the June 1 attack at Cold Harbor, when the climactic effort was ordered and twice postponed, the Official Records show only minimal further instructions—for corps commanders to "examine the ground on their fronts and perfect their arrangements for an assault," plus two sentences addressed to Warren and Burnside. While Lee's army was digging deeper, making ready, there was nothing more explicit from Grant or Meade about objectives, about what to do if the assault broke through, or about any other contingencies. No one took seriously Meade's pro forma orders to reconnoiter the field, a measure that should have made clear the futility of an unplanned attack all along the front. As a result, the Army of the Potomac went forward to the most lopsided defeat in its honorable history.

The state of communications between Grant's and Meade's headquarters was so poor that not until June 11, almost six weeks after the spring campaign had begun, did Meade discover that his brooding resentment against Grant was misplaced. Too late to affect what happened at Cold Harbor, he found out that Grant was not responsible for the way his name had overshadowed Meade's in the press.

"It is from Mr. Dana's telegrams that Mr. Stanton's despatches to General Dix are made up," Meade told his wife—and those reports to Dix served as the War Department's official communiqués. "This I learned accidentally," Meade wrote, ". . . in a conversation with Grant, in which I commented on some of Mr. Stanton's despatches. Grant agreed fully with me in my views, and then told me he had never sent a despatch to Mr. Stanton since crossing the Rapidan, the few despatches he had sent being directed to General Halleck. I was glad to hear this, because it removed from my mind a prejudice I had imbibed, on the supposition that Mr. Stanton was quoting Grant, and arising from the fact that I have mentioned, that in all Mr. Stanton's despatches from Grant's headquarters my name was never alluded to; for which I had held Grant responsible, without cause."[20]

Meade did not say that if he had understood this weeks earlier, he would not have gradually become "determined to let General Grant plan his own battles," and would either have seen that the June 3 attack was properly conceived and directed or urged Grant to call it off. To his wife, Meade admitted his prejudice. He could not confess the rest, even to her, and perhaps not even to himself.

UNDERSTANDING Meade's attitude does not absolve others of blame. It was Grant who ordered the army's ill-advised pause after crossing the Pamunkey, and either he or Rawlins who sent Baldy Smith's force marching uselessly to and from New Castle Ferry. Captain Paine, the engineer officer, misguided and delayed Hancock's corps on its way into attack position. Grant, still egged on by Comstock's advice to "Smash 'em up!," stood by his assault order after Hancock's late arrival gave Lee another day to dig in. And Meade ordered his corps commanders to persist after the effort was hopeless.

Meade's chief of staff, Humphreys, could have added specifics to the bare bones of the attack order. Each corps and division commander could have scouted his front closely enough to issue detailed instructions accounting for peculiarities of ground—or to plead that the whole operation be canceled. Hancock could have pushed Birney's division forward in immediate support of Barlow's assault, before the Confederates had time to counterattack. Birney could have taken that initiative on his own. But it is doubtful that reversing what happened at any point after the thoughtless order to attack all along the front, against an army as thoroughly prepared as that under Lee, could have changed the final result.

While distributing the blame among Union generals, beginning at the top, soldiers and historians have paid little attention to the deftness with which Lee handled his much smaller force, through the overland campaign and specifically at Cold Harbor. He did not merely dig in and squat, waiting for the Federals to attack. He threw enough counteroffensive jabs to delay and confuse their tactical moves, and repeatedly shuffled his own scant reserves to the right place at the right time. And his presence, even when he was sick and unable to ride horseback, gave his troops more confidence in the defense than Grant's soldiers could muster for the attack.

GRANT MAINTAINED that before June 3, his unrelenting offensive had changed the earlier attitude of Rebel troops toward soldiers of the Union: "They seemed to have given up any idea of gaining any advantage of their antagonist in the open field." He conceded that the climactic fight "seemed to revive their hopes temporarily," and "the effect upon the Army of the Potomac was the reverse." Yet he maintained that the boost to Confederate morale "was of short duration," and that "when we reached the James River . . . all effects of the battle of Cold Harbor seemed to have disappeared."[21]

For weeks to come, the words and performance of his soldiers, from private to general, would deny that claim. John Gibbon wrote that his division was so worn and torn that the troops, who "at the commencement of the campaign were equal to almost any undertaking, became toward the end of it unfit for almost any." But on the second Saturday after the great battle, spirits in the Union army did lift, if only briefly: at last, something was about to happen. Movement was about to replace the demoralizing inertia of hugging the earth, of digging deeper into the field of defeat. On June 11, Grant's secret plan was disclosed to his corps commanders when Meade issued marching orders drawn up by his chief of staff, Humphreys. They were vastly more detailed than the orders that had sent his army against Lee's lines eight days earlier.[22]

The move to the James River would begin at nightfall on Sunday, June 12, when a brigade of General Wilson's cavalry would cross the Chickahominy to clear the roads for Warren's Fifth Corps. Later that evening, the Second and Sixth would fall back to the prepared line in the rear, holding it until the Fifth passed and deployed to protect their march toward the James. Burnside's Ninth Corps would move south by different roads, taking care not to interfere with other commands. Ferrero's division of the Ninth Corps would continue to cover the army's wagon trains as they moved. At the same time, Smith's Eighteenth Corps would march to White House and sail for Bermuda Hundred, hurrying toward Petersburg before the rest of the army, to try to seize the town before Lee could reinforce its defenders.

Wilson's other cavalry brigade, on the army's right, would withdraw last, protecting the army's rear on the march. Before dawn on Monday, June 13, the whole Union army would be in motion, and pickets left behind to mask the start of the move would pull out to join their commands.

Meade's order specified which roads and bridges would be used by each command, which corps would take precedence where, and how many pontoons would move with whom. It ordered the depot garrison at White House to stay put until the expected arrival of Sheridan and Hunter. Then the supply base would be broken up and transferred downriver to Yorktown. "Corps commanders will see that every precaution is taken to insure the rapid execution of this movement, and that the troops move promptly and quickly on the march," Meade ordered.[23]

This time, the Army of the Potomac needed no prodding to hurry.

17

Across the Last River

GRANT WAS EDGY as he waited for Cyrus Comstock and Horace Porter to return from visiting Ben Butler and scouting the route for the Union army's move across the James. When they rode up from White House in the morning darkness of Sunday, June 12, he immediately asked them into his tent. Porter thought him much more "wrought up" than usual; as the general listened, he smoked his cigar for a few minutes, put it down, picked it up, relit it, and repeated this as the conference went on. Yes, he said, yes, yes, meaning go on, go on. For nearly an hour, he pumped them for information.

The engineer Comstock advised crossing the James at Fort Powhatan; near there, the river was only 2,100 feet wide between Weyanoke Neck on the north bank and Windmill Point on the south. From Cold Harbor to that crossing was about twenty-two straight miles, farther by indirect roads that must take the army first across the Chickahominy. Grant told the two aides that he had already ordered the move to start that very evening.[1]

Even then, the plan was closely held, and each Federal headquarters still tried to keep up a semblance of routine business. Seeing the shortening of lines and shifting of divisions behind them, the troops understood that something was about to happen, but were still unsure what and when. In the Forty-ninth Pennsylvania, David A. Stohl guessed that the troops remaining in the breastworks would hold off the enemy "while some other part of our Army makes a strike; or perhaps till every thing is ready along the whole line and the whole army strike simultaneously. . . . we are still putting guns in good positions. . . ." The Rebels were tracking them over their rifle sights: "It is a very remarkable fact that men here become so accustomed to bullets whistling by them, that they dont mind them and if one chances to

come very close, they will stand and cuss it and the Johnnie that sent
it," Stohl wrote. "I have seen men cut down while they were cussing."[2]

Across no-man's-land, Southern soldiers watching were even fog-
gier about what was happening. "The enemy are massing their troops
& throwing up very strong works immediately in our front which
looks very much like preparations for a siege . . . ," wrote Tom Strayhorn of Heth's division. At higher levels, Confederate thinking
seemed little clearer than in the ranks. Brigadier General W. N.
Pendleton, Lee's artillery chief, reported "both armies entirely quiet"
that morning except for sharpshooting and an occasional cannon firing. "What Grant means, exactly, we can not divine," Pendleton said.
"In order to carry out his programme he must either break through us
or get around again. The former he has already tried here, to his severe
cost, the latter he seems to dread, as it may expose him to injurious
attack from Genl Lee. On the whole he appears ruminating upon the
difficulties of his task."[3]

GENERAL PATRICK, the provost marshal responsible for policing the
Union army in camp and on the march, got up early Sunday to conduct a routine cavalry inspection. On rising, he found a circular from
Meade, asking the commander's staff to show up at headquarters at
8:00 a.m. for a group picture by the famed photographer Mathew
Brady. When he got there, Brady was so busy with other generals that
Patrick had to wait an hour for a sitting. He was not by nature a cheerful man; in his diary, he said, "I doubt if it [will] prove a very good picture," and he was right. But the series of portraits made by Brady and
his assistants on that visit to the Army of the Potomac tells as much
about the Union generals' personalities and attitudes after Cold Harbor as most of them would ever disclose in writing.[4]

Grant, with his left hand on his hip, stands beside a young pine
outside his headquarters tent, a mile and three-quarters back of Cold
Harbor toward Old Church. The other hand almost touches a tent
rope wrapped casually about the tree—no neat sailor's knots
demanded here. The shadows are short; the time is near midday.
Grant wears his broad-brimmed campaign hat square on his head, letting filtered light onto his face. His pose is all defiance and determination, but there is deep weariness about his mouth and eyes, which
seem sad and sunken. Rather than staring boldly into the camera lens,
his eyes angle away to his left. There is little gray in his close-cropped
beard, but he seems older than his forty-two years. One wonders

whether the worry so visible on his face is for what he has just done, or what he is about to do.

In another exposure, the general-in-chief sits in a folding camp chair beside his chief of staff and overseer, the straightforward, black-bearded John Rawlins. Grant pretends to scan a map or newspaper. Behind them stands his adjutant, Major Bowers, his uniform and demeanor making clear his junior status. Then Grant is on his feet again, before a dozen of his staff officers, leaning against the pine and holding what might be a dispatch from Washington.

Few photographs of the war capture the look of esprit de corps more eloquently than the one of Hancock and his division commanders, outside a headquarters much less elaborate than the general-in-chief's. Unlike Grant and his staff, all of these Second Corps generals wear their swords, as if they were accustomed to using them. Hancock, suffering from a flare-up of the old Gettysburg wound in his groin, is seated, his hat tilted confidently forward, hands clasped over the hilt of his sword. The others are standing hatless; Gibbon, on Hancock's left, leans lightly on his sword, and Birney, behind Hancock, seems willing to recede, in keeping with his division's role at Cold Harbor. Barlow stands forward, as his command has done so often. At twenty-nine, he still looks like the "highly independent newsboy" that Lyman described, wearing that trademark checked shirt and a cavalry saber more than half his height—a choice of weapons he explained by saying, "When I hit a straggler I want to hurt him." But Barlow's familiar sarcastic smile is missing. In its place is an I-dare-you stare, the expression of a youth just whipped but ready to take on the world again.[5]

Horatio Wright was the only ranking general pictured during Brady's visit who could not resist falling into the classic Napoleonic pose with hand in tunic, so eagerly adopted earlier in the war by the "Young Napoléon," George McClellan. That pose is a less accurate symbol of Wright's personality than of McClellan's; Wright was efficient and sometimes bold, but never a man of imperial pretensions. Neither, certainly, was Ambrose Burnside, snapped unawares by Brady's assistant while seated on a bag of oats, reading a newspaper just arrived from Washington. He was still stinging from what he considered the insulting treatment by Swinton of the *Times*.

The last portraits of the series may have been those made at Meade's headquarters, in which the commander of the Army of the Potomac sits before thirty-one of his staff, including Provost Marshal Patrick with a full white beard. In this group photograph, Meade discloses a high, pale dome usually covered by his droopy hat. But in the best known, most typical of these pictures, he has that hat on again, shading his eyes. He stands before his tent with one hand at his belt, wearing cavalry boots, ready to head south across the James, but not happy about it or anything else.[6]

DURING THEIR LAST meal before breaking camp, Grant and his staff talked again about the cost of the campaign, and how many troops remained for the march across the James. By Horace Porter's figures, there had been 54,926 Union casualties since crossing the Rapidan, and not all of the reinforcements sent by Washington had ever reached the army. The number of sick, deserters, stragglers, and discharged soldiers had seriously cut Union strength on the way—as Lincoln had said earlier, "It's like trying to shovel fleas in a barnyard; you don't get 'em all there." Grant recalled that in the midst of battle at Shiloh in 1862, Sherman had encountered a colonel who weepingly said he had lost all but a fraction of his regiment. Later, when danger was past and rations were issued, nearly all of the lost hundreds reappeared from beneath a nearby riverbank and set about boiling coffee.[7]

At 3:00 p.m. Sunday, the Union commanders gladly left behind the neighborhood that Captain Adams called "the meanest of the mean— sandy and full of pine barrens, exhausted by man and not attractive by nature . . . sparsely peopled, broken, badly watered, heavily wooded with wretched timber, and wholly uninteresting." But the Federals' pleasure at leaving had less to do with geology, topography, hydrology, and forestry than with history; their memories of 1862 at Fair Oaks, Beaver Dam Creek, and Gaines's Mill, of 1864 at the Totopotomoy, Bethesda Church, and Cold Harbor, would always be tinged with blood. Adams's interest in the land between the Pamunkey and James rivers, and the later interest of Northern historians, might have been greater if the Union army's experience there had been more uplifting.[8]

Grant and Meade, along with their headquarters entourages, made such a parade as they departed that officers en route expected Confederate batteries to spot them and open fire. They marched for about two hours, past Dispatch Station to Moody's farm, arriving as Warren and his staff were leaving to cross the Chickahominy. Grant's orderlies built a big fire to await the headquarters train, which was delayed when several wagons tumbled into a millpond as they crossed its dam. Grant, without his usual comforts, lay down on a board, with a bag under his head, and tried to make up the sleep he had missed in early morning.[9]

Within minutes after darkness fell, the rest of the Union army started its move toward Charles City Court House—all but Smith's Eighteenth Corps, which headed for White House Landing, and the units left to screen the withdrawal. As the Sixth Corps marched away, its troops looked back and laughed to see the Rebels still throwing rounds into their deserted positions. The moon rose bright, just right for marching, and lent an eerie glow to the dust clouds stirred by men and horses ahead.[10]

Wilbur Fisk and most of his comrades of the Second Vermont guessed where they were going, but "our calculations were a little puzzled when, instead of marching off to the left, we started out 'right in front' and marched back on to the right flank." Soon they realized that they were assigned temporarily to the reserve works as rear guard; at midnight, they pulled out toward the Chickahominy. Men of the 110th Ohio were just as confused when they marched out to the right, turned right again along the second line, reversed course to where they had started, and then did it over again. This marching and counter-marching was meant to fool the Confederates into thinking the Yankees were merely relieving their front line rather than pulling out permanently, which they did at 2:00 a.m.[11]

But the last Federal troops to go were the pickets, who waited out beyond the main works with a "sense of loneliness and peril . . . with the knowledge that our preservation depended solely upon the ignorance of our wary foe." Confederate pickets close by were wide-awake, keeping the Yankees nervous by crowing like roosters, quacking like ducks, barking like dogs, imitating "all the songs of a farmyard at dawn." Troops of the Twenty-first Connecticut, left behind by the Eighteenth Corps, were sure the Rebels suspected something, but that they feared a trap and so made no inquiring probes in the darkness. Between 3:00 and 4:00 a.m., as the sky began to pale, Union officers whispered orders to their pickets to pull out quietly and rendezvous in the rear.[12]

As usual, some pickets got left behind. Lieutenant John E. Reilly of the 187th Pennsylvania was in charge of a detail from the Fifth Corps, posted along the Chickahominy where it flowed as a network of narrow streams, divided by little islands. He had placed his pickets at intervals on a narrow trail that ran from island to island. For hours, they heard the regiments behind them marching away, until in early morning there was silence. When no one came to notify them to

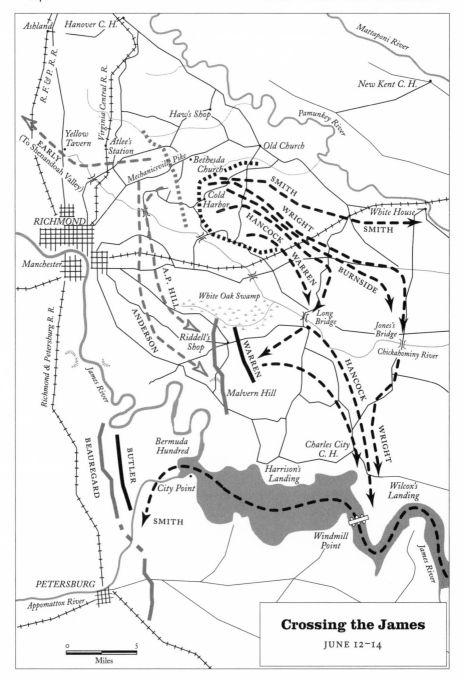

Crossing the James

JUNE 12–14

*In a brilliantly planned and executed move, Grant's army pulls out of Cold
Harbor during the night of June 12. Warren protects the Union flank in a
skirmish at Riddell's Shop. Smith's corps leaves via White House while others
cross the James on a pontoon bridge and ferry boats near Windmill Point.*

leave, Reilly brought his men in, but in the gloom they could not find the trail. They plunged into a swamp, alerting Confederate pickets, who chased them until the pursuers bogged down. At daylight, Reilly's men made it onto solid ground, not knowing which way to go. Reilly figured that Grant must have been heading for the James River as McClellan had done in 1862, and that the river must be off to their right. Sending most of his detail that way, he laid an ambush for Rebel cavalry pressing close behind. He and his ambushers surprised and scattered the horsemen, but did not straggle up to their regiment until near midnight on Monday.[13]

REBEL ARTILLERY officer Robert Stiles wrote that "when we waked on the morning of the 13th and found no enemy in our front we realized that a new element had entered into this move—the element of uncertainty."

At each turn of the campaign, when Grant had seemed to disappear, the Confederates had been confident that they would meet him again trying to get between their army and Richmond. "Not so now," said Stiles; "even Marse Robert, who knew everything knowable, did not appear to know what his old enemy proposed to do or where he would be most likely to find him."[14]

But Stiles could not read Lee's mind. Marse Robert was not surprised, as many have contended, by Grant's move to the James. He expected it, had discussed it with Jeff Davis. They were aware that the Federals had been bringing pontoons up the James, but this was not conclusive: pontoons would be needed to replace destroyed bridges on the lower Chickahominy as well as to cross the much wider James. Lee had to block the way in case the Federals made another drive at Richmond between the Chickahominy and the James, which was the route McClellan had tried. He could not be sure whether Grant would take his entire army across the James or hold a substantial force on the north, to operate on both sides and so force Lee to divide his smaller army still further.[15]

By Monday, Lee had been without most of his cavalry for five days. He had already sent Breckinridge's division to the Shenandoah Valley. On Thursday, June 9, the patched-together defenders of Petersburg had driven off a feeble attack by Butler's troops, and on Saturday, after Beauregard forwarded a rumor that a column of Yankees had crossed to renew the assault there, Lee had sent one of his borrowed brigades back below the James. Then, just before Lee learned that the Union army had disappeared from Cold Harbor, Early's entire corps had set out for the Valley. For Lee to overreact to the unproven suspicion that Grant was taking his whole army south of the James would risk leaving Richmond wide open to the Yankees. He was not willing to take that chance.[16]

At dawn Monday, as soon as Confederate pickets reported the extensive Federal works at Cold Harbor empty, Lee ordered his troops out of their lines in pursuit. His two remaining corps, under Anderson and Hill, hurried across the Chickahominy. During the afternoon, Jeff Davis rode out looking for Lee to discuss what all this meant, but the general was on the move and the president could not find him. Davis was so concerned that he sent a message asking Lee whether they should call Early's corps back before it was too far on the way to the Shenandoah. Lee said that Early might do more good by proceeding, might ease pressure on Richmond by defeating Hunter in the Valley and threatening Washington.

Toward evening, A. P. Hill's troops caught up with Confederate cavalry screening the south flank, which had struck a strong Union force, including infantry, between the Chickahominy and the James. This was Warren's Fifth Corps, carrying out its assignment to protect the Union march route. After sharp skirmishing near Riddell's Shop, Lee deployed his army from Malvern Hill to White Oak Swamp, blocking the way to Richmond between the rivers. Here his troops were within half a day's march of the Confederate pontoon bridge to Drewry's Bluff, in case Lee confirmed that Grant was crossing the James. He directed Hill to attack the Federals facing him Tuesday morning, but once again they pulled away during the night.[17]

Lee advised Davis at noon Tuesday that "I think the enemy must be preparing to move South of the James River." He told what his scouts had reported about Grant's movements, noting that among other options, the Union commander could pull in at Harrison's Landing, where McClellan had entrenched after the Seven Days. Lee would not want to attack him in the deep breastworks left there. "Still," he wrote, "I apprehend that [Grant] may be sending troops up the James River with the view of getting possession of Petersburg before we can reinforce it"—an apprehension that was precisely correct.

The situation called for extreme watchfulness, Lee advised; unless he heard something different by evening, he would move Hoke's division back near the pontoon bridge, ready to cross if needed. "The rest of the army can follow should circumstances require it," he told Davis. Three and a half hours later, he advised the president that he had already ordered Hoke toward the bridge because Grant's "facilities for crossing the River and taking possession of Petersburg are great, and . . . I think it will more probably be his plan. . . ."[18]

As these messages prove, Lee was not fooled by what Grant did. But beyond doubt, he was surprised by the secrecy, speed, and efficiency with which Grant did it. On Tuesday, when Lee told Davis, "I think the enemy must be preparing to move South of the James River," Hancock's Second Corps was already crossing the river aboard ferryboats shuttling between Wilcox's Landing and Windmill Point. Just downstream, in one of the most impressive pioneering feats of the war, Yankee engineers took little more than eight hours to build a 2,100-foot pontoon bridge spanning the eighty-five-foot-deep tidal river between Weyanoke Neck and Fort Powhatan. Baldy Smith, bringing his Eighteenth Corps by boat from White House, reported to Butler on the south side on Tuesday afternoon. By Wednesday morning, most of Grant's hard-marching infantry was across the James and his guns and supply train were on the way.[19]

WHEN WARREN's Fifth Corps rear guard caught its first view of the James River, A. M. Judson of the Eighty-third Pennsylvania thought that "the long wished for goal of our pilgrimage had at last been attained. For six weeks we had been wandering among the wilds of Virginia, shut off from intercourse with the rest of the world. 'If we can only get to the James, we will be all right,' was the universal expression of the soldiers." Judson compared the troops' feeling at seeing the river with the joy of Xenophon's ten thousand Greeks on reaching the Black Sea after their long trek through Asia Minor. "Even the whistle of a locomotive brings delight to the heart of a soldier after a long campaign amidst the wilds of an enemy's country, but the sight of the ocean or a river lifts him out of the depths of melancholy and inspires him with new vigor and new life." Many a Union soldier, including the general-in-chief, agreed with Judson. "When we reached the James River . . . all effects of the battle of Cold Harbor seemed to have disappeared," wrote Grant. The feeling was very temporary.[20]

Grant arrived at the river with his personal entourage on Tuesday, and was gratified to see Hancock's troops loading onto boats and construction of the pontoon bridge going well. From Wilcox's Landing, he took a steamer to Bermuda Hundred, and there told Butler that as soon as Baldy Smith's force landed, he should reinforce it and send it against Petersburg as quickly as possible. Before recrossing the river, Grant reported to Halleck that the enemy had shown no signs yet of bringing troops to the south side, and that "I will have Petersburg secured, if possible, before they get there in much force."[21]

The next morning, he got a telegram from President Lincoln: "Have just read your dispatch of 1 p.m. yesterday. I begin to see it. You will succeed. God bless you all."[22]

When Baldy Smith arrived at Bermuda Hundred, Butler passed on Grant's orders to march against Petersburg at daylight on Wednesday, June 15. Smith's ten thousand soldiers, moving by boat, were fresher than the other four corps marching from Cold Harbor to cross the James. Strengthened by some 2,400 cavalry and 3,700 U.S. Colored Troops of Butler's command, Smith's force had to cover only six or seven miles from its landing on the Appomattox River to the outer defenses of Petersburg. He started his advance early Wednesday but was slowed by a stubborn Confederate cavalry outpost, and did not approach the Rebel works until afternoon.

Beauregard's defenders had had plenty of time to prepare those works, and Smith was impressed by them. Though he could see few infantry troops between the artillery emplacements, he proceeded carefully. In late afternoon, he was advised that Hancock's Second Corps was on its way to join him, and sent word for it to hurry forward.

Remembering what had happened less than two weeks earlier at Cold Harbor, Smith took time for a meticulous reconnaissance before ordering a heavy artillery bombardment on an exposed salient, followed by a rush of skirmishers. At about 7:00 p.m., his troops went forward against brisk cannon and rifle fire, taking two or three hundred prisoners and part of the first line of defensive redans, including sixteen artillery pieces. Most of this success was won by the attached U.S. Colored Troops of Brigadier General Edward W. Hinks's division, who had not been through the experience of Cold Harbor. Rawlins, who had doubted their ability, wrote that in their first serious combat, "they did nobly, and are entitled to be regarded as among the best of soldiers."

Smith did not realize that when he struck the Petersburg defenses, he outnumbered the Confederates before him by roughly five to one. The only force facing him was Brigadier General Henry A. Wise's brigade of 2,400 troops, plus a few home guards and cavalry. But Smith was unwilling to risk pressing on against an enemy of unknown strength. He decided to hold what he had taken and wait till morning to resume the offensive together with Hancock.[23]

By 9:00 p.m., two of Hancock's Union divisions had come up. If they had come sooner, or if Hancock and Smith had shown some of their earlier boldness when they did arrive, the two could have carried Wise's works, captured Petersburg, and probably shortened the war by months. This was just what Grant had in mind, but the otherwise brilliantly executed operation failed because the general-in-chief did not inform either Meade or Hancock that he intended the Second Corps to join Smith in that day's assault on the town. Thus, Hancock dawdled on the way, and when he arrived, Smith asked him merely to relieve his troops at the front. By the time that was done, Hancock decided that despite bright moonlight, it was too late to renew the attack. Except for the Colored Troops' attack, all the boldness at Petersburg that day was on the Confederate side; in Smith and Hancock and their soldiers, the memory of Cold Harbor was too vivid.[24]

On Wednesday evening, Hoke's Confederate division, returned from Lee's control, filed into the Petersburg defenses, and early Thursday, Beauregard summoned another division that had been bottling up Butler at Bermuda Hundred. Lee himself crossed the pontoons bridging the James at Drewry's Bluff that morning with Pickett's division, followed by Field's and later by Kershaw's. But Hill's corps—nearly half of Lee's remaining army—was still north of the river, guarding the way to the capital between the James and the Chickahominy. It was watching part of Wright's Sixth Corps, the last Union infantry to depart the north bank, a force large enough to keep Lee in doubt about whether all of Grant's army was over the river. With most of the Confederate cavalry elsewhere, Lee was unable to mount a strong reconnaissance to settle the question.[25]

That was the situation in late morning, when Lee wrote to Beauregard, "I do not know the position of Grant's army and cannot strip north bank of James River. Have you not force sufficient?" That afternoon, he told him again, "Have not heard of Grant's crossing James River," and half an hour later, he said, "The transports you mention have probably returned Butler's troops. Has Grant been seen crossing James River?"[26]

Standing alone, those messages leave a wrong impression. Lee did not send them in isolation; they were replies to Beauregard's continuing pleas for help. Although Beauregard reported taking a prisoner from the Union Second Corps, Lee still suspected that the troops that had crossed were only Baldy Smith's force, returning to Butler's command, rather than men of Meade's Army of the Potomac. Determined not to leave the front door to Richmond open, he kept resisting the idea that all of Grant's troops were across for almost two more days, until he was convinced that the whole Union force was at the back door, concentrated against Petersburg.[27]

By that time, the gathering Federals had made two more attacks on Beauregard's shrinking lines, each time with greater strength. Finally, after an effort by Burnside's corps was turned back on June 17, Lee was convinced of the danger to Petersburg and sent Anderson's and Hill's corps into the city's defenses. He followed and took command there on the morning of June 18. Grant, facing these Rebel reinforcements, called off further attacks and settled into a siege. Thanks to the efforts of Beauregard and Wise—and the malaise that had overtaken Grant's generals—Petersburg and Richmond were safe until another spring.

GRANT, MEADE, and the Union army were just where they might have been weeks earlier had the general-in-chief decided to approach Richmond from below, the route that McClellan had tried and Grant himself had initially favored. Coming that way, the Federals would have been stronger by more than fifty thousand fresh, spirited men when they moved on Petersburg and the Rebel capital. Many of the Federal troops who crossed the river after Cold Harbor, grieving for missing friends, would never forget the human cost and hardship imposed by Grant's decision to fight his way overland.

The historical debate over that decision and the way he carried it out merges into the long-running dialogue over who won the 1864 spring campaign. Unlike Meade after victory at Gettysburg, Grant after defeat at Cold Harbor was never subjected to second-guessing and harassment by the Committee on the Conduct of the War. As Joshua Chamberlain would write, Grant "was like Thor, the hammerer, striking blow after blow, intent on his purpose to beat his way through, somewhat reckless of the cost." He could proceed that way because he was given more freedom and discretion than any of his predecessors: "He had somehow, with all his modesty, the rare faculty of controlling his superiors as well as his subordinates." The strictest reviews of his generalship came not from above, from Washington, but from those who served below.[28]

The most adept defenders of Grant's strategy have been nimble, skipping in argument from one justification to another. Reminded that Grant had not captured Richmond, they could quote his instructions to Meade before the campaign began: "Lee's army will be your objective point. Wherever Lee's army goes, you will go also."

Responding to that, challengers could cite Rawlins's statement, seven weeks later on the Totopotomoy, that "the reduction of Richmond" was the Union army's original goal, and "thus far there has been no deviation" from it. And to answer that, defenders could produce Rawlins's diary entry, as the army left Cold Harbor: "from the commencement of this campaign General Grant has not deviated at all from his written plan, but has steadily pursued the line he then marked out."[29]

Lee's army was still fighting, but Grant's partisans could say that his offensive had damaged it severely, to which the obvious answer was that Grant's own army had suffered many more casualties than Lee's. On the way south, Grant had said repeatedly that he wanted to tempt Lee out of his trenches to fight in the open, but after Cold Harbor, his aim was to hold Lee in place while the Federals swung across the James. Claims and counterclaims, of goals and successes, varied with the circumstances of the moment.

Tactically, and in the short run strategically, it is possible to say that Lee won the Virginia campaign of 1864. He frustrated both of Grant's objectives—defeating Lee's army and capturing Richmond. Between the Rapidan and the James, Lee inflicted approximately as many losses on the Union forces as he had men in his entire army. By casualty count, he defeated Grant and Meade at the Wilderness. Then he fought them to better than a draw at Spotsylvania and checked them brilliantly on the North Anna. Yet when the Federals crossed the Pamunkey, they still had a chance to achieve both their objectives. But seemingly minor breaks and mistakes, combined with Lee's skillful juggling of his smaller army, brought the campaign to its climax at Cold Harbor.

There, Grant's initial blunder as general-in-chief, placing himself over the shoulder of the already abused Meade, overshadowing him in the eyes of the army and the nation, brought on what now seems a predictable result. With two generals in command, no one properly managed the assault at Cold Harbor. There Grant suffered his worst defeat and Lee won his last great victory, and what happened there determined what happened across the James.

On reaching the river, Warren's artillery chief, Charles Wainwright, wrote in his diary that "it is impossible not to be reminded of 1862, and to be comparing the incidents of that campaign with this. They both had the same objective—Richmond; and both ended in the same way, failure and the James River." Grant, Wainwright said, started with more men than McClellan had, against a smaller Confederate force;

he had experienced officers, superb logistical support, and full backing from Washington, rather than being "thwarted at every step." He lost twice as many men as McClellan did. Yet "the people wildly laud Grant to the skies and call McClellan a traitor. . . . The army sees through spectacles of another colour. . . . the men are getting tired of this constant jamming, and unless General Grant finds some other way of fighting them they will show but little spirit in the matter."

Wainwright's prejudice, compounded by events, was clear, but such feelings were widespread after Cold Harbor. Years later, when the bitterness had faded, General Wilson would write that "it had become painfully apparent that [the army's] fighting impulse had been greatly diminished. It was as though the loss of blood it poured out so freely was distinctly lowering its fighting temper and decreasing its confidence of success. These facts were freely admitted by all. . . ."[30]

A Cold Harbor syndrome, a reluctance to charge enemy breastworks, a memory of comrades left dying in the sun, hung over Grant's soldiers, and especially his generals. It held them back when they could easily have overrun the puny Confederate force at Petersburg. Meade himself said that that effort failed "principally owing to the moral condition of the army; for I am satisfied, had these assaults been made on the 5th and 6th of May, we should have succeeded with half the loss we met. . . . I regret to see symptoms of a discontent which, if persisted in, must paralyze our cause." Thus, instead of ending that summer, the war dragged on and morale in the North plunged.[31]

But in the longer run, by bleeding Lee's army and pinning it down, Grant had ended the war of slash and maneuver at which the Confederate commander excelled and begun the war of siege, which Lee could not win. By Lee's own standard, expressed to Jubal Early in May, the Confederates had failed in the campaign. "We must destroy this army of Grant's before he gets to the James River," he had said then. "If he gets there it will become a siege, and then it will be a mere question of time."[32]

As Captain Blackford of Virginia had written on the way south, the Confederates won fight after fight, but "we are being conquered by the splendor of our own victories, and Grant accepts defeat with that consolation. . . ." Grant had not destroyed Lee's army, as he set out to do. But, more important, Lee had not destroyed Grant's. Thus it became "a mere question of time"—and food, and munitions, and manpower. To that question, the inevitable answer came at Appomattox Court House, ten months and many thousands of lives after Grant pulled away from the grisly field of Cold Harbor.[33]

Epilogue

Dust to Kindly Dust

ON THE BRIGHT morning of June 1, 1865, a hundred of the Union troops occupying the capital of the defeated Confederacy, unarmed and wearing fatigue uniforms, marched out the Mechanicsville Pike. Ahead of them, a mule team drew a white-covered wagon carrying picks, shovels, and long-handled spades. The soldiers, longing to go home for almost seven weeks since Appomattox, were glad to have a day off from the monotony of drill and the routine of policing their camps. As they left the city limits, they joked with each other, feeling light and frivolous without their usual burden of weapons and equipment. Then they turned down the road toward Gaines's Mill and Cold Harbor, and the reality of why they had come took hold, silencing their banter.

They were assigned to burial duty, the bringing of peace to the remains of comrades that had lain untended or upturned on the battlefield during the past year. The Federal troops, still bitter, blamed the Confederates who had held the ground after the campaign of 1864 for not paying decent respect to the fallen. "All the summer and winter and spring have our unburied heroes lain at the mercy of wind and storm, exposed to the fowls of the air and the beasts of the field," a Connecticut soldier wrote. "Their corpses have been overturned, their clothing has been stripped off, every pocket has been cut out and rifled, but no hand has offered to return the dust to kindly dust once more."

Among the many bodies, the burial detail came upon two men, perhaps brothers, who had died in each other's arms. They still clutched each other, and their belts still bore U.S. buckles tarnished green by the weather. "Take up the twain as tenderly as a mother would her babe," the soldier wrote. "Lay them side by side, that e'en in burial their embrace may be unbroken. And so these wasted forms were shielded at last, when the cruel war was over, and after many days of labor this great potter's field was made clean."[1]

But neither man nor the elements would leave it undisturbed.

Five years after Cold Harbor, Russell Conwell, a Massachusetts veteran of the campaign, wrote of visiting the field and remembering its horrors. "Even to an American who knows full well the strength of our army, the magnitude of this battle is seldom comprehended," he said. Tramping the fields, ravines, and overgrown breastworks, he thought of how many men had died there in so short a time. "No other battle of the war has such a history as that. Ah, that was a terrible day!" Conwell tried to enumerate the Massachusetts regiments that had fought there, but gave up, for there was "hardly a State or town in the North that did not lose a valuable citizen in the first ten minutes of the fight on the morning of June 3, 1864."

The vast earthworks about Cold Harbor were already disappearing "under the hands of the diligent lead searchers," who carried on a profitable business carting scrap iron and lead from the battlefield into Richmond. But Conwell was more interested in the black men "with large sacks, collecting the bones of dead horses which they sold to the bone-grinders. . . ." He wondered whether all those bones were of horses. "Skeletons and ghosts haunt us in our dreams," he wrote, "and grinning skulls are all we can think of by day."

All the Union dead were believed to have been collected soon after the war and sent home or properly buried in government cemeteries, Conwell wrote—"in one case they were obliged to bury 631 in a single grave, and in another over 300." But "Since then the Negroes have dug up many bodies, and the bones of Union and Confederate soldiers. We found in all parts of the field that skulls, ribs, legs, and arm-bones lay scattered about in fearful array, while the bones of many a poor soldier lay partially exposed through the action of the rain."

Conwell came upon a man who had just exhumed a body, apparently that of a Massachusetts artilleryman, and found with it a silver watch. He bought the watch from the scavenger and sent it to Boston, hoping that it might find its way to the soldier's next-of-kin. The cemetery keeper told him that he had reported the exposed bodies, and "doubtless the government would soon see them properly buried."[2]

Today, the Cold Harbor National Cemetery is surrounded by a low brick wall, and here and there trees have grown out of graves, their roots embracing the plain headstones as if to hasten their crumbling into the soil of Virginia. Occasionally a car stops and someone walks in to look for an ancestor. There are 1,986 Union graves, but only a third of them bear names. The remaining 1,313 are marked "Unknown." Other bones are still being found and counted.

Appendix 1

ORDER OF BATTLE

The flood of new units and the reorganization of old commands before and after the battles of Cold Harbor kept the rosters of the opposing armies in constant flux from day to day. This list is meant to show the command structure during the critical period from May 30 through June 3, 1864. The following designations are used throughout: k—killed; mw—mortally wounded; w—wounded; m—missing; r—relieved from command.

General-in-Chief, U.S. Armies
Lt. Gen. Ulysses S. Grant

Army of the Potomac
Maj. Gen. George G. Meade
Maj. Gen. A. A. Humphreys, Chief of Staff

Provost Guard
Brig. Gen. Marsena R. Patrick
1st Mass. Cav., Cos. C & D
80th N.Y.
3d Pa. Cav.
68th, 114th Pa.

Engineers
50th N.Y. Engineers
U.S. Engineer Bn.

Artillery
Brig. Gen. Henry J. Hunt

Second Corps
Maj. Gen. Winfield S. Hancock

FIRST DIVISION
Brig. Gen. Francis C. Barlow

1st Brigade
Col. Nelson A. Miles
26th Mich.
2nd N.Y. Heavy Arty.
61st N.Y.
81st, 140th, 183rd Pa.
5th N.H.

2nd Brigade
Col. Richard Byrnes (k 6/3)
Col. Patrick Kelly
28th Mass.
63rd, 69th, 88th N.Y.
116th Pa.

3rd Brigade
Col. Clinton D. McDougall
39th, 52nd, 111th,
125th, 126th N.Y.

4th Brigade
Col. John R. Brooke (w 6/3)
Col. Orlando H. Morris (k 6/3)
Col. Lewis O. Morris (k 6/4)
Col. James A. Beaver
2nd Del.
7th N.Y. Heavy Arty.
64th, 66th N.Y.
53rd, 145th, 148th Pa.

SECOND DIVISION
Brig. Gen. John Gibbon

1st Brigade
Col. H. Boyd McKeen (k 6/3)
Col. Frank A. Haskell (k 6/3)
Col. Byron R. Pierce
19th Maine
15th, 19th, 20th Mass.
1st Co. Mass. Sharpshooters
7th Mich.
42nd, 59th N.Y.
82nd N.Y. Bn.
184th Pa.
36th Wis.

2nd Brigade
Brig. Gen. Joshua T. Owen
152nd N.Y.
69th, 71st, 72nd, 106th Pa.

3rd Brigade
Col. Thomas A. Smyth
14th Conn.
1st Del.
12th N.J.
10th N.Y. Bn., 108th N.Y.
4th, 8th Ohio
7th W. Va. Bn.
14th Ind.

4th Brigade
Brig. Gen. Robert O. Tyler (w 6/3)
Col. James P. McIvor
8th N.Y. Heavy Arty.
155th, 164th, 170th, 182nd N.Y.

THIRD DIVISION
Maj. Gen. David B. Birney

1st Brigade
Col. Thomas W. Egan
20th Ind.
3rd Maine
40th, 86th, 124th N.Y.
99th, 110th, 141st Pa.
2nd U.S. Sharpshooters

2nd Brigade
Col. Thomas R. Tannatt
4th, 17th Maine
1st Mass. Heavy Arty.
3rd, 5th Mich.
93rd N.Y.
57th, 63rd, 105th Pa.
1st U.S. Sharpshooters

3rd Brigade
Brig. Gen. Gershom Mott
1st Maine Heavy Arty.
16th Mass.
5th, 6th, 7th, 8th, 11th N.J.
115th Pa.

4th Brigade
Col. William R. Brewster
11th Mass.
70th, 71st, 72nd, 73rd, 74th, 120th N.Y.
84th Pa.

Artillery
Col. John C. Tidball
Mass. Light, 10th Btry.
1st N.Y. Light, Btry. G
11th, 12th Btry. N.Y. Light
4th N.Y. Heavy
1st Pa. Light, Btry. F
1st R.I. Light, Btry. A
4th U.S. Btry. K
5th U.S. Btry. C, I
Maine Light, 6th Btry.
N.H. Light, 1st Btry.
1st N.J. Light, Btry. B

FIFTH CORPS

Maj. Gen. Gouverneur K. Warren

FIRST DIVISION
Brig. Gen. Charles Griffin

1st Brigade
Brig. Gen. Romeyn B. Ayres
Col. Edward S. Bragg
140th, 146th N.Y.
91st, 155th Pa.
11th, 12th, 14th, 17th U.S.

2nd Brigade
Col. Jacob B. Sweitzer
9th, 22nd, 32nd Mass.
4th Mich.
62nd Pa.
21st Pa. Cav. (dismounted)

3rd Brigade
Brig. Gen. Joseph J. Bartlett
20th Maine
18th, 29th Mass.
1st, 16th Mich.
44th N.Y.
83rd, 118th Pa.

SECOND DIVISION
Brig. Gen. Henry H. Lockwood (r 6/2)
Brig. Gen. Samuel W. Crawford (6/2–6/4)

1st Brigade   *2nd Brigade*
Col. Peter Lyle   Col. James L. Bates
16th Maine   12th Mass.
13th, 39th Mass.   83rd, 97th N.Y.
94th, 104th N.Y.   11th, 88th Pa.
90th, 107th Pa.

3rd Brigade
Col. Nathan T. Dushane
1st, 4th, 7th, 8th Md.
Purnell Legion, Md.
6th N.Y. Heavy Arty.
15th N.Y. Heavy Arty., 1st & 2nd Bns.

THIRD DIVISION
Brig. Gen. Samuel W. Crawford

1st Brigade   *3rd Brigade**
Col. Martin D. Hardin   Col. Joseph W. Fisher
1st, 2nd, 6th, 7th, 11th,   Maj. William R. Hartshorne
13th Pa. Reserves†   5th, 10th, 12th Pa. Reserves†
                                                 190th, 191st Pa. Reserves†

Heavy Artillery Brigade
Col. J. Howard Kitching
6th N.Y. Heavy
15th N.Y. Heavy, 1st & 3rd Bns. (5/30–6/2)

* The 2nd Brigade, Third Division, discontinued in May 1863, was not reorganized until June 6, 1864.
† Most of the Pa. Reserves were ordered home on May 31 for mustering out. The 190th & 191st (1st Pa. Veteran Reserves) were made up mainly of troops reenlisted and remaining in the field. A new Third Division was created when the Fifth Corps reorganized on June 6.

FOURTH DIVISION
Brig. Gen. Lysander Cutler

1st Brigade
Col. William W. Robinson
7th, 19th Ind.
24th Mich.
1st Bn. N.Y. Sharpshooters
6th, 7th Wis.

2nd Brigade
Col. J. William Hofman
3rd Del.
46th, 76th, 95th, 147th N.Y.
56th Pa.
157th Pa. (6/2)

3rd Brigade
Col. Edward S. Bragg
121st, 142nd, 143rd, 149th, 150th Pa.

Artillery
Col. Charles S. Wainwright
Mass. Light, 3rd, 5th, 9th Btrys.
1st N.Y. Light, Btrys. B, C, D, E, H, L
N.Y. Light, 15th Btry.
4th U.S., Btry. B
5th U.S., Btry. D
1st Pa. Light, Btry. B

SIXTH CORPS

Maj. Gen. Horatio G. Wright

FIRST DIVISION
Brig. Gen. David A. Russell

1st Brigade
Col. Wm. H. Penrose
1st, 2nd, 3rd, 4th,
10th, 15th N.J.

2nd Brigade
Brig. Gen. Emory Upton
2nd Conn. Heavy Arty.
5th Maine
121st N.Y.
95th, 96th Pa.

3rd Brigade
Brig. Gen. Henry L. Eustis
6th Maine
49th, 119th Pa.
5th Wis.

4th Brigade
Col. Nelson Cross
65th, 67th, 122nd N.Y.
23rd, 82nd Pa.

SECOND DIVISION
Brig. Gen. Thomas H. Neill

1st Brigade
Brig. Gen. Frank Wheaton
62nd N.Y.
93rd, 98th, 102nd, 139th Pa.

2nd Brigade
Brig. Gen. Lewis A. Grant
2nd, 3rd, 4th, 5th, 6th Vt.
11th Vt. (1st Vt. Heavy Arty.)

3rd Brigade
Col. Daniel D. Bidwell
7th Maine
49th, 77th N.Y.
61st Pa.

4th Brigade
Col. Oliver Edwards
7th, 10th, 37th Mass.
2nd R.I.

THIRD DIVISION
Brig. Gen. James B. Ricketts

1st Brigade
Col. William S. Truex (w 6/1)
Lt. Col. Caldwell K. Hall
Col. John W. Schall (w 6/3)
14th N.J.
106th, 151st N.Y.
87th Pa.
10th Vt.

2nd Brigade
Col. Benjamin F. Smith
Col. John W. Horn (6/3–6/11)
6th Md.
9th N.Y. Heavy Arty.,
1st & 3rd Btrys.
110th, 122nd, 126th Ohio
67th, 138th Pa.

Artillery
Col. Charles H. Tompkins
Maine Light, 4th, 5th Btrys.
Mass. Light, 1st Btry.
1st N.J. Light, Btry. A
N.Y. Light, 1st, 3rd Btrys.
1st R.I. Light, Btrys. C, E, G
5th U.S., Btrys. E, M
1st Ohio Light, Btry. H

NINTH CORPS

Maj. Gen. Ambrose E. Burnside

FIRST DIVISION
Maj. Gen. Thomas L. Crittenden

1st Brigade
Brig. Gen. James H. Ledlie
56th, 57th, 59th Mass.
4th, 10th U.S.

2nd Brigade
Col. Joseph M. Sudsburg
3rd Md.
21st, 29th Mass.
100th Pa.

3rd (Provisional) Brigade
Col. Elisha G. Marshall
2nd N.Y. Mounted Rifles (dismounted)
24th N.Y. Cav. (dismounted)
14th N.Y. Heavy Arty.
2nd Pa. Prov. Heavy Arty.

Artillery
Maine Light, 2nd Btry.
Mass. Light, 14th Btry.

SECOND DIVISION
Brig. Gen. Robert B. Potter

1st Brigade	*2nd Brigade*
Col. John I. Curtin	Gen. Simon G. Griffin
36th, 58th Mass.	2nd Md.
2nd N.Y. Mounted Rifles	31st, 32nd Maine
45th, 48th Pa.	6th, 9th, 11th N.H.
7th R.I.	17th Vt.

Artillery
N.Y. Light, 19th Btry.
Mass. Light, 11th Btry.

THIRD DIVISION
Brig. Gen. Orlando B. Willcox

1st Brigade	*2nd Brigade*
Brig. Gen. John F. Hartranft	Col. Benjamin G. Christ
2nd, 8th, 27th Mich.	1st Mich. Sharpshooters
109th N.Y.	20th Mich.
51st Pa.	24th N.Y. Cav.
	46th N.Y.
	60th Ohio
	50th Pa.

Artillery
Maine Light, 7th Btry.
N.Y. Light, 34th Btry.

FOURTH DIVISION
Brig. Gen. Edward Ferrero

1st Brigade	*2nd Brigade*
Col. Joshua K. Sigfried	Col. Henry G. Thomas
27th, 30th, 39th, 43rd	19th, 23rd, 31st
U.S. Colored Troops	U.S. Colored Troops

Artillery
Pa. Light, Btry. D
Vt. Light, 3rd Btry.

Cavalry
3rd N.J., 22nd N.Y., 2nd Ohio, 13th Pa.

EIGHTEENTH CORPS
Maj. Gen. William F. Smith

FIRST DIVISION
Brig. Gen. William T. H. Brooks

1st Brigade
Brig. Gen. Gilman Marston
61st, 81st, 96th, 98th, 139th
N.Y.

2nd Brigade
Brig. Gen. Hiram Burnham
8th Conn.
10th, 13th N.H.
118th N.Y.

3rd Brigade
Col. Guy V. Henry
21st, 40th Mass.
92nd N.Y.
58th, 188th Pa.

SECOND DIVISION
Brig. Gen. John H. Martindale

1st Brigade
Brig. Gen. George J. Stannard
23rd, 25th, 27th Mass.
9th N.J.
89th N.Y.
55th Pa.

2nd Brigade
Col. Griffin A. Stedman, Jr.
11th Conn.
8th Maine
2nd, 12th N.H.
148th N.Y.

THIRD DIVISION
Brig. Gen. Charles Devens, Jr.

1st Brigade
Col. William B. Barton
47th, 48th, 115th N.Y.
76th Pa.

2nd Brigade
Col. Jeremiah C. Drake (mw 6/1)
Lt. Col. Z. H. Robinson
13th Ind.
9th Maine
112th, 169th N.Y.
10th N.Y. Heavy Arty.

3rd Brigade
Brig. Gen. Adelbert Ames
4th N.H.
3rd, 117th, 142nd N.Y.
97th Pa.

Artillery
1st U.S., Btry. B
4th U.S., Btry. L
5th U.S., Btry. A

CAVALRY CORPS
Maj. Gen. Philip H. Sheridan

FIRST DIVISION
Brig. Gen. Alfred T. A. Torbert

1st Brigade
Brig. Gen. George A. Custer
1st, 5th, 6th, 7th Mich.

2nd Brigade
Col. Thomas C. Devin
4th, 6th, 9th N.Y.
17th Pa.

Reserve Brigade
Brig. Gen. Wesley Merritt
19th N.Y. (1st Dragoons)
6th Pa.
1st, 2nd, 5th U.S.

SECOND DIVISION
Brig. Gen. David McMurtrie Gregg

1st Brigade
Brig. Gen. Henry E. Davies, Jr.
1st Mass.
1st N.J.
10th N.Y.
6th Ohio
1st Pa.

2nd Brigade
Col. J. Irvin Gregg
1st Maine
2nd, 4th, 8th, 13th,
16th Pa.

THIRD DIVISION
Brig. Gen. James H. Wilson

1st Brigade
Col. John D. McIntosh
1st Conn.
3rd N.J.
2nd, 5th N.Y.
2nd Ohio
18th Pa.

2nd Brigade
Col. George H. Chapman
3rd Ind.
8th, 22nd N.Y.
1st Vt.
1st N.H.

HORSE ARTILLERY

1st Brigade
Capt. James M. Robertson
N.Y. Light, 6th Btry.
2nd U.S., Btrys. B, D, L, M
4th U.S., Btrys. A, C, E

2nd Brigade
Capt. Dunbar R. Ransom
1st U.S., Btrys. E, G,
H, I, K
2nd U.S., Btrys. A, G
3rd U.S., Btrys. C, F, K

Army of Northern Virginia
Gen. Robert E. Lee

FIRST CORPS
Lt. Gen. Richard H. Anderson

KERSHAW'S DIVISION
Maj. Gen. Joseph B. Kershaw

Kershaw's Brigade
Col. Lawrence M. Keitt (mw 6/1)
Col. John W. Henagan
2nd, 3rd, 7th, 8th, 15th, 20th S.C.
3rd S.C. Bn. Sharpshooters

Wofford's Brigade
Brig. Gen. William T. Wofford
16th, 18th, 24th Ga.
Cobb's (Ga.) Legion
Phillips (Ga.) Legion
3rd Ga. Bn. Sharpshooters

Humphreys' Brigade
Brig. Gen. Benjamin G. Humphreys
13th, 17th, 18th,
21st Miss.

Bryan's Brigade
Brig. Gen. Goode Bryan
Col. James P. Simms
10th, 50th, 51st, 53rd Ga.

FIELD'S DIVISION
Maj. Gen. Charles W. Field

Bratton's Brigade
Brig. Gen. John Bratton
1st, 2nd, 5th, 6th S.C.
Palmetto (S.C.) Sharpshooters

Law's Brigade
Brig. Gen. Evander M. Law (w 6/3)
Col. Pinckney D. Bowles
4th, 15th, 44th, 47th, 48th Ala.

Anderson's Brigade
Brig. Gen. George T. Anderson
7th, 8th, 9th, 11th,
59th Ga.

Gregg's Brigade
Brig. Gen. John Gregg
3rd Ark.
1st, 4th, 5th Texas

Benning's Brigade
Col. Dudley M. DuBose
2nd, 15th, 17th, 20th Ga.

PICKETT'S DIVISION
Maj. Gen. George E. Pickett

Kemper's Brigade
Brig. Gen. William R. Terry
1st, 3rd, 7th, 11th,
24th Va.

Barton's Brigade
Col. Wm. R. Aylett
9th, 14th, 38th,
53rd, 57th Va.

Corse's Brigade
Brig. Gen. Montgomery D. Corse
15th, 17th, 29th, 30th,
32nd Va.

Hunton's Brigade
Brig. Gen. Eppa Hunton
8th, 18th, 19th,
28th, 56th Va.

ARTILLERY
Brig. Gen. E. Porter Alexander

Huger's Battalion
Lt. Col. Frank Huger
Fickling's (S.C.)*
Moody's (La.)
Parker's, J. D. Smith's,
Taylor's, Woolfolk's (Va.)

Haskell's Battalion
Maj. John C. Haskell
Flanner's, Ramsey's (N.C.)
Garden's (S.C.)
Lamkin's (Va.)

Cabell's Battalion
Col. Henry C. Cabell
Callaway's, Carlton's (Ga.)
McCarthy's (Va.)
Manly's (N.C.)

---

* Confederate artillery batteries are designated here by commander's name and state only.

Second Corps
Lt. Gen. Jubal A. Early

ramseur's division
Maj. Gen. Stephen D. Ramseur

Toon's Brigade
Brig. Gen. Thomas F. Toon
5th, 12th, 20th,
23rd N.C.

Pegram's Brigade
Col. Edward Willis (k 5/30)
13th, 31st, 49th,
52nd, 58th Va.

Lewis's Brigade
Col. William G. Lewis
6th, 21st, 54th, 57th N.C.
1st N.C. Bn. Sharpshooters

gordon's division
Maj. Gen. John B. Gordon

*Hays's Brigade**
Brig. Gen. Zebulon York
5th, 6th, 7th, 8th,
9th La. & remainder of
Stafford's La. Brigade

*Terry's Brigade**
Brig. Gen. William Terry
Remainder of Stonewall,
Jones's, & Steuart's
Va. brigades

Gordon's Brigade
Brig. Gen. Clement A. Evans
13th, 26th, 31st, 38th, 60th, 61st Ga.
12th Bn. Ga. Arty.

rodes's division
Maj. Gen. Robert E. Rodes

Grimes's Brigade
Brig. Gen. Bryan Grimes
32nd, 43rd, 45th, 53rd N.C.
2nd N.C. Bn.

Doles's Brigade
Brig. Gen. George Doles (k 6/2)
4th, 12th, 21st, 44th Ga.

Ramseur's Brigade
Brig. Gen. William R. Cox
2nd, 4th, 14th, 30th N.C.

Battle's Brigade
Brig. Gen. Cullen A. Battle
3rd, 5th, 6th, 12th, 61st Ala.

* Reorganized after heavy losses at Spotsylvania Court House.

ARTILLERY
Brig. Gen. Armistead L. Long

Hardaway's Battalion
Lt. Col. Robert A. Hardaway
Dance's, Graham's,
C. B. Griffin's, Jones's,
H. B. Smith's (Va.)

Braxton's Battalion
Lt. Col. Carter M. Braxton
Carpenter's, Cooper's,
Hardwick's (Va.)

Nelson's Battalion
Lt. Col. William Nelson
Kirkpatrick's, Massie's (Va.)
Milledge's (Ga.)

Cutshaw's Battalion
Maj. Wilfred E. Cutshaw
Carrington's, A. W. Garber's,
Tanner's (Va.)

Page's Battalion
Maj. Richard C. M. Page
W. P. Carter's, Fry's, Page's (Va.)
Reese's (Ala.)

Third Corps
Lt. Gen. Ambrose P. Hill

MAHONE'S DIVISION
Brig. Gen. William Mahone

Perrin's Brigade
Brig. Gen. John C. C. Sanders
8th, 9th, 10th, 11th,
14th Ala.

Mahone's Brigade
Col. David A. Weisiger
6th, 12th, 16th,
41st, 61st Va.

Finegan's Brigade
Brig. Gen. Joseph Finegan
2nd, 5th, 8th, 9th, 10th,
11th Fla.

Harris's Brigade
Brig. Gen. Nathaniel H. Harris
12th, 16th, 19th,
48th Miss.

Wright's Brigade
Brig. Gen. Ambrose R. Wright
3rd, 22nd, 48th Ga.
2nd, 10th Ga. Bns.

HETH'S DIVISION
Maj. Gen. Henry Heth

Davis's Brigade
Brig. Gen. Joseph R. Davis
2nd, 11th, 26th, 42nd Miss.
55th N.C.
1st Confed. Bn.

Cooke's Brigade
Brig. Gen. John R. Cooke
15th, 27th, 46th, 48th N.C.

Kirkland's Brigade	*Walker's Brigade*
Brig. Gen. William W. Kirkland	Brig. Gen. B. D. Fry
Col. George H. Faribault	40th, 47th, 55th Va.
11th, 26th, 44th, 47th,	22nd Va. Bn.
52nd N.C.	13th Ala.
	1st, 7th, 14th Tenn.

WILCOX'S DIVISION
Maj. Gen. Cadmus M. Wilcox

Lane's Brigade	*Scales's Brigade*
Brig. Gen. James H. Lane (w 6/2)	Brig. Gen. Alfred M. Scales
Col. John D. Barry	13th, 16th, 22nd, 34th,
7th, 18th, 28th, 33rd,	38th N.C.
37th N.C.	

Conner's Brigade	*Thomas's Brigade*
Brig. Gen. James Conner	Col. Thomas J. Simmons
1st, 12th, 13th, 14th S.C.	14th, 35th, 45th, 49th Ga.
Orr's Rifles (S.C.)	

ARTILLERY
Col. R. Lindsay Walker

Poague's Battalion	*Pegram's Battalion*
Lt. Col. William Poague	Lt. Col. William J. Pegram
Richards's (Miss.)	Brander's, Cayce's,
Utterback's, Wyatt's (Va.)	Ellett's, Marye's (Va.)
Williams's (N.C.)	Zimmerman's (S.C.)

McIntosh's Battalion	*Cutts's Battalion*
Lt. Col. David G. McIntosh	Col. Allen S. Cutts
Clutter's, Donald's, Hurt's,	Patterson's, Ross's,
Price's (Va.)	Wingfield's (Ga.)
Dement's (Md.)	

Richardson's Battalion
Lt. Col. Charles Richardson
Grandy's, Landry's, Moore's, Penick's (Va.)

(Units Not Assigned to Corps)

BRECKINRIDGE'S COMMAND
Maj. Gen. John C. Breckinridge

Echols's Brigade
Brig. Gen. John Echols
Col. George S. Patton
22nd Va.
23rd, 26th Va. Bn.

Wharton's Brigade
Brig. Gen. Gabriel C. Wharton
45th, 51st Va.
30th Va. Bn. Sharpshooters

Maryland Line
2nd Md. Bn.

HOKE'S DIVISION
Maj. Gen. Robert F. Hoke

Martin's Brigade
Brig. Gen. James G. Martin
17th, 42nd, 66th N.C.

Clingman's Brigade
Brig. Gen. Thomas L. Clingman
8th, 31st, 51st, 61st N.C.

Hagood's Brigade
Brig. Gen. Johnson Hagood
11th, 21st, 25th,
27th S.C.
7th S.C. Bn.

Colquitt's Brigade
Brig. Gen. Alfred H. Colquitt
6th, 19th, 23rd, 27th,
28th Ga.

Read's Artillery Battalion
Maj. John P. W. Read
Blount's, Caskie's, Macon's, Marshall's (Va.)

CAVALRY CORPS

HAMPTON'S DIVISION
Maj. Gen. Wade Hampton

Young's Brigade
Brig. Gen. Pierce M. B. Young
7th Ga.
Cobb's Legion (Ga.)
Phillips Legion (Ga.)
20th Ga. Bn.
Jeff Davis Legion (Miss.)

Rosser's Brigade
Brig. Gen. Thomas L. Rosser
7th, 11th, 12th Va.
35th Va. Bn.

Butler's Brigade
Brig. Gen. Matthew C. Butler
4th, 5th, 6th S.C.

FITZHUGH LEE'S DIVISION
Maj. Gen. Fitzhugh Lee

Lomax's Brigade
Brig. Gen. Lunsford L. Lomax
5th, 6th, 15th Va.

Wickham's Brigade
Brig. Gen. Williams C. Wickham
1st, 2nd, 3rd, 4th Va.

W. H. F. LEE'S DIVISION
Maj. Gen. William Henry Fitzhugh (Rooney) Lee

Chambliss's Brigade
Brig. Gen. John R. Chambliss, Jr.
9th, 10th, 13th Va.

Gordon's Brigade
Col. John A. Baker
1st, 2nd, 3rd, 4th N.C.

JOHNSON'S COMMAND
1st Md. Cav. Bn.

Horse Artillery
Maj. R. Preston Chew

Breathed's Battalion
Maj. James Breathed
Hart's (S.C.)
Johnston's, McGregor's, Shoemaker's, Thompson's (Va.)

This Order of Battle is based on a list compiled by Charles J. Calrow from the Official Records, Vol. 36, Pt. 1, with later revisions by the historian staff at Richmond National Battlefield Park.

Appendix 2

CASUALTIES

ACCURATE tabulation of Civil War casualties became more difficult as the war wore on. Throughout the struggle, Union lists were more complete than those compiled by the Confederates. But they were seldom precise, partly because troops killed outright were sometimes listed separately from those mortally wounded, and the bodies of many soldiers initially listed as missing were later recovered or buried anonymously on the field. Confederate reports often did not even refer to the missing, and most of those for the latter stages of the war were either not filed at all or lost in the evacuation fire at Richmond and the retreat to Appomattox.

Specifying Union casualties of the Cold Harbor campaign, from crossing the Pamunkey to crossing the James, is complicated by the way reinforcing units as small as batteries and as large as corps came and went from the Army of the Potomac. On a lesser scale, the same problem exists for the Army of Northern Virginia. Union reports, though extensive and detailed, are confused by overlapping dates. One Union account (see page 278) purportedly covers the North Anna, Haw's Shop, Totopotomoy, and Bethesda Church through June 1. But on close reading, we find that it places losses in the heavy fighting at Cold Harbor on June 1 under the heading of June 2 to 15—dates that take Grant's troops through their first appearance before Petersburg. Such discrepancies prevent the tabulation of directly comparable figures for each army. As John Bigelow, Jr., admitted in his 1910 study of the Chancellorsville campaign, even careful casualty counts must be "in a measure conjectural."

WHATEVER their exact figures, all historians acknowledge that Union losses at and around Cold Harbor far exceeded those for Lee's army, just as they did in Grant's entire spring offensive, from the Rapidan across the James. But casualty figures for the sixteen-day Cold Harbor campaign are not nearly as lopsided as the margin of almost five to one so often cited for the climactic battle of June 3 alone.

Major General Andrew A. Humphreys, for example, Meade's chief of staff and author of *The Virginia Campaign of '64 and '65*, relied mainly on the contemporary reports of the Army of the Potomac's chief surgeon, Thomas A. McParlin. He arrived at lower totals than later analysts such as William Freeman Fox, author of *Regimental Losses in the Civil War*, whose extensive work took in postwar revisions, after most of the dead and missing were traced down. There is no such authoritative source for Confederate losses, which are much rougher estimates.

Humphreys offered a total of 12,970 Union soldiers killed, wounded, and missing from crossing the Pamunkey on June 27 through the battle of June 3. This figure omitted those lost in the skirmishing, sharpshooting, and artillery duels in the remaining nine days before the Federals departed for the James on June 12.

Fox said that Union losses at Totopotomoy were 671, in cavalry clashes 656, at Bethesda Church 1,366, and at Cold Harbor 12,737, which totals 15,430.

Charles J. Calrow, writing in 1933, came close when he approximately split the difference between Humphreys and Fox, estimating that Union losses from the Pamunkey to the James were "slightly over 14,000."

Thomas L. Livermore, whose *Numbers and Losses in the Civil War in America* was published in 1909, frankly admitted that Confederate losses at Cold Harbor were "unknown."

Humphreys could do no more than guess at the "probable number" of Southern casualties for the period, which he put at between four and five thousand.

Calrow believed that they "probably did not exceed 3,000 of all classes." Most of these came at Bethesda Church, in cavalry engagements, and at Cold Harbor on May 31 and June 1—but not on June 3, when the Southern loss was "comparatively small."

Comparatively is the key word, for in the minutes, then hours, when the Union attack ground down against Lee's lines that Friday morning, between 6,500 and 7,000 Federal soldiers were killed, wounded, or missing. The Confederates who repulsed them so efficiently suffered between a thousand and fifteen hundred casualties in that action.

THE TABLES below are extracted from contemporary returns published in the Official Records. The explanatory footnotes (OR I 36, pt. 1: 153–164, 166–180) illustrate the near-impossibility of providing exact figures for specific engagements within the overall campaign. Some army totals exceed the sum of corps figures because they include casualties among staff and unattached units.

Union Losses

NORTH ANNA, PAMUNKEY, & TOTOPOTOMOY
MAY 22–JUNE 1*

	Killed	Wounded	Missing/Captured	Total
Second Corps	259	1,132	260	1,651
Fifth Corps	135	759	181	1,075
Sixth Corps	11	68	9	88
Ninth Corps	76	322	113	511
Cavalry Corps	110	453	98	661
Army of Potomac	591	2,734	661	3,986

* "Embracing the march from Spotsylvania and operations along the line of the North Anna; thence across the Pamunkey and along the line of the Totopotomoy (including Bethesda Church, up to June 1, inclusive). . . . The several combats of the period were known under the names of North Anna River, Quarles' Mills, Ox Ford, Jericho Bridge (or Ford or Mills), Hanover Junction, Sexton's Station, Totopotomoy River, Mount Carmel Church,

Dabney's Ferry (Pamunkey River), Hanovertown, Little River, Pole Cat Creek, Salem Church, Aenon Church, Jones' Farm, Crump's Creek, Haw's Shop, Matadequin Creek, Old Church, Mechump's Creek, Shady Grove, Shallow Creek, Turner's Farm, Armstrong's Farm, Ashland, Bethesda Church, &c."

Cold Harbor, Bethesda Church, etc.

June 2–15*

	Killed	Wounded	Missing/Captured	Total
Second Corps	494	2,442	574	3,510
Fifth Corps	149	749	442	1,340
Sixth Corps	483	2,064	168	2,715
Ninth Corps	219	1,126	356	1,701
Eighteenth Corps	449	2,365	206	3,020
Cavalry Corps	51	328	70	449
Army of Potomac	1,845	9,077	1,816	12,735

* "Embracing the operations at and about Cold Harbor and Bethesda Church, and the march across the Chickahominy and James Rivers to the front of Petersburg. The losses of the Cavalry Corps at Cold Harbor, May 31 and June 1, and of the Sixth Corps and detachment of the Army of the James at the same place, June 1, are included. The casualties of the First and Second Divisions, Cavalry Corps, up to June 6 only are included. During the remainder of the period covered by the tables these divisions were detached on an expedition. . . ."

As Hancock's Second Corps experienced more casualties (3,510) than any other Union corps, his lead divisions in the June 3 assault suffered more than any other divisions: Barlow lost 1,561 and Gibbon 1,674. Hancock's third division, under Birney, lost only 221 in the same period.

But by percentage, Baldy Smith's much smaller Eighteenth Corps suffered most: his eight brigades, one of them left behind at White House, lost 86 percent as many men as Hancock's thirteen brigades. Hancock's corps included five of the huge heavy artillery regiments, three of them intensively engaged, while the Heavies assigned to Smith missed the most serious action.

Those fresh heavy artillery regiments were at least three times as large as the standard infantry regiments worn down by constant campaigning, so several of them were put out front in the Federal attacks. Because of their size and their role, these outfits took more casualties than any other regiments in either army. Brigadier General Robert O. Tyler's brigade of Gibbon's division was the most heavily damaged at Cold Harbor, and of its 922 casualties, 505, including 207 killed, were in the Eighth New York Heavy. The Seventh New York Heavy, which led Barlow's assault, lost 418, including 127 killed; the Second Connecticut Heavy, which led Upton's attack with Russell's division of the Sixth Corps on June 1, lost 386, including 129 killed.

The Fifth New Hampshire, of Nelson A. Miles's brigade, Gibbon's division, Hancock's corps, suffered more casualties than any infantry regiment at Cold Harbor. Of 577 men engaged, it lost 231, or 40 percent, of whom 69 were killed. By percentage, the smaller Twenty-fifth Massachusetts, of Brigadier General George J. Stannard's brigade, Martindale's division, Smith's corps, lost much more heavily—69 percent, or 215 men of the 310 engaged, 74 of them killed. The Eighty-first New York, of Brigadier General Gilman Marston's brigade, Brooks's division, Smith's corps, also lost 215, of whom 46 were killed.

According to Fox, 45 of the 1,696 infantry regiments recruited for the Union army lost two hundred or more killed or mortally wounded in the course of the war. Of the first ten, six were from the Second Corps, three of them from its First Division, with the Fifth New Hampshire leading the entire list. Of the 45, sixteen were from the Second Corps, including seven of the First Division. Of 22 Union regiments with 15 percent or more of their total enrollment killed in the war, seven were from the Second Corps.

Surgeon McParlin's report, much more detailed than any of the generals' contemporary accounts, broke down Union casualties by location and type of wound. It showed that more men were hit in the lower extremities than in the torso or arms, which suggests that the Confederates were not seriously guilty of overshooting, a mistake often made by defenders firing from behind breastworks. McParlin also showed that many more Union troops were hit by bullets than by artillery fire. This was true in every corps of the Army of the Potomac (the surgeon's report did not include the Eighteenth Corps, temporarily assigned from Butler's command). But the proportion of wound types varied, depending on what role the individual corps played between the Pamunkey and the James. In the Second Corps, bullet wounds outnumbered artillery wounds by twenty-eight to one, and in the Sixth Corps, by fourteen to one. But in the Fifth Corps, which was less involved in the attacks and whose front was overseen largely by Confederate cannon, fully a quarter of the wounds came from artillery fire. Despite some of the dramatic accounts by individual soldiers, McParlin listed no bayonet wounds at all for this period.

Notes

A key to abbreviations and full bibliographical description
of all entries will be found in Sources, page 295.

Prologue: The Circumstances of the Case

1. George G. Meade (hereafter GGM), *Life and Letters* 2:172–173.
2. OR I 32, pt. 3:49.

1. The Rising Sun

1. Andrew A. Humphreys to Mrs. Humphreys, 10 March 1864, Humphreys papers.
2. Mark Mayo Boatner II, *Civil War Dictionary*, p. 659.
3. GGM to Margaret Meade, 9 March 1864, GGM papers.
4. U. S. Grant, *Personal Memoirs* 2:116–117; GGM, *Life and Letters* 2:177–178; Freeman Cleaves, *Meade*, pp. 227–228.
5. Grant, pp. 177–178.
6. John D. Follmer, diary, 24 April 1864.
7. Wilbur H. Proctor, diary, 1 May 1864.
8. Interrogation report, "James Bellew," Comstock papers. The author has been unable to find a Captain James Bellew in any Confederate artillery unit. It is possible that James Bellem, listed as a bugler in Letcher's Virginia artillery battalion, misrepresented his rank when he crossed the lines. His service record shows him absent without leave in early 1864, and later as a deserter.
9. GGM endorsement, George H. Sharpe to A. A. Humphreys, 27 April 1864, Comstock papers.
10. Douglas Southall Freeman, *R. E. Lee* 3:267.
11. Adam Badeau, *Military History* 2:47.
12. Grant 2:131–134.
13. Horace Porter, *Campaigning with Grant*, p. 72.
14. OR I 32, pt. 3:49.
15. Charles S. Wainwright, *A Diary of Battle*, p. 38; Theodore Lyman, *Meade's Headquarters*, p. 83.
16. Porter, pp. 69–70, 74–76.
17. James Harrison Wilson, *Under the Old Flag*, 390–391; Lyman, p. 102.
18. Frank Wilkeson, *Recollections*, p. 79.
19. Morris Schaff, *The Battle of the Wilderness*, p. 41; Lyman, p. 73.
20. Cleaves, pp. 52, 355–358.

21. Joint Committee Report, 2nd Session, 38th Congress, pp. 295–329.
22. George Cary Eggleston, "Notes on Cold Harbor," *B&L* 4:230.
23. OR I 36, pt. 1:4; Marsena R. Patrick, *Inside Lincoln's Army*, p. 373.
24. OR I 36, pt. 1:1020; GGM, *Life and Letters* 2:197.
25. Martin T. McMahon, "Death of General Sedgwick," *B&L* 4:175.
26. Douglas Southall Freeman, *Lee's Lieutenants* 3:432.
27. OR I 36, pt. 1:789.
28. James Harrison Wilson, *The Life of John A. Rawlins*, pp. 227–228.
29. Porter, p. 84.
30. Schaff, p. 47.
31. GGM to Margaret Meade, 13, 18 April 1864. GGM papers.
32. GGM to Margaret Meade, 26 April 1864. GGM papers.
33. Henry H. Humphreys, *Andrew Atkinson Humphreys*, p. 219.
34. Porter, pp. 114–115.
35. Ibid.
36. GGM to Margaret Meade, 16, 19 May 1864. GGM papers.

2. We Must Strike Them a Blow

1. Jesse M. Frank to father, 19 May 1864; Edward Porter Alexander, *Fighting*, p. 265.
2. C. S. Venable, *The Campaign*, p. 8; Robert Stiles, *Four Years*, p. 267.
3. Dudley Landon Vaill, *The County Regiment*, pp. 27–28.
4. Milton H. Myers, diary, pp. 26–34.
5. Stiles, p. 268.
6. John Haley, *The Rebel Yell*, pp. 161, 163.
7. Sylvanus Cadwallader, *Three Years*, pp. 205–206.
8. R. E. Lee to Jefferson Davis, 18 May 1864, in Robert E. Lee, *Lee's Dispatches*, pp. 183–187.
9. John Gibbon, *Personal Recollections*, pp. 223–224.
10. OR I 36, pt. 1:206; Lee to Davis, 23 May 1864, in Lee, pp. 194–197.
11. Theodore Lyman, *Meade's Headquarters*, p. 126.
12. *New York Times*, 29 May 1864.
13. Douglas Southall Freeman, *R. E. Lee* 3:356.
14. Ibid., p. 359.
15. Venable, pp. 13–14.
16. Samuel Thomas McCullough, diary, 24 May 1864; H. H. Cunningham, *Doctors in Gray*, pp. 185–188.
17. William H. Taylor, "Some Experiences," p. 105.
18. OR I 25, pt. 2:811.
19. A. P. Hill to J. E. B. Stuart, 14 November 1862, Stuart papers.
20. Walter A. Montgomery, quoted in Gordon C. Rhea, *The Battles for Spotsylvania Court House*, pp. 255–256.
21. OR I 36, pt. 3:843–844.
22. J. William Jones, *Reminiscences of . . . Lee*, p. 40.

3. Rely Upon It the End Is Near

1. OR I 36, pt. 3:206.
2. Charles McK. Leoser, "Personal Recollections—Ride to Richmond," in *From Everglade to Canon*, ed. Theo. F. Rodenbough, pp. 308–309.

3. OR I 36, pt. 3:183.

4. Ibid., pp. 206–207.

5. OR I 36, pt. 1:79.

6. GGM to Margaret Meade, 24 May 1864, GGM papers.

7. *New York Times*, 26 May 1864.

8. Albert E. H. Johnson, "Reminiscences," p. 74.

9. U.S. Grant, *Personal Memoirs* 2:143–145.

10. James Cornell Biddle to his wife, 16 May 1864, Biddle papers.

11. OR I 36, pt. 3:813.

12. Ibid., p. 183.

13. Wilbur Fisk, "Soldier's Letter—No. 63" to *Montpelier* (Vermont) *Green Mountain Freeman*, 25 May 1864, Fisk papers.

14. Committee of the Regimental Association, *History of the Thirty-Sixth Regiment Massachusetts Volunteers*, p. 184; James Madison Stone, *Personal Recollections*, pp. 168–169.

15. Delos S. Burton, "An Eyewitness," p. 27; Milton H. Myers, diary, p. 40.

16. OR I 36, pt. 1:804.

17. Samuel Thomas McCullough, diary, 28 May 1864.

18. Frank Wilkeson, *Recollections*, p. 124; Theodore Lyman, *Meade's Headquarters*, p. 98.

19. OR I 36, pt. 1:80.

20. Ibid., p. 854.

21. *Charleston Daily Courier*, 22 June 1864; John Cumming to "My Dear Carrie," 26 May 1864, Cumming papers.

22. Joseph R. Haw, "The Battle of Haw's Shop, Va.," p. 374.

23. OR I 36, pt. 1:821; Haw, p. 375; U. R. Brooks, *Butler and His Cavalry*, p. 210.

24. OR I 36, pt. 1:820–821, 829–830, 861; N. Davidson, "Battle of Haw's Shop," *New York Herald*, 2 June 1864; "Butler's Cavalry," *Charleston Daily Courier*, 21 September 1864.

25. Haw, p. 375.

26. St. George Tucker Brooke, autobiography, pp. 46–53.

27. Joseph William Eggleston, memoir, p. 33.

28. Ibid.

29. George Cary Eggleston, "Cold Harbor," *B&L* 4:232.

30. William Swinton, *Campaigns*, p. 481.

31. Fred. Mather, "Under Old Glory," *National Tribune*, n.d.

32. OR I 36, pt. 3:290.

33. Douglas Southall Freeman, *R. E. Lee* 3:365–366; OR I 36, pt. 1:82.

4. Damn Them Let Them Kill Me Too

1. Richard L'Hommedieu, diary, 29 May 1864; W. P. Derby, *Bearing Arms*, p. 294; OR I 36, pt. 1:998; Asa W. Bartlett, *History of the Twelfth Regiment*, p. 199.

2. William F. Smith, "The Eighteenth Corps," *B&L* 4:221–223.

3. OR I 96, pt. 1:998, 999; U.S. Grant, *Personal Memoirs* 2:264.

4. James Cornell Biddle to his wife, 4 June 1864, Biddle papers; Charles A. Dana, *Recollections*, pp. 72–73; Morris Schaff, *The Battle of the Wilderness*, p. 49.

5. Dana, p. 73.

6. Smith, p. 223.

7. William Band to his wife, 30 May 1864, Band-Martin papers.

8. Robert Stiles, *Four Years*, p. 269; OR I 36, pt. 3:278.

9. Robert E. Lee, *Lee's Dispatches*, pp. 198–199.

10. OR I 36, pt. 3:818–819; Lee, p. 199.

11. Lee, pp. 202–203.

12. Ibid., p. 205.

13. Ibid., p. 209.

14. Charles S. Venable, "General Lee," *B&L* 4:244.

15. OR I 36, pt. 3:850.

16. Ibid., p. 857.

17. John Bakeless, *Spies,* pp. 114–115.

18. Douglas Southall Freeman, *Lee's Lieutenants* 1:646; Freeman, *R. E. Lee* 3:239.

19. OR I 36, pt. 3:850–851.

20. Ibid., p. 851.

21. OR I 36, pt. 1:564; pt. 3:339, 854.

22. OR I 36, pt. 3:353, 354; Milton H. Myers, diary, p. 43.

23. OR I 36, pt. 1:365; William H. Reeder to his parents, 31 May 1864, Reeder papers; Francis A. Walker, *History of the Second Army Corps,* pp. 501–502.

24. Theodore Lyman, *Meade's Headquarters,* p. 133.

25. George Breck, "From Battery L—In the Southward," *Rochester Union & Advertiser,* 21 June 1864.

26. *Charleston Daily Courier,* 21 September 1864.

27. *Litchfield* (Connecticut) *Enquirer,* 9 June 1864.

28. William G. Hinson, "Diary," p. 18.

29. Edward Wells, *A Sketch,* pp. 54–55; OR I 36, pt. 1:848; U. R. Brooks, *Butler and His Cavalry,* pp. 227–229; James Michael Barr, *Confederate War Correspondence,* p. 245.

30. OR I 36, pt. 3:353.

31. Charles S. Wainwright, *A Diary of Battle,* p. 393.

32. OR I 51, pt. 1:244; William Allan, memoir.

33. William Henry Locke, *The Story of the Regiment,* p. 346.

34. Freeman, *R. E. Lee* 3:370–371.

35. Breck; Clifford Dowdey, *Lee's Last Campaign,* pp. 279–280; Buckner Magill Randolph, diary, 30 June 1864; C. B. Christian in "The Battle at Bethesda Church," *Richmond Times-Dispatch,* 13 August 1905.

36. Charles H. Minnemeyer, journal, 30 May 1864.

37. OR I 51, pt. 1:244; pt. 2:974.

38. OR I 36, pt. 3:854; pt. 1:1058.

39. OR I 36, pt. 3:329, 355.

40. John O. Casler, *Four Years,* pp. 221–222.

41. OR I 36, pt. 3:371.

42. J. B. Thompson, "Reminiscences," pp. 1–2.

43. Lee, *Lee's Dispatches,* p. 207.

44. Lyman, pp. 136–137; Charles J. Calrow, "Cold Harbor," pp. b–c; OR I 36, pt. 1:293.

5. Hold Cold Harbor at All Hazards

1. Horace Porter, *Campaigning,* pp. 157–160.

2. Jack Coggins, *Arms and Equipment,* p. 28; Francis A. Lord, *They Fought,* p. 164.

3. 21st Connecticut, *The Story of the Twenty-first,* p. 229.

4. Delavan S. Miller, *Drum Taps,* p. 105; Theodore Lyman, *Meade's Headquarters,* p. 136; Henry Colley March, *Cold Harbour,* pp. 3–6.

5. Bruce Catton, *Grant Takes Command,* pp. 257–258.

6. James Harrison Wilson, *The Life of John A. Rawlins,* p. 223.

7. Henry H. Humphreys, *Andrew Atkinson Humphreys,* p. 228.

8. OR I 36, pt. 3:399, 402.

9. Ibid., pp. 381, 382; John Haley, *The Rebel Yell,* pp. 164–165.

10. OR I 36, pt. 3:406, 408.

11. Ibid., p. 858.

12. Charles H. Minnemeyer, journal, 31 May 1864.

13. Avery Harris, Reminiscence, n.p..

14. OR I 36, pt. 3:858; Walter Clark, *North Carolina Regiments* 1:404–405.

15. OR I 36, pt. 1:783, 794, 805.

16. Clark, pp. 404–405; Clifford Dowdey, *Lee's Last Campaign,* p. 285.

17. OR I 36, pt. 1:805–806, pt. 3:411.

18. OR I 36, pt. 1:805–806, pt. 3:469.

19. Edward Porter Alexander, *Fighting,* p. 398; Charles J. Calrow, "Cold Harbor," pp. 85½, 86.

20. OR I 36, pt. 3:400, 403, 404, 393, 394.

21. OR I 36, pt. 1:999–1000.

22. Asa W. Bartlett, *History of the Twelfth Regiment,* p. 200.

23. Charles H. Berry, *Xenia* (Ohio) *Torch-Light,* 20 July 1864.

24. Bartlett, pp. 200–201.

25. William P. Derby, *Bearing Arms,* p. 296; Fred. Mather, "Under Old Glory," *National Tribune,* n.d.; Richard L'Hommedieu, diary, p. 5.

26. Derby, pp. 296–297.

27. John Gibbon, *Personal Recollections,* pp. 228–229.

28. Lyman, pp. 99–100.

6. *The Splendor of Our Victories*

1. *Charleston Daily Courier,* 21 April 1863.

2. Lawrence M. Keitt to "My dear, dear Susie," 30, 31 May 1864, Keitt papers.

3. Charles Minor Blackford, *Letters from Lee's Army,* p. 249.

4. OR I 51, pt. 2:974

5. Edward Porter Alexander, *Fighting,* p. 399.

6. Theo. F. Rodenbough, "Sheridan's Richmond Raid," *B&L* 4:193.

7. D. Augustus Dickert, *History of Kershaw's Brigade,* pp. 369–370.

8. Rodenbough, p. 193; Isaac Dunkelberger, memoir.

9. Robert Stiles, *Four Years,* p. 274.

10. Theo. F. Rodenbough, ed., *From Everglade to Canon,* p. 310.

11. Dickert, p. 370.

12. S.D.S. to Mrs. Keitt, 5 June 1864; A. S. Salley to "Alex," 8 June 1864, Keitt papers.

13. Alexander, *Fighting,* p. 399; James H. Clark, *The Iron Hearted Regiment,* p. 126; *Ballston* (New York) *Journal,* n.d.

14. OR I 36, pt. 1:1049.

15. Alexander, pp. 399–400.

16. T. L. Clingman, "Second Cold Harbor," in Walter Clark, *North Carolina Regiments* 5:198–204.

17. Andrew A. Humphreys, *The Virginia Campaign,* p. 172; Howard Coffin, *Full Duty,* p. 254.

18. James H. Clark, p. 125.

19. T. C. Morton, "Incidents of the Skirmish," pp. 48–53.

20. OR I 36, pt. 3:864–865.

21. OR I 36, pt. 1:874, 900.

22. OR I 36, pt. 3:864.

7. You Cannot Conceive the Horror

1. Dudley Landon Vaill, *The County Regiment,* p. 29; A. Jackson Crossley to "Sam," 6 June 1864.

2. OR I 36, pt. 2:883–896.

3. Vaill, p. 29; *Dictionary of American Biography* 10:129; Theodore Vaill to "Brother Charles," 16 June 1864.

4. *The Connecticut War Record,* September 1864; Dudley Landon Vaill, pp. 29–30.

5. James Deane, "Following the Flag," n.p.

6. Vaill, pp. 31–33; OR I 36, pt. 1:671.

7. Deane.

8. Andrew A. Humphreys, *The Virginia Campaign,* pp. 176–177; Winthrop Phelps to "Dear Lucy," 1 June 1864.

9. OR I 36, pt. 1:734, 739.

10. Ibid., p. 1059.

11. Walter Clark, *North Carolina Regiments* 5:198–202.

12. Ibid.

13. Ibid.

14. John Keely, "Narrative of the Campaign."

15. T. L. Clingman, *Richmond Whig,* 5 June 1864.

16. Charles Sanders to "Sis Deany," 8 June 1864.

17. A. B. Simms to "Dear Sister," 4 June 1864, in A. B. Simms, "A Georgian's View."

18. J. B. Kershaw to E. P. Alexander, 9 July 1868, E. Porter Alexander papers.

19. Ibid.; OR I 51, pt. 2:976.

20. Kershaw to Alexander, 9 July 1868; OR I 36, pt. 1:1049; *Savannah Morning News,* 13 June 1898; Robert Stiles, *Four Years,* pp. 275–276.

21. OR I 36, pt. 1:671, 1059.

22. William Meade Dame, *From the Rapidan to Richmond,* pp. 199–201.

23. OR I 36, pt. 3:456–457, 467.

24. OR I 36, pt. 1:87.

25. W. S. Hubbell, in 21st Connecticut, *The Story of the Twenty-First,* pp. 232–233.

26. Charles A. Currier, "Recollections of Service," pp. 103–103a; OR I 36, pt. 1:1013.

27. OR I 36, pt. 3:440, 441.

28. OR I 36, pt. 1:344.

29. *Richmond Times-Dispatch,* 30 January 1993.

30. OR I 36, pt. 3:449; OR I 36, pt. 3:722.

31. Morris Schaff, *The Battle of the Wilderness,* p. 30; Charles S. Wainwright, *A Diary of Battle,* p. 396.

32. Austin C. Stearns, *Three Years,* pp. 276–277; OR I 36, pt. 3:451–452; Charles J. Calrow, "Cold Harbor," pp. 109–110.

33. Calrow, pp. 127–128.

34. OR I 36, pt. 1:1001.

35. Theodore Lyman, *Meade's Headquarters,* p. 138.

36. *New York Times,* 30 May 1864.

37. GGM to Margaret Meade, 1 June 1864, George Gordon Meade papers.

8. Richmond Dead in Front

1. Martin T. McMahon, "Cold Harbor," p. 217.
2. John B. Jones, *A Rebel War Clerk's Diary*, pp. 384–385; *Richmond Whig*, 22 April 1862.
3. OR I 36, pt. 3:528; Jones, p. 386; *New York Times*, 1 June 1864.
4. *Richmond Examiner*, 3 June 1864.
5. Kate Mason Rowland, diary, vol. 2, 9 May 1865; *Richmond Examiner*, 3 June 1864.
6. *Richmond Examiner*, 1, 3, 4 June 1864.
7. Ibid.
8. Jones, p. 387; Charles Minor Blackford, *Letters*, p. 250.
9. Gideon Welles, *Diary* 2:44.
10. Horace Porter, *Campaigning*, pp. 172–173; *The Story of the 21st Regiment*, p. 235.
11. A. Jackson Crossley to "Friend Sam," 29 May 1864.
12. Porter, pp. 165–166.
13. OR I 36, pt. 3:441–442.
14. John Gibbon, papers, 13 April 1864, p. 82; Morris Schaff, *The Battle of the Wilderness*, p. 42.
15. Glenn Tucker, *Hancock*, p. 232; Theodore Lyman, *Meade's Headquarters*, p. 107.
16. OR I 36, pt. 1:344; Francis A. Walker, *Great Commanders: General Hancock*, p. 218.
17. Walker, pp. 218–219; OR I 36, pt. 3:481.
18. OR I 36, pt. 3:479, 482.
19. Douglas Southall Freeman, *R. E. Lee* 3:381–383.
20. OR I 36, pt. 3:491.
21. Edward P. Tobie, *First Maine Cavalry*, p. 280.
22. John William Ford Hatton, memoir, p. 578; George H. Mills in Walter Clark, *North Carolina Regiments* 4:198–200.
23. T. C. Morton, "Incidents of the Skirmish," pp. 55–56.
24. Lyman, p. 107.
25. OR I 36, pt. 3:484; pt. 1:1050.
26. William P. Hopkins, *The Seventh Regiment Rhode Island Volunteers*, p. 182; Ephraim E. Myers, "Trials and Travels." *National Tribune*, 24 December 1925.
27. William S. Long to Breckinridge Long, 3 March 1903, Breckinridge Long papers.
28. Survivors' Association, *History of the Corn Exchange Regiment*, p. 460.
29. OR I 36, pt. 3:493; William H. Osborne, *The History of the Twenty-ninth Regiment*, p. 300.
30. Augustus Buell, quoted in 5th Massachusetts Battery, *History of the Fifth Massachusetts Battery*, pp. 859–860.
31. OR I 36, pt. 3:479, 494.
32. Lyman, "Operations of the Army of the Potomac," p. 9.
33. E. M. Law, "From the Wilderness to Cold Harbor," *B&L* 4:138–139; William H. Smith, diary, 2 June 1864.
34. Lyman, p. 8.
35. Hatton, p. 572.
36. Porter, pp. 174–175.

9. It Was Not War, It Was Murder

1. James Madison Stone, *Personal Recollections*, pp. 172–173.
2. Delavan S. Miller, *Drum Taps*, p. 106.
3. Frank Wilkeson, *Recollections*, pp. 128–129.

4. John William Ford Hatton, memoir, pp. 579–580; OR I 36, pt. 1:1050.

5. Zack C. Waters, "All That Brave Men Could Do," p. 15; C. W. Humphreys, "Another Account," *Atlanta Journal,* 22 February 1902.

6. "Second Maryland Battalion: Second Cold Harbor," *Baltimore Telegram,* n.d. 1879, Civil War Miscellaneous Collection, USAMHI.

7. David L. Geer, "Memoirs"; James Eldred Phillips, memoir, p. 54.

8. Eppa Hunton, *Autobiography,* p. 113.

9. William C. Oates, *The War Between the Union and the Confederacy,* pp. 365–366.

10. John Gibbon, *Personal Recollections,* pp. 231–232; OR I 36, pt. 1:433.

11. Harvey Clark, *My Experience,* pp. 65–66.

12. Fred. Mather, "Under Old Glory," *National Tribune,* n.d.

13. OR I 36, pt. 1:345, 414; Mather.

14. A. Du Bois, "Cold Harbor Salient," 27 April 1902; Mather.

15. OR I 36, pt. 1:390.

16. Wilkeson, p. 129; OR I 36, pt. 1:366.

17. OR I 36, pt. 1:433.

18. Charles D. Page, *History of the Fourteenth Regiment,* p. 266; OR I 36, pt. 1:452.

19. OR I 36, pt. 1:345, 433; Theodore Lyman, *Meade's Headquarters,* p. 154.

20. OR I 36, pt. 1:435–436.

21. Hatton, pp. 580–581.

22. John K. Thompson to George M. Edgar, 22 July 1902, George Matthew Edgar Collection; Dubois.

23. Council Bryan to "My Dear Wife," 3 June 1864, Bryan Collection; Charles G. Elliott, "Martin's Brigade," p. 193; Humphreys.

24. Hatton, pp. 581–582; "Cold Harbor: from a Member of the Battalion" and "Second Maryland Battalion," *Baltimore Telegram,* n.d. 1879; John Goldsborough White, "Recollections of Cold Harbor," *Baltimore Sun,* 2 June 1929; Lamar Hollyday, "Maryland Troops," p. 135.

25. Geer; Waters, p. 16.

26. Council Bryan to "My Dear Wife," 3 June 1864; A. F. Gomillion to "Dear Friend Rogero," 7 June 1864.

27. "Eighteenth Paper—Second Series," *Baltimore Telegram,* n.d. 1879; Waters, p. 16; James William Thomas, diary.

28. Oates, pp. 366–337.

29. *Macon Daily Telegraph,* 14 June 1864.

30. E. M. Law, "From the Wilderness to Cold Harbor," *B&L* 4:139–141.

31. OR I 36, pt. 1:671, 662–663.

32. Charles J. Calrow, "Cold Harbor," pp. 174–175.

33. OR I 36, pt. 1:689, 708.

34. OR I 51, pt. 1:1254.

35. Clark, pp. 66–67.

36. D. Augustus Dickert, *History of Kershaw's Brigade,* pp. 372–373.

37. Asa W. Bartlett, *History of the Twelfth Regiment,* pp. 202–204; OR I 51, pt. 1:1254, 1261, 1265.

38. Clark, pp. 66–67.

39. OR I 36, pt. 1:1003, 1006.

40. Ibid., pp. 930, 932, 937, 1050.

41. Ibid., pp. 946, 952.

42. Ibid., p. 565; pt. 3:538, 539.

43. Joseph William Eggleston, memoir, p. 34.

44. W. P. Derby, *Bearing Arms,* p. 306.

45. Law, p. 142.

10. A Simple and Absolute Impossibility

1. Theodore Lyman, *Meade's Headquarters,* pp. 144–145.

2. OR I 36, pt. 3:524–525.

3. Ibid., p. 526.

4. Ibid., p. 530.

5. Ibid., pp. 530–531.

6. Ibid., pp. 536, 544, 553.

7. Ibid., p. 538; GGM to Wright, 4 June 1864 (misdated).

8. OR I 36, pt. 3:554; William F. Smith, "Eighteenth Corps," *B&L* 4:227.

9. OR I 36, pt. 3:538–539.

10. Ibid., p. 539.

11. Ibid., pp. 539, 547–548.

12. Ibid., pp. 560–561.

13. Edward Porter Alexander, *Fighting,* p. 404.

14. OR I 36, pt. 1:1032, 1059; John Esten Cooke, *Wearing of the Gray,* p. 406; E. M. Law,
    "From the Wilderness to Cold Harbor," *B&L* 4:141; Alexander, pp. 539–540.

15. OR I 36, pt. 3:869–870.

16. John H. Reagan, *Memoirs,* pp. 191–194.

17. Robert E. Lee, *Lee's Dispatches,* pp. 212–213; OR I 36, pt. 3:870–872.

18. *New York Times,* 7 June 1864; OR I 36, pt. 1:1004.

19. OR I 36, pt. 3:526.

20. Ibid., p. 528.

21. Asa W. Bartlett, *History of the Twelfth Regiment,* p. 202.

22. William Swinton, *Campaigns,* p. 487.

23. OR I 36, pt. 1:345.

24. C. D. MacDougall to Major John Hancock, n.d. Francis Barlow papers.

25. Martin T. McMahon, "Cold Harbor," *B&L* 4:217–218.

26. GGM to Margaret Meade, 4 June 1864, GGM papers; *New York Times,* 7 June 1864.

27. McMahon, p. 218.

28. *New York Times,* 7 June 1864; *Macon Daily Telegraph,* 14 June 1864.

11. All a Weary, Long Mistake

1. E. A. Shiver, "North Anna and Cold Harbor," *Atlanta Journal,* 25 January 1925.

2. *Florida Index,* 2 February 1902.

3. D. Augustus Dickert, *History of Kershaw's Brigade,* p. 375; John William Ford Hatton,
    memoir, pp. 583–584.

4. *New York Times,* 8 June 1864.

5. James F. Tucker, ("J.F.T."), "Some Florida Heroes," p. 363; H. W. Long, "Reminis-
    cence"; James F. Tucker to Daniel B. Bird, 2 April 1892; Zack C. Waters, "All That
    Brave Men Could Do," pp. 18–20.

6. OR I 36, pt. 1:11.

7. Robert E. Lee, *Lee's Dispatches,* p. 213.

8. Kinloch Falconer to William H. Jackson, 3 June 1864; Josiah Gorgas, *The Civil War
    Diary,* p. 112.

9. Robert Stiles, *Four Years,* p. 290; Geer.

10. Jack Coggins, *Arms and Equipment,* pp. 37–39.

11. Dickert, p. 377.

12. Francis P. Fleming, *Memoir of Capt. C. Seton Fleming,* pp. 100–105; Long; Alfred Lewis Scott, memoirs.

13. OR I 51, pt. 2:963

14. OR I 36, pt. 3:548.

15. Ibid., p. 541; OR I 51, pt. 1:246.

16. OR I 36, pt. 3:556, 545, 534.

17. Theodore Lyman, *Meade's Headquarters,* pp. 146–147.

18. George E. Pickett, *The Heart of a Soldier,* pp. 132–133.

19. OR I 36, pt. 1:1032.

20. Lyman, p. 149.

21. Kinloch Falconer to William H. Jackson, 3 June 1864; U. H. Hane, "Finegan's Florida Brigade," p. 540; Council Bryan to his wife, 3 June 1864, Bryan Collection; "Civil War Letters of Colonel David Lang," quoted in Waters, p. 14; *Selma Daily Reporter,* 20 June 1864; "Eighteenth Paper—Second Series," *Baltimore Telegram,* n.d. 1879.

22. W. P. Derby, *Bearing Arms,* p. 319.

23. Dickert, p. 373; OR I 36, pt. 1:990–991.

24. Horace Porter, *Campaigning,* p. 179.

25. 21st Connecticut, *The Story of the Twenty-first Regiment,* p. 240.

26. Stiles, pp. 301–302.

27. Dickert, p. 375; James William Thomas, diary, 4 June 1864.

28. A. B. Simms, "A Georgian's View," p. 108; Dickert, pp. 375–376.

29. Henry Van Leuvenigh Bird to "My darling," 3 June 1864, Bird Family papers; Lyman, pp. 147–148.

30. Lyman, pp. 147–148.

31. Shelby Foote, *Civil War* 3:290.

12. You Kneed Not to Be Oneasy

1. *Confederate Veteran* 36, p. 307.

2. H. W. Long, "Reminiscence"; G. H. Dorman, *Fifty Years Ago,* p. 11.

3. Robert Stiles, *Four Years,* pp. 290–292.

4. A. B. Simms to his sister, 4 June 1864, in A. B. Simms, "A Georgian's View."

5. William H. Brotherton to his father, mother, and sister, 4 June 1864, Brotherton papers.

6. Peter S. Michie, *The Life and Letters of Emory Upton,* pp. 108–109.

7. James Harrison Wilson, *Under the Old Flag,* p. 448.

8. Charles S. Wainwright, *A Diary of Battle,* pp. 405–406.

9. James C. Biddle to his wife, 4 June 1864, Biddle papers.

10. Ibid.

11. John Haley, *The Rebel Yell,* p. 166.

12. OR I 51, pt. 2:986.

13. OR I 36, pt. 3:570.

14. OR I 36, pt. 1:314; pt. 3:576–577, 584–585.

15. OR I 36, pt. 1:367.

16. Theodore Lyman, *Meade's Headquarters,* pp. 148–149.

17. John G. Perry, *Letters from a Surgeon,* p. 187.

18. OR I 36, pt. 1:166–169.

19. Ibid., p. 245.
20. Robert E. Denney, *Civil War Medicine,* p. 294.
21. OR I 36, pt. 1:249–252, 271–272; P. C. Prugh, *Xenia Torch-Light,* 22 June 1864.
22. Gideon Welles, *Diary* 2:44–245.
23. OR I 36, pt. 1:246.
24. Ibid., p. 247; G. Van Santvoord, *The One Hundred and Twentieth Regiment,* pp. 135–136.
25. George W. Bagby to *Atlanta Register,* 4 June 1864.
26. Jefferson Davis to "My Dear Madam," 25 May 1864, in William C. Davis, *Jefferson Davis,* p. 559; John B. Jones, *A Rebel War Clerk's Diary,* p. 388.
27. R. E. Lee to his wife, 4 June 1864, Lee papers.
28. Horace Porter, *Campaigning,* p. 179.
29. Worthington Chauncey Ford, ed., *A Cycle of Adams Letters,* p. 141.
30. OR I 36, pt. 3:570–573.

13. Like a Scene in an Opera

1. E. B. Long, *The Civil War,* p. 515.
2. Charles Francis Adams, Jr., to R. H. Dana, Jr., 5 June 1864, Dana, Jr., papers.
3. David Coon to his daughter Emma, 5 June 1864; Coon to his son Herbert, 6 June 1864, Coon papers; Harold Holzer, ed., *Witness to War,* p. 151.
4. Charles Francis Adams, Jr., to R. H. Dana, Jr., 5 June 1864; OR I 36, pt. 3:656.
5. Clarence Edward Macartney, *Grant and His Generals,* p. 201.
6. James Harrison Wilson, *The Life and Services of General Smith,* p. 98.
7. James Harrison Wilson, *Under the Old Flag,* p. 445; James Harrison Wilson, *The Life of John A. Rawlins,* pp. 227–228.
8. Wilson, *Under the Old Flag,* p. 446.
9. Robert E. Lee, *Lee's Dispatches,* pp. 215–216.
10. Cyrus B. Comstock, diary, 5 June 1864.
11. OR I 36, pt. 3:603, 610, 616.
12. Charles S. Wainwright, *A Diary of Battle,* p. 411; Robert Stiles, *Four Years,* p. 308.
13. OR I 36, pt. 3:598.
14. Ibid., pp. 598–599; Clarke Baum to "My Darling," 11 June 1864.
15. OR I 36, pt. 3:599.
16. OR I 36, pt. 1:89; pt. 3:603, 618, 624.
17. GGM, *Life and Letters* 2:201.
18. OR I 36, pt. 1:434; William C. Oates, *The War Between the Union and the Confederacy,* p. 367.
19. OR I 36, pt. 3:603; *New York Times,* 10 June 1864.
20. OR I 36, pt. 3:604.
21. OR I 36, pt. 3:600.
22. Theodore Lyman, *Meade's Headquarters,* pp. 149–153; Theodore Lyman, "Operations of the Army of the Potomac," pp. 11–15; OR I 36, pt. 1:367–368.
23. Lyman, *Meade's Headquarters,* pp. 149–153; Lyman, "Operations of the Army of the Potomac," pp. 11–15; OR I 36, pt. 1:367–368; pt. 3:600.
24. OR I 36, pt. 3:638.
25. Ibid.
26. Ibid., pp. 638–639.
27. Ibid., pp. 639, 666.
28. Ibid., p. 877; OR I 51, pt. 1:247.

29. Lee, pp. 216–218.

30. Ibid., pp. 219–220.

31. OR I 36, pt. 3:646–647.

32. Ibid., p. 643.

33. Ibid., pp. 653, 657–658, 660.

34. *New York Times,* 1 June 1864.

35. GGM to Margaret Meade, 6 June 1864, GGM papers.

14. Killing Without Any Battle

1. Robert Stiles, *Four Years,* pp. 293–294; Gideon Welles, *Diary* 2:53.

2. Stiles, pp. 295–297.

3. OR I 36, pt. 3:666–667.

4. Francis A. Walker, *Great Commanders: General Hancock,* pp. 225–226.

5. Asa W. Bartlett, *History of the Twelfth Regiment,* p. 209.

6. OR I 36, pt. 3:669–670.

7. Theodore Lyman, *Meade's Headquarters,* p. 154.

8. Delavan S. Miller, *Drum Taps,* pp. 111–113.

9. Winthrop Phelps to "Dear Lucy," 7 June 1864.

10. Oliver Wendell Holmes, Jr., *Touched with Fire,* pp. 142–143.

11. OR I 36, pt. 3:672, pt. 1:346; Gilbert Thompson, journal, p. 276; Daniel Chisholm, *The Civil War Notebook,* p. 118.

12. *Mobile Advertiser & Register,* 21 June 1864.

13. OR I 36, pt. 3:675; 5th Massachusetts Battery, *History of the Fifth Massachusetts Battery,* p. 866.

14. S. Millett Thompson, *Thirteenth Regiment,* p. 370.

15. Charles S. Wainwright, *A Diary of Battle,* p. 409.

16. Charles J. Calrow, "Cold Harbor," p. 267; John Rumsey Brinckle to "Dear Sister," 8 June 1864; Brinckle to "Dear Brother," 9 June 1864, Brinckle papers.

17. Cyrus B. Comstock, diary, 7 June 1864.

18. Austin C. Stearns, *Three Years,* pp. 27–28.

19. Avery Harris, Reminiscence, n.p.

20. James P. Coburn to "My Dear Parents," 7 June 1864, Coburn papers.

21. John Cumming to "Dear Carrie," 9 June 1864, Cumming papers.

15. A Nice Friendly Chat

1. Sylvanus Cadwallader, *Three Years,* p. 207; Frank Wilkeson, *Recollections,* p. 146.

2. *Philadelphia Inquirer,* 2 June 1864.

3. GGM to Margaret Meade, 9 June 1864, GGM papers; Freeman Cleaves, *Meade,* p. 252; Isaac R. Pennypacker, *General Meade,* pp. 317–318.

4. GGM to Margaret Meade, 9 June 1864.

5. OR I 36, pt. 3:670.

6. GGM to Margaret Meade, 9 June 1864.

7. J. Cutler Andrews, *The North Reports,* pp. 547–548; Whitelaw Reid to *Cincinnati Gazette,* n.d., Reid papers.

8. OR I 36, pt. 1:94; pt. 3:722.

9. *New York Times,* 8 June 1864.

10. Lafayette S. Foster to wife, 4 June 1864, Foster papers.

11. *New York Times,* 7 June 1864.

12. Ibid.

13. OR I 36, pt. 3:751.

14. U.S. Grant, *Personal Memoirs* 2:145.

15. William C. Davis, *Jefferson Davis*, p. 559.

16. OR I 36, pt. 3:879; OR I 51, pt. 2:997, 998.

17. Henry H. Hopkins to "Mary," 8 June 1864, Hopkins papers.

18. OR I 36, pt. 3:695.

19. George Breck, *Rochester Union & Advertiser*, 23 June 1864.

20. Horace Porter, *Campaigning*, p. 194.

21. OR I 36, pt. 1:1059; pt. 3:880.

22. Clarke Baum to "My Darling," 11 June 1864.

23. S. H. Walkup, diary, 9 June 1864; James E. Bassett, journal, 9 June 1864.

24. Wilkeson, pp. 149–150.

25. OR I 36, pt. 1:1059; pt. 3:736.

26. OR I 36, pt. 3:709, 711.

27. OR I 36, pt. 1:302; pt. 3:730, 736, 888.

28. William Hyndman, *History of a Cavalry Company*, p. 203.

29. OR I 51, pt. 2:1003.

30. Ibid.

31. Charles J. Calrow, "Cold Harbor," p. 293.

32. OR I 36, pt. 3:897.

16. The Heavens Hung in Black

1. Wilbur Fisk, "Soldier's Letter No. 64" to *Montpelier* (Vermont) *Green Mountain Freeman*, 11 June 1864, Fisk papers.

2. Joshua Lawrence Chamberlain, *The Passing*, p. 3.

3. Noah Brooks, *Washington, D.C.*, p. 157.

4. William Swinton, *Campaigns*, p. 492.

5. Charles S. Wainwright, *A Diary of Battle*, p. 410.

6. Philip Van Doren Stern, ed., *The Life and Writings of Abraham Lincoln*, pp. 816–818.

7. OR I 36, pt. 1:21–22.

8. U.S. Grant, *Personal Memoirs* 2:276.

9. Charles A. Dana, *Recollections*, pp. 209–211.

10. Lewis Bissell, *The Civil War Letters*, p. 254.

11. William F. Smith, "The Eighteenth Corps," *B&L* 4:225.

12. John C. Ropes, "Grant's Campaign," pp. 394–395, 398.

13. Theodore Lyman, "Operations of the Army of the Potomac," p. 6.

14. Ropes, p. 372; Adam Badeau, *Military History* 1:85.

15. John Gibbon, *Personal Recollections*, pp. 239–240.

16. Ropes, p. 377.

17. GGM to Margaret Meade, 9 June 1864, George Gordon Meade papers.

18. Smith, p. 228.

19. Clarence Edward Macartney, *Grant and His Generals*, pp. 46–47, cites "the astonishing fact that [Meade] ordered a general assault without careful planning and reconnaissance because he was irritated at the position he occupied under Grant and now intended to allow the latter to make his own plans."

20. GGM to Margaret Meade, 12 June 1864, George Gordon Meade papers.

21. Grant, pp. 276–277.

22. OR I 36, pt. 1:434.

23. OR I 36, pt. 3:747–749.

17. Across the Last River

1. Horace Porter, *Campaigning,* pp. 189-190.
2. David A. Stohl to Col. H. C. Eyer, 12 June 1864, Susan Boardman Collection.
3. Thomas J. Strayhorn to "Dear Sister," 12 June 1864, Mrs. John Berry Collection;
    W. N. Pendleton to "My darling love," 12 June 1864, Pendleton papers.
4. Marsena R. Patrick, *Inside Lincoln's Army,* p. 382.
5. Theodore Lyman, *Meade's Headquarters,* p. 107.
6. William A. Frassanito, *Grant and Lee,* pp. 174-194.
7. Porter, pp. 191-193.
8. Worthington Chauncey Ford, ed., *A Cycle of Adams Letters* 2:138-139.
9. Theodore Lyman, "Operations of the Army of the Potomac," pp. 18-19.
10. Henry Keiser, diary, 12 June 1864.
11. Wilbur Fisk, "Soldier's Letter No. 65," *Montpelier Green Mountain Freeman,* n.d.,
    Fisk papers.; Fred. LaRue, "From the 110th Regiment," *Xenia Torch-Light,* 20 July
    1864.
12. 21st Connecticut, *The Story of the Twenty-first Regiment,* p. 248.
13. James M. Gibbs, *History of the First Battalion,* pp. 86-89.
14. Robert Stiles, *Four Years,* p. 308.
15. OR I 40, pt. 2:653.
16. OR I 36, pt. 3:889, 896; OR I 51, pt. 2:1003-1004.
17. OR I 36, pt. 1:1035, 1052; pt. 3:1059-1060; Robert E. Lee, *Lee's Dispatches,* pp. 229, 240;
    Douglas Southall Freeman, *R. E. Lee* 3:402-403.
18. Lee, pp. 226-233.
19. Andrew A. Humphreys, *The Virginia Campaign,* pp. 205-206.
20. A. M. Judson, *History of the Eighty-third Regiment,* p. 103; U. S. Grant, *Personal
    Memoirs* 2:277.
21. Humphreys, pp. 196-197; OR I 40, pt. 2:18-219.
22. Abraham Lincoln, *Collected Works* 7:393.
23. Humphreys, pp. 206-210; James Harrison Wilson, *The Life of John A. Rawlins,* p. 233.
24. Humphreys, pp. 207-210.
25. G. T. Beauregard, "Four Days of Battle," *B&L* 4:540-542; Edward Porter Alexander,
    Fighting, pp. 426-430; Humphreys, p. 220.
26. OR I 51, pt. 2:1078.
27. OR I 40, pt. 3:659; Lee p. 229.
28. Joshua Lawrence Chamberlain, *The Passing,* p. 22.
29. Adam Badeau, *Military History* 2:47; Wilson, *The Life of John A. Rawlins,* pp. 223,
    231.
30. Charles S. Wainwright, *A Diary of Battle,* pp. 419-420; James Harrison Wilson,
    Under the Old Flag, p. 447.
31. GGM, *Life and Letters* 2:207.
32. J. William Jones, *Reminiscences of . . . Lee,* p. 40.
33. Charles Minor Blackford, *Letters from Lee's Army,* p. 249.

Epilogue: Dust to Kindly Dust

1. 21st Connecticut, *The Story of the Twenty-first Regiment,* pp. 248-249.
2. Russell H. Conwell, *Magnolia Journey,* pp. 21-24.

Sources

I am grateful for the cooperation of all the libraries and museums hold-ing the manuscripts cited, especially to the staffs of the Richmond National Battlefield Park and the institutions abbreviated below.

For soldiers whose manuscript letters, diaries, or personal reminis-cences are quoted, I have tried to list their units during the Cold Har-bor campaign. When the documents of a single participant have been collected or edited by someone else, I have listed them by writer rather than by editor. The following abbreviations are used for the collections and publications most frequently cited:

B&L	*Battles and Leaders*
Duke	William R. Perkins Library, Duke University, Durham, North Carolina
HSP	Historical Society of Pennsylvania, Philadelphia
LC	Manuscript Division, Library of Congress, Washington
MC	Museum of the Confederacy, Richmond
MHS	Massachusetts Historical Society, Boston
OR	War of the Rebellion, Official Records
RNBP	Richmond National Battlefield Park
SHC	Southern Historical Collection, University of North Carolina, Chapel Hill
SHSP	Southern Historical Society Papers
USAMHI	U.S. Army Military History Institute, Carlisle, Pennsylvania
VHS	Virginia Historical Society, Richmond

Manuscripts

Allan, William. Memoir. Folder 11, Allan papers. SHC.
Adams, Charles Francis, Jr., 1st Massachusetts Cavalry. Letter. R. H. Dana, Jr., papers. MHS.
Anderson, James S., 5th Wisconsin. Journal. Anderson papers. State Historical Society of Wisconsin, Madison.

Arnold, John C., 49th Pennsylvania. Letters. Arnold Family Papers. USAMHI.

Bailey, C. O., 9th Florida. Papers. SHC.

Band, W. D., 3rd Pennsylvania Cavalry. Letters. Band-Martin papers. USAMHI.

Barker, Orville A., 39th Massachusetts. Diary, "The Valley of the Shadow." Vol. 54. RNBP.

Barlow, Francis C. Letters. Barlow papers. MHS.

Barlow, Joseph, 23rd Massachusetts. Letters. Barlow Collection. USAMHI.

Barnum, George G., 100th New York. Letters. Vol. 26. RNBP.

Baum, Clarke, 50th New York Engineers. Letter. Vol. 38. RNBP.

Beach, Alvah, 14th New York Artillery. Letter. Vol. 25. RNBP.

Beaver, James W. Letter. Civil War Library and Museum, Philadelphia.

Benjamin, William, 4th Delaware. Benjamin papers. USAMHI.

Biddle, James Cornell. Civil War letters. Biddle papers. HSP.

Bird, Henry Van Leuvenigh, 12th Virginia. Letters. Bird Family papers. VHS.

Boatwright, George W., 12th Georgia Light Artillery. Letters. Vol. 15. RNBP.

Brevard, T. W., 2nd Florida Battalion. Letter. George Fairbank papers. Tampa Historical Society, Tampa.

Brinckle, John Rumsey, 5th U.S. Artillery. Letters. Brinckle papers. LC.

Brock, James D., 12th Georgia Battalion. Letter. Vol. 68. RNBP.

Brooke, St. George Tucker, 2nd Virginia Cavalry. Autobiography. VHS.

Brooker, Albert, 1st Connecticut Heavy Artillery. Letter. Torrington Historical Society, Connecticut.

Brooks, Brig. Gen. William T. H. Letter. Brooks papers. USAMHI.

Brotherton, William H., 23rd North Carolina. Brotherton papers. Duke.

Bryan, Council, 5th Florida. Bryan Collection. Florida State Archives, Tallahassee.

Burrage, Henry S., 36th Massachusetts. Reminiscences. MOLLUS Unpublished Files. USAMHI.

Burrows, James A., 14th North Carolina. Letter. Burrows papers. Duke.

Campbell, H. S., 2nd U.S. Sharpshooters. Letter. Anna B. Campbell papers. Duke.

Cartwright, James W., 56th Massachusetts. Letters. Civil War Times Illustrated Collection. USAMHI.

Chancellor, William F., 14th Georgia. Letter. Civil War Miscellaneous Collection. USAMHI.

Chipman, Charles, 29th Massachusetts. Letters. Chipman papers. USAMHI.

Coburn, James P., 141st Pennsylvania. Letters. Coburn papers. USAMHI.

Comstock, Cyrus B. Diary and letters. Comstock papers. LC.

Coon, David, 36th Wisconsin. Letters. Coon papers. LC.

Crockett, Edward R., 4th Texas. Diary. University of Texas, Austin.

Crossley, A. Jackson, U.S. Engineer Battalion. Letters. Petersburg National Battlefield Park, Virginia.

Crowley, John M., 56th Massachusetts. Letter. Cartwright Collection. USAMHI.

Cumming, John, 5th South Carolina Cavalry. Letters. Cumming papers. Duke.

Currier, Charles A., 40th Massachusetts. "Recollections of Service with the Fortieth Massachusetts Infantry Volunteers." MOLLUS Unpublished Files. USAMHI.

Dana, Charles A. War dispatches. James H. Wilson papers. LC.

Davis, Creed Thomas, Richmond Howitzers. Diary. VHS.

Deane, James, 2nd Connecticut Heavy Artillery. Memoir, "Following the Flag." Connecticut Historical Society.

Derrick, Clarence, 23rd Virginia Battalion. Letter. George Mathews Edgar Collection. SHC.

Draper, George W., 89th New York. Norwich Civil War Round Table Collection. USAMHI.

Dunkelberger, Isaac. 1st U.S. Cavalry. Memoir. Winey Collection. USAMHI.

Dunn, Washington L., 27th Georgia. Diary. John B. Gordon Chapter, United Daughters of the Confederacy, Thomasville, Georgia.

Eggleston, Joseph William, Lamkin's battery, Haskell's artillery. Memoir. VHS.

Elam, William, 18th Virginia. Letters. Alderman Library, University of Virginia, Charlottesville.

Elliott, Joseph P., 71st Pennsylvania. Diary. Vol. 12. RNBP.

Falconer, Kinloch, Army of Tennessee. Letter. 3 June 1864. M331, General and Staff Officers, CSA, Record Group 94. National Archives.

Fisk, Wilbur, 2nd Vermont. Diary and letters to *Montpelier* (Vermont) *Green Mountain Freeman*. Fisk papers. LC.

Follmer, John E., 16th Pennsylvania Cavalry. Diary. HSP.

Foster, Lafayette S. Letters. Foster papers. MHS.

Frank, Jesse M., 48th North Carolina. Letters. Duke.

Gibbon, John. Papers. HSP.

Gomillion, A. F., 1st Florida Battalion. Letter. P. K. Yonge Library of Florida History, University of Florida, Gainesville.

Guyton, R., 139th Pennsylvania. Letters. Guyton-Heaslet papers. Duke.

Hall, Henry E., 2nd Maine Battery. Letter. Lewis Leigh Collection. USAMHI.

Harris, Avery, 143rd Pennsylvania. Reminiscence, 1910. Harris papers. USAMHI.

Harris, Nathaniel. Letter. Virginia State Library.

Haskell, S. W., 1st Vermont Heavy Artillery. Letter. Lewis Leigh Collection. USAMHI.

Hatton, John William Ford, 1st Maryland Battery, CSA. Memoir. Hatton papers. LC.

Hawkes, George P., 21st Massachusetts. Morning Report Book. Coco Collection. USAMHI.

Hayward, Albert M., 7th Massachusetts. Letter. Lewis Leigh Collection. USAMHI.

Herd, J. J., 2nd South Carolina Rifles. Letter. Vol. 46. RNBP.

Hill, A. P. Letter. J. E. B. Stuart papers. VHS.

Hoffman, John, 10th New Jersey. Diary. Vol. 24. RNBP.

Hopkins, Henry H., chaplain, 120th New York. Letter. Hopkins papers. Duke.

Humphreys, Andrew A. Papers. HSP.

Johnson, Charles F., 4th New York Heavy Artillery. Letters. Johnson Family papers. USAMHI.

Johnston, Mary Sayre Macon. Memorandum of Ingleside. VHS.

Jones, Peleg G., 7th Rhode Island. Diary. Civil War Times Illustrated Collection. USAMHI.

Joyner, Joseph D., 7th North Carolina. Letter. Joyner Family papers. SHC.

Keiser, Henry, 96th Pennsylvania. Diary. Harrisburg Civil War Round Table Collection, USAMHI.

Keitt, Lawrence M. Letters. Keitt papers. Duke.

Kershaw, Joseph B. Letters. E. Porter Alexander papers. SHC.

Knowles, Francis W., 36th Massachusetts. Journal. Knowles papers. J. Y. Joyner Library, East Carolina University, Greenville, North Carolina.

Lambeth, Joseph Harrison, 14th North Carolina. Diary. VHS.

Latta, James W., 119th Pennsylvania. Diary. LC.

Lee, Robert E. Letters. Lee papers. LC.

L'Hommedieu, Richard, 139th New York. Diary. Vol. 56. RNBP.

Lockhart, Samuel P., 27th North Carolina. Letters. Hugh Conway Browning papers. Duke.

Long, H. W., 9th Florida. "Reminiscence of the Battle of Cold Harbor." United Daughters of the Confederacy Scrapbooks. Florida State Library, Tallahassee.

Long, William S., 44th North Carolina. Letter. Breckinridge Long papers. LC.

Lyman, Theodore. Journal and letters. Lyman Family papers. MHS.

MacDougall, C. D., 111th New York. Report. Francis Barlow papers. MHS.

Marks, Samuel J., 2nd U.S. Artillery. Letters. Civil War Miscellaneous Collection. USAMHI.

Madill, Henry J., 141st Pennsylvania. Diary. Coco Collection. USAMHI.

McCarthy, Dennis., 104th New York. Letters. USAMHI.

McConnell, John Daniel, 5th South Carolina. "Recollections of the Civil War." Winthrop College, Rock Hill, South Carolina.

McCullough, Samuel Thomas, 2nd Maryland, CSA. Diary. Hotchkiss-McCullough papers. LC.

McIntosh, David Gregg. Notes concerning a tour of battlefields around Richmond, Virginia. VHS.

Meade, Capt. George. Letters. George Gordon Meade papers. HSP.

Meade, George Gordon. Dispatch to Horatio Wright, n.d. Vol. 64. RNBP.

Meade, George Gordon. Papers. HSP.

Miles, Abanijah, 67th Pennsylvania. Diary. Vol. 42. RNBP.

Miles, Nelson A. Letter. Miles papers. USAMHI.

Minnemeyer, Charles H., 11th Pennsylvania Reserves. Journal. Save the Flags Collection. USAMHI.

Morse, Frank C., chaplain, 37th Massachusetts. Papers. MHS.

Mullen, Joseph, Jr., 27th North Carolina. Diary. MC.

Myers, Milton H., 110th Ohio. Diary. Vol. 59. RNBP.

Myers, Robert Pooler, assistant surgeon, 16th Georgia. Diary. MC.

Myers, William Barksdale. Letter. Gustavus Adolphus Myers papers. VHS.

Oberlin, William Penn, 148th Pennsylvania. Letter. Penn papers. Civil War Miscellaneous Collection. USAMHI.

Ocker, Thomas, 6th Maryland, USA. Letter. Gist Family Collection. LC.

Parsons, Charles Moses, 8th Connecticut. Memoir, "My Soldier Life for 22 Months: A First Person Account by C. M. Parsons." Civil War Times Illustrated Collection. USAMHI.

Partridge, L. T., 76th New York. Letter. Partridge Family papers. Civil War Miscellaneous Collection. USAMHI.

Pendleton, Alexander S. (Sandie). Letters. W. N. Pendleton papers. SHC.

Pendleton, W. N. Letters. W. N. Pendleton papers. SHC.

Phelps, Winthrop, chaplain, 2nd Connecticut Heavy Artillery. Letters. Litchfield Historical Society, Connecticut.

Phillips, James Eldred, 12th Virginia. Diary and memoir. VHS.

Pierce, Joseph H., 36th Massachusetts. Letter. Lewis Leigh Collection. USAMHI.

Pingree, Samuel E., 2nd Vermont. Letters. Vermont Historical Society.

Pitt, John S., unidentified New York regiment. Letter. RNBP.

Pollack, Curtis C., 48th Pennsylvania. Letter. Civil War Miscellaneous Collection. USAMHI.

Potter, Jared J., 7th Rhode Island. Coco Collection. USAMHI.

Proctor, Wilbur Washington, 10th New York Battalion. Diary. LC.

Randolph, Buckner Magill, 49th Virginia. Diary. VHS.

Rea, James L., 52nd New York. Letter. Civil War Miscellaneous Collection. USAMHI.

Reardon, J. W., 115th New York. Letter. Vol. 39. RNBP.

Reeder, William H., 20th Indiana. Letters. Reeder papers. USAMHI.

Reid, Whitelaw. Papers. LC.

Rew, Francis E., 2nd Vermont. Letters. RNBP.

Rich, Stephen, 32nd Massachusetts. Letters. Civil War Miscellaneous Collection. USAMHI.

Richardson, Samuel A., 6th Vermont. Bilby Collection. USAMHI.

Robinson, John G., 14th Pennsylvania Cavalry. Diary. Civil War Times Illustrated Collection. USAMHI.

Root, Samuel G., 24th Massachusetts. Memoir. Civil War Miscellaneous Collection. USAMHI.

Rowland, Kate Mason. Memoirs of the War: Diary and Correspondence, edited by a Virginian. MC.

Rumrill, Haskell B., 3rd Vermont. Letter. Rumrill Family papers. USAMHI.

Sanders, Charles, Cobb's Legion. Letter. Civil War Miscellany. Georgia Department of Archives and History.

Sawtelle, Orlando P., 9th Maine. Letter. Civil War Miscellaneous Collection. USAMHI.

Sawyer, O. G. Letters. James Gordon Bennett papers. LC.

Scott, Alfred Lewis, 9th Alabama. Memoirs. VHS.

Scott, John Zachary Holladay. Memoirs 1891. VHS.

Seibert, James, 93rd Pennsylvania. Letter. Vol. 12. RNBP.

Sharpe, George H. Letter. Cyrus B. Comstock papers. LC.

Sherril, G. M., 32nd North Carolina. Diary, continued by P.C. Shuford. MC.

Smith, William F., 1st Delaware. Letters. Lewis Leigh Collection. USAMHI.

Smith, William H., 23rd Georgia. Diary. Vol. 15. RNBP.

Snook, James M., 50th New York Engineers. Diary. Maryland Historical Society.

Sorrell, Moxley. Diary and maps. MC.

Soule, Horatio, assistant surgeon, 56th Massachusetts. Diary. Civil War Miscellaneous Collection. USAMHI.

Stackhouse, William, 19th Pennsylvania. Diary. HSP.

Steele, M. B. Diary. Henry Carter Lee papers. MC.

Stephens, Thomas White, 20th Indiana. Diary. Thomas White Stephens Collection. USAMHI.

Stevens, Hazard. Letters. Knight Library, University of Oregon, Eugene.

Stillwell, William Ross, 53rd Georgia. Letter. United Daughters of the Confederacy Typescripts, vol. 14, Georgia Department of Archives and History.

Stiner, William H. Letters. James Gordon Bennett papers, LC.

Stohl, David A., 49th Pennsylvania. Letters. Susan Boardman Collection. USAMHI.

Stowitz, George H., 100th New York. Letter. Vol. 25. RNBP.

Strayhorn, Thomas J., 27th North Carolina. Letters. Mrs. John Berry Collection. SHC.

Strickland, W. B., 10th Georgia. Letter. VHS.

Stuart, Franklin L., 23rd North Carolina. Letter. Lewis Leigh Collection. USAMHI.

Stuart, J. E. B. Letter. Stuart papers. VHS.

Tanfield, John O., 2nd Pennsylvania Provisional Heavy Artillery. Letter. Tanfield papers. USAMHI.

Terrell, Nicholas, Ashland (Virginia) Artillery. Letter. Vol. 62. RNBP.

Thatcher, Mahlon W., 40th Massachusetts. Letters. Vol. 37. RNBP.

Thomas, James William, 1st and 2nd Maryland, CSA. Diary and notes. RNBP.

Thompson, Eugene A., 10th Georgia. Letters. Vol. 15. RNBP.

Thompson, Gilbert, Topographic Engineers. Journal and memoir. LC.

Thompson, J. B., 1st Pennsylvania Rifles. "Reminiscences of Prison Life in the South." Civil War Miscellaneous Collection. USAMHI.

Thompson, John K., 22nd Virginia. Letter. George Mathews Edgar Collection. SHC.

Tibbetts, Albert H., 147th New York. Letter. Lewis Leigh Collection. USAMHI.

Tilton, William S. Diary. MHS.

Tucker, James F., 6th Florida Battalion. Letter. Special Collections. Florida State University, Tallahassee.

Unknown Confederate artilleryman, defenses of Richmond. Letter. Lewis Leigh Collection. USAMHI.

Vaill, Theodore, 2nd Connecticut Heavy Artillery. Letters. Vol. 35. RNBP.

Veil, Charles H., 1st U.S. Cavalry. Memoir. Civil War Miscellaneous Collection. USAMHI.

Verdery, James P., 48th Georgia. Letter. Eugene and J. P. Verdery papers. Duke.

Walkup, S. H., 48th North Carolina. Diary. Samuel H. Walkup Collection. SHC.

Waller, Francis A., 6th Wisconsin. Civil War Miscellaneous Collection. USAMHI.

Wheeler, W. H., 16th Massachusetts. Memoir. Wheeler Collection. Duke.

White, Lewis C., 102nd Pennsylvania. Reminiscences. Save the Flags Collection. USAMHI.

Wilson, James H. Diary and draft biography of Charles A. Dana. Wilson papers. LC.

Published Firsthand and Contemporary Accounts

Adams, Francis C. *A Trooper's Adventures in the War for the Union.* New York: Hurst & Co., n.d.

Albert, Allen D., ed. *History of the Forty-fifth Regiment, Pennsylvania Veteran Volunteer Infantry 1861–1865.* Williamsport, Pennsylvania: Grit Publishing Company, 1912.

Alexander, Edward Porter. *Fighting for the Confederacy: The Personal Recollections of Edward Porter Alexander.* Ed. Gary W. Gallagher. Chapel Hill: University of North Carolina Press, 1989.

Anderson, John. *The Fifty-seventh Regiment of Massachusetts Volunteers in the War of the Rebellion.* Boston: E. B. Stillings, 1896.

Bache, Richard Meade. *Life of General George Gordon Meade, Commander of the Army of the Potomac.* Philadelphia: Henry T. Coates, 1897.

Badeau, Adam. *Military History of Ulysses S. Grant, from April 1861, to April, 1865.* 3 vols. New York: D. Appleton, 1881.

Bannard, L. W. "Fighting Them Over." *National Tribune,* 28 August 1884.

Barr, James Michael, 5th South Carolina Cavalry, and Rebecca Ann Dowling Barr. *Confederate War Correspondence.* Ed. Ruth Barr McDaniel. Taylors, South Carolina: Faith Printing, 1963.

Bartlett, Asa W. *History of the Twelfth Regiment, New Hampshire Volunteers, in the War of the Rebellion.* Concord, New Hampshire: I. C. Evans, 1897.

Battle, Cullen A. "A Letter Which Caused a Desertion." *Confederate Veteran* 7 (1899):547–548.

Baylor, George. *Bull Run to Bull Run; or, Four Years in the Army of Northern Virginia, Containing a Detailed Account of the Career and Adventures of the Baylor Light Horse,*

Company B, Twelfth Virginia Cavalry, C.S.A., with Leaves from My Scrapbook. Richmond: B. F. Johnson, 1900.

Beauregard, G. T. "Four Days of Battle at Petersburg." *B&L* 4:540–544.

Bennett, Edwin C., 22nd Massachusetts. *Musket and Sword, or the Camp, March, and Firing Line in the Army of the Potomac.* Boston: Coburn Publishing, 1900.

Berry, Charles H. "With the 110th." *Xenia* (Ohio) *Torch-Light,* 20 July 1864.

"Bibb." "Fight of the 1st and 3rd—Colquitt's Brigade." *Macon* (Georgia) *Daily Telegraph,* 14 June 1864.

Bidgood, Joseph V., 32nd Virginia. "Further Recollections of Second Cold Harbor." *SHSP* 17 (1909):319–320.

Bissell, Lewis. *The Civil War Letters of Lewis Bissell.* Ed. Mark Olcott, with David Lear. Washington, D.C.: Field School Educational Foundation Press, 1981.

Blackford, Charles Minor. *Letters from Lee's Army, or Memoirs of Life in and out of the Army in Virginia During the War Between the States.* Ed. Susan Leigh Blackford. New York: Scribner's, 1947.

Blythe, T. M., 50th New York Engineers. "From the 50th Regiment." *Corning* (New York) *Journal,* 2 June 1864.

Bosbyshell, Oliver Christian. *The 48th in the War; Being a Narrative of the Campaigns of the 48th Regiment, Infantry, Pennsylvania Veteran Volunteers, During the War of the Rebellion.* Philadelphia: Avil Printing Company, 1895.

Bradwell, L. G. "Cold Harbor, Lynchburg, Valley Campaign, Etc., 1864." *Confederate Veteran* 20 (1912):138–139.

Breck, George, 1st New York Light Artillery. Letters to *Rochester Union & Advertiser.*

Brooks, Noah. *Washington, D.C., in Lincoln's Time.* Ed. Herbert Mitgang. New York: Rinehart, 1958.

Brooks, U. R. *Butler and His Cavalry in the War of Secession 1861–1865.* Columbia, South Carolina: The State Company, 1909.

Burton, Deloss S. "An Eyewitness." *Civil War Times Illustrated,* April 1983, p. 27.

Cadwallader, Sylvanus. *Three Years With Grant.* Ed. Benjamin P. Thomas. New York: Knopf, 1956.

Casler, John O., 33rd Virginia. *Four Years in the Stonewall Brigade.* Reprint. Dayton, Ohio: Morningside Bookshop, 1971.

Chamberlain, Joshua Lawrence. *The Passing of the Armies: An Account of the Final Campaign of the Army of the Potomac, Based Upon Personal Reminiscences of the Fifth Army Corps.* Reprint. New York: Bantam, 1993.

Chisholm, Daniel. *The Civil War Notebook of Daniel Chisholm: A Chronicle of Daily Life in the Union Army 1864–1865.* Ed. W. Springer Menge and J. August Shimrak. Reprint. New York: Ballantine, 1989.

Clark, Harvey. *My Experience With Burnside's Expedition and 18th Army Corps.* Gardner, Massachusetts: n.p., 1914.

Clark, James H. *The Iron Hearted Regiment, Being an Account of the Battles, Marches and Gallant Deeds Performed by the 115th Regiment N.Y. Vols.* Albany: J. Munsell, 1865.

Clegg, H. C. Sr. "War Record for 1862 to 1865." *Chatham Record* (Pittsboro, North Carolina), 1924. VHS.

Committee of the Regimental Association. *History of the Thirty-fifth Regiment Massachusetts Volunteers, 1862–1865.* Boston: Mills Knight, 1884.

———. *History of the Thirty-sixth Regiment Massachusetts Volunteers, 1862–1865.* Boston: Rockwell & Churchill, 1884.

Cone, A. J. "A Close Call." *Confederate Veteran* 27 (1919):372, 396.

Confederate Veteran. "Charles M. Miller." *Confederate Veteran* 36 (1928):307.

21st Connecticut. *The Story of the Twenty-first Regiment, Connecticut Volunteer Infantry, During the Civil War 1861–1865.* Middletown, Connecticut: Stewart Printing, 1900.

The Connecticut War Record. "Col. Elisha S. Kellogg." New Haven: Morris & Benham, September 1864.

Conwell, Russell H. *Magnolia Journey: A Union Veteran Revisits the Former Confederate States.* (Letters to the *Daily Evening Traveller,* Boston.) Ed. Joseph C. Carter. Reprint. University, Alabama: University of Alabama Press, 1974.

Cook, Roy Bird. "The Last Time I Saw General Lee." *Confederate Veteran* 35 (1927):287.

Cooke, John Esten. *Wearing of the Gray, Being Personal Portraits, Scenes and Adventures of the War.* Ed. Philip Van Doren Stern. Bloomington: Indiana University Press, 1959.

Coppee, Henry. *Grant and His Campaigns: A Military Biography.* New York: Charles A. Richardson, 1866.

Coxe, John. "Last Struggles and Successes of Lee." *Confederate Veteran* 22 (1914):356 ff.

Cushman, Frederick E. *History of the 58th Regt. Massachusetts Vols. From the 15th day of September, 1863, to the Close of the Rebellion.* Washington, D.C.: Gibson Brothers, 1865.

Dame, William Meade. *From the Rapidan to Richmond and the Spotsylvania Campaign: A Sketch in Personal Narrative of the Scenes a Soldier Saw.* Baltimore: Green-Lucas, 1920.

Dana, Charles A. *Recollections of the Civil War.* New York: D. Appleton, 1898.

———, and J[ames] H[arrison] Wilson. *The Life of Ulysses S. Grant, General of the Armies of the United States.* Springfield, Massachusetts: Gurdon Bill, 1868.

Davis, Varina. *Jefferson Davis, Ex-President of the Confederate States of America: A Memoir.* 2 vols. New York: Bedford, 1890.

Derby, W. P. *Bearing Arms in the Twenty-seventh Massachusetts Regiment of Volunteer Infantry During the Civil War, 1861–1865.* Boston: Wright & Potter, 1883.

Derby, William P. "War Memories—XII: Charge of the Star Brigade at Cold Harbor." *Springfield* (Massachusetts) *Daily Republican,* 5 July 1886.

Dickert, D. Augustus. *History of Kershaw's Brigade.* Newberry, South Carolina: E. H. Aull, 1899.

Dorman, G. H. *Fifty Years Ago: Reminiscences of '61–65.* Tallahassee: T. J. Appleyard, 1911.

Doyle, W. E. "Fresh Soldiers." *Confederate Veteran* 24 (1916):544.

Du Bois, A. "Cold Harbor Salient." *Richmond Dispatch,* 27 April 1902.

Early, J. A. "The Relative Strength of the Armies of Generals Lee and Grant." *SHSP* 2 (1876):6–21.

Early, Jubal Anderson. *Jubal Early's Memoirs: Autobiographical Sketch and Narrative of the War Between the States.* Philadelphia: J. B. Lippincott, 1912.

Eggleston, George Cary. "Notes on Cold Harbor." *B&L* 4:230–232.

Elliott, Charles G. "Martin's Brigade, of Hoke's Division, 1863–64." *Raleigh State,* 6 November 1895, reprinted in *SHSP* 23 (1895):189–198.

Field, C. W. "Campaign of 1864 and 1865." *SHSP* 14 (1886):542 ff.

Fleming, Francis P. *Memoir of Capt. C. Seton Fleming of the Second Florida Infantry CSA, Illustrative of the History of the Florida Troops in Virginia During the War Between the States.* Jacksonville: Times-Union, 1884.

Ford, Worthington Chauncey, ed. *A Cycle of Adams Letters.* 2 vols. Boston: Houghton Mifflin, 1920.

Galpin, Henry. Letter from "near Coal Harbor." *Herkimer County* (New York) *Journal & Courier,* 15 June 1864.

Galwey, Thomas Francis. *The Valiant Hours: Narrative of "Captain Brevet," an Irish-American in the Army of the Potomac.* Ed. W. S. Nye. Harrisburg, Pennsylvania: Stackpole, 1961.

Geiger, Aaron. "An Interesting Letter Written During the War." *Plant City* (Florida) *Courier,* n.d.

Gibbon, John. *Personal Recollections of the Civil War.* New York: Putnam, 1928.

Gibbs, James M. *History of the First Battalion Pennsylvania Six Months Volunteers and 187th Regiment Pennsylvania Volunteer Infantry: Six Months and Three Years Service, Civil War 1863–1865.* Harrisburg, Pennsylvania: Survivors' Association, 1905.

Goldsborough, W. W. "Grant's Change of Base: The Horrors of the Battle of Cold Harbor." *Richmond Dispatch,* 17 November 1901, reprinted in *SHSP* 29 (1901):285–291.

Gordon, John B. *Reminiscences of the Civil War.* New York: Scribner's, 1903.

Gorgas, Josiah. *The Civil War Diary of General Josiah Gorgas.* Ed. Frank E. Vandiver. Tuscaloosa: University of Alabama Press, 1947.

Gould, Joseph. *The Story of the Forty-eighth: A Record of the Campaigns of the Forty-eighth Regiment Pennsylvania Veteran Volunteer Infantry During the Four Eventful Years of Its Service in the War for the Preservation of the Union.* Philadelphia: Regimental Association, 1908.

Grant, U.S. *The Papers of Ulysses S. Grant.* Ed. John Y. Simon. 18 vols. Carbondale: Southern Illinois University Press, 1967.

———. *Personal Memoirs of U.S. Grant.* 2 vols. New York: Charles L. Webster, 1886.

Grimes, Bryan. *Extracts from the Letters of Major-General Bryan Grimes to His Wife.* Compiled by Pulaski Cowper; ed. Gary W. Gallagher. Wilmington, North Carolina: Broadfoot Publishing, 1986.

Haley, John. *The Rebel Yell and the Yankee Hurrah: The Civil War Journal of a Maine Volunteer.* Ed. Ruth L. Silliker. Camden, Maine: Down East Books, 1985.

Hane, U. H. "Finegan's Florida Brigade." *Confederate Veteran* 15 (1917):540.

Haskell, John Cheves. *The Haskell Memoirs.* Ed. Gilbert M. Govan and James W. Livingood. New York: Putnam, 1960.

Haw, Joseph R. "The Battle of Haw's Shop, Va." *Confederate Veteran* 33 (1925):373–376.

Hinson, William C. "The Diary of William C. Hinson During the War of Secession." *South Carolina Historical Magazine,* January 1974.

Hollyday, Lamar. "Maryland Troops in the Confederate Service." *SHSP* 3 (1877):130 ff.

Holmes, Oliver Wendell, Jr. *Touched with Fire: Civil War Letters and Diary of Oliver Wendell Holmes, Jr., 1861–1864.* Cambridge: Harvard University Press, 1946.

Hopkins, William P. *The Seventh Regiment Rhode Island Volunteers in the Civil War 1862–1865.* Providence: Providence Press, 1903.

Humphreys, Andrew A. *Address of Maj. Gen. A. A. Humphreys on the Military Service of the Late Maj. Gen. George Gordon Meade, United States Army, Made at the Meade Memorial Meeting of the Citizens of Philadelphia, November 18, 1872.* Washington, D.C.: Gibson Brothers, 1872.

———. *The Virginia Campaign of '64 and '65: The Army of the Potomac and the Army of the James.* New York: Scribner's, 1883.

Humphreys, C. W. "Another Account of Breckinridge's Brigade at the Cold Harbor Battle." *Atlanta Journal,* 22 February 1902.

Humphreys, Henry H. *Andrew Atkinson Humphreys: A Biography.* Philadelphia: John C. Winston, 1924.

Hunton, Eppa. *Autobiography of Eppa Hunton.* Richmond: Privately printed, 1933.

Hyndman, William. *History of a Cavalry Company: A Complete Record of Company "A," 4th Penn'a Cavalry.* Philadelphia: James A. Rodgers, 1870.

Ingraham, John. "From the 121st." *Little Falls* (New York) *Journal & Courier,* 23 June 1864.

James, Henry B. *Memories of the Civil War.* New Milford, Connecticut: Franklin S. James, 1898.

Johnson, Albert E. H. "Reminiscences of the Hon. Edwin M. Stanton, Secretary of War." *Records of the Columbia Historical Society* 13 (1910), pp. 69–97.

Johnson, Robert Underwood, and Clarence Clough Buel, eds. *Battles and Leaders of the Civil War.* (Cited as *B&L.*) 4 vols. New York: Century Co., 1889.

Johnston, J. Stoddard. "Sketches of Operations of General John C. Breckinridge. No. 2." *SHSP* 7 (1879):317 ff.

Jones, A. C. "Thrilling and Amusing War Episode." *Confederate Veteran* 18 (1910):214.

Jones, J. William. *Personal Reminiscences, Anecdotes and Letters of Gen. Robert E. Lee.* New York: Appleton, 1876.

Jones, John B. *A Rebel War Clerk's Diary.* Ed. Earl Schenck Miers. New York: A. S. Barnes, 1961.

Judson, A. M. *History of the Eighty-third Regiment Pennsylvania Volunteers.* Erie, Pennsylvania: B. F. H. Lynn, 1881.

Keely, John. "Narrative of the Campaign of the 19th Georgia Volunteer Infantry. Third Installment." *Atlanta Constitution Magazine,* 15 March 1941.

King, W. C., and W. P. Derby, eds. *Camp-Fire Sketches and Battlefield Echoes.* Springfield, Massachusetts: King, Richardson, 1889.

Lane, Mills, ed. *"Dear Mother: Don't grieve about me. If I get killed, I'll only be dead": Letters from Georgia Soldiers in the Civil War.* Savannah: Beehive Press, 1977.

LaRue, Fred. "From the 110th Regiment." *Xenia* (Ohio) *Torch-Light,* June 29, July 20, 1864.

Law, E. M. "From the Wilderness to Cold Harbor." *B&L* 4:118–144.

Lee, Robert E. *Lee's Dispatches: Unpublished Letters of General Robert E. Lee, C.S.A., to Jefferson Davis and the War Department of the Confederate States of America 1862–65.* Ed. Douglas Southall Freeman. New York: Putnam's, 1915.

———. *Wartime Papers of R. E. Lee.* Ed. Clifford Dowdey and Louis H. Manarin. Boston: Little, Brown, 1961.

"Letter from Virginia." *Selma* (Alabama) *Daily Reporter,* 20 June 1864.

Lincoln, Abraham. *The Collected Works of Abraham Lincoln.* Ed. Roy P. Basler. 9 vols. New Brunswick: Rutgers University, 1953.

Litchfield (Connecticut) *Enquirer.* "Our Army Correspondence." 4, 21, 30 June, 7 July, 1864.

Livermore, Thomas L. "Grant's Campaign Against Lee." *Military Historical Society of Massachusetts Papers,* vol. 4. Boston: The Society, 1887.

Locke, William Henry, Chaplain, 11th Pa. *The Story of the Regiment.* Philadelphia: J. B. Lippincott, 1868.

Lyman, Theodore. *Meade's Headquarters 1863–1865: Letters of Colonel Theodore Lyman from the Wilderness to Appomattox.* Ed. George R. Agassiz. Boston: Atlantic Monthly, 1922.

———. "Operations of the Army of the Potomac, June 5–15, 1864." *Papers of the Military Historical Society of Massachusetts,* vol. 5. Boston: The Society, 1906.

Lynch, John W., ed. *The Dorman-Marshbourne Letters, with Brief Accounts of the Tenth and Fifty-third Georgia Regiments, C.S.A.* Senoia, Georgia: Down South Publishing, 1995.

Macon Daily Telegraph. "Anderson's Brigade." 14 June 1864.

1st Maine Cavalry. *Record of Proceedings at the Eighth and Ninth Annual Reunions, Held at Lewiston and Pittsfield, 1879–80.* Augusta, Maine: Sprague & Son, 1881.

March, Henry Colley. *Cold Harbour.* Reprint from "Transactions of the Lancashire and Cheshire Antiquarian Society," vol. 9. Manchester, England: Richard Gill, 1892.

5th Massachusetts Battery. *History of the Fifth Massachusetts Battery, Organized October 3, 1861, Mustered Out June 12, 1865.* Boston: Luther E. Cowles, 1902.

Mather, Fred. "Under Old Glory." *National Tribune,* n.d. Vol. 5, RNBP.

Maury, Dabney H. "Grant as a Soldier and Civilian." *SHSP* 5 (1878):227–229.

McMahon, Martin T. "Cold Harbor." *B&L* 4:213–220

———. "The Death of Gen. John Sedgwick." *B&L* 4:175.

McNeilly, James H. "Four Years Under Marse Robert." *Confederate Veteran* 23 (1915):538 ff.

McWhirter, George I. E. "Freak of Lightning in the Sixties." *Confederate Veteran* 13 (1925):462.

Meacham, Henry H. *The Empty Sleeve, or the Life and Hardships of Henry H. Meacham in the Union Army.* Springfield, Massachusetts: Privately printed, n.d.

Meade, George G. *The Life and Letters of George Gordon Meade, Major-General United States Army.* Ed. George Meade. 2 vols. New York: Scribner's, 1913.

Medical and Surgical History of the War of the Rebellion. 3 vols., 6 parts. Washington, D.C.: Government Printing Office, 1870–1888.

Michie, Peter S. *The Life and Letters of Emory Upton, Colonel of the Fourth Regiment of Artillery, and Brevet Major–General, U.S. Army.* New York: D. Appleton, 1885.

Miller, Delavan S. *Drum Taps in Dixie: Memories of a Drummer Boy, 1861–1865.* Watertown, New York: Hungerford-Holbrook, 1905.

Moore, Edward A. *The Story of a Cannoneer Under Stonewall Jackson, in Which Is Told the Part Taken by the Rockbridge Artillery in the Army of Northern Virginia.* Lynchburg, Virginia: J. P. Bell, 1910.

Morton, T. C. "Gave His Life for His Flag." *Confederate Veteran* 12 (1914):70–71.

———. "Incidents of the Skirmish at Totopotomoy Creek, Hanover County, Virginia, May 30, 1864." *SHSP* 16 (1888):47–56.

Moyer, H. P., ed. *History of the Seventeenth Regiment Pennsylvania Volunteer Cavalry, or One Hundred and Sixty-second in the Line of Pennsylvania Volunteer Regiments.* Lebanon, Pennsylvania: Sowers Printing Co., 1911.

Myers, Ephraim F. "Trials and Travels of the 45th Pa." *National Tribune,* 24 December 1925.

Nichols, George W. *A Soldier's Story of His Regiment (61st Georgia) and Incidentally of the Lawton-Gordon-Evans Brigade, Army of Northern Virginia.* Reprint. Kennesaw, Georgia: Continental Publishers, 1961.

Oates, William C. *The War Between the Union and the Confederacy and Its Lost Opportunities, with a History of the 15th Alabama Regiment and the Forty-eight Battles in Which It Was Engaged.* New York: Neale, 1905.

6th Ohio Cavalry. *Souvenir, Fiftieth Annual Reunion of the Sixth Ohio Veteran Volunteer Cavalry Association.* Warren, Ohio, 1915.

Olsen, Bernard A., ed. *Upon the Tented Field.* Red Bank, New Jersey: Historic Projects, 1993.

Osborne, William H. *The History of the Twenty-ninth Regiment Massachusetts Volunteer Infantry in the Late War of the Rebellion.* Boston: Albert J. Wright, 1877.

Osgoode, J. A. "Grant, the Magnanimous." *Confederate Veteran* 34 (1926):365–366.

Page, Charles D. *History of the Fourteenth Regiment, Connecticut Vol. Infantry.* Meriden, Connecticut: Horton Printing, 1906.

Parker, Francis J. *The Story of the Thirty-second Regiment Massachusetts Infantry: Whence It Came; Where It Went; What It Saw; and What It Did.* Boston: C. W. Calkins, 1880.

Patrick, Marsena R. *Inside Lincoln's Army: The Diary of Marsena Rudolph Patrick, Provost Marshal General, Army of the Potomac.* Ed. David S. Sparks. New York: Thomas Yoseloff, 1964.

1st Pennsylvania Cavalry. *History of the First Reg't. Pennsylvania Reserve Cavalry, from Its Organization, August, 1861, to September, 1864.* King & Baird, 1864.

155th Pennsylvania Regiment. *Under the Maltese Cross: Antietam to Appomattox: The Loyal Uprising in Western Pennsylvania 1861–1865.* Pittsburgh: 155th Regimental Association, 1910.

Perry, John G. *Letters from a Surgeon of the Civil War.* Ed. Martha G. Perry. Boston: Little, Brown, 1906.

Perry, Leslie J. "A Parallel for Grant's Action: Here Is a Comparison of His Campaign in 1864 and Lee's in 1862." *Philadelphia Times,* 14 March 1896.

Pickett, George E. *The Heart of a Soldier as Revealed in the Intimate Letters of Genl. George E. Pickett, CSA.* Ed. Lasalle Corbett Pickett. New York: Seth Moyle, 1913.

Plowden, John Covert. *The Letters of Private John Covert Plowden 1862–1865.* Ed. Henry B. Rollins. Sumter, South Carolina: Wilder & Ward Printing, 1970.

Polley, J. B. "J. B. Polley to 'Charming Nellie.'" *Confederate Veteran* 5 (1897):425–426.

Porter, C. "Cold Harbor: Did Soldiers Refuse to Charge?" *National Tribune,* 7 March 1889.

Porter, Charles H. "The Battle of Cold Harbor." *Military Historical Society of Massachusetts Papers,* vol. 4. Boston: The Society, 1905.

Porter, Horace. *Campaigning With Grant.* New York: Century, 1897.

Prugh, P. C. "Letter from Rev. Prugh." *Xenia* (Ohio) *Torch-Light,* 22 June 1864.

Reagan, John H. *Memoirs, With Special Reference to the Civil War.* New York: Neale, 1906.

Reid, James E. "Cold Harbor." History of 115th New York in *Ballston Journal.* Saratoga Springs (New York) Public Library.

Rodenbough, Theo. F., ed. *From Everglade to Canon with the Second Dragoons (Second United States Cavalry): An Authentic Account of Service in Florida, Mexico, Virginia and the Indian Country.* New York: D. Van Nostrand, 1875.

———. "Sheridan's Richmond Raid." *B&L* 4:188–193.

Rowland, E. E. "Cold Harbor." Ed. Louis H. Manarin. *Mechanicsville* (Virginia) *Local,* 23 June 1993.

Sanford, George B. *Fighting Rebels and Redskins: Experiences in Army Life of Colonel George B. Sanford 1861–1892.* Ed. E. R. Hagemann. Norman: University of Oklahoma Press, 1969.

Schaff, Morris. *The Battle of the Wilderness.* Boston: Houghton Mifflin, 1910.

Sheridan, Philip. *Personal Memoirs of P. H. Sheridan, General, United States Army.* 2 vols. New York: C. L. Webster, 1888.

Shiver, E. A. "North Anna and Cold Harbor." *Atlanta Journal,* 25 January 1902.

Simms, A. B. "A Georgian's View of the War in Virginia: The Civil War Letters of A. B. Simms." Ed. Jane Bonner Peacock. *Atlanta Historical Journal,* Summer 1979.

Smith, William F. "The Eighteenth Corps at Cold Harbor." *B&L* 4:221–230.

Southern Historical Society Papers. "A Northern Opinion of Grant's Generalship," vol. 12 (1884):20–22.

———. "Editorial Paragraphs," vol. 6 (1878):142–144.

———. "Strategic Points: Their Value in the War Between the States, 1861–5, and How Fiercely They Were Fought For," vol. 21 (1893):376 ff.

Stearns, Austin C. *Three Years With Company K.* Rutherford, New Jersey: Fairleigh Dickinson University Press, 1976.

Stevens, George T. *Three Years in the Sixth Corps.* Albany: S. R. Gray, 1866.

Stiles, Robert. *Four Years Under Marse Robert.* New York: Neale, 1910.

Stone, James Madison. *Personal Recollections of the Civil War.* Boston: Privately printed, 1888.

Storke, C. A. "A Green Squad at Totopotomoy Creek." *National Tribune,* 27 May 1925.

Stuart, E. S. *Pennsylvania at Cold Harbor, Virginia: Ceremonies at the Dedication of the Monument Erected by the Commonwealth of Pennsylvania in the National Cemetery at Cold Harbor, Virginia.* Harrisburg, Pennsylvania: C. F. Aughinbaugh, 1912.

Survivors' Association. *History of the Corn Exchange Regiment 118th Pennsylvania Volunteers from the First Engagement at Antietam to Appomattox.* Philadelphia: J. L. Smith, 1892.

Swinton, William. *Campaigns of the Army of the Potomac.* New York: C. B. Richardson, 1866.

Taylor, William H. "Some Experiences of a Confederate Assistant Surgeon." *Transylvania College Physician* 28 (1906):103 ff.

Thomas, Henry W. *History of the Doles-Cook Brigade, Army of Northern Virginia, CSA.* Atlanta: Franklin Printing, 1903.

Thomas, Wm. M. "Nelson's Battalion: One of the Heroic Commands of the Confederate Army." *Charleston* (South Carolina) *Sunday News,* 8 August 1897.

Thompson, S. Millett. *Thirteenth Regiment of New Hampshire Volunteer Infantry.* Boston: Houghton Mifflin, 1888.

Tobie, Edward P. *History of the First Maine Cavalry 1861–1865.* Boston: Emory & Hughes, 1887.

Tucker, James F. ("J.F.T.") "Some Florida Heroes." *Confederate Veteran* 11 (1903):363.

U.S. Congress, Joint Committee on the Conduct of the War. *Report,* 2nd Session, 38th Congress.

U.S. War Department. *The War of the Rebellion: A Compilation of the Official Records of the Union and Confederate Armies.* (Cited as OR). 127 vols. Prepared under the direction of the Secretary of War by Robert N. Scott. Washington, D.C.: Government Printing Office, 1880–1901.

Vaill, Dudley Landon. *The County Regiment: A Sketch of the Second Regiment of Connecticut Volunteer Heavy Artillery, Originally the Nineteenth Volunteer Infantry, in the Civil War.* Litchfield, Connecticut: Litchfield County University Club, 1908.

Van Santvoord, G. *The One Hundred and Twentieth Regiment New York Volunteers.* Rondout, New York: *Kingston Freeman,* 1894.

Vautier, John D. *History of the 88th Pennsylvania Volunteers in the War for the Union, 1861–1865.* Philadelphia: J. B. Lippincott, 1894.

Venable, C. S. *The Campaign from the Wilderness to Petersburg: Address of Col. C. S. Venable (formerly of Gen. R. E. Lee's Staff), of the University of Virginia, Before the Virginia Division of the Army of Northern Virginia.* Richmond: George W. Gary, 1879.

Venable, Charles S. "General Lee in the Wilderness Campaign." *B&L* 4:240–246.

Wainwright, Charles S. *A Diary of Battle: The Personal Journals of Colonel Charles S. Wainwright 1861–1865.* New York: Harcourt, Brace & World, 1962.

Walker, Francis A. *Great Commanders: General Hancock.* New York: D. Appleton, 1895.

———. *History of the Second Army Corps in the Army of the Potomac.* New York: Scribner's, 1886.

Ward, George W. *History of the Second Pennsylvania Veteran Heavy Artillery (112th Regiment Pennsylvania Volunteers) from 1861 to 1866, Including the Provisional Second Penn'a Heavy Artillery.* Philadelphia: Geo. W. Ward, 1904.

Watson, George William. *The Last Survivor: The Memoirs of George William Watson, A Horse Soldier in the 12th Virginia Cavalry (Confederate States Army).* Ed. Brian Stuart Kesterson. Washington, West Virginia: Night Hawk Press, 1993.

Weld, Stephen Minot. *War Diary and Letters of Stephen Minot Weld, 1861–1865.* Boston: Massachusetts Historical Society, 1979.

Welles, Gideon. *The Diary of Gideon Welles.* 3 vols. Boston: Houghton Mifflin, 1911.

Wells, Edward E. *A Sketch of the Charleston Light Dragoons from the Earliest Formation of the Corps.* Charleston, South Carolina: Lucas Richardson, 1888.

White, John Goldsborough. "Recollections of Cold Harbor and Petersburg." *Baltimore Sun*, 2 June 1929.

White, William S. *Contributions to a History of the Richmond Howitzer Battalion. Pamphlet No. 2: A Diary of the War or What I Saw of It.* Richmond: Carlton McCarthy, 1883.

Wilkeson, Frank. *Recollections of a Private Soldier in the Army of the Potomac.* Reprint. Freeport, New York: Books for Libraries Press, 1987.

Willsey, Berea M. *The Civil War Diary of Berea M. Willsey: The Intimate Daily Observations of a Massachusetts Volunteer in the Union Army, 1862–1864.* Bowie, Maryland: Heritage Books, 1995.

Wilson, Clarence. "Move to Petersburg." *National Tribune*, 29 December 1910.

Wilson, James Harrison. *The Life and Services of General Smith.* Wilmington, Delaware: John M. Rogers, 1904.

———. *The Life of John A. Rawlins, Lawyer, Assistant Adjutant-General, Chief of Staff, Major General of Volunteers, and Secretary of War.* New York: Neale, 1916.

———. *Under the Old Flag.* New York: D. Appleton, 1912.

Newspapers

Atlanta Constitution

Atlanta Journal

Atlanta Register

Ballston (New York) *Journal*

Baltimore Sun

Baltimore Telegram

Bangor (Maine) *Daily Whig & Courier*

Boston Daily Evening Traveler

Boston Journal

Charleston (South Carolina) *Sunday News*

Charleston (South Carolina) *Daily Courier*

Cincinnati Gazette

Corning (New York) *Journal*

Florida Index (Lake City, Florida)

Herkimer County (New York) *Journal & Tribune*

(Lake City) *Florida Index*

Litchfield (Connecticut) *Enquirer*

Little Falls (New York) *Journal & Courier*

Macon Daily Telegraph

Mechanicsville (Virginia) *Local*

Mobile Advertiser
Montpelier (Vermont) *Green Mountain Freeman*
National Tribune
New York Times
New York Herald
Philadelphia Inquirer
Philadelphia Times
Pittsboro (North Carolina) *Chatham Record*
Plant City (Florida) *Courier*
Raleigh State
Richmond Dispatch
Richmond Examiner
Richmond Sentinel
Richmond Times-Dispatch
Richmond Whig
Rochester Democrat & American
Rochester Union & Advertiser
Savannah Morning News
Selma (Alabama) *Daily Reporter*
Springfield (Massachusetts) *Daily Republican*
Washington Star
Winsted (Connecticut) *Herald*
Xenia (Ohio) *Torch-Light*

Secondary Sources

Anderson, Nancy Scott, and Dwight Anderson. *The Generals: Ulysses S. Grant and Robert E. Lee.* New York: Knopf, 1987.

Andrews, J. Cutler. *The North Reports the Civil War.* Pittsburgh: University of Pittsburgh Press, 1955.

Bakeless, John. *Spies of the Confederacy.* Philadelphia: J. B. Lippincott, 1970.

Boatner, Mark Mayo III. *The Civil War Dictionary.* New York: David McKay, 1959.

Bradford, Gamaliel, Jr. "Lee as a General." *South Atlantic Quarterly,* July 1911, pp. 232–247.

Buell, Tom. *The Warrior Generals: Combat Leadership in the Civil War.* New York: Crown, 1997.

Burne, Alfred H. *Lee, Grant and Sherman: A Study in Leadership in the 1864–65 Campaign.* New York: Scribner's, 1939.

Calrow, Charles J. "Cold Harbor: A Study of the Operations of the Army of Northern Virginia and the Army of the Potomac from May 26 to June 13, 1864." Unpublished typescript, completed in 1933 by a former operations officer in the U.S. First Army in World War I. RNBP.

Catton, Bruce. *Grant Takes Command.* Boston: Little, Brown, 1968.

Clark, Walter, ed. *Histories of the Several Regiments and Battalions from North Carolina in the Great War, 1861–65.* (Cited as *North Carolina Regiments*). 5 vols. Raleigh: E. M. Uzzell, 1901.

Cleaves, Freeman. *Meade of Gettysburg.* Norman: University of Oklahoma Press, 1960.

Coffin, Howard. *Full Duty: Vermonters in the Civil War.* Woodstock, Vermont: Countryman Press, 1993.

Coggins, Jack. *Arms and Equipment of the Civil War.* Garden City, New York: Doubleday, 1962.

Cunningham, H. H. *Doctors in Gray: The Confederate Medical Service.* Baton Rouge: Louisiana State University Press, 1958.

Curtis, G., ed. *A Memorial Record of St. Lawrence County, N.Y.* Syracuse: D. Mason, 1894.

Davis, William C. *Jefferson Davis: The Man and His Hour.* New York: HarperCollins, 1991.

Denney, Robert E. *Civil War Medicine: Care & Comfort of the Wounded.* New York: Sterling, 1994.

Dowdey, Clifford. *Lee's Last Campaign: The Story of Lee and His Men Against Grant—1864.* Reprint. New York: Bonanza, 1960.

Foote, Shelby. *The Civil War.* 3 vols. New York: Random House, 1958.

Forrester, Richard H., Jr. "Letters of Rawleigh W. Dunaway." B.A. project, Randolph-Macon College, 1957.

Fox, William Freeman. *Regimental Losses in the American Civil War.* Albany: Albany Publishing, 1889.

Frassanito, William A. *Grant and Lee: The Virginia Campaigns, 1864–1865.* New York: Scribner's, 1983.

Freeman, Douglas Southall. *Lee's Lieutenants: A Study in Command.* 3 vols. New York: Scribner's, 1944.

———. *R. E. Lee: A Biography.* 4 vols. New York: Scribner's, 1935.

Fuller, J. F. C. *The Generalship of Ulysses S. Grant.* Bloomington: Indiana University Press, 1958.

———. *Grant and Lee: A Study in Personality and Generalship.* Bloomington: Indiana University Press, 1957.

Holzer, Harold, ed. *Witness to War: The Civil War 1861–1865.* New York: Perigee, 1995.

Keegan, John. *The Mask of Command.* New York: Penguin, 1987.

Livermore, Thomas Leonard. *Numbers and Losses in the Civil War in America, 1861–1865.* Boston: Houghton Mifflin, 1909.

Loderhose, Gary. "Letter of W. A. Hunter, 9th Fla." M.A. thesis, University of Richmond, 1987.

Long, E. B. *The Civil War Day by Day: An Almanac 1861–1865.* Garden City: Doubleday, 1971.

Lord, Francis A. *They Fought for the Union: A Complete Reference Work on the Federal Fighting Man.* Reprint. New York: Bonanza Books, 1971.

Macartney, Clarence Edward. *Grant and His Generals.* Reprint. New York: McBride Company, 1953.

McPherson, James M. *Battle Cry of Freedom: The Civil War Era.* New York: Oxford University Press, 1988.

McWhiney, Grady, and Perry D. Jamieson. *Attack and Die: Civil War Military Tactics and the Southern Heritage.* University, Ala.: University of Alabama Press, 1982.

Nolan, Alan T. *Lee Considered: General Robert E. Lee and Civil War History.* Chapel Hill: University of North Carolina Press, 1991.

Pennypacker, Isaac R. *General Meade.* New York: D. Appleton, 1901.

Rhea, Gordon C. *The Battles for Spotsylvania Court House and the Road to Yellow Tavern.* Baton Rouge: Louisiana State University Press, 1997.

Rhodes, James Ford. *History of the Civil War.* New York: Macmillan, 1917.

Ropes, John C. "The Battle of Cold Harbor." In *Military Historical Society of Massachusetts Papers,* vol. 4. Boston: The Society, 1883.

———. "Grant's Campaign in Virginia in 1864." In *Military Historical Society of Massachusetts Papers,* vol. 4. Boston: The Society, 1884.

Stern, Philip Van Doren, ed. *The Life and Writings of Abraham Lincoln.* New York: Modern Library, 1940.

———, ed. *Soldier Life in the Union and Confederate Armies.* Reprint. New York: Bonanza, 1961.

Tap, Bruce. *Over Lincoln's Shoulder: The Committee on the Conduct of the War.* Lawrence: University of Kansas Press, 1998.

Trudeau, Noah Andre. *Like Men of War: Black Troops in the Civil War, 1861–1865.* Boston: Little, Brown, 1998.

Tucker, Glenn. *Hancock the Superb.* Indianapolis: Bobbs-Merrill, 1960.

———. *High Tide at Gettysburg.* Indianapolis: Bobbs-Merrill, 1958.

Waters, William C., and Carlotta S. Tait. *Georgia Bennetts: Their History and Their Heritage.* Jonesboro, Georgia: Martin Johnson, 1976.

Waters, Zack C. "All That Brave Men Could Do: Joseph Finegan's Florida Brigade at Cold Harbor." *Civil War Regiments* 3, no. 4 (1994):1–23.

———. "Tell them I Died Like a Confederate Soldier: Finegan's Florida Brigade at Cold Harbor." *Florida Historical Quarterly* 69 (1990):156–177.

Waugh, John C. *Reelecting Lincoln: The Battle for the 1864 Presidency.* New York: Crown, 1997.

Weisberger, Bernard A. *Reporters for the Union.* Boston: Little, Brown, 1952.

Wert, Jeffry. "One Great Regret: Cold Harbor." *Civil War Times Illustrated,* February 1979, p. 22.

Wiley, Bell Irvin. *The Life of Johnny Reb.* Indianapolis: Bobbs-Merrill, 1943.

Williams, T. Harry. *Lincoln and His Generals.* New York: Knopf, 1952.

Index

A Note About the Author

Ernest B. "Pat" Furgurson, author of the widely praised *Ashes of Glory* and *Chancellorsville 1863,* is a native of Virginia and descendant of Confederate soldiers. He was an officer in the U.S. Marine Corps before beginning a long career as Washington and foreign correspondent for the *Baltimore Sun.* He and his wife live in Washington, D.C.

A Note on the Type

This book was set in Caslon, a typeface named after William Caslon (1692-1766). The first of a famous English family of type designers and founders, he was originally an apprentice to an engraver of gunlocks and gun barrels in London. In 1716 he opened his own shop, for silver chasing and making book-binders' stamps. He began typefounding in 1720. A specimen sheet of typefaces, issued in 1734, established Caslon's superiority to all other letter cutters of the time, English or Dutch, and soon his types, or types modeled on his style, were being used by most English printers, supplanting the Dutch types that had formerly prevailed. Caslon's characteristics are remarkable regularity and symmetry, and beauty in the shape and proportion of the letters; its general effect is clear and open but not weak or delicate. It is of interest to note that the first copies of the Declaration of Independence were printed in this typeface.

Composed by North Market Street Graphics,
Lancaster, Pennsylvania
Printed and bound by Quebecor Printing,
Fairfield, Pennsylvania
Designed by Anthea Lingeman